THE CRISIS

OF

GERMAN IDEOLOGY

INTELLECTUAL ORIGINS
OF THE THIRD REICH

BY GEORGE L. MOSSE

Schocken Books · New York

First published by Schocken Books 1981
10 9 8 7 6 5 4 3 2   84

Copyright © 1964 by George L. Mosse
Preface copyright © 1981 by Schocken Books Inc.

Library of Congress Cataloging in Publication Data

Mosse, George Lachmann.
   The crisis of German ideology.
   Reprint of the ed. published by Grosset & Dunlap,
New York.
   Includes bibliographical references and index.
   1. Germany—Intellectual life—20th century.
2. Nationalism—Germany—History. 3. National
socialism—History. 4. Ideology—History. I. Title.
[DD67.M67   1981]   943.08   80-54141

Manufactured in the United States of America
ISBN 0-8052-0669-8

Contents

Preface to the Schocken Edition

THIS BOOK attempts to analyze the history of Volkish thought and to define Adolf Hitler's German revolution. It focuses upon German nationalism at its most extreme, on those who advocated Volkish ideas and on how they penetrated into the population. To be sure, the curious notions analyzed in this book and the bizarre scholars who advocated them would have remained in well-deserved obscurity had Adolf Hitler not given Volkish thought pride of place in National Socialism. Yet Hitler would never have succeeded in demonstrating the political effectiveness of the Volkish world view had this perception of reality not already been shared by a great many Germans. True Volkish believers may never have represented the majority of the nation. Nevertheless, most Germans collaborated willingly enough with a regime based on Volkish foundations. This book attempts to analyze the development and dissemination of Volkish ideas from their beginnings through their realization in the Third Reich.

I want to touch briefly upon the chief criticisms which have been leveled against the book and at the same time indicate what I would do differently were I writing today. Some critics have objected to my central argument for the continuity of Volkish thought and the uniqueness of German fascism. I cannot, however, join them in regarding National Socialism as a break with the German past, as a unique response to specific events such as the lost war and the Great Depression. It seems to me that to concentrate solely on the play of social, political, or economic forces, as some historians have done, is to eliminate the difficult issue of personal responsibility. Why so many Germans possessed a false Volkish consciousness cannot be explained through such historical forces alone, for in the final analysis, a broad choice of political alternatives was available before Hitler's seizure of power.

National Socialism was not an aberration; it was, rather, the product of a dialectical historic process of economic, social, and political forces on the one hand, and human hopes and longing for the good life on the other. National Socialism was successful as a mass movement precisely because it was able to turn long-cherished myths and symbols to its own purposes. Human beings seek a future bright with promise, yet they dread a flight into the wild blue yonder. Adolf Hitler mixed traditional and acceptable Volkish thought with his own obscure brand of racism, a form which up to that time had existed only on the margins of history. Men like Guido von List or Lanz von Liebenfels, to be met in this book, occupied the outer edges of politics; the racial theosophy to be discussed was an esoteric *weltanschauung* until it influenced Hitler's own thought. Others such as Julius Langbehn or Paul de Lagarde, discussed at some length in the book, were closer to the center of political debate. It was my foremost objective to explain how the obscure and irrational world view advocated by such isolated individuals or small groups could ultimately determine the political discussion of a nation. For this process to occur, Volkish thought had to penetrate into so-called respectable social circles, while a specific historical situation provided the proper environment.

If I were to write this book today, however, World War I, which prepared the breakthrough of Volkish thought, would be given greater space. Not only because the myth of the war experience proved susceptible to Volkish ideas, but because, as a result of the lost war and its consequences, Germany became the nation in which the Volkish dream was to be realized. This could not be foreseen before the war. Racism and radical nationalism were, after all, also deeply rooted in France: if there had been speculation before World War I as to where the radical right would have a chance to gain power, the finger would have been pointed at France and not at Germany.

What, then, was unique about Germany? I attempted to distinguish the German from other forms of fascism in the last chapter of this book. This does not mean, however, that I negate the possibility of a general theory of fascism. (I later elaborated such a theory in *Man and Masses*.) Every country developed a fascism appropriate to its own specific nationalism. For example, the racist and Volkish component of National Socialism must be distinguished from Italian fascism. To be sure, similar currents existed in Italy, but the idea of "romanitá" was never dominant and all encompassing, and racial thought came late and lacked a national tradition. To be sure, Volkish thought also influenced other Central and East European nations and even the United States with its populist tradition, its idealization of the frontier spirit, and its Ku Klux Klan. But Germany was the nation where Volkish thought had the greatest impact.

The National Socialist government of Germany was the first European government in history to base its internal policies upon racism. Volkish thought and racism, however, were not necessarily identical. For example, some Volkish thinkers were willing to take Jews into the fold, provided they conformed in looks and manner. Racism as a scavenger ideology annexed diverse ideas, even those which, like early socialism, traditional Christianity, or some of the sciences, rejected a narrow Volkish outlook upon the world. In contrast to Volkish thought, racism could ignore the existence of individual nations for broader categories like "Caucasian" or "European." Yet in Germany the alliance between racism and Volkish thought triumphed. The anti-Jewish revolution, the climax of this book, was the unique result. One should not lose sight of this when reading about the eccentric scholars and the many organizations in these pages.

Surveying the latest research, I would have said more about *Bund* and eros, as I would have further explicated the relationship between Volkish thought and modern technology. The chapter on *Bund* and eros would have been expanded in order to place increased emphasis on the role of the male stereotype in the myths and symbols of Volkish thought. I had not yet realized that in the age of mass politics, symbols and political liturgies were of central importance in making abstract ideas effective and concrete. These were used by the National Socialists as a form of self-representation, and through them Volkish ideas were transformed into a new religion. As in all religions, ideals of beauty played a central role, and not least the ideal of classical male beauty. The new concern with nudity as part of the rediscovery of the human body, so popular at the turn of the century, was co-opted by nationalism in defining the purity and beauty of its male stereotype. More could have been said about the nationalist attempt to strip all sexuality from these Volkish symbols of manliness. (I have analyzed the relationship between nationalism, mass politics, and ideals of beauty in *The Nationalization of the Masses*.)

In addition, I argued in this book that the rejection of modernity was characteristic of Volkish thought. However, recent research has begun to emphasize the connection between Volkish ideas and technology. The Nazis made use of the most up-to-date technology in all fields, from transport to propaganda. Here we must distinguish between natural sciences and technology. National Socialists rejected the latest developments in physics as "Jewish," but their program "Beauty of Labor" modernized the work place. Pre-industrial forms were often applied to the industrial process as successful modernization: Volkish art, clear and simple architectural design, fresh air, lawns, and trees were to transform working conditions. The aesthetics of politics through rituals and symbols went hand in hand with the aesthetics of labor. Volkish ideology transformed the fear of the machine into a glorification of technology. We should not be tempted, however, to place this aspect of Volkish thought in the center of a basically anti-modernist nationalism. Were I writing today, I would have expanded this book in order to better define the complex relationship between Volkish thought and modernity.

Finally, this book appears to have left the impression among some readers that Volkish thought must inevitably lead to National Socialism. But that was not my intention. It could have continued to vegetate on the margins of history, or it could have come to power through some other nationalist movement. As I hope to show, German conservatives and their most important political party, the *Deutschnationale Volkspartei*, were deeply infected by Volkish thought. Moreover, Volkish thought was not necessarily aggressive or racist: it was possible to think in Volkish categories, and yet grant each people its own contribution to humanity, to accept the Volk, not as something that is eternally given, but as a step toward the unification of mankind. "Why," asked the anti-authoritarian socialist Gustav Landauer, "should we call for the end of all specific bonds and with them for the end to all differences among humanity?" The Volk as a democratic community among equals is an idea which also appears in this book. But Landauer's Volkish socialism found little echo in Germany. The relationship between Volkish and socialist movements remains to be properly investigated. Socialists of all countries made efforts to combine Volkish and socialist thought; had such a blend been successful, National Socialism might not have triumphed so easily.

After World War II, Volkish thought shared the fate of National Socialism. From the center of political events it was once again forced to the margins. Again the question arises: what could propel Volkish thought back into the center of politics? Are conservatives still susceptible to such ideas? Most post–World War II conservatives were good liberals who opposed Volkish tendencies. The youth movement no longer exists in Germany, unlike the student fraternities, which continue to carry on old traditions. While Volkish thought is no immediate threat in today's Germany, it is latent in all modern nationalism. By analyzing the Volkish triumph in the past perhaps we can prevent its victory in the future.

Madison, 1981

Acknowledgments

THE THESIS of this book was both sharpened and modified through invaluable criticism by fellow members of the interdisciplinary seminar on European studies sponsored by the Department of History at Stanford University. Three of my students at the University of Wisconsin must be singled out for special acknowledgment, for they made the writing of this book an enjoyable intellectual experience: André Martinsons, Michael Ledeen, and Carl Weiner. Howard Fertig proved to be a rigorous and understanding editor, beyond the call of duty. Jack Lynch was most helpful in matters of style.

The research for this book took me to three continents, a reflection of the dispersal of Volkish materials. In Germany the Institut für Zeitgeschichte in Munich and the Bayrische Staatsbibliothek freely extended their facilities. Interviews with individuals were of great assistance, though some of them must unfortunately remain anonymous. I owe a special debt to the archives of the German Youth Movement at Burg Ludwigstein and to its learned archivist, Hans Wolf. The Bundesarchiv in Koblenz made it a pleasure to work on the materials there. In Jerusalem, both the Library of the Hebrew University and the Jewish National Archives were treasure troves for materials bearing on the Volkish movement. On this side of the Atlantic the Hoover Institution on War, Revolution and Peace and especially Mrs. Agnes F. Peterson greatly facilitated my researches. The substantial collections of the University of Wisconsin library were indispensable.

The Social Science Research Council made a grant toward the completion of my investigations abroad. My debt to the graduate school of the University of Wisconsin for support of my research is very great; indeed, it is difficult to see how without its generosity this book could have been completed

I have left to the last that institution where most of the spade work for this book was done and whose librarian, Ilse R. Wolff, put her vast knowledge freely at my disposal. To the Wiener Library in London, truly a scholars' home, I wish to dedicate this book.

G. L. M.

Madison, Wisconsin
July 1964

Introduction

THE HISTORY OF GERMANY in the past century has been discussed at great length by historians and laymen alike. All have wondered whether men of intelligence and education could really have believed the ideas put forward during the Nazi period. To many, the ideological bases of National Socialism were the product of a handful of unbalanced minds. To others, the Nazi ideology was a mere propaganda tactic, designed to win the support of the masses but by no means the world view of the leaders themselves. Still others have found these ideas so nebulous and incomprehensible that they have dismissed them as unimportant.

This work will attempt to analyze these ideas, for it is a fact of history that they were embraced by many normal men. It is important to keep in mind that the Nazis found their greatest support among respectable, educated people. Their ideas were eminently respectable in Germany after the First World War, and indeed had been current among large segments of the population even before the war.

What differentiated the Germany of this period from other nations was a profound mood, a peculiar view of man and society which seems alien and even demonic to the Western intellect. Yet to understand the growth of such ideas, the role they played, and the longings they gratified during nearly a century of German life is to go far toward an explanation of Germany's unique development. Racial thought, Germanic Christianity, and the Volkish nature mysticism will all receive serious consideration here. Historians have not given them much serious attention, for they have regarded this ideology as a species of subintellectual rather than intellectual history. It has generally been regarded as a façade used to conceal a naked and intense struggle for power,[1] and therefore the historian should be concerned with other and presumably more important attitudes toward life. Such, however, was not the case. It was precisely that complex of particularly German values and ideas which conveyed the great issues of the times to important segments of the population.

Much of this ideology has been characterized as "apolitical," and indeed, at first glance it is hard to see how one can justify calling nature mysticism, sun worship, and theosophy parts of a political ideology. But the problem here is one of perspective. For the ideologists who will be our chief concern, traditional politics was seen as exemplifying the worst aspect of the world in which they lived. They rejected political parties as artificial, and representative government was swept aside in favor of an elitism which derived from their semi-mystical concepts of nature and man. This type of thinking is only apolitical if "politics" is restricted to a description of traditional forms of activity and belief. If "politics" is so defined, then the ideology with which we are concerned is more properly termed *anti-political*, for the revolution it called for was to sweep away the old *Rechtsstaat* in favor of the thousand-year Reich, and the *Führer-prinzip* was to triumph over parliamentary forms of government. Ironically enough, an ideological movement which has been termed "apolitical" eventually came to define what was politically acceptable. That this occurred demonstrates the danger of applying stereotyped concepts to a case which is so clearly not part of the general pattern. It will be our task in this work to trace the unfolding of the ideology and thereby help to explain the transformation of German politics.

This approach to the German catastrophe does not deny the concrete factors which underlay the development of such attitudes. It is probably impossible to determine why people believe all the things they do, but certainly the transformation of Germany from a semi-feudal collection of principalities to a nation-state, and the parallel transformation of the regional economy from agricultural to industrial could not help but leave profound impressions on the psyches of German citizens. Both changes were remarkably rapid, and the change in perspective which they effected was consequently greater than it would have been had the rate of change been slower. Moreover, the unification of Germany had a special impact since it came after more than half a century of unsuccessful attempts.

Germany's prolonged quest for national unity had the effect of turning her best minds toward problems of national destiny. This unity could have come about at the Congress of Vienna after the fall of Napoleon, but instead a loose German Confederation emerged which left the individual German states to pursue their independent ways. As a result, those Germans who wanted unity looked increasingly to the formation of a cultural cohesion among their people, rather than to a political unity which seemed far distant. They conceived this cultural unity in terms of national roots and of opposition to the foreigner. The revolutions of 1848, which seemed at first to give Germany another chance for unity, only resulted in frustration. The search for national roots, for a national stability upon which to form a true union was intensified between 1848 and 1870, and was accompanied by an increasing opposition to modernity. The modern world had denied to the Germans the unity which they had possessed long ago, and many felt that the movement for unity must draw its strength from those distant times rather than from the unpromising present.

When in 1871, at Versailles, Bismarck proclaimed the Prussian King to be the Emperor, unity seemed won at last. But the political unity of the new Prussian-dominated federation proved a disappointment to many Germans. It was prosaic, concerned with everyday problems, whereas the movement toward that unity had been highly idealistic and indeed utopian.

Experiences rarely, if ever, turn out exactly as anticipated, and this is especially true if the anticipation has gone on for a long time. For many German thinkers the anticipation of unity had grown to almost messianic dimensions, and the confrontation with Bismarck's bloodless *Realpolitik* was a tremendous disappointment. At first, the new Reich was greeted with great enthusiasm. But the kind of enthusiasm it received is more properly reserved for religious experiences, not political ones, and the business of government is hardly designed to produce a continuing state of ecstasy. Confidence in the newly won national identity was sapped by a feeling that Bismarck's Reich had failed to sustain the dynamic momentum which had led to unification. The preoccupation with the fate of Germany which had become a habit of mind before unification, could not suddenly be abandoned once this goal had been achieved. Indeed the problem persisted: it seemed that political unification had not brought with it that national self-awareness which many Germans had always desired. Instead the newly unified people engaged in material pursuits —making money and building up cities—and thus were destroying those ancient German traditions which to many minds had been the real driving force behind the movement for unification.

National unity triumphed at a time when the Industrial Revolution was rapidly cutting into German lands. The subsequent economic maladjustments added to the disappointment with national unification. A united Germany had not produced the good society for all of its people, but instead old problems had merely given way to new dilemmas. It was thus easy for many people to apply the same cast of mind which had stood them in good stead during the struggle for unity to the new problems of industrialization. They now sought solutions by deepening and intensifying their Germanic faith as they called for a more "genuine" unity. It is small wonder that such men ultimately rejected industrial society altogether, believing it irreconcilable with national self-identification. In the end, they called for a "German revolution" to liquidate the dangerous new developments and to guide the nation back to its original purpose as they conceived it. In this manner political unity and industrialization produced a crisis in German thought which led directly up to the "German catastrophe" of our times.

This crisis had its actual starting point in the 1870's. By 1873 the pressures of the increased tempo of industrialization had already produced the first grave economic crisis. By this time, too, it seemed clear to many that the great promises of national unity had somehow gone sour. Modern industrial Germany was being born and rapidly propelled forward, and the cry for a new "German" revolution that accompanied this growth was a reaction to modernity. Although the ideology with which we are concerned can be traced back to the beginning of the nineteenth century, to the struggle for national unity, the events of the last decades of the century infused it with a new life and a new dynamic.

The set of ideas with which we are concerned in this work has been termed "Volkish"—that is, pertaining to the "Volk." "Volk" is one of those perplexing German terms which connotes far more than its specific meaning. "Volk" is a much more comprehensive term than "people," for to German thinkers ever since the birth of German romanticism in the late eighteenth century "Volk" signified the union of a group of people with a transcendental "essence." This "essence" might be called "nature" or "cosmos" or "mythos," but in each instance it was fused to man's innermost nature, and represented the source of his creativity, his depth of feeling, his individuality, and his unity with other members of the Volk.

The essential element here is the linking of the human soul with its natural surroundings, with the "essence" of nature. The really important truths are to be found beneath the surface of appearances. An example—and one that is ultimately crucial in the development of Volkish thought—will serve to illustrate what is meant by this linking. According to many Volkish theorists, the nature of the soul of a Volk is determined by the native landscape. Thus the Jews, being a desert people, are viewed as shallow, arid, "dry" people, devoid of profundity and totally lacking in creativity. Because of the barrenness of the desert landscape, the Jews are a spiritually barren people.

They thus contrast markedly with the Germans, who, living in the dark, mist-shrouded forests, are deep, mysterious, profound. Because they are so constantly shrouded in darkness, they strive toward the sun, and are truly *Lichtmenschen*.

It has often been asserted that not until after defeat in the First World War and the founding of the Weimar Republic did the Volkish ideas really come into their own. To be sure, it was at this time that these ideas acquired a mass political base. However, the prewar developments were also of great importance, for it was during this period that the ideology was elaborated and diffused. The Volkish ideas were not spread primarily through organized movements, but rather through personal relationships and small groups which infiltrated the official establishment itself. Above all, this period witnessed the institutionalization of the ideas, a factor overlooked by those who see them as existing in virtual isolation before 1918.[2] In order to be truly effective, a system of ideas must permeate important social and political institutions. And before 1918 the Volk-centered ideology penetrated one of the most important of such institutions, the educational establishment.

Education and youth play an important role in our story. German youth had stood in the forefront of the struggle for unification. Ever since the time of Father Jahn and the founding of the fraternity movement at the beginning of the nineteenth century, the cause of national unity had aroused their enthusiasm. Friedrich Ludwig Jahn, professor at the University of Berlin, had founded the fraternity movement (*Burschenschaften*) in order to propagate "Germanic culture" and to encourage young Germans to build up their bodies so that they could fight for their country's unity. This enthusiasm for unity reached its high point in 1817, when the fraternities assembled at the Wartburg castle to burn "foreign" books which had poisoned the genuine culture of the Volk.

For many young people such nationalism offered the only proper solution to the many social and economic problems that confronted them. Their disappointment with the results of the long-awaited unity, combined with the effects of the Industrial Revolution, produced a longing for a more genuine unity of the Volk. With the impatience characteristic of their age, youth became the vanguard of a truly Germanic revolution. The educational establishment constantly encouraged such a solution to the crises of German thought. The Youth Movement after 1918 continued the searching which the prewar Youth Movement had begun: a search for new social and political forms for Germany which would, to their way of thinking, correspond more truly to Germanic longings. This Youth Movement was uniquely German, a microcosm of modern Germany. Starting around 1900, it captured the loyalty and imagination of youth until the Nazi seizure of power ended its story. At first the young people banded together for mere rambles in the countryside, but their activities soon became fraught with ideological purpose: to reconstruct the Volk along more genuine and natural principles than modernity offered. Before the war the youth groups had a membership of about 60,000; after the war this swelled to over 100,000. This was the elite of the bourgeois youth, and the Movement was a formative influence for many of the intellectual leaders born between the 1880's and 1920. The Youth Movement's influence was substantial among teachers and students, and we shall have occasion to devote much attention to it.

These are some of the principal ingredients which provided the dynamic for the uniquely German developments of our century. Their link with National Socialism may, at times, have been indirect, but the Nazi movement developed out of this context, adopting the slogan of the "German revolution" and making good use of its popular appeal. Here the trend in German thought which demands an ideology as the basis of all concrete action becomes important. What the National Socialists shared with other Volkish groups and with many of the youth was their mood, which in turn depended upon the ideological presuppositions we are discussing. For these presuppositions gave men and women their idea of their place in their country and society. It determined their image of themselves and of the world in which they lived. Such considerations seem much more important than the search for some individual precursors of National Socialism, which historians have detected in various figures from Herder to Wagner and Nietzsche.

The basic mood of the ideology is well summarized by the distinction between Culture and Civilization which was constantly on the lips of its adherents. A Culture, to recall Oswald Spengler's words, has a soul, whereas Civilization is "the most external and artificial state of which humanity is capable." [3] The acceptance of Culture and the rejection of Civilization meant for many people an end to alienation from their society. The word "rootedness" occurs constantly in their vocabulary. They sought this in spiritual terms, through an inward correspondence between the individual, the native soil, the Volk, and the universe. In this manner the isolation that they felt so deeply would be destroyed. The external was equated with the present, disappointing society; the state was opposed to the Volk, and the divisive parliamentary politics contrasted with that organic unity for which so many Germans longed. Moreover, the external signified a society which had forgotten its genuine, Germanic purpose in its rush to amass the benefits of the Industrial Revolution. This critique was directed at the comfortable and complacent bourgeois society, which was satisfied with Germany as it was and gave little thought to Germany as it should be. Their preoccupation with the external was materialistic, for those who had a true concern for the Volk believed in an inner spiritual revival which would bring about the true flourishing of the German Volk.

The critique was that Civilization had captured the bourgeois, and yet it was the bourgeois themselves who had made this critique. To be sure, it was not the haut bourgeois or the newly rich who objected, but those whom the Industrial Revolution had squeezed to the wall—the retail merchant, but not the department-store owner; the small, tradition-oriented entrepreneur, but not the director of the expanding industries or of the large banks, in whose hands economic power seemed to center. These middle-class bourgeois were joined by the artisan classes, who were rapidly sinking to working-class status and who felt themselves isolated as early as 1848. For both, modernity threatened to destroy their bourgeois status. They found ready allies in the landowners who saw their food monopoly threatened by demands for a reduction of tariffs and for expanded world trade. Thus those who advocated a return to Culture, who embraced a "German revolution," did not come from the lower classes of the population. On the contrary, they were men and women who wanted to maintain their property and their superior status over the working classes. The notion of a genuine social revolution was anathema to these people, yet they were profoundly dissatisfied with their world. The tension between their desire to preserve their status and their equally fervent desire to radically alter society was resolved by the appeal to a spiritual revolution which would revitalize the nation without revolutionizing its structure. Ultimately, the Nazi revolution was the "ideal" bourgeois revolution: it was a "revolution of the soul" which actually threatened none of the vested economic interests of the middle class. Instead Volkish thought concentrated upon another enemy within. This is why the Jews and the Jewish question will bulk so large in these pages, for the Jew was seen as the enemy. He stood for modernity in all its destructiveness. Thus we will find that Volkish thought sharpened and focused itself against, and in relation to, the supposed "Jewish menace." It can be justly argued that the attitude toward the Jew provided much of the cement for this thought and gave it a dynamic it might otherwise have lacked. The Jew, or rather the stereotype which Volkish thought made of him, is therefore central to any analysis and understanding of this ideology.

Moreover, in this instance the connection with National Socialism is a direct one. Hitler gave focus to his "German revolution" by making it into an anti-Jewish revolution. In a situation where revolutionary social and economic changes were excluded, the Jew became a welcome and necessary substitute toward which the revolutionary fervor could be directed.

Gerhard Ritter, the German historian, was far from the mark when he asserted that the ideological evolution which led to National Socialism was not typically German and that other countries also contained such movements.[4] Although anti-parliamentarianism was a general European attitude between the wars (as was the longing for a society that would be neither Marxist nor capitalist), it took different forms in different nations. As ideologies varied so did their results. German Volkish thought showed a depth of feeling and a dynamic that was not equaled elsewhere.

The Volkish movement triumphed in Germany because it had penetrated deeply into the national fabric. Rather than trying to explain away this fact, it would seem more profitable to ask how this could have been accomplished. This book will argue that the triumph grew out of a historical development, helped along by concrete causes, which resulted in an attitude of mind that was receptive to the solutions offered by Volkish thought; that January 1933 was not an accident of history, but was prepared long beforehand; and that if National Socialism had not taken the lead, other Volk-oriented parties stood ready to do so, for by that time Volkish ideas had captured almost the entire powerful German right.

Not that the triumph of a different section of the right would have led to the same results, or that the fall of democracy could not have been avoided. But democracy had faltered ever since its founding and millions had sought refuge in Volkish attitudes. To say that January 1933 was not an accident of history does not mean to deny the importance of the actual mechanism of the Nazi seizure of power. But the way was prepared and we must look beneath the actual political context to understand the attitudes which led both to support and to acceptance.

Those who have stated that Germany was "unprepared" for Hitler's sudden rise to power are reacting against attempts to see in this event the logical culmination of all of German history.[5] Our object is not such historical determinism. It is rather to show how one trend of German thought could become so strong that millions of people accepted it as the only solution to Germany's dilemma. Moreover, Volkish attitudes permeated the entire German right. Only eventually did the Nazi movement blanket the diverse Volkish longings of all those who saw their spiritual roots dislodged through industrialization and the atomization of modern man.[6]

Although, in this book, an attempt has been made to relate the unfolding ideology to the actual political, social, and economic developments in Germany, it should be kept in mind that there is no necessary, precise relationship between these events and Volkish ideas. The Volkish thinkers did not respond to "real" developments in the manner of political commentators. In fact, the nature of their ideas tended to detach them from real events rather than to compel them to take new developments into consideration.

Volkish thought was, after all, heir to a long development in German thought which tended toward abstract rationalism and idealism. The combination of romanticism and the popularizations of German idealism produced intellectuals whose ideal was to view the world *sub specie aeternitatis*. Their concern was hardly with mundane, day-to-day affairs. The Volkish thinkers were cut from the same cloth. If at times our discussion seems to be detached from the realities of the time, it is because the figures with whom we deal were so detached. Again, the paradoxical nature of Volkish thought forces itself upon us. An ideology that was only vaguely relevant to the real problems confronting the German people ultimately became normative for the solutions to those problems. As we shall see later, it was the genius of Adolf Hitler to wed the Volkish flight from reality to political discipline and efficient political organization.

Although millions of Germans, mostly of the left, were never captives of Volkish ideology, there were other millions who were, and these were the ones who triumphed in the end or who by their consent made that triumph easier. It would have been simpler to write a book such as this in the heat of moral indignation. However, such emotion might not only have obscured a serious historical analysis, but, what is worse, it might have given the impression that the ideas treated here were an aberration, something abnormal and indeed satanic. Yet the important fact to bear in mind is that many of the men and women who came to hold these ideas were normal in any usual definition, people whom one might have considered good neighbors.

In a sense this study is a historical analysis of people captured to such an extent by an ideology that they lost sight of civilized law and civilized attitudes toward their fellow men. Eventually a majority of the nation was taken in by such self-deception. That this was no mere accident or short-term reaction should be plain at first glance. Nor is our story necessarily over and done with. Volkish ideas are still with us, beneath the surface, ready to be used in those extreme crises which mankind constantly manufactures for itself. In the United States, for example, extremist groups who want to segregate Negro from white at all costs embrace the Volkish ideology, fusing anti-Negro with anti-Jewish sentiment. They hope to penetrate the right in the United States as the Volkish groups penetrated the right in Germany. Quite consciously they steal much of their material from German sources, thus helping to keep them alive in a new environment.[7] Moreover, isolated Volkish groups continue to exist in Germany itself. These attitudes of mind are easier to instill than to erase from the national ethos.

Yet it is said that all of these are small fringe groups who have no chance of coming to power. History, it is said, does not repeat itself. However, in the history of the Volkish movement it was never the actual size of the Volkish groups which counted, but rather the institutions they infected and the mood that they spread and maintained until the time was ripe. This also is worth remembering, however low the fires may be burning at a given time. We can only hope, but not predict, that nowhere in the world will the Volkish ideology again serve as a solution to a crisis in human thought and politics; that it did so in modern Germany has been catastrophic for Germans and non-Germans alike.

PART I

The Ideological Foundations

CHAPTER 1

From Romanticism to the Volk

THE INTELLECTUAL and ideological character of Volkish thought
was a direct product of the romantic movement of nineteenth-
century Europe. Like romanticism, Volkish ideas showed a distinct
tendency toward the irrational and emotional, and were focused
primarily on man and the world. This outlook found a receptive
audience. Rationalism had been discredited. The fine distinctions and
restrictions of the intellectual systems and rational ideologies of the
eighteenth century had been inundated by what many men took to
be inevitable social and historic forces. The patient experimentation
and intellectual discipline of the Enlightenment were succeeded by
the ideal of revolution, and the concept of an intelligible God gave
way to a pantheistic view of the universe.

A further and more basic impetus was given to the romantically
inspired Volkish movement by the turmoil that accompanied the social, economic, and political transformation of Europe. Stimulated
or shocked—depending upon one's partisanship—by the recurring
revolutions in France, surrounded by an encroaching industrial society, men and women looked for a deeper meaning in life than the
transitory reality of their present condition. The rapid process of
European industrialization was indeed bewildering to them, accompanied as it was by the dislocation of the population, by the sudden
obsolescence of traditional tools, crafts, and institutions, and by social
maladjustment and political upheaval. The demands of an increasingly industrial society, with its new opportunities and restrictions,
tended to strengthen the individual's feeling of isolation. This isolation, man's alienation from both himself and his society, occupied
men as divergent as Tocqueville and Karl Marx.

Bewildered and challenged, men attempted to re-emphasize their
own personality. But, since the rate of industrial transformation, as

well as its effects, seemed to evade the grasp of reason, and men could not easily make themselves part of the new social order, many turned from rational solutions to their problems and instead delved into their own emotional depths. The longing for self-identification, the individual's desire to fulfill his capacities, ironically heightened by the process of alienation, was accompanied by the contradictory urge to belong to something greater than oneself, a striving that inevitably circumscribed the individual's independence. The human condition was conceived as straddling two spheres—that of the individual on earth as well as a larger unit outside society in which man could find a universal identity. The latter came to represent the "real" reality, and since existing social conditions were bewildering and oppressive, romantics sought to find the larger, all-encompassing unity outside the prevalent social and economic condition of man. This larger unity was defined in terms of the cosmos. The universe itself was thought to embody the "higher reality," which inspired all that took place on earth. From a pantheistic perspective, in romantic, emotional terms, the world was viewed as tied to the cosmos by the transfer of the "living force" which radiated earthward and infused those who were attuned to it. As this life force flowed from cosmos to man, self-fulfillment was thought possible only to the extent to which man was imbued with this force and was in harmony with the cosmos from which it sprang.

These romantics, however, were not pure mystics concerned only with their own intensely personal connection with the universe—though they did esteem such German mystics as Meister Eckhart as precursors of their own spirit. Though they rejected their social environment, they did not exclude the possibility that it could be reconstituted along more harmonious lines. In Germany especially, where foreign occupation and the wars of liberation coincided with the wave of romanticism, an intermediary between the extremes of individuality and the quest for cosmological identity was found in the form of the Volk. Men like Father Jahn, Arndt, and Fichte began to conceive of the Volk in heroic terms during the wars of liberation against Napoleon. After the Congress of Vienna the idea of the Volk assumed added significance. It seemed as if the cold calculations of Continental power politics had triumphed over the quest for national unity: Napoleon had only initiated the process of Germany's subjugation; the Congress of Vienna completed it. Opposition to the social chaos of industrialization and urbanization was then reinforced by thwarted national aspirations. Some sought an outlet for their frustrations by linking the Volk to the cosmos as the true and deeper reality.

Idealized and transcendent, the Volk symbolized the desired unity beyond contemporary reality. It was lifted out of the actual conditions in Europe onto a level where both individuality and the larger unity of belonging were given scope. The Volk provided a more tangible vessel for the life force that flowed from the cosmos; it furnished a more satisfying unity to which man could relate functionally while being in tune with the universe. Volkish thought made the Volk the intermediary between man and the "higher reality."

But if the individual was tied to the Volk, which, in turn, as the repository of the "life force," found a unity with the "higher reality," how was this trinity actually expressed? Common to both the individual and the Volk was the romantic pantheistic concept of nature. For the romantics, nature was not cold and mechanical, but alive and spontaneous. It was indeed filled with a life force which corresponded to the emotions of man. The human soul could be in rapport with nature since it too was endowed with a soul. Every individual could therefore find an inner correspondence with nature, a correspondence which he shared with his Volk. In this way the individual linked himself with every other member of the Volk in a common feeling of belonging, in a shared emotional experience. Yet, after all, the Volk did not have universal dimensions, but was limited to a particular national unit. Not all of nature, therefore, but only its regional manifestations gave the Volk its character, potential, and unity. Nature was defined as landscape: those features of the environment peculiar and familiar to the members of one Volk and alien to all others.

The landscape thus became a vital part of the definition of the Volk through which it retained continuous contact with the life spirit of the transcendent cosmos. In this respect, the desired reality was charged with both emotional values and rural aspirations, reflecting quite explicitly the Volkish desire to escape from and to negate the validity of the century's increasingly industrial and urban values. Man was seen not as a vanquisher of nature, nor was he credited with the ability to penetrate the meaning of nature by applying the tools of reason; instead he was glorified as living in accordance with nature, at one with its mystical forces. In this way, instead of being encouraged to confront the problems cast up by urbanization and industrialization, man was enticed to retreat into a rural nostalgia. Not within the city, but in the landscape, the countryside native to him, was man fated to merge with and become rooted in nature and the Volk. And only in this process, taking place in the native environment, would every man be able to find his self-expression and his individuality.

The term "rooted" was constantly invoked by Volkish thinkers—and with good reason. Such rootedness conveyed the sense of man's correspondence with the landscape through his soul and thus with the Volk, which embodied the life spirit of the cosmos. It provided the essential link in the Volkish chain of being. Moreover, rural rootedness served as a contrast to urban dislocation, or what was termed "uprootedness." It also furnished a convenient criterion for excluding foreigners from the Volk and the virtues of rootedness. In addition, the concept of rootedness provided a standard for measuring man's completeness and his inner worth. Accordingly, having no roots stigmatized a person as being deprived of the life force and thus lacking a properly functioning soul. Rootlessness condemned the whole man, whereas rootedness signified membership in the Volk which rendered man his humanity.

In addition to the restrictions imposed by the landscape and the region, the Volk was circumscribed in other respects as well. The romantics' increased interest in nature had been accompanied by a revival of the notion that history provided an explanation and a goal for man's development. In the Volkish interpretation of history, the Volk was a historical unit that had come down to the present from a far and distant past. As the nostalgia for the medieval past had played a cardinal role in romanticism, so the Volkish thinkers tended to contrast the idyllic medieval Volk with the actual modern present. In giving the Volk roots in the remote past, history also seemed to endow it with endurance. Napoleon and the European political reaction which opposed nationalism might be victorious, but only temporarily, for the Volk that had endured for centuries could not be destroyed nor permanently subjugated. This concept of historicity gave the individual a further link with the landscape and with membership in the Volk. It also expanded the concept of the landscape to include not only the mountains, valleys, trees, and fields, but also the legendary exploits of those who had lived within this "genuine" environment for centuries. The small towns, the villages, the peasant and burgher inhabitants, symbolized the connection between the history of the Volk and its fusion with the landscape. Historicity, consequently, joined nature in defining the Volk and gave it a foundation in observable fact. The concept of rootedness was also enriched by history in that it acquired a broader base: nature and historical tradition.

Such then were the components of the ideology that called itself "Volkish," a foundation for a mode of thought, an attitude toward life, which was to become of ominous importance in the development of modern Germany. In essence it was an ideology which stood opposed to the progress and modernization that transformed nine-teenth-century Europe. It used and amplified romanticism to provide an alternative to modernity, to the developing industrial and urban civilization which seemed to rob man of his individual, creative self while cutting him loose from a social order that was seemingly ex-hausted and lacking vitality. Volkish thought revitalized the social framework by charging it with the energy of the Volk. It simul-taneously gave new life to the possibility of individual self-ful-fillment by making it part of the creative process of a higher life force. As this force, which streamed from the cosmos, was transmit-ted through the Volk, it was imperative that the individual be a mem-ber of the Volk unit. This process of thought answered the problem of alienation from society by positing a suprasocial unity to which it was vital to belong. It also made belonging to something larger than oneself a positive virtue indispensable to personal salvation. Thus rootedness, both in nature (defined as the native landscape) and in the history of the Volk's evolution, was viewed as the regenerative natural state of man which transformed the individual into a crea-tive being—while this state also reconstructed the contemporary na-tion according to the model of the Volk.

The Volkish ideology, as it emerged fully armed toward the close of the nineteenth century, was closely tied to the popularization of one of its central ideas: the peculiar and unique concept of nature and the associated idea of rootedness. From this base, Volkish thought was elaborated into a world view. The distinction between nature and landscape was summed up by Otto Gmelin, a writer of historical novels, in *Die Tat*, at that time one of the principal or-gans of romantic-Volkish thought: "A countryside becomes a land-scape insofar as it is a coherent whole with its own characteristics. But this can happen only when it becomes the experience of the hu-man soul, if the soul recognizes the rhythm of the countryside as its own rhythm." He continues, significantly, to reduce nature in gen-eral to a distinct regional and intelligible entity: "For each people and each race a countryside thus becomes its own peculiar landscape." [1] A further elaboration of the subject, written on the eve of the First World War, declared: "The landscape is something objective, neutral, and becomes of value only when we see it through our own spirit. It attains value through the strength of the life of our own soul, the vessel, of which the landscape becomes the object." [2] Nature in the rough must be tamed, the wild landscape sublimated. In the Ro-mance-language countries, nature retained elements of a primitive energy and furnished the romantics with that exalting correspond-ence between itself and their souls which enabled the young Berlioz to receive greater inspiration from the Roman Campagna than from the Roman conservatories of music. In Germany, however, that energy was reconstituted to produce more specific effects. Within the context of German Volkish thought, young Berlioz could not have been inspired by the Italian landscape. It was not his native land, which alone could stimulate the fusion of souls in creative expression.

In taming nature, Volkish thinkers rehabilitated it as a landscape filled with flora, fauna, villages, and small rustic peasant farms, entities which had lived within nature so long that they had become an integral part of the countryside. In 1896, Friedrich Ratzel, an often quoted writer, made this important point explicit, when in talking about the romantic awakening of a feeling for nature he viewed the process as "only a sign of the increased reacquaintance with our country, that is to say, with ourselves as a Volk. For how could you divorce from the very being [of nature] a Volk which for half a thousand years has worked, lived, and suffered on the same soil." He continues in the same vein to characterize nature as spontaneous, infusing it with the character and personality of the Volk. In denying that the German landscape is similar to that found in eastern France, the Netherlands, Jutland, Poland, Austria, and Switzerland, Ratzel remarks that this was true only "if one regards the landscape as merely nature, if one sees in man living within it only decoration, a bit of scenery." But, he concludes, the German landscape is different, for in it "a people inscribes its spirit and its fate as it does in its towns and houses." [3]

Ratzel's statement was significant, for he believed that the historical roots of the Volk were an integral part of nature, that, indeed, they had fused with nature's truly "genuine" qualities. This idea of a pantheistic integration was further extended by the prominent historian Heinrich von Sybel in his *Die Deutschen bei ihrem Eintritt in die Geschichte (The Germans at Their Entry into History)* (1863), in which he presented his thesis that "the source of Germanic religion is nothing else than a deep, warm sense of nature which alone introduced this Volk into human history and culture." [4] But more famous and influential than Sybel's work was Theodor Fontane's *Wanderungen durch die Mark Brandenburg (Ramblings through Brandenburg)* (1862–82). Fontane's description of Brandenburg fused the history, architecture, and landscape of Prussia into an indivisible whole—the people as well as the land they cultivated and inhabited. At a high literary level, this work summarized the intrinsic connection between the creativity and politics of a people and the unique nature which encompassed them and gave them their roots. Fontane's book became required reading for the German Youth Movement and, indeed, has maintained its popularity until this day.

However, it was not Fontane or Sybel or Ratzel but an earlier writer whose work became normative for a large body of Volkish thought, for he constructed a more completely integrated Volkish view of man and society as they related to nature, history, and landscape. In his famous *Land und Leute* (*Places and People*), written in 1857–63, Wilhelm Heinrich Riehl discussed the organic nature of a Volk which he claimed could be attained only if it fused with the native landscape. Riehl himself, whose life spanned most of the century (1823–97), was a professor at the University of Munich and later curator of Bavarian antiquities. Like most of the men whose thought we will deal with, he came from a settled middle-class background. Riehl analyzed the various population groupings of Germany in terms of the landscape they inhabited. The genuineness of the natural environment was held up to praise and credited with engendering in the population such qualities as sincerity, integrity, and simplicity. The culture of a Volk rooted in nature was posited as the very opposite of a mechanical and materialistic civilization. Riehl rejected all artificiality and defined modernity as a nature contrived by man and thus devoid of that genuineness to which living nature alone gives meaning. Such a contrivance—a city and its factories, for example—was seen as lacking genuineness and therefore as contributing to the disharmony among the population. For example, Riehl pointed to the newly developing urban centers as the cause of social unrest and the democratic upsurge of 1848 in Hessia.[5] For Riehl, as well as for subsequent Volkish thinkers, only nature was genuine, since it was infused with both the life force and historical meaning for the Volk. Any merely man-made improvement upon it would destroy the ordained meaning of nature and thereby rob both the individual and the Volk of significance and regenerative powers.

But Riehl went beyond contemplating the simple interpenetration of nature, Volk, and cosmos. He formulated important precepts for the society that the Volkish ideology envisaged. Starting once more with the ideal of nature, Riehl held up the unspoiled countryside as the model for the social structure he desired. He saw in the natural contrast between field and forest a justification for preserving the equally natural difference between social estates.[6] Contrasts that were an integral part of the unspoiled countryside were invoked as a basis for maintaining the distinctions among social classes. The society Riehl desired was hierarchical in nature and patterned after the medieval estates.[7] It reflected the romantic nostalgia for medieval times and found its justification in the historic tradition of the Volk residing in its landscape, an ideal which seemed to have been fulfilled in the Middle Ages. For Riehl this historicity was plainly evident in the web of ancient custom, which once had determined every man's place in society—and should do so again. The respective positions of lord and peasant had been fixed by time-honored customs as clearly as nature had divided field from forest. Riehl viewed the peasantry and nobility as the two estates which still lived according to the prescribed customs and which were, furthermore, an integral part of the landscape out of whose soil they drew their living.[8]

This medieval and rural utopia symbolized the intrinsic unity of people and landscape. But even Riehl realized that for his time the ideal had one glaring fault: it could not accommodate the "estates" which had joined the ancient groupings since the Middle Ages. In reflecting upon the changes and dangers of contemporary society, Riehl was aware that the old order had been drastically disturbed. To him, the bourgeoisie was a disruptive element that had challenged the "genuine" estates. In *Die bürgerliche Gesellschaft* (*Bourgeois Society*) (1854), he accused that class of disturbing ancient customs and thus disrupting the historicity of the Volk. Moreover, this new element was composed mainly of merchants and industrialists who had no close connection with nature. But not all hope was lost. The bourgeoisie could still be tamed and accommodated within the Volk. The small town, which had been a part of the historical landscape for centuries, had furthered the growth of indigenous traders, settled burghers, and small-scale merchants. Respectable and established merchant houses that could be traced back to those inauspicious beginnings could, therefore, find an honorable place among the original estates. Writers increasingly gave these merchant establishments a place alongside the peasantry who cultivated the soil. For Riehl himself it was axiomatic that the vast majority of Germany's great men had sprung from either the small town or the countryside.[9] From this point of view, by virtue of the antiquity and solid virtues of the established merchant families the bourgeoisie acquired rootedness and integration into the harmony and the "genuineness" of the Volk. Many literary works portrayed the middle class in this favorable light. Gustav Freytag, in *Soll und Haben* (*Debit and Credit*) (1855), the most popular German novel of the century, wrote of just such a merchant house and glorified it above those members of the nobility who had regarded their estates solely as a source of wealth to support their dissolute lives and had consequently become uprooted.

Having found a place for the middle class, Riehl and subsequent Volkish thinkers faced another problem in their structuring of the social order of the Volk: the workers. Here was an essentially new class, the product of the last century, which was increasingly accounting for a sizable portion of the population. In dealing with the working class, Riehl presented the same arguments he had employed for the bourgeoisie; they too could be tamed and could acquire rootedness. However, in one respect he favored them above the merchants: by regarding them as a genuine estate. This distinction permitted the workers to act in concert, to some extent, in the Volkish society, since, historically, estates had acted as a unit to gain their own ends. In this vein Riehl praised the first of Germany's workers' cooperative home-building societies and even had a good word for Robert Owen's cooperatives.[10]

Riehl regarded such cooperative efforts on the part of the workers as analogous to the medieval guilds in which master, journeyman, and apprentice were parts of a supposedly harmonious order. Typically enough, Riehl praised Robert Owen, above all, for gathering the workers and management into one big family which ran his industrial enterprises at New Lanarck. This was not a Communist family in which all members were supposedly equal, but a patriarchal family in which the factory owner played much the same role which the master craftsman had played in the past. This theory of the working class divested the workers of characteristics associated with industrial functions and became normative for the whole Volkish movement.

Workers were transformed into artisans so that they would fit in more closely with the image of their medieval counterparts. As artisans they would acquire the distinction of being settled and rooted craftsmen—partaking of the same honor granted the ancient merchant houses. Taking into consideration the problems of the contemporary industrial workers, Riehl advocated a reform, not along the line of unionization, but in the form of a grant which would parcel out a small piece of land to each worker. This measure was not designed to improve the worker's living conditions but rather to enhance his contact with nature, to root him in the landscape, and thus to transform him into an integral part of the Volk. His benefits would be those shared by all his fellows: natural simplicity, removal of the frustrations inflicted by an artificial urban way of life, genuineness of emotions and their uninhibited expression, and the rewarding sense of belonging within both a historically and cosmically sanctioned whole.

Rooted in the Volk, the worker would recapture his individual and creative self, and would thus be able to function as a medieval artisan rather than as an alienated modern proletarian. In the eyes of Riehl and other Volkish thinkers, this nostalgic image of harmony between worker and master, of the industrial worker transformed into the rooted artisan, provided the solution to the social and economic tensions that erupted periodically. Cooperation was justified by history, Volk interests, and cosmic life forces, and hence was the alternative to class warfare. This idea grew in popularity and received increased expression throughout the history of Volkish thought—from Riehl in the mid-nineteenth century to August Winnig after the First World War.

Yet for Riehl a third class, dangerous to the body politic and unfit to be accommodated within Volkish society, had come into being. This group, identified as true "proletariat," consisted of the totally disinherited. Riehl differentiated this third group from the "genuine" working class by stigmatizing it as a pariah caste which not only was the unfortunate product of modernization but which itself entertained an anti-Volkish malevolence. Consequently, it was futile to extend them a saving hand. On the contrary, the proletariat was the enemy to be vanquished.

What precluded the integration of the proletariat into the system of estates was its instability, its restlessness. This group was a part of the contemporary population which could never sink roots of any permanence. In its ranks was the migratory worker, who, lacking a native residence, could not call any landscape his own. There was also the journalist, the polemicist, the iconoclast who opposed ancient custom, advocated man-made panaceas, and excited the people to revolt against the genuine and established order. Above all, there was the Jew, who by his very nature was restless. Although the Jew belonged to a Volk, it occupied no specific territory and was consequently doomed to rootlessness.[11] These elements of the population dominated the large cities, which they had erected, according to Riehl, in their own image to represent their particular landscape. However, this was an artificial domain, and in contrast to serene rootedness, everything it contained, including the inhabitants, was in continuous motion. The big city and the proletariat seemed to fuse into an ominous colossus which was endangering the realm of the Volk: "dominance of the big city will be equivalent to the dominance of the proletariat."[12]

Such then was the threat that disturbed Riehl as well as subsequent Volkish thinkers. In their frame of reference the city came to symbolize the industrial progress and modernity that all adherents to the Volkish ideology rejected. It was the very opposite of rootedness in nature and, therefore, antithetical to the spirit of the Volk. Worse still, it represented the accomplishments of the proletariat; it was the concrete expression of proletarian restlessness. The fear of encroaching urban centers became synonymous with apprehension over the alarming rate at which the proletariat increased in numbers and asserted itself. The image of the city always conjured up the dread of the rootless elements, their incompatibility with the Volk, and an antagonism to foreign persons or cultures. Volkish thinkers saw the specter of internationalism in the rapid expansion of the cities. Riehl, who was credited with this apocalyptic vision, criticized big cities for wanting to become international urban centers, to achieve equality with all the large cities in the world and form a community of interest. Within such a union, Riehl feared, the "world bourgeoisie" and the "world proletariat" would recognize their mutual compatibility and exercise a suzerainty over a world in which all that was natural had been destroyed, especially the estates.[13]

This animosity toward the city was an integral part of the rise of Volkish thought. At times it was expressed in the slogan "Berlin is the domain of the Jews," or in the remark of another writer that "cities are the tombs of Germanism." [14] Not until the big cities were devastated in the Second World War did this hostility end. Then, in 1944, Joseph Goebbels made a statement which itself demonstrated the depth and duration of anti-urban influence on Volkish thought: it is necessary to respect the rhythm of life in the big cities which had survived the bombings. "Here the vital powers of our Volk are anchored as securely as in the peasantry." [15] It is indeed ironic that only with their annihilation did the cities attain equal ideological status with the rooted peasantry.

Such ideas secured a place for Riehl in the history of Volkish thought. Although the statements of many famous men were misconstrued and their thought distorted by extremists in the later Volkish movement, he was not among them. Such superficial actions as the founding of the Riehl Bund (1920) and the Riehl Prize for German *Volkskunde* (1935) only symbolized a more profound influence. References to Riehl and restatements of his ideas are found throughout the history of the Volkish movement. He was revered for his standardization of many of the basic precepts of Volkish thought. He was a pioneer in localizing the cosmic spirit within the confines of the Volk. He also limited the romantic concept of the infinite forms of individual expression when he rejected the restlessness peculiar to the true mystics who sought to link their souls directly to the creator's. Instead he emphasized that the very life force that infused the individual demanded rootedness and abhorred motion. This circumscription of the individual's striving may well have accounted for the attraction he exercised upon those who wanted to link themselves to a higher reality and at the same time find rest in a rapidly changing society. Indeed, this was his most lasting and most appreciated contribution to the Volkish movement. A leading German educator, in his defense of National Socialism, summed up this feeling almost a century after Riehl: "With the victory of National Socialism the limitations upon the dynamic spirit of man, which at first frightened us, are transformed into a feeling of restfulness. Freedom, for whose fate we feared, is renewed as it rises upward from a close-knit consciousness of Volk and Culture; our world of feeling had found fulfillment." [16] Riehl's thought came to symbolize an end to the fear of alienation and chaos since it substituted the Volkish sense of individuality through belonging. The Volk was transformed into the vessel of the cosmic spirit and contained definite social limits within it.

In this formulation of the Volkish ideology, the concept of the peasantry came to play a cardinal role. Riehl himself had hopefully observed that Germans were beginning to sense how important the peasantry was for the nation. Writers were prophesying what statesmen were refusing to see with their own eyes: through novels and stories of village life the peasantry was knocking at the doors of political power. Riehl came to believe that through such literature the influence of the peasantry was becoming a real political force and that the process of national degeneration might yet be halted.[17] Indeed, by the middle of the nineteenth century, German literature increasingly began to glorify the peasant as the man nearest to nature and therefore nearest to both cosmos and Volk. Writers began to construct the plots of their novels against the background of the native landscape. Thus Droste Hülstof made the Westphalian Heide a particular domain of her fiction and Adalbert Stifter, another celebrated writer, laid his plots in the Bohemian mountains. Depicting the peasant as a Volk hero as well as an ideal German, Berthold Auerbach (1812–82) became the most influential chronicler of peasant life. In his stories he stressed the appealing simplicity of the peasants, with their reverent sense of tradition and their closeness to nature. He linked these qualities to the virtues of honesty, uncomplicated integrity, and love of family. This catalogue of virtues was part of the Volkish belief that those closest to the soil were the most genuine human beings, since they alone partook of nature and the historical landscape of the Volk; only they were attuned to the life spirit.

In Auerbach's writings the pantheistic life force took on religious overtones. Sketching one of the peasants as a "real German," Auerbach says of him that "even today he is a simple and just man, loyal and filled with faith." [18] This faith which should be professed by the simple and just man was exemplified, in one of Auerbach's stories, by a parson who ministered to the peasants' spiritual needs. A thoroughly good man, of a "pure and beautiful nature"—as Auerbach depicts him—the minister is unalterably opposed to Protestant orthodoxy, believing that true Christianity is signified solely by the possession of a "sanctified heart." With his undogmatic faith, the parson is able to tame even the wildest and most unruly peasants. The simplicity of his religion also allows the parson to live and work among the simple and good peasants on an equal basis and to infuse the lives of peasant heroes with the same undogmatic faith.[19] Whereas Auerbach's work represents only an early literary expression of the fusion of peasant virtues and faith, later Volkish thought more explicitly combined the glorification of the peasant with a simple heartfelt religion, a Christianity not hemmed in by theological orthodoxy and thus free to fuse with the life spirit originating in the pantheistic cosmos.

Auerbach's works, however, convey another early aspect of Volkish thought. In his stories, the good and benevolent always vanquishes evil. The virtues he acclaims and attributes to his characters are peaceful by nature and recognizable to all men. But as the century progressed, writers endowed their peasant heroes with an additional moral distinction, a virtue of ferociousness, making them rather less lovable than Auerbach's men and women. An element of force, even of cruelty, was introduced into the character of the "ideal German."

Jürg Jenatsch, the peasant hero of Conrad Ferdinand Meyer's novel of the same name (1876), has been called the kind of nationalist who bore within himself the seeds of the First World War.[20] There is much truth in this. Jenatsch worshipped force, wished his enemies dead, and did his best to fulfil that wish by any and all means. Although Jenatsch struggled for the just and noble cause of Swiss independence, the emphasis on the necessary violence was so distorted that it transformed force from a tolerated means to a desirable end in itself. Force, which was previously invoked only under extreme conditions, now became a positive and lasting virtue.

In *Der Wehrwolf* (1910), the most famous German peasant novel, Hermann Löns eventually carried the glorification of brute force to its heights. Löns' "wolves" were peasants who, accepting the fact that rapine and pillage had become the law of the land during the Thirty Years' War, executed their own judgment upon their enemies and those of the Volk. There is little historically wrong in this, given the horrible age which Löns describes. But as the novel unfolds it becomes increasingly clear that the peasants' cruelty was not required solely for self-defense but that it represented one of their valid and genuine virtues. The bloodthirsty deeds are enveloped in an aura of satisfaction, as when a peasant recalls the days of the were-wolves as "so terrible and yet so beautiful." [21]

The peasant type that came to typify the truly Volkish individual not only embodied the virtues of simple justice and goodness but also was fascinated by force. This was a significant development which may well have arisen from the frustrations of those who wanted to actualize the Volk but whose hopes were continuously thwarted by the increasing tempo of industrialization. The story of the peasants who defended themselves against the bandits and ma-rauders of the Thirty Years' War may well have been intended to il-lustrate the heroic Volkish personality defending the true order against the inroads of a materialistic and industrial society.

This evolution of the peasant image, however, also symbolized the fusion of something very basic in nature with the Volk hero. It glori-fied not only a rural but, more pertinently, a primitive civilization. In this case, the historical, the genuine, came to be associated with a primitivism which alone had strength enough to strip off the artificial veneer of man-made civilization: "What is culture, what meaning does civilization have? A thin veneer underneath which nature courses, waiting until a crack appears and it can burst into the open." [22] The crevice had opened with the disintegration of society during the Thirty Years' War. The peasants had discovered their ag-gressive, warlike instincts and broke through the superimposed layer of civilization. The author permits them to look down upon the other classes of the population and say to the bourgeoisie and the workers: "I am the tree and you are the leaves, I am the source and you are the flood, I am the fire and you are its reflection." [23]

In Volkish thought the image of the tree was constantly used to symbolize the peasant strength of the Volk, with roots anchored in the past while the crown aspired toward the cosmos and its spirit. The same symbol was easily transformed to represent the peasant as the Faustian man persistently striving to relate himself to the spirit of life. Dietrich Eckart, the man who exercised the greatest influence on Adolf Hitler in the immediate postwar years, adapted *Peer Gynt* with just such an idea in mind. The peasant boor of the original play became, in Eckart's hands, a simple, just, and genuine man strug-gling for salvation and giving himself to the cosmic spirit. With the addition of the Faustian aspect, the character of the ideal peasant was complete. Rootedness and proximity to nature embraced the simple social virtues as well as the elemental strength derived from primitiv-ism. What emerged was the model for a Volk hero who alone, according to Volkish ideology, could shatter the complex of contemporary society.

As the Volkish hero was concretely objectified in this manner, so was the enemy. At the beginning of the movement, Riehl had designated the uprooted proletariat as the antagonist. After his day it became still more firmly centered upon the Jew. Popular literature, mainly novels (which sold into the millions), portrayed the alien Jew in growingly distasteful stereotypes. Peasant novels in increasing volume depicted the Jew as descending from the city into the countryside in order to deprive the peasant of his wealth and land. This was a most insidious development, for the Jew, in depriving the peasant of his landed property, severed his bonds with nature, the Volk, and the life force, and thus would inevitably bring about his death. One of the most important books of this genre will serve as an illustration—Wilhelm von Polenz's *Der Büttnerbauer* (*The Peasant from Büttner*) (1895), a book Hitler felt had somewhat influenced his thought. The outlines of its plot were to become conventional. A peasant becomes indebted to a Jew and has his land foreclosed. The Jew sells the property to a captain of industry, who in turn builds a factory on it. The peasant hero hangs himself in the end, his eyes reverently focused on his former land, soon to vanish beneath machines and factories: "The eyes which were leaving their sockets stared at the soil, the soil to which he had dedicated his life, to which he had sold his body and his soul." [24] In this framework the Jew was identified with modern industrial society, which uprooted the peasant, deprived him of his land, caused his death, and thereby destroyed the most genuine part of the Volk. However, the animosity toward the Jew had a further component, linked to the hatred of him as the representative of industrial society (after all there were German Gentile capitalists too), its agent who came into direct contact with the peasants. And, of course, he was a foreigner. In this conception of the Jew's role, the tree symbol of the sturdy, rooted peasant served a vivid function: the Jew was usually pictured as the snake at the root of the tree, seeking to destroy it.

This image of the tension between Jew and peasant was not merely based on abstraction but had some foundation, however slight, in concrete reality. The Jew functioned as middleman in many of Germany's agricultural regions. Usually it was in his capacity as cattle dealer or merchant of small products that he came into contact with peasants who relied on his services or goods. As a moneylender he was hated most when the peasants were in greatest financial difficulties and relied on him to tide them over, as after a bad harvest. In these capacities the Jew filled a need in the economic structure of many areas and represented a distinct and separate economic reality within the peasant world. The peasants were his debtors, and in bad times, no doubt, he collected his debts legally by foreclosure. There were many generous and charitable Jews engaged in such commerce; nevertheless, to the debt-ridden peasant, the Jew represented the most easily identifiable and immediately present element of the greedy power of modern capitalist civilization. Given these conditions, it is no coincidence, for example, that the first truly popularly organized anti-Semitic movement arose in the predominantly agricultural section of Hesse under the leadership of Otto Böckel. Nor is it astonishing that the large organization of agriculturalists, the Bund der Landwirte (Farmers' Union), was both Volkish and anti-Semitic. Thus the Jew's role in society, however exaggerated and distorted, identified him as the enemy of the peasant, and therefore also as the cause of the German people's misfortune. The Volkish cure was vividly presented: if the snake could be removed from the root of the tree, it would flourish and the strength of the Volk would cease to be sapped.

Besides being the enemy of the peasant, the Jew was also viewed as embodying rootlessness, the force most antagonistic to Volkish values. Indeed, the uprootedness of the Jew, castigated by Riehl and others, was the clue to his true nature, which made him the enemy of the Volk. The increasingly violent attacks on the poet Heinrich Heine during the late nineteenth century merit attention in this context, for Heine came to symbolize the rootlessness of the Jew as contrasted with the rootedness of the Volk. In such accusations as "One never knows where one is with him," Heine's constantly questioning, inquisitive, and critically analytic mind was brought under attack. His search for solutions to contemporary problems that would usher in a progressively better society was viewed with repugnance by Volkish thinkers. In their minds this constituted advocacy of a violent change in the direction of modernity. Heinrich von Treitschke even went so far as to accuse Heine of having prepared the way for the Revolution of 1848.[25] The modern society that was brought in by such a liberal revolution was a negation of all Volkish values; it represented the uprootedness of Riehl's apocalyptic vision of encroaching big cities.

Heine's advocacy of change betokened a dissatisfaction with the past and constituted an attack on the hallowed historicity of the Volk. Worse, this attitude at times ran counter to Volkish aesthetic values. Heine's rootlessness, it was felt, compelled him to be dissatisfied with knowing what "powerful, good, and beautiful" meant; instead, he desired to know only the superlative, "the most powerful, the most beautiful, and the best." [26] This was dangerous presumptuousness. For, according to Volkish values, the good and the beautiful were products of man's self-identification with the cosmos through the intermediacy of the Volk, which, as a "higher reality" established in the ancient and historical past, could not change any more than nature could negate its essence.

Volkish critics equated Heine's attitude with a lack of reverence. They demanded that homage be rendered to the historic manifestations of the cosmic forces and the life spirit they embodied. Constant dissatisfaction signified irreverence, a sacrilegious disposition. Indeed, one Volkish critic pictured Heine, as the Jew, standing irreverently, hands in pockets, before a picture of the Madonna. [27] Heine was thereby linked to a shallow materialism which ignored the existence of the "higher reality." His posture once more typified rootlessness and a constant longing for change.

Ironically, in a sense, while Heine was condemned for inspiring a revolution, Volkish thinkers themselves considered it essential that the contemporary society undergo a revolutionary change. However, it was not Heine's kind of change or social goals which the Volkish movement advocated. Their idea of a revolutionary dynamic was centered upon a breakthrough of nature's primitive forces and the life spirit into the existing society: a radical transformation which would revitalize the Volk. This change would not aim at "the best and the most beautiful," but would simply reveal the *eternally* good and beautiful. These values had always existed and had manifested themselves in the idyllic past; they needed only to be actualized anew in a society conducive to their growth. Heine was accused of advocating modernity while the Volkish movement aspired to reconstruct the society that was sanctioned by history, rooted in nature, and in communion with the cosmic life spirit. These were not new forces or uncharted seas, but realities obscured by the society Heine symbolized so well. This was the desired revolution. Modern restlessness was to be abolished by that rootedness which the peasant hero symbolized. To attain it, it was necessary only to exterminate the snake at the root of the tree and for men to recapture their self-identification within the Volkish ideology. Then the Volk would emerge victorious.

The initial forces of Volkish thought did not rest content with delineating its heroes, enemies, and goals. The movement developed rapidly, adding to its basic structure many new facets while making necessary emendations. Indeed, it acquired a dynamic of its own. The ideology was elevated into a Germanic faith, an achievement for which two men bear a large share of the responsibility: Paul de Lagarde and Julius Langbehn. An analysis of their thought will show how the Volkish ideas were rapidly diffused through the population, a process that led ultimately to their triumph over all other ideologies.

CHAPTER 2

A Germanic Faith

THE FIRST SIGNIFICANT organization of Volkish ideas into a system designed to realize the good society was achieved in the works of two late-nineteenth-century German writers. What had earlier been expressed in terms of nostalgia or as a literary and visual contrast to the jarring aspects of modernity, now was fitted out with the trappings of a program. Here concepts of religion, national creativity, and education fostered a positive identification of the individual with a collective enterprise that strove to bring into being a nation structured on Volkish principles.

If the Volkish movement can be said to have had a founder, it was a cranky scholar who had changed his name from Paul Böttischer to Paul de Lagarde; if the founder, in turn, had a prophet, that role was filled by Julius Langbehn. Until recently both men were almost unknown outside Germany,[1] though Lagarde and Langbehn played a central role in popularizing Volkish concepts, some of which they fashioned themselves. Their importance is emphasized by the many references that were made to them in later Volkish literature. Above all, subsequent scholars, educators, and politicians thought they were acting in accordance with the principles both men had advanced.

Significantly, Lagarde's life spans the second half of the nineteenth century, years which saw Germany develop into a modern military and economic power. Many of his fundamental impressions were gained in his youth, which coincided with the heyday of romanticism. He decided to enter the world of scholarship and eventually became a leading authority in Oriental studies; some of his contributions are still valid today. However, Lagarde had sufficient cause to be bitter toward the establishment, for it was not until late in life that he received his professorial appointment at Göttingen. Prior to

that he had earned his living as a teacher at a gymnasium, an occupation he came to consider wasteful of his talents. Langbehn, many
years his junior, also had academic ambitions, but they remained un-
fulfilled. Thus, both men were disappointed academicians. They expressed a resentment against the established educational order that
was shared by many subsequent Volkish thinkers, among them
Guido von List and Alfred Schuler, who will be the subjects of later
chapters. This rancor on the part of Lagarde and Langbehn was not
without significance in the shaping of their lives and theories.

Ironically, the prophets of the Volkish movement belonged to the
academic proletariat—a distinction shared by many of their fellow
writers and publicists. Both men fulminated against the academic
scene, and their disappointments spurred them on to a heightened
opposition to the prevalence of positivism and rationalizing intellectualism in academic circles. Their view of the contemporary society
as a conspiracy of evil forces was undoubtedly reinforced by their
exclusion from the social sphere to which they aspired. Their failure
to gain admission to the establishment served only to heighten their
already inflated sense of their own significance. They believed themselves to be learned in the essence of life, more learned than the professors who were comfortably occupying their endowed chairs. This
sense of uniqueness, practically verging on a feeling of mission, persisted even after Lagarde finally obtained his professorship. At the
university he refrained from close contact with his fellows and believed that his colleagues were persecuting him.[2]

To Lagarde's personal disappointments was added a disappointment in the form that the unification of Germany had taken. Lagarde
had desired a united Germany, but after it had come about he saw in
it only another step toward hateful modernity. Political unity did not
necessarily reflect a corresponding inner, spiritual unity. The superficial cohesion achieved through political means did not prevent or
disguise the decline of the Volk through the agencies of industrialism, increasing democratization, and urbanism. A true unity was
needed; but there seemed to be precious little time left in which to
effect it.

Deeply disturbed and concerned with the solution to this problem,
Lagarde offered his analysis and remedy in a collection of essays
published under the title *Deutsche Schriften* (*German Writings*)
(1878). He styled himself a conservative because he desired to
achieve the unity of the German state in a more elemental manner:
through the preservation and vitalization of the life force to be found
in the genuine nation and Volk.[3] This life force came to be his para-

mount concern, since it alone, finding expression in the spirit of the nation, could provide the fabric of national unity. Neither a committed political leadership nor economic growth nor national prosperity necessarily reflected a unity and contentment among the general population.[4] These were only superstructures, and false ones at that, which had been imposed without regard for the spiritual character and needs of the German nation. Reflecting this thought, Lagarde coined a sentence that was to echo and re-echo in all Volkish writings: "Germanism lies not within the blood but in the character."[5] It was a matter of inner attitudes, inherent in the individual German, his Volk, and the nation—the modern political vehicle of the Volk.

When Lagarde wrote this he was unaware of the developments in racial thought that equated the outward expression of shape and form with the inner qualities of spirituality, making the one symbolic of the other. To be sure, racial thought was developing throughout the nineteenth century. But its real diffusion did not come until after 1870, when Lagarde's outlook on the world had already been formed. However, when later writers quoted Lagarde they assumed that he had been working within the context of racial thought and had simply emphasized the inner attitudes of the Aryan race. But this was not Lagarde's original, broader meaning. His concern was solely with the appropriate spiritual attitude necessary for the regeneration of the nation. For Lagarde viewed the nation as a spiritual essence, an ideal which bound the people together.[6] Correspondingly, lacking genuine unity, the German state required a realignment of the spiritual forces to effect a true unity of the Volk. This requirement, in turn, would be met by a Germanic faith, which, in replacing contemporary materialism, would permit the flourishing of national institutions that reflected true inner attitudes. The advocacy of this religious doctrine was Lagarde's most important contribution to Volkish thought.

Lagarde's Germanic religion was founded on the rejection of traditional Christianity, which, he thought, had been stifled in orthodoxy. The spontaneous native piety of the Biblical fathers, which had imbued them with a natural sense of proximity to the Creator, had been displaced and abrogated by the introduction of laws, of prescribed traditions and practices. The law had been substituted for the spirit. In common with most Volkish thinkers, Lagarde blamed St. Paul for having enveloped untainted Christianity in sterile Hebrew law, thus stifling the original dynamic aspects inherent in the faith of Jesus Christ. Christ, Lagarde claimed, had stressed the dynamism of the inner spirituality of man and the importance of personal revelation. Within this framework, Lagarde set himself to re-discover the original Christianity in order to apply it to the regen-eration of his fatherland.[7]

In Lagarde's spiritual dogma, history (conceived in peculiarly Volkish terms) played a cardinal role. Historical development in-volved progression from an original source, similar to the dynamic evolution of the religious spirit within the individual: from revela-tion and inner faith to a conscious mystical relationship with God. History, for Lagarde, was the expression of a religious spirit, which manifested itself through a continuous revelation. Yet, this revelation was not to be confused with personal mysticism. Like all Volkish thinkers, Lagarde thought that the individual could be genuine only in a circumscribed form, that his uniqueness was derived from the peculiar character of the larger unit, the Volk. Personal revelation could come only within the confines of the community, a concept justified by Christ's proclamation of the Gospel to the community of the Apostles. In Lagarde's framework, the Apostles were assimi-lated into the concept of the Volk which was to serve as the organic receptacle for the continuous unfolding of the vital, religious spirit. In this manner, the Volk and its members were indeed the recipients of a constantly renewing spirituality and of all creativity. God's king-dom was the Volk.[8]

The revelation of God through the mediation of Jesus was not considered to be fixed and immutable. St. Paul, the dogmatism of the institutionalized church, and modern orthodoxy were held responsi-ble for this belief. Instead, Lagarde's Volkish precepts extolled the process whereby an inner religious dynamic led each Volk to its own peculiar destiny. Through such a religion, each man was linked di-rectly to God,[9] and the German Volk was endowed with a particu-larly vital spiritual revelation, a correspondence with the creative Demiurge more valid than that of other peoples. This Germanic faith provided the cohesive fabric of the Volk, but it also attributed to individual Germans the virtues of integrity and simplicity that were glorified in the peasant novels. When fused with the Volkish concept of nature, such a religion would guide man out of the dis-cord of modernity back to his true and creative self. For inspiration and inner contentment, Lagarde wrote, man should listen to the voice of nature unfolding within the trees of the wood and the har-vest in the fields.[10]

Possessing a revealed faith and spontaneous piety, the Volk could erect a national edifice that would truly reflect its character and in-ner attitudes. The unity of the nation, correspondingly, would not be re-established according to political dictates, but rather as the concrete expression of the common spiritual, emotional, and mystical qualities of the German people. The roots of Lagarde's ideas, of course, were anchored in his opposition to contemporary society. His appreciation of German history led him to propose a social structure similar to the one advocated by Riehl. The leadership of the nation was to rest with a responsible and reinvigorated aristocracy. Although Lagarde did call for a charismatic figure as his bitterness toward contemporary society increased, such a leader was envisaged in terms of the existing monarchy. For Lagarde, as for Riehl, all of society was to be organized into medieval estates, with the working classes transformed into artisans.[11] This nostalgia found almost lyrical expression: "Oh, what a delightful time the Middle Ages were, when everything was learned under the guidance of masters."[12] This Old Germanic life, Lagarde thought, was delightful because it had been endowed with the genial harmony of personalized customs and traditions, instead of the alienation and impersonalism that were characteristic of contemporary modern society. The industrial age and modern values had fossilized the individual, just as St. Paul had deprived Christianity of creativity through his rigid laws.[13] Supported by a feudally structured social hierarchy, the Germanic religion was the antidote that would regenerate the Volk.

In this context, the concepts of freedom and individualism found an appropriately Volkish expression. Rather than the tradition-defying bourgeois-capitalist individual, it was the personality circumscribed by Volkish forces of life and creativity that defined Lagarde's image of freedom and individualism. By stressing the creative and religious aspects which shape the individual, Lagarde further expanded Volkish ideology. Man derived another advantage in belonging to the Volk: "Free is he who is able to follow the creative principle of life; free is that man who recognizes and makes effective innate principles which God put within him."[14]

Beyond providing such safeguards as tradition, the historicity of the Volk, the genuineness of nature, and direct correspondence with God, Lagarde hoped to guide the German nation to its destiny while simultaneously guarding it from the disruption of revolution. It was true, according to Lagarde, that men who put their faith in a mystical, God-inspired unity did indeed abhor radical change. In fact, revolution, like an illness, was considered punishment for neglecting the inner self. Successful revolutions, like those in France, had destroyed the organic nature of the people and led to national suicide.[15] However, Lagarde's rejection of revolutionary change had to be taken advisedly. In principle he attempted to preserve the organic character of the Volk, and accordingly denounced the radical forces that promoted modernity, democracy, and socio-economic progress. But the Volk was an exception. Imbued with a destiny, it retained the prerogative to effect a violent transformation of contemporary society—but only if it did so in accordance with the precepts of history.

In speaking of Germany as a political entity Lagarde used the term "nation" instead of "Volk"—but he meant the same thing. However, he always made a distinction between "nation" and "state." The latter denoted a mere political mechanism, a superstructure insufficiently representative of the national character. If the political structure tended to obscure the inner attitudes of the Volk, it was imperative that the structure be suitably transformed.[16] As in revolution, so here: the license to use physical force was determined solely by the needs of the Volkish movement. If the state opposed the realization of the national destiny, it had to be crushed like an eggshell. According to Lagarde, man was a creature of the will. And once that will was revitalized through the religious inspiration of the Volkish soul, it would ruthlessly seek out victory.[17]

The enemy, modernity in all its ramifications, was epitomized by the Jews. Through their own national religion they had retained a cohesiveness which easily identified them as a separate segment of the population.

Lagarde wrote during the second generation of Jewish emancipation. Before 1812 Jews had been treated as a separate group on German soil, and while they were permitted to carry on their business activities under special "privileges," they had to pay special taxes for the honor. But even after 1812 professorial chairs were barred to Jewish intellectuals and no Jew could become an officer in the army. These were serious disabilities in a society where the "officer of the reserves" became an important status symbol and where academic posts guaranteed great esteem and stability.

Even though the ghetto walls were never to rise again after the Napoleonic occupation, emancipation faced a rocky road. With the fall of Napoleon, the German states hurried to impose restrictions upon their Jews once more, and it took the Revolution of 1848 to proclaim a fuller emancipation. By that time many Jews realized that the liberals, so instrumental in the revolution, were their firmest champions. Thus the close connection between Jews and liberals, both of whom were denounced by Lagarde and other Volkish thinkers.

Jewish emancipation was not really consummated until 1918. Without baptism, Jews could become neither officials nor professors.

Emancipation became bound up, in the end, with both the advance of liberalism and the existence of the Weimar Republic.

Jewish assimilation had been opposed by many Gentiles from the very beginning, and the Jews tried to counter the opposition in a variety of ways. During the first part of the nineteenth century many sought acceptance through baptism, while others tried to modernize Judaism—rejecting many old customs in favor of a "religion of reason." The first approach to the problem was the more successful, although many Gentiles regarded baptism as a mere ruse to gain acceptance. Nevertheless, baptized Jews were equal citizens, and they obtained posts in universities and even in the military.

But, however great their efforts to assimilate, Jews for the most part were thought to be a "state within a state." To be sure, they did organize themselves, not just into religious communities, but also into larger groups whose purpose was to battle against the infringements on Jewish rights. Typically enough, the chief organizations of this nature did not begin on a national scale until the wave of anti-Semitism at the end of the century had once more endangered the hard-won Jewish equality. The Verband Deutscher Juden (Union of German Jews) was founded in 1904, but it eventually gave way to the so-called Central Verein (Central Organization), which became the principal non-religious German-Jewish organization until Hitler dissolved it. The Central Verein was a special target for the Volkish movement. It was, typically enough, dominated by liberalism, which seemed to confirm the suspected liberal-Jewish symbiosis which symbolized Jewish "materialism" to those concerned with national unity. But in Lagarde's time this organizational structure did not yet exist, and he saw Jewish separateness in religious terms.

Lagarde felt that their religion kept Jews separate, and that they were in fact a coherent and dangerous minority within the Christian state. We shall have occasion to refer to the view of Judaism as both mysterious and without ethical roots. If Jews wanted to be Germans, why did they not throw off a spiritually valueless faith which made them so obviously separate? The stronger the longing for national unity, the more burning became the preoccupation with the Jewish question. After the failure of 1848, anti-Semitism acquired a new momentum. This is the background against which Lagarde wrote, for his prime concern was with national unity. Here again the fact that this unity was described in spiritual and not merely political terms must be given due weight. The Jews did not form a separate political or economic group. Indeed, they voted for the usual parties and admired Bismarck's work. But spiritually they seemed to be bound together by a non-Christian and non-Germanic religion. And it was in specifically religious, not racial, terms that Lagarde opposed the Jews. From a historical perspective, Lagarde admired the early Hebrews, seeing in them a people welded together in a true, spontaneously inspired, non-dogmatic religious spirit. However they had fallen from this state of beatitude as the spiritual cement was displaced by law and dogma. As was seen earlier, Lagarde felt that St. Paul the Jew had extended this selfsame legalism into the body of Christianity. For the Jews of his own day, Lagarde had only castigation. They had lost all true connection with the ancient Hebrews; they were fossilized, a living example of the spirit run dry. Pharisaical fundamentalism was now the essence of Judaism, based as it was on the literal observance of the laws. Since such a sterile religious attitude was incompatible with a vital mysticism, it could never fuse with the living and developing Germanic religion. By the same token, the Jews could never be Germans.[18]

Not only was the essential nature of the Jews incompatible with the inner character of the German Volk, but their national religion made them an irreconcilable foreign element on German soil. It also made them a danger to the regeneration of the Volk. While regarding Judaism as spiritually empty, Lagarde attributed conspiratorial motives to contemporary Jewry. The lack of a true religion meant a turning toward evil, a substitution of materialistic desires for inward faith. Lagarde seems to have believed that the Jews practiced ritual murder and he even declared that the Talmud and its prescriptions rendered the Jews a powerful weapon in the unavoidable power struggle.[19] The Jewish question was therefore not to be met with tolerance. Instead it was reducible to a mortal contest: either the Jewish or the "true" German way of life must prevail in the end. Since Lagarde saw the final struggle as a test of both physical and spiritual strength, he considered it imperative that the Germanic religion gain public acceptance, as only such a faith would infuse the Volk with the strength necessary for victory.

If at times Lagarde seemed to display an ambivalence toward the Jews, his less venomous attitude was by no means engendered by humane considerations. Rather, it was simply because he did not work within a framework of racial thought and was unfamiliar with the latest developments in that "science"; he thus lacked a vehicle for a more systematic vituperation. Then, too, several of the accusations against the Jews were not original with him. His willingness to believe the charge of ritual murder, for instance, came at a time when the Catholic professor August Rohling had thrown Central European Jewry into a panic by charging them with the practice and Lagarde might very well have based his accusations on the analysis of the Talmud put forward by this fellow professor from Prague. On several occasions, however, he entertained the possibility that a select number of exceptionally well assimilated Jews might be converted to Germanism. But these lapses of "kindness" grew increasingly rare. In direct proportion to his growing bitterness against the *status quo*, the Jew became the incarnation of evil. Any humaneness Lagarde possibly possessed was eventually obscured by his call for the extermination of the Jews like bacillae.[20] This outburst clearly paralleled his advocacy of physical force and violence to crush the recalcitrant contemporary state "like an eggshell."

Eventually, Lagarde's thought came to contain the fundamental ideas of Volkish ideology—the primacy of the Volk and the abhorrence of the Jew. However, two contributions to the movement distinguish him as a principal theorist: his overriding emphasis on spirituality, upon a Germanic faith that knit the individual Germans into the fabric of the Volk and joined the complex to God; and the outlines of the various forms of anti-Semitism that became the heritage of the later Volkish movement. The first contribution endowed the Volk with a dynamic faith which led the nation to know and grasp its destiny. The second, which accused the Jews of possessing a sterile religion and a consequently materialistic nature, of entertaining an international conspiracy, and of being incompatible aliens on German soil, led to the prophecy of a mortal struggle between Germans and Jews.

The influence of Lagarde is partly attributable to his literary style—short, pithy phrases that were easily memorized and quoted. He corresponded with many important contemporaries, but this was less significant than the more general influence he wielded on the whole of the Volkish movement.[21] Here he played a cardinal role, and was widely acclaimed and recognized to the extent that after the First World War agricultural settlements were founded specifically to enshrine and maintain Lagarde's Germanic religion. Homage was rendered by many distinguished people, but most important in its implication was that of Eugen Diederichs. This influential publisher, who coined the phrase "New Romanticism," so basic to future developments of Volkish thought, stated that the works of Paul de Lagarde were the finest of all the books he had published in his attempt to contribute to the vitalization of the Volk.[22]

Where Lagarde was often pedantic and scholarly, Langbehn, his junior, had a volatile style and message. Though twenty-four years apart in age (Lagarde was born in 1827, Langbehn in 1851), they knew each other socially and communicated many thoughts in writing. Langbehn himself has given us an appreciation of Lagarde which tells us something of the differences in approach between the two. He speaks of Lagarde's "sober and practical" methodology, which depressed him.[23] This evaluation was corroborated by Langbehn's closest friend and biographer, who commented that Lagarde lacked an "intuitive" sensibility.[24] This sense Langbehn certainly possessed. His *Rembrandt als Erzieher* (*Rembrandt as Educator*) (1890), written in an almost Nietzschean ecstasy, attracted a wide public, and not just among those committed to Volkish ideas. For Langbehn's work could be read chiefly for aesthetic reasons, as a clarion call for a new artistic creativity opposed to the sterility of German Wilhelmine art. Yet for Langbehn himself, such a call was an integral part of a world view both Germanic and creative, and as such it excited most of his contemporaries. More popular than Lagarde's work, for a time Langbehn's book was practically required reading among the young. Although his influence did not penetrate as deeply as Lagarde's, nor did it endure as long, it was spread more broadly. By the time the book had become passé, around the First World War, it had been read by millions. Many Germans today will still admit to the profound influence Langbehn exerted on their youth.

It was the absence of the historical dimension that distinguished Langbehn's contribution to the growth of Volkish, Germanic religious thought. Less historical-minded than Lagarde, Langbehn did not share that reverence for the past which permitted the scholar from Göttingen to rest his case on the existence of true spirituality among the ancient Hebrews or the genuine spiritual harmony epitomized by the Middle Ages in Germany. Similarly, lacking Lagarde's scholarly authority and objectivity, Langbehn substituted a veritable paean in praise of intuition, stressing the irrational, the mystical, and the subjectively intuitive.

Langbehn, too, was concerned with the incompleteness of German unity and the stifling of the Volk's true expression by the prevalent political and social institutions. This state of affairs, he thought, could be overcome if Germans were transformed into "artists," if they possessed a creative sensibility which would enable them to mold their individual characters in concert with the forms of nature and landscape. These artists would be creative solely because they understood the true nature of the Volk. Through it they would be infused with a "primal energy," the life spirit descending from cosmos to man, made assimilable as it passed through the Volk. Since Langbehn went further than his illustrious predecessor in rejecting the supremacy of reason in man, the life spirit he invoked was a truly mystical, an irrational force. Of course, Lagarde had also rejected

dogmatism and his Germanic religion had been launched on an uncharted pantheistic course, but in comparison with Langbehn's mysticism, his pronouncements were confined in a historical frame of
reference and weighted with scholarly pedantry. With the younger
man, the life spirit became a purely mystical and emotional dynamic:
"With a dose of mysticism one can gild the life of a nation." [25]

By elevating his mysticism into a Germanic religion, Langbehn
transcended Lagarde's theology and closely tied his ideas to the
spiritualism current in his day. This was a peculiarly nineteenth-century spiritualism, a theosophy which shared the Volkish interpretation of the life spirit. The theosophists Langbehn turned to looked
upon nature as eternally transmitted through a mysterious, omnipresent vital ether. They held that the extrasensory world was the true
world and that its mysteries could be discovered only through the
"true science" of theosophy. Madame Blavatski, who came to be the
foremost representative of this school of thought, described the science of theosophy as a revelation of reality by disembodied "voices"
from the beyond. Langbehn, while accepting the primacy of the
extrasensory world, specifically rejected Blavatski's occultism as
superstitious, for he could not accept the actual existence of ghosts.[26]

He was, however, fascinated by the cult of Emanuel Swedenborg,
the remarkable Swedish engineer who by the middle of the eighteenth century had turned into a religious mystic. Recognized by
Madame Blavatski as a forerunner of her own theosophical beliefs,
Swedenborg also upheld the primacy of the extrasensory world and
himself communed with those whom death had brought closer to that
genuine reality. However, there was another aspect to Swedenborg's
theosophy that directly appealed to Langbehn: the concept that God,
man, and the world were one unity, that all shared in the same essence.
According to the Swedish mystic, all extensions of mind and body
and nature were spiritual phenomena. Consequently, there exists a
perfect correspondence between outward manifestations and the inner spiritual world. Man's soul, the sentient substance, was the link in
the correspondence, since it stood at the center of the process
whereby the life-giving fluid flows between outward manifestations
and the God of the universe without whom nothing could live or be
wise.[27] In this manner Swedenborg stressed the substantial quality of
spiritual things; for to judge reality by material outward appearances
was a deception of the senses.[28]

Langbehn's peculiar appreciation of Swedenborg further reflected
the influence of the Swede on the whole Volkish movement. Swedenborg's view that every man was a microcosm containing within itself
a world or a heaven tended to portray the individual in the terms of

Volkish ideology. The "cosmic thinker" anthropomorphized the world, gave it a human form and sensibility by considering individuals as spiritual phenomena that were integral parts of the whole cosmos. Moreover, Swedenborg believed that there existed many heavens whose relative proximity to God was due to the spiritual intensity of the particular society man had inhabited while on earth. For Langbehn this allowed for a more extensive elaboration of Volkish individuality. The lives of cosmos and man were seen as parallel to each other.[29] Langbehn believed that such a concept of man and the universe provided the solution to the "riddle of the world." Above all, it provided an organic approach to life, an intimately mystical, a creative approach: "the organic is the artistic." [30]

Whereas Swedenborg had applied his mysticism on a universal basis, Langbehn restricted the fusion of the individual with the spiritual world to the region of northern Germany. To the Volkish thinker it came as no surprise that Swedenborg had spent a great deal of his life in that region. In fact, it was proof that man, the environment, and the idea were mysteriously interdependent—as kindred spirits in interplay with a kindred soil. In this respect, the Swede was considered the embodiment of the "ideal German type." The mystical ideas formulated by Swedenborg were appropriated by Langbehn, but they were regarded as appropriate only to the northern German landscape, where, in Langbehn's view, the spirit of the Volk continued to function in a vital manner. Correspondingly, only individual members of this Volk could become truly organic, creative partners in the cosmic relationship.[31] Swedenborg, transformed by Langbehn into a German mystic whose function was equated with that performed by the medieval mystic Meister Eckhart, became pivotal in providing the Volk with the spiritual mysticism that would lead it to its goal.

This fascination with Swedenborg was to continue throughout the development of Volkish thought, complemented by an equal attraction to the theosophy of Madame Blavatski. These theories were akin to the Volkish ideology which defined and clarified the mystical connection between the individual and the cosmos. They, too, could be reinterpreted in a way that made the Volk a necessary intermediary in the vital transfusion of spiritual substances. The soul was viewed as the essential spontaneous element—and only the Germans possessed a soul, since, according to the Germanic faiths of Lagarde and Langbehn, the Jews had long ago forfeited their souls, whereas the French had lost theirs in a revolutionary conflict. Though the existence of ghosts was denied by Volkish thinkers, whatever remained of such spiritualistic theories was incorporated in the dominant ideology. In Swedenborg's case, interestingly enough, in addition to rejecting disembodied spirits Langbehn also discarded the Christ-centeredness of the doctrine. This exhibited another tendency in Volkish thought—namely, to substitute the image of the Volk for the person and function of Christ. In Langbehn's theology, dupli-cated in other Germanic religions, the Volk and the God of the uni-verse participate in a direct relationship.[32] This distortion of orthodox Christianity was facilitated, it will be remembered, by the earlier popularity of pantheism and various spiritualist cults which stressed the primacy of a Creator whose existence subsumed that of Christ. However, in whatever manner such spiritualistic superstitions were transformed, for Langbehn and his successors the Germanic religion was a mystical union of individual, Volk, and cosmos.

Basing his arguments on these mystical tenets, Langbehn called for the regeneration of the individual through membership in the Volk. This regeneration, this belonging and molding oneself according to the ethos of the Volk, was to make man creative. The Volk was to enhance the development of the native aesthetic instinct even if it manifested itself only in the construction of a peasant hut, the layout of a garden, or the enjoyment of traditional dances, songs, and tales. Rembrandt was chosen as the example, the epitome of the simple, or-ganic artist. As with Swedenborg, so here, Rembrandt was viewed in relation to the geographical and social environment, the landscape and the popular peasant traditions that shaped his inner spiritual char-acter.[33] Langbehn had selected a Dutch painter to epitomize German creativity, because he came from Niederdeutschland, a borrowed geographical expression which denoted northern Germany and the Netherlands. Here the Volk had provided that pulsating, organic vi-tality which linked man to the universe and the Demiurge. Here the nature-Volk relationship was still intact; the peasants and nobility were the pillars of political and spiritual life, while ancient customs governed their mutual relationships.[34]

In addition to sharing Riehl's and Lagarde's emphasis on the role of nature in the social relationships of the Volk, Langbehn, like them, also admired the Middle Ages. He came out in strong support of monarchy as the proper form of government and changed the earlier concepts of nobility only to include those who had transformed themselves into artists as a "natural aristocracy." [35] However, whereas earlier Volkish thinkers like Riehl had nostalgically located traditions, social customs, peasant virtues, and Volk bravery in the feudal era, Langbehn regarded this historical period as representing the embodi-ment of a Germanic religion which rested on a mystical life force that came from the extrasensory world and revealed itself in the forces of nature and landscape. These forces, in turn, had eternally imprinted themselves on the character of the Volk and race.

Ideas of race played a greater role in Langbehn's theology than in Lagarde's. Race and the vitality of nature were viewed as equivalent forces. To support his position, Langbehn quoted Benjamin Disraeli as saying that "race is everything." Consequently, if nature and race are identical, then the Germanic life spirit must perforce be racial. All Volkish virtues, the physical as well as spiritual, were considered nature's eternal gifts transmitted through blood inheritance. Race was a pervasive and decisive force.[36] The outward appearance of the Volk, as expressed in its physical and spiritual culture, was seen as bearing the imprint of the inner qualities, as the signature of the soul. Langbehn even told his readers that investigations into human facial characteristics were a valid part of historical research.[37] Gone was the possibility that as long as only cultural differences prevented assimilation into the Volk, all who lived in Germany, Jews excepted, could become true Germans. The essentially non-racial anti-Semitism of Lagarde had been superseded; emphasis upon racial incompatibility had become an indelible part of Volkish ideology.

As regards the Jews, there was a distinct intensification of antagonism in Langbehn's thought. In his earlier writings he had expressed a tolerance of orthodox Jews living within the boundaries of the German nation. He considered them a separate people who abided by and maintained their own unique law. Assimilated Jews, however, had trespassed beyond their natural limitations and by infiltrating the body of the Volk they were polluting the purity of its blood inheritance. These Jews, identified as the "pest and cholera," had to be exterminated.

In later editions of his book this "finely discriminating" prejudice was obliterated. Instead he expanded the section on the Jews and wrote a condemnation that included all of Jewry.[38] Indeed, he became increasingly obsessed with anti-Semitism. As his utopia failed to materialize, his frustrations drove him to imagine that there existed powerful interests deliberately obstructing the fulfillment of the Volk. The Jews bore the brunt of his frustrated hate. They were pictured as the archfiends opposed to the regeneration of German "artists." Embodying materialism and modernity, the Jews automatically opposed the inner character of the German nation. And that was clearly understandable, for they had become estranged from the vital flow of the life spirit and their souls had petrified. Since they lacked a soul and could not re-establish contact with the life force, it was impossible for them to retain basic virtues like honesty and loyalty. These virtues were part of the "genuine" force of nature which the Germanic race alone had retained and could exemplify. Jews were simply the would-be oppressors and eternal enemies of the Germans.[39]

Whereas Lagarde had been merely crotchety, Langbehn was personally unstable. His admiring biographer, Momme Nissen, attributed to him an inflexibility that excluded compromise and prevented his coming to terms with anything.[40] He quickly went to extremes. Thus he shocked his friends by advocating the subjugation of the "lower" races and the reintroduction of slavery.[41] However, an opinion such as this would not seem to be inconsistent with a logical extension of his theories on race, and that is precisely the light in which Volkish posterity viewed Langbehn's message.

Moreover, Langbehn was dictatorial, both in his personal life and in the socio-political theories he advanced. His disciple Benedict Momme Nissen, who lived with him, wrote that "when he commanded, I had to obey," indicating that there was a master-apprentice relationship between them, contracted when they had become friends.[42] This personal idiosyncrasy was transmuted in his ideology into a yearning for a leader who would ruthlessly actualize the longings of the Volk. In the end, in fact, his medieval social ideal dissolved into the dictatorship of the Volk.[43] This substitution occurred frequently in Volkish literature, as in the writings of one of Langbehn's contemporaries, the Viennese Guido von List, who called for the appearance of "the great one who comes from above." At times, Langbehn, living in dire poverty, regarded himself as just such a Messiah, an idea that found expression in his messianic style of writing.

Eventually, the prophet and Messiah gave up his quest. The tension produced by a life spent in constant pursuit of security in a mystical world view was resolved by a submergence into orthodox Christianity. Langbehn converted and joined a Catholic order. Undoubtedly this conversion was due to the attraction which the medieval glory of the Church[44] exercised upon him. In the folds of the Church, his hysterical and erratic spirit found rest, and there he died while still a young man, in 1907.

In their respective works Langbehn and Lagarde provided a systematic framework for future Volkish ideas. They had sensed that Germany was undergoing rapid change in all areas of life—in society, politics, culture, and economy. The two Volkish prophets transformed this crisis, actually the birth pangs of modernity, into a crisis of ideology. They accepted the romantic impetus and its premise: the primacy of man's inner emotions, which were the genuine indicators of his personality. As a corollary they stated that this inner spiritual nature of man, properly circumscribed by the Volk, could transform the evil world of contemporary reality. Thus, actual reality was rejected and relegated to the background: not the state but the Volk was of paramount importance as the true fabric of the German nation. Religion—specifically a Germanic religion—was the expression of a romantic longing. Irreconcilable racial differences were pushed to the foreground, both as marks of a superior distinction possessed by the Germans and lacking in the Jews and as the sacred core around which the Volk could unite in eternal opposition to a pernicious and God-given foe.

Lagarde and Langbehn were exceptionally lucid exponents of an undercurrent that pervaded much of German society. That the two fathers of the Germanic religion rejected the dogmatic bases of orthodox faiths and identified with a dynamic spiritual force that worked within the individual and the Volk, only reflected a general condition of religious life in an industrializing German state. Their approach to the predominant Protestant faith prefigured a change that eventually came about toward the end of the century. A frustrated and emotional rejection of the materialistic social norms and values that were increasingly being adopted in society led to a similar discarding of religious orthodoxy, which seemed unable to grapple with the problem of modernity. The vogue of spiritualism and theosophy exemplifies this attitude, and, as we saw, Langbehn (and through him subsequent Volkish thinkers) made full use of these doctrines. Then, too, several trends of thought detached the specifically Christian component of Christianity from its historical moorings and transformed the religious commands into ethical imperatives. The historical Christ became merely a symbol of appropriately pious and moral behavior, or, as with Lagarde, the symbol of a person infused with the dynamic life spirit. In general, Volkish thought made use not only of mystical ideologies such as spiritualism and theosophy—which could hardly be considered Christian religions—but also of the tendency to reduce Christianity to a symbolism for a generalized standard of ethical behavior.

This tendency supplied the basis for the Ethische Gesellschaft (Ethical Society), founded in 1892. Wilhelm Förster, its moving spirit, expanded the doctrine of the primacy of ethical behavior into a pantheistic humanism embracing all mankind. Inspired by Kantian precepts, his society presupposed a goodness in man which obviated any reference to mysterious and occult elements. Moritz von Egidy shared some of these ethical presuppositions, yet he refused to join Förster's society precisely because its ethical emphasis was too "scientific" and excluded a mystical religious feeling from its world view.[45] Egidy, a contemporary of Langbehn, had been an officer in the army. After undergoing a religious conversion, he renounced his military career and proclaimed a humanist religion which was also pacifist. No wonder that in Wilhelmine Germany this created a sensation.

By gathering around him in his Berlin apartment a small circle of friends, Egidy exerted an influence on the Volkish movement that made it more readily acceptable to more sophisticated young people. Though personally Egidy would have been appalled, his doctrine of religious mysticism nonetheless contributed to the view that the Volk was the profound receptacle of the spiritual forces. His further, and in many respects greater, contribution to mystical thought which the Volkish movement adopted, was the stress he placed on the cardinal role that education must play in initiating youth into the ethical-religious spirit. In one sense Egidy's role is particularly significant, for it illustrates how an idea may be absorbed by a movement and used in a way that belies its original intent. Egidy's ethical mysticism and Volkish thought had some precepts in common; in fact, some of his disciples gravitated toward the Volkish movement and ended up by adopting its conclusions as well.

Egidy advocated the dispersion of Christianity among all of humanity through the medium of a humanistic ethic which stressed good actions.[46] There was nothing explicitly Volkish about this idea; indeed, the world Egidy envisaged would have been soft and distasteful to those who believed the Volk to be the exclusive vessel of God's spiritual gifts. Egidy considered all men capable of good and moral deeds; they had only to live according to God's precepts, which prescribed the proper ethical behavior. Accordingly, men could renounce the use of force in their relationships and realize their mutual equality in private as well as public life.[47] In this respect, he differed with the advocacy of force and power in Volkish thought—something the former army officer abhorred. However, there were some important similarities, especially in connection with the utopian ideal, which, for both, embodied standards set by the mystical forces of nature. Actually, these were the only remaining criteria, once the Volkish thinkers and Egidy had renounced the ethical norms of the contemporary scientifically oriented society.

Egidy stressed certain additional elements within this general framework which are similar to the Germanic religions of Langbehn and Lagarde. In contrast to Förster's purely humanistic ethic of behavior, Egidy posited the "mystery" of religious faith; in opposition to a mathematical, positivistic configuration of man, he pictured the human essence as a "secret" organism.[48] He thought man was subject to an instinctive urge to attain a state of genuine righteous-

ness on a higher plane of life. This urge, springing from his inner secret self, propelled man toward a fulfillment of his ethical potential.[49]
Its motivation was not impulsive but developmental—that is, the urge
unfolded according to an "eternal law of development" which had its
source in man and culminated in man's conforming to the laws of
God. In this system the only sin man could commit was to transgress
against the sacred law and consequently to inflict injury on his own
nature.[50]

Egidy saw salvation in the establishment of an ethical society on
earth. This could only be achieved through a continually developing
religion which stressed virtues that only a society that lived by the
laws of nature could possess. Egidy identified this as the process
whereby mankind could erect the ethical society, but he too went to
the Volk as the higher reality. Egidy even specified the Volk as the
framework and vehicle for a God-given freedom. Instead of using
the coercive methods of the modern state, the ideal society would
have the Volk elect men who would not rule but merely execute the
wishes of the Volk—the ruler would indeed be a *primus inter pares*.[51]

It is significant that even this humanitarian ended up by linking
his ideas with those that stressed the primacy of the Volk. Perhaps
he saw in it the only remaining political structure which would allow
for the functioning of the theories of human equality in the ethical
society. There were few alternatives left after he had rejected industrialization, urbanization, modern science, and the ethical values
that modernity demanded. Once he had exalted the Volk in this manner Egidy could not escape defining individual freedom as circumscribed by the peculiar attributes of the Volk, which it had developed
from its interplay with the spiritual life force. Although he shared
this view with the Volkish thinkers, he hoped to see different results.
Egidy believed that the true nature of the Volk would engender an
ethical nation that could unite with all humanity.

Nevertheless, he considered the Volk a cohesive unit. Egidy's pro-
foundest influence may well have been his view that the necessary
cohesiveness was to be attained not by force but through education.
Youth, he claimed, must develop freely in a natural and uninhibiting
environment in order to realize its ethical potential for good, and the
school must foster a feeling of togetherness. To this end he advocated the abolition of rigid rules in education, which he hoped to
realize in the establishment of *Einheitschulen* (unitary schools) that
would cater to all Germans regardless of wealth or status.[52] In this
manner, Egidy supplemented his religious concepts with an educational imperative. In doing so he added a practical prescription to
Langbehn's ecstatic and Lagarde's somber Germanic religions. Al-

though Lagarde had also condemned German school systems, he had been less specific about the way these institutions might be used to bring about the triumph of his religion.

On the whole, Egidy left his theories open to several interpretations. His humanitarianism, for instance, could be regarded as subordinate to his emphasis upon the Volk. Likewise, the virtues of his ethical society could be interpreted as those genuine virtues which the Volkish movement strove to achieve through its Germanic faith. Above all, there were Egidy's educational ideas, which could become powerful weapons in the hands of the Volkish movement. Egidy himself sought his ethical goals in a Volkish political structure.

Several important men who were directly influenced by Egidy made just such interpretations. Hermann Lietz, one of Egidy's closer disciples, played a key role, as we shall see, in institutionalizing Volkish thought through education.[53] Others joined in as well, men such as Ferdinand Schöll [54] and Kurt Wilhelmi.[55] We shall hear more of these men later; they are mentioned here only to show that the men around Egidy were concerned with educational problems. All in all, Egidy proved to be a catalyst whose advocacy of school reform became, in spite of itself, a Volkish cause. That his influence came to be felt indirectly, through his disciples, does not detract from the Volkish tendency inherent in his mystical ideas.

However, there was a third realm—in addition to spiritualism and education—that drew Egidy into closer identification with the Volkish movement: the Jewish question. On this subject he shared something of Lagarde's ambivalence. Egidy ridiculed the assertion that half a million Jews could possibly corrupt fifty million Germans.[56] Applying his ethical presuppositions, he claimed that those Jews who had a capacity for an inner spiritual development would fuse with Germanism, thereby negating their distinguishing Jewish traits. But it was this, his acceptance of the supposedly objective uniqueness of the Jews—an acceptance that necessitated the qualifying consideration: "those nobler Jews who had a capacity for inner spiritual development"—that indicated Egidy's view of the Jews in general.[57] He accepted the stereotype of the Jew and in that context asked the typically Volkish question: How could the Jews, with their spirit of usury and love of ostentatious materialism, have gotten the upper hand in Germany? The conclusion was simple, and also Volkish: the German people must share the guilt for such a state of affairs and consequently must expiate their sin.[58] "If we fifty million Germans can purify ourselves, Jewry will wither away." [59] Whether or not Egidy's concept of purification was bound up with the triumph of ethical humanitarianism did not in the end matter for the Jews who would have to vanish one way or another. Of course, it was the Volkish movement which laid claim to the sole, correct formula for exorcising the Jewish minority: force and a Germanic faith engendered by the cohesiveness of the Volk.

In much the same way as Volkish theorists found nourishment and fertile ground in Egidy's ethical mysticism, they also appropriated other ideologies which had based themselves on undogmatic religious expression. All of these shared the belief in the mystical, the irrational. And even when the leaders abhorred the Volkish movement, some of their followers gradually shifted into the Volkish camp.

A case in point is Wilhelm Jatho's Freireligiöse Gemeinde (Free Church Community). Like Egidy, Jatho was a humanitarian, even a Social Democrat, who advocated a totally spontaneous, direct, non-dogmatic relationship with God. Because of his belief that the essence of God and the depth of the soul were one, Gottfried Traub, his disciple, likened him to ancient German mystics such as Eckhart and Tauler.[60] Jatho had been a pastor in the Lutheran consistory of Westphalia, but had been expelled in 1911, whereupon he founded his own congregation. Out of the immediate group that formed around him, and in spite of his own abhorrence of nationalism, three of his followers emerged to become leaders in the Volkish movement by 1920: Gottfried Traub, Max Maurenbrecher, and Wilhelm Stapel. Jatho's daughter was quite correct when, much later, she accused Traub of having betrayed her father's heritage.[61] But that Traub could have embraced Volkish precepts was more than a coincidence. Like Egidy's mysticism, Jatho's was stripped of all theological discipline. It lacked a firm and principled framework of thought. As it tended to become irrationally mystical and ambiguous in regard to real values, this faith could easily be reinterpreted in terms of the growth of the inner spirit and character within a Germanic image.

Clearly articulated by Lagarde and Langbehn, the Germanic religion fed on the several undogmatic religious themes that flourished in the last decades of the century. Christianity, already weakened by a prolonged attack by the school of Biblical higher criticism, stripped of dogma and historicity, was sucked into the all-pervasive Germanic faith. Religious liberalism suffered this fate nowhere else in Europe. It was one more sign of the very real difference that separated Germany from the West. With banners raised Germanic faith met the crisis of modernity head on. Action was advocated in the name of a religion that combined the idea of creative individual development with mysticism, nature, and a nostalgia for medieval social relationships. Educational ideas, especially those of Egidy, were also incorporated and added a special dimension of practicality. The resulting religious ideas had great appeal because they combined the best of all possible worlds. Romanticism, and the concomitant idealization of nature, the peasantry, and the Volk, had facilitated a favorable reception. Now it could afford to level a trenchant criticism reflecting the disenchantment of displaced elements against a unified modern state. The accusations ranged from betrayal of inner national character to the destruction of genuine creativity by the impinging morass of a materialistic civilization. A change was imperative; the crisis raised by modernity had to be resolved. Lagarde and Langbehn saw themselves as catalysts in the Volkish transformation of society. Others of equal importance were to implement it.

CHAPTER 3

The New Romanticism

WHAT HAD ACTUALLY CHANGED in the romantic outlook once German unification had been effected? Basically, one is tempted to say, very little. Even in the beginning romanticism in Germany had an irrational base which tended toward emotional and political extremes. Enmeshed in Volkish ideology, it was applied to the growing problems of the modern age. A pantheistic vision of the cosmos had turned into a Germanic religious striving; national distinctions traced along historical and cultural lines took on racial dimensions. Two new factors characterized the forward thrust of Volkish thought in the new nation well into the twentieth century: first, a rapid assimilation of racial ideas systematized in a pseudo-science, and second, a heightened urgency to put the Volkish ideology into practice. These aspects went into the making of the more extreme trend in the Volkish movement, and as such will occupy us in subsequent chapters.

However, more immediately important was another trend, which perpetuated Volkish ideas by making them respectable. Under the banner of the "New Romanticism," it furnished a respectable impetus in thought and ideology which worked hand in hand with racial typology and Germanic fantasies. The extensive fusion of the "New Romanticism" with the more extreme trends shows that it was not so innocent as it might at first appear.

This relationship can be better understood through an analysis of the character and intent of the man who coined the phrase "New Romanticism"—Eugen Diederichs. This highly influential publisher brought a great deal of respectability to certain Volkish ideas. He himself is no longer famous. Historians ignore him and philosophers do not discuss his mystical and social theories. Yet he was one of the most celebrated publishers from the first decade of the century until his death in 1927. He did not conceive of publishing as merely a business. He worked within an older tradition which allowed him to publish primarily those books which reflected his own philosophy. His books enjoyed a wide audience and consequently it can be argued that his own tastes and philosophical idiosyncrasies were sucessfully communicated to a large number of readers. Moreover, his influence penetrated more deeply still after 1912, when he became the editor of the reputable journal *Die Tat*. In its pages he encouraged controversy between diverse currents of thought, except, typically enough, those of the left.

Personally, Diederichs was a man of unbounded energy, with a zest for life, for the eccentric, and for entertaining a wide and diverse acquaintanceship. His house, idyllically located in the small university town of Jena, became the headquarters for a group of intellectuals who worshipped at the shrine of the "New Romanticism." Significantly enough, it was also frequented by members of the growing Youth Movement. At these meetings, Diederichs would display his love for the eccentric and his infatuation with the mystical essence of life. Presiding over his "Sera Circle," he wore zebra-skin pants and a Turkish turban. In this atmosphere the meetings were transformed into Greek feasts pervaded by a spirit of Dionysian abandon. Such behavior, of course, left the sincerity of his own social and philosophical ideas open to doubt.

Actually, Diederichs' personal deportment was of greater importance than it would seem at first glance. More than most people, Germans have always tended to equate ponderous behavior with seriousness of purpose. Because of this eccentric behavior, a close associate doubted Diederichs' ability to be sincere in anything,[1] while another, whose work was published by Diederichs, thought that he lacked a clearly-worked-out system of ideas.[2] However, others, using the same evidence, formed a different opinion. Gustav Wyneken, the famous educator, who knew him well, thought that Diederichs possessed an open mind and a tolerance for different and opposing ideas.[3] The articles that Diederichs published in *Die Tat* reinforced this interpretation, since they led to a healthy controversy between conflicting schools of thought. But Diederichs' own works run counter to all of these interpretations. His own writings as well as those he published embraced a definite system of ideas.

Diederichs coined the term "New Romanticism" to describe the revitalized nature of romanticism in the last years of the nineteenth and the early part of the twentieth century. Many of the essentially mystical forces and much of the Volkish framework it had retained are already familiar to us. But Diederichs restated these views, this "New Romanticism," with a forceful emphasis at a time when positivism had made deep inroads in German scientific, industrial, and political life, when materialism, the urge for aggrandizement, engrossed an increasingly larger part of the population. The specter confronting him was the generation of economic empire builders, in mid-passage in Europe as well as the United States. In reaction to this gilded age, Diederichs and his New Romantics did not resort to muckraking as had their American colleagues. Instead, they called for a return to the higher, transcendent reality, and for intuition as a vehicle of communication with that world. This ideology attracted to its ranks not advocates of social welfare or enterprising men in search of personal wealth, but people who stood in danger of being swept away by this new wave of materialism—those who were emotionally or materially tied to traditional ways.

Diederichs, with his New Romanticism, did not blindly embrace the narrowly circumscribed ideology of the Volk as it had evolved during the nineteenth century. Nor did he entertain a fanatical idealism. The air of respectability that distinguished his approach was due to an analytical and judicious estimate of contemporary German thought and of the direction it could and should take. Diederichs' moderation was thought respectable, in contrast with the fanaticism of a Langbehn. To Diederichs the crisis German ideology was experiencing was apparent: industrial materialism was being opposed by a new spiritual vitality. Mechanism and positivism were being met by truly creative aspirations which would reconstitute the German national character. A new type of thought had been fostered by proximity to the soil, as had a strengthened feeling for the occult.[4] By "occult" neither Diederichs nor Langbehn meant theosophy and spiritualism in a dogmatic sense. Although Diederichs had flirted briefly with theosophy, and had called his publishing house "theosophical," he soon rejected this as too narrow. For Diederichs it was the *Geist* (a word that significantly lacks an English equivalent) which embodied the mystical force of the universe. Earlier romantics had employed a similar concept and the same word to designate human empathy with cosmic vitality. Diederichs used the word in the same way. He styled the *Geist* as the "longing of the soul towards unity." [5] He wrote in his publisher's catalogue of 1920 that the New Romantics wanted to enjoy and behold the world as a whole once more, not as portrayed and dissected by simplistic rationalism.[6] Only intuition could serve as the vehicle for attaining this goal, the visualizing of the "world picture." The guidelines were laid down in the fifteenth and sixteenth centuries, when the vitality of the Volk unfolded within zestful and genuine men of the humanist age, in such figures as Paracelsus and Dürer. However, at an even earlier time, the

German mystics had made a valid contribution toward strengthening the *Geist,* and Diederichs appropriately published Meister Eckhart's complete works. In contrast, he rated Luther's Reformation, with its emphasis on the Bible (secondhand religion), as far inferior to the reformation Eckhart had desired.[7]

Diederichs' New Romanticism was not a dream world removed from reality. Rather, it looked for concrete means for overcoming the materialism and naturalism of his time.[8] The aspiring spiritual forces that whirled around him needed a reshaping, a remolding, in order that they might become alive and realize themselves.[9] Gathered together in an "idealism of deeds," they could construct an environment conducive to the development of the *Geist.* This did not mean a return to the past, to a peasant utopia, which, he held quite rightly, would leave twenty million Germans unemployed.[10] But neither would this idealism tolerate increasing industrialization. Indeed, we are never told how twenty million workers could be kept employed while a spiritual society was being established. This vagueness is partly explained by the precedence that the "idealism" took over the "deed," a transposition inspired by the hatred of positivism. However, the vagueness is also indicative of the presuppositions in Diederichs' thought. After all, it was not necessary to define the process, as the principle was sufficient to communicate the meaning and the consequences of his vision. Indeed, he set the revitalization of Germany through ideology in opposition to the principle of organization. Such a viewpoint will be typical for most of Volkish thought.[11] According to Diederichs, the adoption of an irrational, emotional, and mystical world view by each individual German would automatically produce the desired results. At the very least it would create a new community of thought.

This community and its program, the "idealism of deeds," required a fixed sphere of identity, a set horizon. These would be furnished by the soil and the Volk. Diederichs came to this conclusion through his speculation that the whole cannot be attained until its several parts are first acquired. The soil, the earth, the Volk, were the component parts of a great universal absolute. Through forces that emanated from them, these phenomena attached themselves to the cosmos. Consequently, if the individual desired to fulfill his longings for unity with the eternal and gain an understanding of the secret enveloped in history, he had to have roots.[12] The soil was once more equated with the Volk. Only through roots anchored in the Volk could the German find a release for his religious dynamic—a force subsumed in the *Geist.* The total population of the nation, regardless of occupational or social differences, made up the Volk.

The effectiveness of the *Geist* depended upon this all-embracing quality of the Volk.[13] The community of the Volk constituted that unity for which the soul yearned. Its existence and vitality were a prerequisite for that intuitive grasp of the cosmos which signified the function of the true *Geist*.

Quite naturally, the peasant ideal, historicity, and culture played pre-eminent roles in Diederichs' concept of the Volk, as they had for the other romantic and Volkish thinkers. The publisher was himself of peasant stock. Revealingly, he wrote in a personal memorandum: "I have always felt close to mother nature. Partly out of the tradition of my forebears, partly out of the core of my spiritual orientation: This has involved within me a desire to anchor myself in reality in order to find from it the path to the cosmic-metaphysical." [14] Pride in his peasant origin was combined with an interest in German cultural history. In discussing the science that would probe the origins of the German Volk (*Stammeskunde*), he maintained that its primary evidence consisted of what the peasants had to say about themselves. Furthermore, the historical needs of such a science necessitated the use of old myths and sagas. Only through these media, Diederichs felt, could the soul of the Volk communicate with the city dwellers, who, unfortunately, had lived for too long away from the soil.[15] To further such a cultural revival and integration, Diederichs undertook to edit ancient German myths and sagas, since only these literary forms had captured the spirit of an age when Germanic culture was still pure.[16] In line with this effort, he published *Der Wehrwolf*, whose author, Hermann Löns, he held in high esteem.

All this has the familiar Volkish ring about it. But in certain respects Diederichs differed with the more popular, extremist movement. Although the submergence of the New Romanticism into the Volk provided the answer to the German crisis of ideology even for Diederichs, he drew a line at accepting the narrow Volkish precepts which claimed a special uniqueness for the German nation. For him, the true community of the Volk was not equivalent to a population united simply by powerful political or national interests; nor was racial uniqueness the sole force that cemented the interests of the nation. It was here that Diederichs displayed his greater broadness of mind. What Volkish thinkers restricted to a purely German inheritance and prerogative, Diederichs by the same logic extended to other nations, other peoples. He viewed the new racial theories with some ambivalence, but race, to be sure, was something with which the true metaphysical impulse chose to interact. However, more than race and the metaphysical impulse was required for the formation of the spiritual base of the nation. Although all the necessary elements were possessed by Germans and their *Geist* was an indispensable cosmic entity, there was nothing that had decreed Germany's exclusive rights to such a relationship. Being Germanic, according to Diederichs, meant rendering allegiance to a New Romanticism whose counterparts could be found even among Slavs, Celts, and Jews.[17]

The cosmic orientation of the nation and the Volk was of paramount importance in determining whether they possessed a *Geist*. And though such a feeling could emanate only from a rooted people, the privilege must not be confined too narrowly. In attempting to separate the various cosmic identities that distinguished peoples and their different cultural heritages, Diederichs tried to avoid narrow nationalistic categories. He regarded the nationalistic furor of his time as a stage in the evolution of cosmic law, a process crystalizing otherwise chaotic longings. But such nationalistic aspirations alone were not yet creative. Merely historically oriented and focused upon the past, they tended to ignore the immediate dynamism of those ideals which emanated from the soil. The true community consisted of those who really lived in the *Geist;* its members were bound together by a shared experience of the absolute which gave them strength and heightened their sense of life.[18] As the *Geist* was not the property of one nation or race to the exclusion of others, racial or national purity was not a prerequisite for an enjoyment of the spiritual life. Diederichs' tolerance in this area can be traced partly to his admiration for Chinese, Indian, and Islamic ideas, which, by virtue of their anti-imperialistic orientation, he thought could impart a new life and direction to European culture.[19]

Such ideas seem to contradict the important emphasis upon the soil and the Volk. Indeed, there was a certain ambivalence in Diederichs' thought, a tension best exemplified in his attitude toward the Jews. On the one hand, he rejected anti-Semitism, since the Jews were indispensable to the peoples of Europe—dispersed throughout the continent, they formed a link between the various countries and thus softened the discord produced by the growing nationalism. On the other hand, he treated the Jews as a distinctly different and foreign race. Their ethos was determined by their Near Eastern origins and their cosmic sense derived from a static center, the law, and then diffused outward. In Europe, on the other hand, cosmic feeling had priority and penetrated *inward* to the center, the Volk.[20] Diederichs ascribed to the Jews a characteristic that was similarly projected by the whole Volkish movement: they lived according to a sterile law from which they intellectualized and suffocated their inner spirituality. It is partly in these terms that modern anti-Semitism has to be

understood: Germans searched for a uniqueness to distinguish themselves from aspects of modernity they disliked. They wished to draw
out of their personality and national heritage new forms and insights
whose validity could be proved by their relationship to an eternal,
cosmological entity. Consequently, since they rejected all mechanization and industrialization, they ascribed intellectual and "Oriental"
qualities to the people who had supposedly forced modernity upon
the Germans—the Jews. Since Diederichs ascribed racial differences
to Jews and Europeans but also held that Jews performed an indispensable function in Europe, his views seem ambivalent and indeed
confusing. However, that Diederichs could undisturbedly tolerate
such contradictory ideas can best be understood in the context of
his ever-increasing occultism. Though he would personally reject
such an association, his peculiar emphasis on the cosmic and metaphysical led him precisely in this direction.

At the beginning of his publishing venture, Diederichs had abandoned the concept of theosophy as too narrow and had dropped the
term "theosophical" from the title of his publishing house.[21] Behind
this lay his rejection of the existence of ghosts, a belief entertained
by the kind of spiritualism popular in his day. Nonetheless, the basic
precepts of the cosmological outlook he embraced were close to
theosophical thought. This was especially true when he talked about
forces arising from the earth, extrasensory forces that captivated one's
senses, and he came to believe in mystical fluids that united the individual with the community. To be sure, these were not (as they
were for theosophists) electric currents flowing from the cosmic
ether, but the similarities were undeniably significant. Diederichs
saw the same laws contained in history: history not as a chronicle of
facts but as a thickening of events which exemplified the universally
valid laws of life. The life force, the cosmic reality, was the essence of
the historical process.[22] In entertaining such concepts, Diederichs
came close to sharing Langbehn's identification with spiritualism
and with the theosophical painter Fidus' view that the artistic impulse to produce a painting and the stimulation communicated by the
completed work of art are matters of extrasensory perception.[23] Indeed, Fidus came to be associated with Diederichs professionally,
illustrating many books brought out by his publishing house.

The sun was another image with theosophical connotations that
Diederichs used, but he preferred to regard the cult he built around
it as traceable to the Volk rather than to spiritualism. The festival
of the changing sun, an old Germanic custom, was endowed by
Diederichs with new meaning and was celebrated yearly among
his circle of young adherents. Thus, a Volk custom and spiritualistic

symbolism became intertwined. Diederichs himself wrote to a friend: "My view of God is this, that I regard the sun as source of all life." The rays of the sun represented material infused with the *Geist*, a visible substance transferring invisible heat. After all, the rays came from the cosmic beyond and bestowed actual warmth upon man. He added, typically without really committing himself: "I do not want to think about this. I only want to experience within me the growth of the *Geist*." [24]

This trend in Diederichs' philosophy contained an element of great importance in the development of the New Romanticism. Sun worship will occupy us again, for in the Volkish movement it was acclaimed as an authentic religious expression with cosmic and Germanic meaning. In a mythological manner, the Germans of the North, who truly yearned for the sunlight to penetrate their perpetual mist and fog, were said to have a special hunger for knowledge of the source of the seemingly sacred light. And even present-day Volkish journals, which still communicate their ideology to a not inconsiderable readership, acclaim the sun as the sole God of the true Germans.[25]

Diederichs' own faith was Christianity according to the teachings of Eckhart, not those of the Bible. In essence it was a mixture of mystical and individualistic precepts, a fusion of solar cultism and Christianity. His argument in favor of this belief stated that only the individual's soul could appreciate and understand the life forces that emanate from the sun. And since the soul was linked to the Volk, the knowledge it gains from a personal mysticism can have meaning only in the framework of a Germanic Christianity.[26] Diederichs, like Lagarde and Langbehn, saw Christianity split along the lines of spontaneous faith and strict dogma. Christ, accordingly, could not have been simply a law giver, even though he was a Jew, and divine at that. Instead, he was the sign and symbol of the cosmic spirit, a spirit that could be apprehended only in a quasi-mystical union with it. This was true Christianity according to Diederichs. How then had it been perverted? Here the publisher again echoed Volkish reasoning. He accused St. Paul of encasing the true theology in a strangling dogmatism.[27] This line of thought, of course, was truly Volkish and provided an added rationale for a deepened anti-Semitism.

Diederichs' attitude toward conventional Christianity was quite hostile and he even admitted that the very name of Christ made him nervous.[28] He published works demonstrating the falsity of the historical and traditional concept of Christ. His own metaphysical ideals, on the other hand, not only found ideological expression but were also taken up by enthusiastic young adherents who, at Jena, joined together in what was called the Sera Circle. The circle, under Diederichs' guidance, celebrated the yearly festival associated with the changing of the sun, and since its members were part of the Youth Movement, it also emphasized folk music and dancing. Diederichs himself never disguised the circle's essentially heathen aspects. On the contrary, he reveled in its pseudo Greek and Roman settings, its wild Dionysian dances, and its colorful red banner with a flaming gold sun in the center.[29] Part of this display was geared to shock the philistines in the small university town, to give the circle an anti-bourgeois bent. But the greater part was a direct expression of Diederichs' sincere belief in the genuinely spiritual, or *geistige,* nature of the cult.

Diederichs' penchant for the occult significantly colored other areas of his ideology, as it related to culture, civilization, social organization, and politics. Specifically, he envisaged that his "idealism of deeds" would be effected by a small group of initiates who had perceived and fully comprehended the mystical intermingling of active, tangible forces with the cosmological elements that were symbolized by the sun. These men, imbued with their mystical concepts, would form what Diederichs called the "secret yet open *Bund* of those who have the *Geist.*" [30] They were secret insofar as they constituted a self-conscious and dedicated cell; open in that they created a public forum to propagate their views. The effectiveness of such organizations was clearly perceived by Diederichs in records of analogous sects drawn from the annals of the sixteenth and seventeenth centuries. It was indeed to this age that he went for inspiration on the subject and found a historical parallel in the order of the Rosicrucians and the *illuminati* which had flowered during the seventeenth century.[31] It is surely significant that ideas, cults, and theories which in the rest of Europe were simply passing fads became associated in Germany with serious world views.

That only a small number of men were required to form the circle of initiates also reflected Diederichs' elitist tendencies. Indeed, he believed that as few as a dozen metaphysically oriented men could make a decisive impact on the public. To initiate greater numbers would be to spoil the uniqueness and individuality of the cult as well as to contradict the natural division that raised the noble few above the common multitude. In this respect, it is not surprising that Diederichs proclaimed his adherence to the romantic notion of the inherent superiority of culture over civilization and the comparable values of their origins: "Democracy is civilization, while aristocracy equals culture." [32] Needless to say, Diederichs considered himself part of the aristocracy with a commensurate responsibility to revitalize the cultural life of Germany. This obligation, he felt, was already being implemented. For did not the initiates form the Sera Circle, and the publishing house and *Die Tat* provide the public forum?

Diederichs applied a similar framework and system of values to the state. Culture and the aristocracy were to form the bulwark of the nation, since jointly they reflected the interests of the Volk and alone could implement the "idealism of deeds" which would permit the revitalization of the Volk.[33] The state and political activity were considered merely means to an end, a view that was basic to a large segment of the Volkish movement, though it was not shared by the powerful, super-patriotic organization called the Alldeutsche (Pan-Germans), who opposed Diederichs in this respect.[34] At best, the state was a servant of the *Geist*, of the Volk and its interests. After all, he wrote, one cannot place the forms of organization and the soul of a living organism on an equal plane.[35] If the two phenomena were indeed different, then they could also be viewed as incompatible. Like his Volkish counterparts, Diederichs made exactly such a division when he called for an open confrontation between the state and the profound cultural forces inherent in the Volk. In ideological terms, neither his cult nor the Volkish movement ever advocated the acceptance of the *status quo*. In fact, before and especially after 1918 they persistently demanded a revolutionary overthrow of the state.

As a replacement for the state, Diederichs envisaged a culturally grounded nation guided by the initiated elite. The society would be a hierarchy established according to estates, or corporations, composed of professions, trades, skills, and other occupations. Though he allowed for universal suffrage, the dominant body in the new nation would be the chamber of corporations, which would provide the indispensable aristocratic principle of government.[36] In this respect his writings and the ideas of the Volkish movement shared an important elitist tinge: on the one hand, there were the select, the initiates and the intelligentsia; on the other, the vast mass of outsiders who had to be educated and led. Both ideologies, Diederichs' and that of the Volkish movement, were aristocratic in nature. With their rejection of the modern, industrial, mass society they denied themselves the great advantage of the modern mass movements— the power of large numbers. Their opposition to the "masses" as part of modernity deprived them of the only really effective means for realizing the revolution they desired. But that, of course, was due to the intrinsic nature of their elitist presuppositions. The Nazis, whose elitism did not suffer from the same handicap, were able to succeed where they had only laid the ideological basis. When the National Socialists assimilated the Volkish ideology, this obstacle was removed and both swept on to victory under the banner of a thousand-year future for the Volk.

However, there was a difference between Diederichs' elitism and that of the rest of the Volkish movement which made his own more positive and effective in the propagation of their mutual ideological precepts. It contained an activist drive, a messianic dynamism, to effect certain changes in the immediate situation. In some respects this ingredient could be compared with the stress Egidy placed upon education. Diederichs realized that even though a mystical disposition on the part of individuals would produce some changes in the group character, by itself the metaphysical impulse that would illuminate life could effect nothing. Consequently, he was prone to admonish the older romantics for having ignored the fact that this impulse had to be transformed into an "idealism of deeds." [37] *Logos* would have to become a deed, a determined act. A dialectical interchange, a tension between matter and spirit, was inevitable, and indeed desirable. It rendered the individual's inwardness more dynamic and made his urge toward unity in the community of the Volk all the more meaningful.[38] In short, Diederichs was more cognizant of the reality around him and made use of its malleability more so than the earlier Volkish prophets.

But the Volkish movement was quick to grasp the initiative and make up for lost time. Its emphasis on effecting a change in "external reality," in the here and now, increased and became an important element in the popular appeal of the ideology. In the years during which Diederichs wrote—before, during, and after the First World War—the Volkish movement felt compelled to act against its enemies, domestic and foreign. After all, this was the time when Germany's economic and social problems were aggravated, when a general disorientation and chaos seemed to have reached a climax, when the prophecies of Germanic apostles like Langbehn and Lagarde seemed verified.

Diederichs, as we have described him so far, was of course important in other respects besides his direct connection with the Volkish thinkers. Some of his ideas did in fact run parallel to—albeit on a more respectable, intellectual, and moderate plane—the more extreme ideas of the Volkish movement. But although his ideas at times were too subtle for the movement and although, significantly, he never belonged to the association of Volkish publishers, Heinrich von Gleichen's influential journal, *Gewissen*, could write after Diederichs' death that he had been in profound harmony with the spirit of his times.[39] It was, above all, through his contacts in the publishing world, among authors and artists, that he wielded a wide, if not always tangible, influence.[40]

Many of his authors reflected the same concern for mystical forces as Diederichs did himself. Generally they were of the same moderate and even scholarly character, except for those of Hermann Löns, who indulged in a more extreme and irrational expression. Through the concept of "mythos" some of these authors formulated what seemed to be the crux of the world's problems and of Diederichs' attempt to solve them. Martin Buber, more of a friend than one of his authors (though Diederichs published one of his many books), whose early work and thought was linked to this school, gave a relatively precise formulation of the meaning of "mythos" within a Jewish context. He considered it an eternal function of the soul through which concrete events grasped by the senses were interpreted by the soul as divine and absolute. Correspondingly, a man whose soul functioned genuinely, necessarily experienced a heightened feeling for nature's irrational forces as communicated and contained in each particular experience.[41] Thus he would be sensitive to and cognizant of all his experiences as lying within the context of the absolute, of the divine. The mythos, then, linked man to the absolute through the continuous intervention of the divine and cosmic forces which stand behind it. Although this is also Diederichs' concept of metaphysical experience, it was Buber who elucidated it and further defined the mythos as the elemental state of being from which the soul surges forth in the quest for unity outside itself.

The elemental mythos was contained in the Volk, where alone it could acquire the stature commensurate with its potential power. For Buber, it was not contemporary Jewry, but rather the medieval Jewish mystics from Poland, the Chassidim, who typified the mythos of the Jewish Volk. Similarly, for Diederichs only German mystics like Eckhart truly understood the metaphysical impulse of the Germanic Volk. With the Volk as the receptacle, Buber tells us, the mythos drives the soul on to ever deeper unity with the cosmic reality. The God Yahweh, who already was cast in the role of a national cosmic deity, is now broadened to become the God of "all," the God of humanity, the Lord of the soul.[42] In many respects, Buber's longing for unity and submergence into the spiritual essence goes further than that of Diederichs. For Diederichs the containment in the Volk was and remained more central than for Buber. The difference notwithstanding, the ideas that went into Buber's Zionism paralleled those which went to comprise the New Romanticism.

It was not Diederichs himself but one of his authors who exercised considerable influence upon Martin Buber. Arthur Bonus is forgotten today, but in Diederichs' and Buber's early years his impact was extensive. He was one of the original cosmic thinkers in search of the mythos, which he too hoped would resuscitate the suppressed emotional nature of humanity; and he too thought that it had finally manifested itself in the form of the New Romanticism to become the wave of the future. For Bonus the mythos also had its roots in the proximity of man to the "all," to nature, to his own life, and to fate. It was an ethereal force, which in neither Bonus' nor Diederichs' cosmology could find a place within legal formulations or the dogmatism of orthodox Christianity. And although the older mythos, that of the Biblical fathers and the ancient Germans, had tolerated terms and emotions such as "guilt," "repentance," and "grace," since then the mythos had undergone historical transformations that had made it unreceptive to the old, confined piety.[43] Even in the form of the Reformation, which it had assumed when it burst into human history on one of its rare occasions, the mythos was unacceptable to contemporary needs. All these previous manifestations had been merely transitory episodes; but they were nonetheless the true moments from which humanity had drawn its breath and life.[44] For Bonus as for Diederichs, the Volk comprised the primary community through which the mythos expanded to manifest itself as the ideal love of all mankind.[45]

The religious undercurrents of the mythos were twofold: Christianity and a Germanic faith. As the metaphysical impulse emanated from the Volk, where alone it found a basis for self-realization, its character would bear the mark of particular peoples. Christianity would inevitably have to undergo a process of Germanization, in which the true mythos of the age could come into being and the individual could manifest his ethical potential. Clearly then, for Bonus, as for the Volkish ideologues and prophets, a Germanic Christianity was an integral part of the New Romanticism.

Bonus, however, deserves more detailed consideration on two additional counts that distinguish him from Diederichs. First, he placed great emphasis on the importance of the human will. According to him, it was this faculty which facilitated man's contact with the mythos and strove for community in the Volk. For Bonus, as for the Volkish thinkers to a lesser degree, the will signified that personal dynamic which was the cement of the Volk's faith.[46] Such considerations reflected a Kantian influence, on the one hand, and a Nietzschean re-emphasis, on the other. The latter had indeed been appropriated by the New Romantics. Karl Joel's book *Nietzsche und die Romantik* (*Nietzsche and Romanticism*) (1905), published by Diederichs, praised Nietzsche as the most romantic soul of all times, as a man who had an unlimited passion for the *Geist*. This distortion was achieved by equating Nietzsche's power of will with the passion of the soul to penetrate the cosmic essence. Here, according to the New Romantics, was a soul full of great tensions, capable of fantastic moral fluctuations, and able to feel that lust and sorrow which alone could produce an irresistible urge toward the infinite. Diederichs' tension between the material and the spiritual forces, as well as Bonus' emphasis upon the will, became boundless romantic passions. Thus Nietzsche was adopted into the pantheon of New Romanticism, and furthered the trend toward activism that was so much a part of New Romantic yearnings.

Small wonder that it was possible for Ernst Bertram in his *Nietzsche* (1918) and, later, Alfred Bäumler to take the next logical step: the transformation of the passion into an advocacy of force. The Nietzsche of National Socialism was the great battler for whom life was senseless without the good fight. The New Romantics' accent upon the internal became, in the end, a blatant praise of force, of the necessity of struggle to realize the new utopia. The tension between the material and the spiritual, a dichotomy accepted by both Diederichs and Bonus, was then resolved into the glorification of violent struggle. The element of force engrained in the Volkish ideology, as depicted in Hermann Löns' *Der Wehrwolf*, had moved to the foreground. Hitler was to call this urge an expression of the "heroic will" in the service of the Volk.

Bonus' second important contribution was his sharp separation of science from true reality. By science he meant the knowledge of history, religion, and nature that is acquired through scholarly study and disciplined learning. He considered the insights gained in this manner to be technical information of value only to the herd.[47] The scholarly examination of religion, for example, would provide merely quantitative information; it could never solve the higher problems of existence.[48] If the achievement of formal knowledge had a recognizable purpose, it was essentially negative. It only encouraged man's intellect to strive against his visions. That is, it fossilized man's sensitivity to the cosmic forces. However, such knowledge might perform an auxiliary function if it permitted man to perceive those aspects of the cosmic vision which created doubts and fears within him. These hindrances could then be overcome by a will steeled to deal with them.[49] Thus, acquired knowledge, at its best, supplemented the strength of the will; at its worst, it was a petty accomplishment. The rejection of empiricism implied here amounted to a rejection of science—indeed, of all human knowledge—as insignificant and meaningless. In this respect, the New Romanticism followed its predecessor in exhibiting a strong streak of anti-intellectualism.

For the numerous parallel developments to be found in the Volkish ideology and in the ideas of Diederichs and Bonus, there are a significant number of dissimilarities. Racial ideas, for example, figured minimally in the thought of these men. They would have deplored, as did some of the Volkish thinkers, the crude racial ideas of the Nazis—ideas which nonetheless had thrived within the Volkish movement and eventually ripened for the Nazi harvest. But, above all, the elitism of these men was irreconcilable with the use of the mass movement introduced by some later Volkish groups and carried to victory by the Nazis. In the end though, one is tempted to ask whether there really did not exist a logical development from one to the other. What had been an element of anti-intellectualism in Bonus and Diederichs was transformed by the National Socialists into an irrationality that the "herd" could grasp and act upon. What had been a sophisticated ideology for these men was for the Nazis a system of thought whose rejection of acquired knowledge facilitated the use of mass propaganda.

Although these differences should be taken into consideration, it is the similarities that are significant. When, as in this case, sufficient material is available, the historian can perceive a trend of causality, of interconnection between similar and especially contemporary phenomena. He can also evaluate the complementary nature of the several systems of thought and the responsibilities they share for the final use to which they were put. Was Germany unique in Europe? Other nations had movements similar to the New Romanticism. Barrès and Maurras in France also called for an internal renewal of their nation, a transformation that would entail both a metaphysical religious conviction and political action.[50] But this impetus never penetrated as deeply as in Germany, nor did it lead to the same end. It is important to clarify this once again, since German historians, of late, have been happy to point out parallels with other Western nations. Yet, even though these may have shared certain elements with the New Romanticism, the chemistry of the German movement was quite different. In Germany, the romantic, Volkish ideology established a frame of reference which reached deeper into the nation.

CHAPTER 4

Ancient Germans Rediscovered

THE SENSE of a glorious past played a leading role in both the old and the New Romanticism. After all, the primary condition of a Volk was its rootedness in nature—an attribute not to be attained overnight. Rootedness implied antiquity, an ancient people set in an equally ancient landscape, which by now bore the centuries-old imprint of the people's soul. Antiquity also conveyed the connotation of youth, of the moment of inception, when the pure, unadulterated, heroic, and virtuous qualities of the Volk had been first thrust into history. The aspirations of the Volk in the modern era would consequently have to become reidentified with its heroic past, with its youth. The historian Heinrich von Sybel, writing in 1867, reaffirmed this imperative when he said that a nation had to cherish its historical ties, that otherwise the Volk would resemble a tree deprived of its roots. This return to Germanic roots required a focusing, a fixation of one's vision upon the ancient, tribal Germany, where traditional virtues had remained intact: "The Germans of Tacitus were the Germans in their youth." [1]

In the Volkish thinkers' efforts to solidify their ideological base, they turned to history for help and applied the images and material of the past to the modern scene. Their favorite source of reference and their favorite authority on the history of the ancient Germans came to be Tacitus. The context in which this distinguished Roman historian wrote was considered irrelevant or was twisted to convey the desired implications. That his book, *Germania*, was a piece of propaganda within a specific context was simply ignored. Where Tacitus was primarily concerned with contrasting the Germanic virtues of fresh strength and endurance with increasing Roman degeneracy, Volkish authors took the contrast at face value and extended the favorable descriptions of the Germans to their culture, their racial stock and purity, as well as to their religious outlook and myth-ology.

The Roman propagandist became the prophet expounding the ancient purity of Germanic virtues. In many respects, it was exactly this emphasis on purity that was stressed by the Volkish movement. After all, in *Germania*, Tacitus had described the Germans as people who had not mixed with other tribes, who, according to modern terminology—precisely the sense in which it was used—had retained the distinction of being a special Volk. Other arguments were derived from this ancient description to substantiate such a rationale. Houston Stewart Chamberlain used such arguments, and as he was the most influential of racial theorists (accepted despite his English origins), what he had to say about Tacitus became normative. For Chamberlain the Roman's work confirmed the racial purity of the original Volk. As additional evidence, Chamberlain cited Tacitus' description of the physical homogeneity that distinguished the Germans.[2] From Tacitus' unfavorable depiction of the Jews—which the Volkish historians connected with the belief that the Jews were racially impure—was derived the concept that enmity between Germans and Jews was time-honored and eternal. It followed that the contrast between good and evil, between being German and being Jewish respectively, was indeed enshrined in antiquity and must be retained as a precept of the modern Volk.

But Volkish thinkers did not rest satisfied with showing that the history of the ancient Germans provided the indispensable antecedent to the present Volk. If the Goths had been so heroic in antiquity, if they had surpassed such prestigious and powerful nations as Greece and Rome in strength and endurance, then they must have represented an absolute value. The Germanic tribe's entrance into historical consciousness, correspondingly, could not have been simply an accidental, fortuitous, or even evolutionary occurrence. It was something greater. Its appearance was motivated by more profound and eternal forces.

It was in this context that Volkish ideologists noted that Tacitus had written at a time when the Germans made their historical debut. His descriptions, therefore, took on an added meaning and constituted more than just a chronology of historical events. They became in practice the prophetic words of an apostle preaching the inception of a government by a great, exceptional people. Thus, Chamberlain could assert that the virtuous, victorious Germanic tribes had appeared on the historical stage just in time. While Rome was deteriorating in its degeneracy, the heroic men from the North scourged the slothful civilization and saved humanity. The envigorating force of the Germans embodied a "saving angel, the giver of a new dawn for humanity." [3] Rome, the seat of a distinguished civilization, and Roman power fell to the inheritance of the Germans. Chamberlain only deplored that the Nordic race had not made more efficient use of this power, that it had failed to completely eradicate all the degeneracy that surrounded it, thereby putting an end to the "chaos of the peoples." In other words, the ancient Germans had unfortunately not established themselves as the sole rulers of the conquered peoples and territory; they had not imposed their superior culture and virtues as the only standards of excellence.[4]

That the Germans had inherited temporal power from the ancient Romans was readily accepted by Volkish thinkers, and if the Germans are taken to be the Goths, it was, in fact, historically true. But they did not accept the view held by the early romantics, that Nordic man had also assimilated the cultures of Rome and Greece. On the contrary, it was now argued, the reverse was the case. The Germans had had a unique culture of their own. Had not Tacitus described it? Moreover, their appearance which dissolved Roman hegemony did not signify that they had lain dormant until then. Prior to this time, it was stated, they had influenced human events in a diversity of ways. As the genuine, as the solely pure race of peoples, the Germans, it was claimed, represented all that was creative since the inception of time. From the very beginning, before they had entered history as a group, Germans had affected the cultures of Greece and Rome. This theoretical assertion transformed the ancient Greeks into Germans and divorced modern Greeks from their classical heritage. Similarly, Rome in its glorious period must have been led by Germanic leaders. In essence, the German Volk was like a tree growing from particularly profound roots: it could not inherit anything; it was the sole repository of all creativity and any genius that had ever existed.[5]

Even before Chamberlain, Volkish thinkers attempted to draw historical lessons, examples, and analogies to apply to the present. The contemporary Germans, in their view, had to reidentify themselves with the virtues that had carried the ancient Germanic tribes to victory over Rome. History was telescoped: the heroic past was transformed into the present to infuse a similar heroism into the modern generation. This process of idealization was especially influential during the period of turmoil that preceded the unification of Germany.

Felix Dahn's immensely popular novel, *Kampf um Rom* (*Fight for Rome*) (1867), illustrates this well. The author, a professor of history at Königsberg, made early German history his specialty. Inspired by the concept of the Volk, he produced a lively rendition of the early trials and achievements of the German people. The novel, overflowing with an enthusiastic passion for the Volk and the fatherland, was distributed by Dahn to isolated German communities in the Tyrol with the express purpose of preventing them from being Italianized and absorbed.[6] The author's enthusiasm for the Germanic forebears, their beliefs and virtues, eventually caused the Catholic Church to charge him with responsibility for a revival of the Wotan cult in Germany. A conscientious Protestant, Dahn disclaimed any such purpose.[7] We can easily believe that Dahn had no formal connections with the cult. However, he cannot evade responsibility for having drawn popular attention to a glorified German past in which the mythology, the moral, ethical, and social values, and the physical qualities of the Goths were extolled. It seemed to him and to his readers that these marks of distinction were sadly lacking in modern Germany.

Written just after Italy had achieved unification, the novel exhorted Germany to do likewise. Through its recital of the struggle for supremacy between the Goths and the Romans, it attempted to depict that celebrated national valor which had carried the Goths (used interchangeably with Germans) to victory. In the account of the German conquest of Italy during the Dark Ages, the novel's protagonist was, in fact, the entire Gothic nation. The blond, manly exterior of these people mirrored a purity of soul, which furnished the sufficient reason for their success (symbolically, the "Italianized" daughter of King Theodoric becomes infected with the debauchery of the Romans and eventually drowns in a Roman bath). Contained within this purity of race were also the elements of honesty and courage which, in the struggle against the rationality and calculating cleverness of the prefect Gethegus, caused the defeat of this Roman. But it was the physical prowess relentlessly employed in the pursuit of victory that distinguished the early Germans from the effete and debauched Romans, and enabled them to serve as models for modern Germany.[8]

Diederichs claimed that the ancient Germanic virtues had been forged, tempered, and strengthened in this mortal and bloodthirsty conflict between the two peoples.[9] Dahn doubtless would have concurred. Indeed, the idealized combat of old rendered more attractive the Volkish idea of the indispensability of the good fight, of the war that steeled the nerves and character of a nation. In a spirit similar to that found later in Löns' Der Wehrwolf, Dahn praised war as creating the heroes that are celebrated in legends, poems, and history. He also stressed an additional quality possessed by the ancients: their peasant roots.[10] The reasoning again runs true to Volkish form; the

Germans are inherently of peasant stock, as reflected in the fusion of the soul and historicity in the roots of the Volk. As one writer of the Nazi period expressed the thought: "At a time when the Semites were still searching for their promised land and Romulus and Remus were fighting each other, our fatherland already possessed a settled peasant culture." [11] Both in the popular mind and in the Volkish movement, this fusion of peasant and ancient Germanic traits led to an adoration of a primitivism that encompassed such virtues as honesty and loyalty as much as it extolled the "righteous" power of the sword.

If Dahn, who styled himself a national liberal, hesitated to espouse the logical consequences of an idealization of the past, others did not. As the ancient Germans represented people closer to the roots of the Volkish tree than their modern counterparts, so the ancient religious beliefs, mythology, and gods also came to represent the unfailing source of primeval strength and genuineness, qualities that were lacking in modern religious doctrine. Consequently, ancient symbolism, such as the rune and the swastika, and old legends, such as that of Mittgart, a place believed to be the original home of Nordic man, assumed an immediate and urgent importance. The eminent sociologist Eugen Dühring only extended Dahn's passionate identification with the past when, in his bitter book against the Jews, *Die Judenfrage* (*The Jewish Question*) (1880), he wrote that the Nordic gods of antiquity were still sentient, vital forces residing in nature as of old. They had endured even through the years of neglect, years in which they were replaced by Christianity.[12] Where men like Diederichs had indulged in talk about a Germanic Christianity, others, who actively longed to recapture the roots of Germanism, displayed a marked trend toward a committed heathenism.

As a central part of this growing paganism, solar occultism experienced a sharp rise in the late nineteenth and the early twentieth century. It played an important role in Diederichs' thought and had adherents as early as 1848. At that time, C. H. Carus reflected on solar symbolism and attributed the inequality of the races to the fact that some had a more positive attitude toward the sun than had others.[13] A common explanation of the origin of sun worship contended that northern peoples, inhabitants of foggy regions, expressed a natural longing for the sun, which, to them, represented light, hope, and the conceptual center of the cosmos. Such is the tenacity of this simplistic argument, most popular at the turn of the century, that it has been invoked as recently as 1955. At that time it was succinctly restated by the National Socialist Johann von Leers, residing in secure exile in Egypt, a man who had learned nothing and forgotten nothing.

Under the Nazis he was a guiding spirit in formulating their racial policy and the author of the violently anti-Semitic book *Juden sehen dich an* (*Jews Look at You*). He claimed that to Nordic peoples the cycle of the sun was symbolic of life in general, as proved by their own particular experience. During the foggy period when the sun was hidden from man it mirrored a brooding contemplative episode in man's inner self. When, however, it broke from the clouds, man's spirit would respond by joyfully and victoriously ascending toward the glowing orb. The gloom of night had given way to the long-awaited festival of the changing sun; again its recurrence had marked the triumph of indomitable and eternal rebirth.[14]

This symbolism of a reborn sun, in which the concept of *karma* (rebirth) played a central role, was found throughout the increasingly popular ancient sagas. The *Edda*, a very ancient collection of German legends, portrayed the old religion and its gods with a startling vitality. Indeed, the *Edda* was an even more popular inspirational source for Volkish ideology than was the *Niebelungenlied*. Brought out by a number of Volkish publishers, it was a special favorite of Diederichs and his followers. Throughout the 1920's, the *Edda* was itself supplemented by a special series of publications devoted to the Eddic religion and world view. Some of these studies transformed Christ into the Germanic sun god and the Virgin Mary into the mother of the Aryans.[15] Others regarded the birthday of Christ as a celebration of the return of Baldur, the god of light, from the kingdom of darkness.[16]

The many hypotheses that grew up around the sun cults and Germanic religion verged at times on the absurdly irrational. They entertained symbols that had lost all relation to a plausible reality—as, for instance, in the patently Volkish reasoning of Leers, who stated that since the sun rose to the right, it is little wonder that those who are degenerate call themselves of the left. Here, Leers did not skirt the edge of irrationality; he was in the center of it.[17] Yet this nonsense was taken seriously, with a deadly seriousness that revealed some of the impact of New Romanticism. Wherever hostility to modern life took root, excesses flourished. What made such ideas attractive and plausible, however, was the popularity of occultist beliefs. The irrationality of these cults, as well as the anti-rationalistic romanticism then in vogue, made an astonishing number of men receptive to equally, and at times more, outlandish theories of national heritage, race, and religion. Occultism, in fact, became essential to another aspect of Volkish thought. For some thinkers it provided a link between the present and the past; it was a bridge that spanned a thousand years of neglect. The past, which Christianity had done its best to destroy, could be recovered and applied to the present needs of the Volk through occultism. Occultism was the chalice that quenched their thirst, and at the same time made irrelevant anything that historical scholarship might do to show events in an entirely different light.

The most influential of such occultist groups gathered in Vienna during the last two decades of the nineteenth century. Their mentor was the Austrian Guido von List, a private scholar obsessed with the desire to prove that Vienna was the holy city of old. (Significantly enough, List's ideas originated in a German border region which was subject to constant interaction with the neighboring Slavic lands.) List, in a manner that should now be familiar, combined nature and history, with nature as the divine guide emanating a continuous life force. Whatever was closest to nature, so ran the formula, was closest to truth. The German Aryan past was closest to all that was true, to all that was laudatory and worthy of emulation. In this Germanic past, materialism and rationalism had found no sanction; indeed, they were purely moden afflictions.[18]

But how was contemporary man to recapture the past? According to List, all that was required was immediate participation in the landscape that still bore the indelible traces of the glorious Germanic civilization. "We must read with our souls the landscape that archeology reconquers with the spade . . . if you want to lift the veil of mystery [that of the past] you must fly into the loneliness of nature."[19] Nature was the guide to the divine, since the search for truth must of necessity follow in the footsteps of her creative will. This appreciation of landscape, however, required a more profound initiation. It was necessary that one become infused with the historical past of the Volk, with the most genuine part of the life force, ancient Germanic wisdom. The wisdom had been suppressed by the strictures of Christianity; indeed, that alien dogma had attempted to eradicate it as a vestige of paganism. But it still existed, permeated with the life force, though in a dormant state. The task of historians and Germanists was to revive it by deciphering the ancient script and symbols, and to convey its meaning to modern Germans. In furtherance of this end, List himself published a study of the runic symbols in 1908 as well as a two-volume work entitled *Deutsch-mythologische Landschaftbilder* (*German Mythological Landscape Pictures*) (1891), in which he reconstructed Austria's Aryan past. The mythology in question was that of the German gods, who, during the Goths' conquest of the Western world, had determined the fate of man. One chapter, for example, dealt with traces of Germanic religious sites in the environs of Vienna—evidence of the presence of ancient Germanic culture in the heartland of Austria.

In his investigation of the language that would pierce the centuries of Christian oppression, List boasted that he had discovered the *kala*, or secret language of the Germans. Since some of the *kala* words also occurred in the Kabala (a series of ancient books of Jewish mysticism), List also claimed that these works were part of the ancient German wisdom that had survived Christian persecution. His *Secret of the Runes* (1908) gave rise to the ideas of his disciple, Philip Stauff, an assiduous writer for German Volkish publications, who thought that this secret language had survived more tangibly in the wooden beams of old buildings. This theory was advanced in Stauff's book, appropriately entitled *Runenhäuser* (*Rune Houses*) (1913).

List's emphasis on using purely mystical means to arrive at a system of intuitive history brought him close to the ideas of the theosophists. Like Madame Blavatski, List claimed to possess a "secret science" which, by means of the life force—in Blavatski's case it was an omnipresent vital ether—unveiled the past. His emphasis on solar symbolism, a belief that all impressions necessarily come from an extrasensory world, and communication with the ghosts of a bygone age further reflected an especially close connection with theosophy. In some instances, both movements were linked by a common membership. Johannes Baltzli, the founder and moving spirit of the Guido von List Society, figured importantly in theosophical publications, while the chief financial supporter of the society was likewise an avowed spiritualist.[20]

However, occultism affected List and his disciples in other ways as well. One of them was in the realm of political theory. List was associated with the Schönerer group of anti-Semitic pan-Germanists and contributed to their official publication.[21] Like Schönerer, he dreamed of a political system that, sanctioned by natural and ancient custom, would revitalize the Volk and institute the appropriately Germanic form of government. At the center of this vision stood the figure of a leader, a "strong man from above," one whose advent was inevitable. He also believed—another indication of the influence of occultism—that this leader would arise reincarnated, "reborn," from among the gallant dead of the ancient battlefields. List shared the concept of *karma*, which was basic to such a belief, with Madame Blavatski, as shown in his account of his dream of the messianic leader published in the pages of *Prana*, a German theosophical journal.[22] This idea of a *Führer* had added significance in that it supplied a goal for List's longings and provided a concrete way out in times of national disturbance and unrest. And it was indeed in the disoriented era of the 1920's that List enjoyed something of a revival. The largest union of white-collar workers, the Deutschnationale Handelsgehilfen Verband (German National Union of Apprentices), praised this "almost forgotten man" for having shed light and hope into the age of darkness.[23]

From Austria, List's ideas filtered into Germany by way of one of those figures one encounters in the Volkish movement who are so difficult to explain to modern readers. Alfred Schuler was a *Luftmensch*, a man who never earned a penny and somehow managed to live in poverty without caring—above all, one who exerted great impact on his fellow men without ever publishing a line. Schuler's milieu was the artists' quarter of Munich, Schwabing, where a whole coterie of like-minded people had gathered at the turn of the century. The poet Stefan George was an important figure in the group, as was a promising young man named Ludwig Klages, later to be one of the ornaments of German philosophy.

This circle in which Schuler moved and was looked up to has been celebrated in Franziska zu Reventlow's autobiographical novel, *Herrn Dames Aufzeichnungen* (*Mr. Dame's Notebook*) (1902). In it she describes the members of this esoteric group, who were known as "the cosmics." They distinctly frowned upon individualism and held the individual, along with his precious idiosyncrasies, in low esteem. Instead, the greatest value was placed upon the primeval substance common to all persons of the same race. It was a racial substance supposedly found in the blood of the peoples.[24] This racial characteristic, in turn, was equated, on a philosophical level, with a cosmic principle that created the true life and was necessarily present in any worthwhile, creative personality. Like List, the members of this circle equated Germanism and race; the life spirit was identical with the racial characteristics exemplified by the common blood of the German Volk. The emphasis on blood was directly derived from the ancient German cult of the Druids, which this group attempted to revive. By so doing, they hoped to become infused with the primeval substance—though their eccentricity was not insignificantly affected by a desire to flaunt their heathenism. George, to be sure, in the end chose a different path, but Schuler and Klages remained loyal to their youthful convictions and experiences. Klages, in fact, went on to elaborate a more detailed cosmic philosophy, but we shall discuss that further on.

Supported financially by Gustav Freytag's son, Schuler eked out a meager existence while giving some public lectures in Munich and

Dresden. The most significant of these may have taken place at the Bruckmanns' private house in Munich in the year 1922.[25] During this year, Adolf Hitler was a regular guest at the house and it is altogether likely that he heard some of Schuler's ideas from the Schwabing oracle himself. In his ideas and lectures, Schuler closely followed the concepts and hypotheses formulated by List. He too rejected all academic scholarship in favor of an inner correspondence with Germanic antiquity. Schuler, however, subtly twisted or reformulated some ideas; for example, he identified the life force inherent in nature more closely with that flowing in the blood. Moreover, he placed greater emphasis on the outward cultural expression of the Volk spirit. For instance, he claimed that the life force could be aroused and vitalized through a participation in heathen rituals and through the medium of spiritualism. He had earlier even tried to cure Nietzsche's madness by means of an ancient Roman rite of spirits.[26]

In his lectures Schuler condemned urbanism and equated it with the intellectual's materialism which perverted true creative thought. In opposition to the cosmopolitan intellectual stood the adept whose "idealism" stemmed from the mysterious call of the blood, from the source of the genuine creative instinct. It was only through the ancient wisdom diffused in the blood, Schuler claimed, that he personally had "lived" antiquity, that he had known it intimately and had actually "seen" the life of long ago. His Germanic blood had allowed him to "see with his soul," to experience deeply what Christianity with its alien dogmatism had for so long repressed. However, this interaction with the Germanic past could not be attained in any meaningful way by the individual on his own. Life, as understood by Schuler and his fellow mystics, could only be lived meaningfully in unity with others, in concert with the "initiates"—that is, the members of the Volk. It functioned best on a wide basis, the way towns and houses together formed a part of the landscape.[27] This organic unity had been known in the heathen times of old. It was the task of the contemporary generation of Germans to strive to recapture it.

Another link between List and Germany was supplied by an eccentric character named Tarnhari. Whereas Schuler was at least sincere, Tarnhari, in all probability, was simply a crook and an opportunist. He introduced himself to List as the reborn leader of the old Germanic tribe of the Völsungen. Enraptured, List attentively lent his ear to Tarnhari's ancient memories of tribal history and found that, "singularly enough," they corresponded with results from his own "research." [28] That he believed Tarnhari itself speaks volumes for the quality of his thought. Tarnhari went on to make a career in the Volkish movement. He made an ideological contribution to the cause by publishing a *Swastika Letter* from Leipzig, whose title page displayed an astral figure with a sun-drenched swastika floating over a man kneeling in a landscape. The combination of sun worship, exaltation of nature, and Volkish faith could hardly have found a better representation. Like many members of the Volkish movement, Tarnhari, around the turn of the century, attempted to organize a sect. And like those of the others, it too broke down, since he quarreled with everyone involved instead of getting down to concerted action. To obtain funds, Tarnhari printed and sold small pictures that could be used as stamps. All were of a Volkish character. One such picture showed Baldur, the Germanic god of light, while another portrayed Thor, the god of action, of strength. (The pictures were executed for him by Ludwig Fahrenkrog, himself an eager advocate of a Germanic ideology, who, oddly enough, had been the favorite student of the Wilhelmine painter Anton von Werner, a model of respectability and correct taste.) But Tarnhari, like Schuler, had his admirers and advocates. In fact, his principal advertiser was Dietrich Eckart, Hitler's mentor in the early days of the National Socialist party.[29] And, indeed, the world view Hitler carried into office was not untainted by Schuler and Tarnhari's Germanic frame of reference.

But still we say that such beliefs verged on the magical, the irrational, the insane. What is important, however, is that at that time these viewpoints were acclaimed precisely *because* they were magical. Schuler himself admitted that the actual realization of the cosmic and primeval forces in a person could make that individual strong and powerful enough to be considered a magician. Not famous for his humility, Schuler attributed such powers to himself.[30] One is reminded of Thomas Mann's *Mario and the Magician* (1929), which showed such ideas in their terrible reality. Was Schuler simply misguided or was he half mad? That either might be true is not really relevant and does not account for his influence. For Schuler was taken seriously by too many "intelligent" persons. Of course, one could go so far as to consider the sanity of the audience just as questionable; but that would fail to explain why such a large sector of respectable society likewise thought that these ideas did reflect reality and could in fact be implemented with honor and justice.

In Germany, List's ideas, spread by Schuler, intermingled with other Volkish precepts. Many people accepted them. Some made subtle changes or emphasized some points while ignoring others. But who participated, and in what manner, in deriving respectable, plausible political alternatives from these ideas? The Volkish movement was like a spiderweb. The men who entertained these mystical ideas knew one another personally and borrowed from one another's works. Moreover, they contributed to one another's journals. When *Die Sonne*, a periodical advocating the Nordic world views we have discussed, was founded in 1923, its contributors represented a number of subtly varying viewpoints, but all were united in the common effort. Among them were the National Socialist Darré, the racial theorist Günther, the ardent Volkish novelist Kapherr, and the conservative Deutschnationale Dr. Paul Bang, who will occupy us later. Furthermore, once the Weimar Republic had been established, the small coteries in Jena, Vienna, and Munich broadened out to include much of the political right. Not all accepted the Germanic visions of a List or a Schuler, but it is astonishing how many did. Beneath the respectable mien of serious gentlemen in top hats coursed a mystical ideology of Germanism and race. The more desperately frightened they were by the direction the Weimar state seemed to be taking —into economic crisis and possibly eventually into Communism— the more they turned to the concepts, slogans, and rationale of the Volk and all that it signified.

Both literature and art effectively diffused the cult of Germanism among the population at large. By this route it penetrated the national bloodstream, especially in popular novels such as Hermann Burte's *Wiltfeber, der ewige Deutsche* (*Wiltfeber the Eternal German*) (1912). The hero rejected the bourgeois values of those around him and took up a search for the Volk, for those of his people who could be vitalized with the true feeling of Germanism. He attempted to resurrect a world that was being strangled by modernity. The world of the past was more genuine and beautiful than contemporary reality. Its civilization was epitomized by the peasants who had tilled the soil for centuries past. In contrast, the hero felt that his own century had become debased, that the ugly was exalted instead of the naturally beautiful, that the herdlike masses dominated religious feeling and aesthetic taste. In Wiltfeber's eyes, this degeneracy symbolized the death of the Christian God and the dissolution of the covenant of the Old Testament. These had to be supplanted by a Germanic Christianity through which the springs of the Volk's salvation could flow again. A Germanic god must rule again; it only remained for Germans who still felt him in their souls to raise him to the appropriate stature. The narration of the story abounded in Germanic symbols and even contained a new version of the *Götterdämmerung:* the hero and his beloved die high on a rock, destroyed and consumed by a thunderbolt. Modeled presumably after the god Thor, Wiltfeber represented a Germanic hero leading a people who were still "healthy" enough to yearn for the Volk leaders and kings, and still opposed rule by the herd.

Burte went on writing, but none of his later novels ever attained *Wiltfeber*'s popularity. Many of his works developed the sun myth, of which he made the Old Testament Samson a physical symbol; Samson was the superman whose power depended upon the strength he received from the warmth of the sun's rays.[31] In his old age Burte became a supporter of Hitler; as Frederick the Great could enlist the admiration of Goethe, so he maintained Hitler should command the allegiance of great national poets. Burte felt that he was superior to Goethe in his grasp of the significance of the organic Volk.[32]

To Hermann Burte we must add the younger Hans Friedrich Blunck, who, if not as popular as Burte, was certainly the most prolific of the Volkish novelists. His approach was similar to Burte's, though he relied more directly on the ancient German sagas. In his *Die Urvatersaga (The Legend of the Primeval Father)* (1934), the sun was portrayed as the mother of all life; according to legend, there existed such a sensitive relationship between the sun and life that when it receded at night the king would be subject to "bad hours." Blunck's heroes also sought after God, the God of German mythology, and it was on behalf of the German Volk that Blunck wanted to see a resurgence of the ancient godheads. "The Romantic who transcends the worldly, as the mystic did the scholastic, is the great contribution of our Volk to the idea of creation." [33]

Blunck came to the Volkish movement as a youth. At school he founded, in 1903, an association called Die Germanen, whose purpose was similar to that of the contemporary Youth Movement— the re-establishment of spiritual and physical contact with Germanic nature. He often expressed a deep admiration for the Youth Movement and frequently published in its journal.[34] Later he went on to contribute to Adolf Stöcker's various publications. His development was fairly typical of many young people who entered and later contributed to the Volkish movement. As we will shortly see in greater detail, Blunck mirrored the predominant radical turn to the right that was typical for German youth. He too went the whole gamut and eventually became the president of the Reichsschriftumkammer (Corporation of Authors) under the Nazis. But not being a racist, as Burte was, he was never fully at ease in the Third Reich.[35] For it was possible to share Volkish attitudes without being a racist. This is a problem which will occupy us in future chapters, for some men and women believed in the Volk but also held that certain privileged and Germanically oriented Jews could become a part of this mystical whole. Blunck's anti-Semitism became muted and subdued and the barbarities of the regime shocked his rather sensitive metaphysical turn of mind.

The Volkish novels of this general tendency were mostly crude, in both a literary and an aesthetic sense. As reflections of reality and contemporary problems they were of less value still. Most of the plots were composed of the stuff of fantasy and easily lent themselves to parody. But we must constantly bear in mind that it was precisely these fantasies that were taken seriously. Here too, a New Romantic attitude was busily at work erecting a metaphysical edifice to substitute for the relentless sway of progress and modernity.

Ernst Wachler's novel, *Osning* (1914), was perhaps one of the most blatantly Volkish Germanic books of the time. Wachler is one more example of the university man who became a Volkish publicist. He interested himself first in the theater, and produced plays in Berlin; this interest was never to leave him. Moreover, he also founded a series of journals through which he formed friendships with many of the leading Volkish figures. He was born a year after the founding of the German empire, and cultural unity seemed vital to him, while he dreamed of a "Nordic Renaissance." *Osning* was meant to further this dream. It depicted the workings of a secret order named after the ancient Goth hero Arminius, which had been convoked to resurrect the Volk. This order carried out its mission underground and its leader appropriately housed himself in a cave in the Teutoburger Forest, whose old Germanic name was Osning. Highly charged with the atmosphere of the forest, which had harbored (and still does) the shrine of the Old Germans (the *Ecksternsteine*) and where Arminius had victoriously ambushed Varus' legions, the book was permeated with reverence for the old gods. The plot bore echoes of Tarnhari—the self-proclaimed ancient leader of the Arminians, centuries old, still remembered the original Germans. Like Burte's heroes, he himself vanishes in a bolt of lightning and thunder.

Ernst Wachler and his penchant for natural environment, musty with the aura of Germanic valor, were important for the Volkish movement in another respect. He was instrumental in introducing a theatrical form closely linked to the Volkish ideology in search of its past: the open-air theater in the forest. His goal was to construct a modernized version of the Germanic "*Thing*," the meeting place where the ancient Germans had worshipped at their religious shrines and administered their laws. Wachler established what he called "a stage for cults," in places that either originally had marked the ancient shrines or resembled them. Here, under an open sky, Volk plays would be performed in natural surroundings that evoked an aura of the past.[36] He realized his idea in 1907, when he founded the Mountain Theater in the Harz, the first theater of its kind. The plays he wanted to stage, however, were not traditional dramas. Actually, they were embodiments of rites which would dramatize the Volkish *Weltanschauung*. The titles themselves indicated the typical content —for instance, Wachler's own *Hohenstaufen* or *Walpurgis*. Other plays dealing with similar themes were also performed, especially the famous *Till Eulenspiegel*.

The importance of this new art form may not, at first glance, be apparent. It was one of the first serious attempts to objectify the ideological by means of the visual arts: to create a public cult for the dramatic presentation and reliving of Germanic themes. National Socialism, in time, adopted and implemented Wachler's ideas on a more ambitious scale. They made them into large popular spectacles wherein the dramatic content of the performances was transformed into intense expressions of mass veneration for the action on the stage. Typically enough, the National Socialists formalized the rites so as to eliminate virtually all aspects of true theater. Theatrical versions of the Nazi ideology's doxology were staged instead, replete with confessions of faith and pledges of allegiance. The drama that was permitted was subordinated in importance to the choral chants that periodically interrupted the action. As the consciousness of the community was considered of greater importance than that of the individual, as one official description had it, so the masses in the Volk drama superseded mere theatrical considerations. According to this prescription, no humor could be permitted to disturb the serene pathos of the unfolding drama.[37]

Several such theaters were founded under the auspices of the National Socialist cultural drive. These outdoor stages and amphitheaters can still be seen in cities such as Heidelberg—places of ghostly convocation after the wreck of a real *Götterdämmerung*. Before the war the Nazis had aspired to endow every town with a similar "*Thing*." These were to be modeled after what was regarded as a particularly favorable site: the Saxon forest at Werdenan, which had been planted with 4,500 trees in memory of the Saxons murdered there by Charlemagne.[38] Quite a few of these theaters were actually built.

Wachler's ideas had bloomed beyond expectation, and his contribution to the objectification of the ideology was of the greatest importance. It is possible that he taught the Nazis some of their most effective techniques—the mass cult and the liturgical framework for a substitute Volk Church. Some of these outdoor theaters were available to the Nazis, as examples, since Wachler's ideas were quickly copied even before the First World War.

Wachler's further literary activities were of minor significance, though we shall turn to them briefly in a discussion of racial eugenics. However, several other aspects of his life are of some importance. Politically and ideologically he was associated with the extremist wing of the Volkish movement. He had ties with Dietrich Eckart and wrote articles for his journal, *Auf Gut Deutsch* (*In Plain German*). Wachler also cultivated the favors of Nietzsche's sister, while his son married a niece of the philosopher. His admiration of Nietzsche was, not surprisingly, based on those transformations in thought wrought by the editorial changes of Elizabeth Förster-Nietzsche. To Wachler too, Nietzsche was the great Germanic seer, the prophet of the reborn race of heroes; not the scathing skeptic and sometime prophet of a dying religion and civilization.[39]

One writer was particularly effective among the landed Volkish interests. Ellegard Ellerbeck was the adopted Germanic name of an eccentric born Erich Leiser. He was spokesman for Schuler's viewpoint even prior to the First World War, but it was not until after the war that he acquired prominence as a Volkish author with his book *Sönne Sönnings Söhne auf Sönnensee* (1919). The title is quite untranslatable, but roughly it means "the sons of sunman in sunland." In wild profusion in this and in his other writings, he mixed theosophy, occultism, spiritualism, astrology, and the more typical Volkish precepts discussed so far. His extremism, almost as unbridled as Tarnhari's, quickly brought him into public notice. Shortly before the assassination of Walther Rathenau, Ellerbeck peremptorily announced the symbolic meaning of a frieze situated in Rathenau's residence. He claimed that it depicted the execution of all living kings, who, according to Schuler, could represent none other than the German nation.[40] In his lectures, Ellerbeck erected a logical construct on the argument that Germanic blood signifies a blood relationship with the gods of yore. "Do you know that you are gods?" he exhorted his audience, and followed with the accusation that the Jews were the malevolent exterminators of Germanism, that they prevented the Aryans from assuming their godlike stature, and that, consequently, they must be eradicated.[41] He wrote in Dietrich Eckart's paper that Jewish poison transforms the creatures of the sun into urbanites.[42] Ellerbeck's slanderous interpretation of the Rathenau frieze created such a furor that some Jews were moved to reply at some length to the charges that it was anti-Gentile.

Ellerbeck's influence, however, was not limited to these two incidents. He made himself well known throughout the country, traveling on behalf of the periodical *Die Sonne* and talking to school audiences on such subjects as "Is there a world of spirits?"—with an answer that always rang out in the affirmative.[43] His associations ranged from Dietrich Eckart to Alfred Rosenberg, who, even as he stood in the shadow of the gallows, found words of qualified praise for Ellerbeck.[44] Ellerbeck was also a constant contributor to the *Deutsche Tageszeitung*, where his articles appeared alongside those that came from the pens of supposedly reputable conservatives of the day. His Volkish praise of peasant culture, of the genuine landed character of the German population, particularly endeared him to the farming interests. The powerful Bund der Landwirte (Farmers' Union) and its organ singled out Ellerbeck for high praise at the end of the war.[45] This sympathy with and even espousal of the Germanic Volkish cause by a powerful political group was of undisputed significance.

The effectiveness of the ideology typified by Ellerbeck was enhanced still further when, after 1918, the Bund der Landwirte became one of the props of the Deutschnationale party, the new embodiment of the old conservatism. In this manner Volkish ideas penetrated to the heart of classical German conservatism. Though they did not come to dominate it, they were decidedly more than an ideological fringe. Moreover, together with other groups that contributed to this ideology, they did become powerful enough to capture one important wing of conservatism for the Volkish movement. The strength of their position was reflected in the eventual character of conservative thought, which, by 1933, was far more Volkish in nature than it was classical Wilhelmine.

The revived consciousness of the historical German grandeur mirrored itself in the visual arts as well as in literature. Here, too, it ran the gamut from blatant copying of Germanic themes to a new and supposedly revolutionary form of Volkish art. At one end there was Hermann Hendrich, who in 1901 elaborately constructed a "German temple" to house his paintings, which depicted "German legends and the beauties of the landscape." The front of the building, the "Hall of Walpurgis," was decorated with the skulls of horses, as on ancient Germanic dwellings, while the one eye of Wotan looked down from the roof. Wotan was the chief figure in his paintings as well. To encourage art similar to his own, Hendrich founded the Värhandibund, named after a part of the *Edda*.[46]

In the arts and crafts movement led by Ferdinand Avenarius, the emphasis on the ancient Germanic was muted even though the ideological foundations of the art were fused with the Volkish movement. Art was tied to the Volk, but a slightly more contemporary one, with more refined aesthetic sensibilities. However, more important for our purposes was the art style initiated by Karl Höppner, who went under the name of Fidus. Though his art was singularly personal and inimitable, his influence was widespread; there was hardly a Volkish publication from the beginning of the century on that did not at some time print one of his pictures. But he was especially popular among the youth, who, enamored of his art, filled their various journals with it. He represented a combination of interest in the Volk, nature, and spiritualism—in this case, theosophy—that inevitably made him an important spokesman of the ideas we have been discussing in this chapter.

Fidus referred to his work as "temple art." It attempted, and according to its claims achieved, the highest form of aesthetic expression. This art was to make visible the invisible; it was to give form to the sacred spiritual and Volkish elements that make up man; it was to impart to people a belief in a "mystical ocean," a belief in worlds beyond and transcending our own, so that they could draw from these worlds the necessary strength to live and to command. Nature alone could not convey sufficient vitality, according to Fidus. Painting had to transmit the quintessence of life; it had to communicate that which was beyond the senses.[47]

In his art Fidus attempted to answer the most sacred of man's questions. He himself believed that the beauty and truth of the higher worlds were transmitted to him through a life force, a mystical impetus derived from the cosmos.[48] This was reflected in the themes of his paintings. Theosophical symbols which concentrated on ethereal forces abounded. His motifs included sun-drenched Egyptian sphinxes, landscapes penetrated by glaring rays of the sun, and naked, golden youths striding into the sun's rays. The last motif was most frequently elaborated. His "Wanderers in the Sun," for example, portrayed a nude boy and girl striding forth, their bodies sun-drenched and surrounded by green plants. His most famous painting depicted the nude figure of a young man on a cliff, poised as though about to fly off into the air, while the sun looms large behind him, drenching his nude form. Fidus thought that this painting had captured the hope of youth in touch with the cosmos. Whether it did or not, it became one of the favorite pictures of the German Youth Movement.

But why was Fidus' work more popular than the other Germanic art forms? First, it had a stimulating intellectual quality which the others lacked. Not a rational intelligence, in the sense that it attempted to portray subjects that could only be understood by applying the tools of reason, stylistic analysis, or biographical and historical background. Fidus and his Volkish confrères vehemently denied the value of such a rationalistic approach; in their view, only purely emotional, intuitive, and irrational forces had any function in the execution and appreciation of a work of art. Rather, there was present in Fidus' work an intelligibility according to which one could easily recognize the symbols and the intended mystical message and communicate them in an intelligent manner to larger and diversified audiences.

Second, Fidus' style worked in his favor. Within the ideological framework his paintings were actually highly realistic. He abhorred impressionism and expressionism, which were then in great vogue.[49] Like all Volkish artists, Fidus drew his impetus from romanticism and romantic art styles, though, as he put it, painting "nature as it is was insufficient"; the cosmic life spirit must enter the picture.[50] Yet only when he pictured the cosmic spirit as a cross of light did he tend toward abstraction. To the romantic genre he added his theosophical symbols and Volkish world view. The figures that dominated his canvasses represented a concept of male beauty that was becoming current in the German Youth Movement and which eventually became the typical Aryan image. Essentially, it combined ideas taken from racial thought, an idealization of ancient Germanic strength, and echoes of the Greek ideal of physical beauty. It exalted a primitive strength, which, as we have seen, often acquired a twist of cruelty; while the Greek ideal of bodily proportions supplied an indispensable harmony to the Germanic form. In all this, intellectual complexity in painting was considered un-German and best left to the degenerate expressionists. The love for the nude body which Fidus helped to further, became important in the Youth Movement as representing the urge for the genuine which required a return to nature; but we shall turn to that aspect shortly.

However, it was not only the Youth Movement but the majority of Volkish sympathizers who felt that Fidus' paintings realized their ideals of beauty. He was praised as highly as Ellerbeck was, and the multitudinous voice of the Deutschnationale Handelsgehilfen Verband joined the chorus.[51] But the National Socialists rejected him. Fidus dolefully complained that when he had stretched out his hand to Adolf Hitler, even before the Nazi seizure of power, he was ignored.[52] The slight was incorporated into official Nazi "aesthetic" policy when Rosenberg treated him with contempt and the Party journals rejected his pictures. The stated reason for this hostile attitude was furnished by a Nazi publication which decried Fidus' occultism as a "trance without a body." It also bemoaned the fact that he had become the "victim of the occult," and had been made to sacrifice his more valuable Volkish didactic talents.[53]

Why suddenly this sophistic distinction? Surely National Socialism had a good dose of the occult within its own ranks. Heinrich Himmler, for instance, believed in *karma* and thought himself a reborn Henry the Fowler of medieval fame.[54] The overriding reason seems to be the Nazis' feeling that Fidus' paintings lacked that obvious one-to-one relationship between image and desired reality provided by more tendentious Volkish and Nazi artists. His specifically theosophical overtones and formulations were his undoing. And although Fidus had attempted to marry theosophy and extrasensory perception to the Volk, the life force of the cosmos, it seemed to the Nazis that this spiritualism could have dangerous separate existence.[55] Moreover, Fidus did not emphasize the blatantly Germanic; his temples lacked the specific Germanic symbols and emblems and his astral symbolism was not purely Volkish in content—though Fidus thought that he, in his own way, had achieved just such a connection. Of course, Hitler's own artistic tastes figured significantly in the rejection of Fidus. The Führer's tastes were more sober; his favorite architectural styles more classical and monumental; he preferred to see occult symbolism confined to cultish party rites, and not allowed to invade everyday artistic expression. Yet, in spite of this official disfavor, the ideal beauty of the proportioned and harmonious figure which Fidus popularized became assimilated in National Socialist stereotypes of the ideal German; however much they rejected Fidus' spiritualist aesthetics, they enthusiastically espoused his Aryan prototypes.

This general and sometimes esoteric discovery of the old Germans had nothing to do with historical scholarship; indeed, scholarship was looked down upon as a tool of research and rejected in favor of the intuitive. It was, as we have seen, a part of the mystical ideology of Volkish thought and New Romanticism. In fact, it accentuated certain elements of these outlooks: the urge for historical identification and spiritualism, now made explicit in occultism and theosophy. All these factors combined to help objectify the Volkish ideology in the use of cultish rites in outdoor theaters. In Fidus, as we have seen, the ideology was communicated with considerable impact through the visual arts. From this consideration, however, although we have touched on it in passing, we have omitted a discussion of the specifically racial component. It was of such importance as to merit separate and detailed analysis. In the Volkish concept, membership in the Germanic society was not solely a matter of fusing oneself with the cosmos; race took precedence. Not everyone was capable of becoming a cosmic personality, an Aryan god.

CHAPTER 5

Racism

WHEREAS THE GERMANIC visions of history, the foundations of a Germanic Christianity, and solar cultism all shared an explicit anti-rationalist base, the concept of race, at least at its inception, did not. As it was conceived, the idea of race was essentially and respectably scientific. It was first used, in the eighteenth century, to classify various species of plants, animals, and tribes. Today anthropologists still use it as a means of classification. Of course, the concept of race has suffered adulteration throughout its history. It has been, and still is, a pernicious concept only when used to derive internal qualities from external differences; in other words, when the concept is transposed from a scientific to a metaphysical level.

Not surprisingly, during the age of romanticism and Social Darwinism just such a transposition was made. After all, the era did emphasize the internal, inherent, and inalienable virtues of man. The external was thought to be only a reflection of deeper spiritual forces. The body mirrored the soul; it was its signature. As we have seen, landscape and geography were considered indispensable to the Volk soul. To these, however, was added the concept that the very physical characteristics of people rested on the nature of their inner selves. Consequently, Volkish thinkers and pseudo-scientists began to detail the various component parts that represented the outward signs of the true racial soul. Artists, as we saw in the last chapter, portrayed the ideal of Aryan beauty; Fidus' depictions, for example, were physical images of inner Germanic beauty modeled after a racially "ideal type."

Philosophically, Volkish authors and racial theorists did not need to go far from their native traditions to find an honorable, respectable basis for their theories. They were inspired in part by certain tenets in Kant's speculations on race which seemed to give them license to elaborate further. Volkish theorists found a theory of race in the writings of Kant which was based primarily on geographic factors and held that geographically determined racial characteristics were accompanied by an "inner life force." This Kantian tenet was applied in correlating landscape and the Volk soul. In the end, however, two relatively recent sciences realized the objectification of the Volkish ideology more fully: anthropology and philology.

Early anthropological thought attempted a racial classification of tribes and nations in which various contingent values of superiority and inferiority were postulated. By the nineteenth century, anthropological concepts were infused with romantic precepts and values which depart from strict scientific criteria. Various techniques were applied in order to relate external characteristics to internal qualities in a more systematic way. The introduction of cranial measurements as a part of anthropology was of major importance in this respect. From the time of Franz Joseph Gall (1758–1828), physical differences such as those found in cranial shape were presumed to indicate inherent differences. Gall, the founder of phrenology, thought he could discover the moral and intellectual predispositions of men through the configurations and protuberances of their heads. This theory did not remain without consequences. When the adepts of Old Germanism announced that the skulls of their ancestors had been long and narrow, this physical distinction soon became a prime criterion for Aryanism. Subsequently, as can be seen in Fidus' art, the whole physical structure of a person was thought to indicate his race.

To the growing body of racial theory, philology contributed the actual "Aryan" distinction. Through an examination of German and English linguistic roots German philologists postulated the theory that both peoples had stemmed from a common root. Max Müller, one of the early proponents of the theory, in his lectures to English audiences during the period 1859–61 expounded on the hypothesis that the Aryan forebears of the Anglo-Saxons had been impelled by an irresistible impulse and had driven westward from their original home in the region of India. The two peoples had developed the desirable qualities of self-reliance and independence as a direct result of the migration.[1] (That the Aryans originated in a mysterious, semi-Oriental land became a favorite theme of writers and later Volkish thinkers. Indeed, it served to interlace the cultural structure with an organic, biological base, to tie the theosophical ideas of *karma* [rebirth] and solar mysticism to the same soil that had nourished the race. The connection was especially emphasized by philologists who fused a large number of mystical Indian symbols with the gods of the ancient Germans. One of the more explicit results was the frequent use of Indian names to designate Germanic societies, as when Willibald Hentschel, in 1923, gave his order for the development of true Aryans the name Artamanen, after the Indian sun god Artam.)

All these factors entered into what some Volkish theorists called the "mystery of race." But it would have been incomplete without that cosmic emphasis which runs through the old and the New Romanticism. A complete theory was first presented in workable form in the writings of the French diplomat Arthur de Gobineau, who employed a specifically racial context as the setting for human history. This mid-nineteenth-century theoretician denied that the institutions of Christianity, governments, and ideas—which he termed "superstitions"—were the functional agents of history, or the causes of the rise and decline of civilizations. Race alone was the deciding factor. To Gobineau, purity of race meant strength for survival, for mastery and domination of lesser races; while intermingling of racial lines would result in a rapid decline of culture and national prowess, culminating in racial death.

According to Gobineau, history showed that races rose to power in their pure state and fell when they had become contaminated. The purest contemporary race, Gobineau noted, was the Aryans, a race whose inward qualities were inseparably linked to its external appearance—a relationship true of all races—and who possessed that vigor and genuine vitality which, to the Volkish thinkers, the German peasant so bountifully exhibited. The desire for force and conquest was part of their nature. In this respect, they represented the aristocracy in a world of lesser, conquered races. However, they too, like earlier anthropologically distinct groups, were subject to contamination by lesser blood, to a process of bastardization by which the lower races infiltrated the ranks of the aristocracy. The historical law that dealt with this recurring process held that admixture of races was inevitable and would result in racial extinction. Characteristically, Gobineau forecast racial death with greater certainty than racial revival. This was amply evident in his major work, *Essai sur l'inégalité des races humaines* (1853), which concentrated on the cause of the decline of civilization. Though he was a prophet of doom and did not, as did his successors, extol the Aryans' coming glory, the message of his theory was quite clear: a race must stay pure. Democracy, an extension of racial admixture, must be prevented at all costs.[2]

Though Gobineau set the stage and supplied all the essential props, his thought remained virtually unnoticed in contemporary Germany. The ideological base had not evolved sufficiently to necessitate such a superstructure. The Volkish version of old romanticism, Germanism, and New Romanticism had to sink roots first. Romanticism had to be deepened and directed toward the Volk. Secondly, anthropological theories had to be refined and made more applicable to cultural matters of interest to the public; they also had to be wedded to a growing Social Darwinism that applied the scientific theory of evolution to the social struggle among men and extolled the virtues of calculated survival. Similarly, political dissatisfaction with the direction that German unity had taken and social tensions arising from commercial and industrial progress had to make themselves felt. Only then was the stage fully set for penetration (modified, to be sure) of his ideas.

Not until 1894 was there a concerted attempt to introduce Gobineau's ideas into Germany. In that year, Ludwig Schemann founded a society to honor his name and revive his theories both in France and in Germany. The French branch received little support and never really flourished.[3] It was not generally popular in Germany either, but there it received the wholehearted support of the Richard Wagner circle, of which Schemann was a member. In addition, Schemann, active on the board of the Pan-Germans, was able to obtain the support of this significant conservative group for the cause of racial theory.[4] In the end, his assertion proved correct: "Only Germany can be the receptacle for Gobineau and his ideas."[5]

Although its membership was small (by 1914 there were 360 members and 50 institutions subscribed), the influence of the society was disproportionately high. However, it was not the popularity of Gobineau's works that accounted for his influence; though his works were distributed gratis to schools and to the army, only a thousand copies of his specifically racist work had been distributed by 1919, whereas the more popular *Renaissance* reached double that number.[6] Thus, neither the size of the society's membership nor the popularity of Gobineau's works really accounted for his impact in Germany. Rather it was the prestige and influence of the groups that supported the society. The Wagner circle, led after the composer's death by his widow, Cosima, and, above all, the Pan-Germans were significant proponents of racial views founded partly on Gobineau's writings. Moreover, a disproportionately large number of the Pan-Germans were schoolteachers. According to a survey made in 1906, no less than 36 per cent of all local chairmen belonged to the teaching profession,[7] out of a membership of about 21,000. The combination was perfect. The support of an important pressure group, the Pan-Germans, which included a large number of teachers, who were in a position to disseminate the racist ideas in the schools.

Personally Schemann gave himself wholeheartedly to the furtherance of the cause. He had a typical Volkish mentality, a private scholar who since his youth had considered science distasteful and looked upon values derived from technology and science as blasphemous manipulations of the forces of nature.[8] His personal nostalgia for the small, idyllic German town of his youth reflected itself in his ideology. In 1925, Schemann asserted that if Germans could rid themselves of the conceit that big cities, machines, and the emancipation of Jews were landmarks in the progress of humanity, then all would be well.[9] For him, the hateful modernity was represented by emancipated Jewry, mechanization, and urbanization, while Gobineau's racial theories and values were a prophetic force for liberation from the nightmare. And though his writings did not meet with outright success, Schemann was not as ineffectual as this criterion might suggest. He admired and was heavily influenced by that apostle of Germanism, Paul de Lagarde. He wrote a biography of Lagarde and helped to popularize his thought. In addition, in books and articles he glorified Wagner as the advocate of the Volk—an image widely propagated by Wagner's wife, Cosima. He also had influence among the Pan-Germans, and especially on their leader, Heinrich Class, a close personal friend.

Like the Pan-Germans, Schemann actively participated in, or extended his support to, many right-wing causes. In 1920 he endorsed the putsch attempted by Wolfgang Kapp and, under Hitler, wrote a eulogy of it.[10] The Nazis called him into the *Reichsinstitut* for modern history and on his eighty-fifth birthday the Third Reich awarded him the Goethe Medal for his services to the nation and the race.[11] Politics figured only peripherally in Schemann's life, which was wholly devoted to an advocacy of the racial ideal. With his impact in the upper social circles and especially among educators, Schemann helped to awaken the younger generation to the ideas of race, directing their receptive minds to reading works extolling racial purity and warning against the dangers of racial degeneration.

As we have already indicated, there were two main reasons why Gobineau did not become the immediate father of German racial thought: the tenor of the times and the lack of the Social Darwinist ingredient. Later on, at the turn of the century, another development interfered. By 1900 there were several rival racial theories current in Germany. Most of them had grown with the refinement of anthropological criteria and had incorporated elements of the "survival of the fittest" axiom of the Social Darwinists. They were correspondingly more optimistic about the direction history was taking. Instead of concentrating on the inevitability of racial contamination and the consequent decline of civilization, these theorists looked toward a developing race that would save Western culture and stamp it with its own uniqueness.

Of these, Houston Stewart Chamberlain was the most important. Unlike Gobineau, Chamberlain analyzed the totality of civilization, not because he was concerned with its decline, but, on the contrary, because he yearned for a better, more beautiful racial future. Chamberlain was the son of an English admiral, but he spent most of his life on the Continent and eventually became a German citizen to symbolize his deep attachment to that country. His attraction to the Continent was heightened by necessity, for he was chronically ill and suffered from nervous disorders which were aggravated by the more severe English climate. Except for long periods in Geneva, he made his home in Germany.

At first he was fascinated by plant pathology, and he might well have become a scientist had it not been for his health. Instead, he fused his scientific training with a mystical love of nature and a Social Darwinism which was so typical of much radical thought. This transformation from scientist to radical racist was catalyzed by his encounter with the work of Richard Wagner. From 1882 on, Bayreuth became the "home of his soul" and later his real home as well, where he devoted himself to the preservation and dissemination of Wagner's world view. He married Wagner's daughter, and his life became dedicated to the development of his racial theories.

Like Schemann's, Chamberlain's ideas were stimulated by the Wagner circle at Bayreuth, with its focus on the *Ring* cycle as the gospel of the Germanic race. Wagner himself was regarded as the prophet of Germanism, and this tradition was carried on by his daughter Winnifred, who transformed the Bayreuth festival into a National Socialist rite after the seizure of power in 1933.

Chamberlain himself was a great admirer of Hitler. In a dramatic scene, Hitler visited the paralyzed and dying apostle of Germanism and kissed his hands. But Chamberlain died in 1927 and did not see the triumph of his prophecies. He wrote as the prophet of the future, righteously indignant against the forces which forestalled the inevitable unfolding of the new race and full of praise for that which would bring it into being. Tenacious in thought and persistent in his claims for the bright future, Chamberlain never showed the slightest trace of resignation in his work.

Without doubt, his inflexible optimism contributed to the tremendous success of Chamberlain's *Die Grundlagen des XIX. Jahrhunderts* (*Foundations of the Nineteenth Century*) (1900). In this work, which had a deep impact on Volkish thought, racism became more than just the explanation of the rise and fall of civilizations. It became the hope of mankind, the fulfillment of its aspirations. Chamberlain's reasoning also transcended that of earlier racists in that it merged the streams of science and mysticism. He provided the New Romanticism with a scientific base and thus lent the tone and the goals of science to his racial theories. In the end, it was the mysticism that won out, eventually doing violence to the scientific method. Even anthropology, the century's new science, had progressively cloaked racial theories in a scholarly and academically respectable mantle. Interestingly enough, another area from which Chamberlain's *Foundations* drew a semblance of respectability was Kantian philosophy —particularly for arguments in favor of the existence of intrinsic racial values. Chamberlain held that Kant, who believed in reason and pragmatism, also postulated an essence of things, the *Ding an sich*, which was outside empirical comprehension. Chamberlain used Kant to the following effect: On the one hand, there was a German science which determined, with the utmost accuracy, that which existed empirically; on the other hand, there was a Germanic religion, which bestowed infinite vistas upon the German soul. In terms of importance, the religion took priority, since it alone could fathom the true essence of things. As it also functioned in the realm of ideas, it served to keep science within its proper limits, and at the same time appropriated empirical evidence in support of itself.[12] Through their inner selves, which were enveloped in a mystical Germanism, Chamberlain asserted, men could determine the meaning of the external world. Thus, throughout his long book Chamberlain called upon the Germans to "drench" the external world with that religion which symbolized their own ideals. As in the New Romanticism, the impetus toward an "idealism of deeds" came from within man through his mystical contact with the cosmos.[13] In a sentence that summed up his thought on the subject, Chamberlain declared that nothing could be more dangerous for man than to possess a science without poetry or a civilization without culture.[14]

However, Chamberlain also thought that science had its merits, though of a limited nature. All his declarations on religion and race were made with a great show of learning, and rested upon a base that had purposely been scientifically researched. In Germanizing Christianity, for instance, he brought forth scholarly arguments which denied the Jewishness of Christ on the grounds that Galilee had been inhabited by heathen, non-Jewish tribes.[15] In regard to race, he used a scientific base to prove its absolute nature, its totality, which encompassed both internal and external appearances. At the end of the nineteenth century, he wrote, no scholar could ignore the fact that skull measurements and the external appearance of the brain decisively influenced the conceptions of aesthetic form that lay within. After all, went the analogy, a building was characterized by the materials used in its construction; they provided the outward form and expressed the "ideas" inherent in the erection.[16]

Chamberlain's thesis became commonplace in racial thought and easily lent itself to excesses. The equation of inner and outer qualities was the subject of many a scientific and academic project, and the most absurd conclusions enjoyed at times a momentary popularity. Such was the case with the work of Dr. Burger-Villingen, a portrait painter, who in 1912 attempted to validate Chamberlain's assertion that a person's physiognomy expressed his inward being.[17] To verify this statement scientifically, Burger-Villingen actually constructed an instrument, called a plastometer, which purported to measure the geography of a human face and thus the cast of a person's soul. For instance, according to his findings, a protruding forehead and a receding chin and mouth indicated a superficial intelligence devoid of any creativity.[18]

In this manner, theoretical statements, theses, and accusations acquired a visual form; the Volkish ideology was objectified. Burger-Villingen's "scientific" discoveries only supplemented the aesthetic impact of Fidus or the distorted literary image of the Jew that was standard fare in the peasant novels. It worked to the advantage of the Volkish movement. Theories of racial distinctions were to be comprehended not only in a mystical sense; on the contrary, they could be made popular through the use of stereotypes. The Aryan was distinguished by a physical form that typified the Germanic ideal of beauty; the Jew was his very opposite. Symbolically, only to be too deeply believed later on, the two represented the polarization of God and the devil. For Chamberlain these categories were sufficient for communicating his racial philosophy in the attempt to produce an authoritative history based on the eternal struggle between races.

What did Chamberlain present as history? Primarily, he presented the history of mankind, especially of Germany, as the story of a bitter, polarized struggle. God was, so to speak, embodied in the Germanic race, and the devil in the Jewish race. These were held to be the two pure races—and between them flourished the "chaos of peoples," bastard mixtures of various races. The Jews had entered the history of the West as alien people who stemmed from an Asiatic environment and subscribed to a strict and dehumanized law. In contradistinction, the Germans had entered the same history as saviors at a moment when the West seemed on the verge of disintegration. The Teutonic peoples had been the carriers of all that was best in Greek and Roman civilization, to which they added a more vital emphasis. The Germans had added the metaphysical element to the Greek ideal of aristocracy and to the Roman concept of justice. Among Germans, heroism represented an inner fortitude that was superior to mere external strength and victory. This virtue made the difference between a Siegfried and a Semitic Samson or even a Greek Achilles. The metaphysical impulse gave harmony to the Germanic race, a harmony that shone forth in the Germanic countenances of Dante (claimed as a German) and Luther alike and was embodied in the profound depths of their beliefs. Moreover, Chamberlain argued that, since Germans were the saviors of world history and the carriers of Western culture, all real cultural achievement in modern times must be permeated with their spirit, a spirit sharpened through incessant struggle.[19]

And the antagonists in this never-ending battle? They were the Jews. This was the only other race that retained its purity, not through the force of an inner conviction or mysticism but as a result of external laws. According to the prophet of the German race, the Jewish people strove to dominate through an ineradicable persistence, an iron will to power that was not graced by any metaphysical impulse, by imagination or ideals. At times, it was said, they were assisted by so-called degenerate Nordics such as the Jesuits. Mostly, however, the Jews concertedly carried out their mechanistic plans to attain the primacy among nations that was guaranteed by their God Yahweh in return for obedience to his laws. This was meant seriously, for Chamberlain did not make light of what he defined as the Jewish menace. Regardless of the popular myth inspired by the ridiculousness of his stereotype, the Jew was not a figure of fun, but an enemy to be fought with deadly seriousness. Chamberlain's *Foundations* ominously maintained that the Germanic race was engaged in a mortal struggle that was to be fought not only with cannon but with every weapon of human life and society.[20]

In some respects Chamberlain was more of a mystic than some Volkish thinkers, and at the same time a greater realist in other ways. For instance, he did not spurn all of modernity, but simply decried its misapplication. While German industry was in the hands of the Jews, it worked against German interests. But when industry and other aspects of modernity were in the hands of the German race, they were infused with a spirit that strove for higher values. Chamberlain thought a revolution necessary for the German race to recognize this state of affairs and to discard a materialism encouraged by Jewish interests. Like that prescribed by Lagarde, it was an inner transformation which would bring about the change. It would leave the external shell intact and would change only the inner nature, endowing it with a new meaning. This concept of revolution, in combination with a stress on the righteousness of struggle and violence, resulted in a formula that was similar to that of most Volkish thinkers. A defeat of the racial enemy would automatically remove all obstacles to a cosmically inspired breakthrough by the Aryan race. The change would not lead to a social revolution—but to a revolution of the spirit which would reduce present reality to its true proportions in the service of the Volk.

The modification Chamberlain placed on the rejection of science, which had been a distinction of early Volkish thought, was significant since it contributed to the greater contemporaneity of the Volkish ideology. Science and technology were not to be discarded, but applied under the direction of the Volk in line with its racial needs.[21] The revolution Chamberlain foresaw was to be a spiritual one nonetheless. In a Volkish sense, it would facilitate a return to a semi-rural, hierarchical ideal; or, rather, it would bring the idyllic past into the perspective of the future good society. Messianically, Chamberlain proclaimed that then Germans would leave the dark and crumbling present in order to enter into the "new, splendid, and light-filled" future: Kant's "pure ideal." [22] The triumph of this vision could come about peacefully and naturally in the wake of a general race consciousness; it did not represent a violent, radical, social upheaval. Culminating in this message of imminent victory for the German race, Chamberlain's *Foundations* became a favorite book in the Volkish movement. In many ways it attained the stature of being the Bible of racial truth, thought, and victory.

When the Volkish movement proclaimed the German revolution to be a spiritual revolution, they looked to Chamberlain for the racial framework. When they talked of the three great revolutions in German history—Luther's, that of the romantics, and the future one of the Volk—they referred to the Volkish revolution as the one inspired by racial thought. New Romanticism and racial ideas worked in tandem: in every respect, it was held, the soul of man represented the motive force in transforming reality, but it was the soul of Aryan man that would sweep the enemy out of the way and mold reality to its correct proportions. The formula called for the subordination of science, mechanization, modernization, and a new ethics to a religious racial goal. Except for its emphasis on the idyllic past, it would not basically change the social and economic structure of society. In the end, this was the argument advanced by National Socialism to justify an increase in industrialization. And though, even then, the true society was to be in close proximity to nature, the sting had been removed from industrialism. It was not a threat so long as

Aryans kept it within bounds through a metaphysical religious impulse that operated in each Aryan soul.

The Volkish movement was essentially elitist-oriented, a factor that the racial ideas of a Chamberlain, a Gobineau, or a Schemann had to take into account. It was not difficult for them. All of them defended the justice of a hierarchical social order in which leadership qualities were of prime importance. Volkish thinkers before 1918 did not direct themselves to an over-all mass appeal, though in some regions, especially the agrarian areas, spontaneous eruptions cultivated by racist demagogues did take place. After the war, attitudes changed and divergent strategies were proposed within the movement. As the movement began to attract growing numbers of students, intellectuals, and white-collar workers, and a different, power-directed emphasis came to be heard from Hitler, the elitist ideas lost favor and the Volkish movement slowly gravitated toward the National Socialists. But to the end, even when the Third Reich had been proclaimed, racial emphases retained an elitist tinge.

This racial elitism was forcefully expressed in the theories of the Volkish thinkers at the turn of the century. They tried to develop a racial elite in accordance with their aristocratic views. And as mass revolution was not their conception of racial progress, they searched for a way that race could be carried to its triumph in accordance with the Germanic spirit. Racial hygiene utilized to develop a racial elite within the nation was their answer. As they had based some of the broader theories of racial progression on the precepts of Social Darwinism, so they called upon it in this respect as well. It was advocated that by a process of selection and breeding the fittest would survive to become leaders and spokesmen of the race. There was nothing new or particularly German about this thought. Some of Darwin's disciples had advocated it. In England, Karl Pearson, writing about the survival of the fittest, held that it was man's obligation to accelerate the progress of religious nature. He quoted with approval Francis Galton's remark that it was a "religious duty" for humans to "see that man is better and better born." [23] If nature's law had it that the fit survived and the unfit perished, then men had to be bred who were fit. Racial thought in the service of the Volk paraphrased the formula with particular emphasis on the elite: if the race was the savior of mankind and if purity of race insured its survival, then men must be bred who are racially pure. These pure Aryan men and women, exponents of the German race's superior qualities, would secure the future and correspondingly advance the mission of their race.

This racial emphasis was current in the last two decades of the nineteenth century. The Frenchman Vacher de Lapouge drew similar conclusions from Darwin's work and likewise applied them to the Aryan race. In his *Les Selections sociales* (1876), he concentrated on the problem of insuring proper racial purity through eugenics. Significantly, like Gobineau, he never really achieved recognition in his native France but was widely admired in Germany.[24] On the whole, the application of Darwinism to society and race had considerable appeal to the Volkish movement.[25] This was so for several reasons. In their view, Darwinism stressed the element of struggle, the good fight that has been mentioned so often in the preceding chapters. Similarly, it provided a pseudo-scientific rationale for the extermination of those unfit to survive: in Volkish eyes, the lower races. Finally, Social Darwinism furnished the impetus for racial hygiene, to those experiments in race purification which one modern historian has termed "utopias of human breeding."

In 1900, Alfred Krupp, the wealthy industrialist, sponsored an essay contest on the topic: "What can we learn from the principles of Darwinism for application to inner political development and the laws of the state?" Most who answered maintained that the biological criterion was of the utmost importance and that within this framework a cadre of the racially fit would be necessary to ensure the continuity of the state. Wilhelm Schallmeyer, who received the first prize, viewed all legal systems, technical advances, morals, and even concepts of good and evil in terms of the struggle for survival. All life and morals must be brought into harmony with this fact. Anything that contributed to the safeguarding of the weak would hasten the degeneration of the white race to the level of Australian aborigines.[26] This would include mental as well as physical degeneration, as both capacities were racially determined. Schallmeyer, a doctor and private scholar, was supported by a fellow practitioner, Dr. A. Plötz, who endorsed the superiority of the Caucasian race in a qualified way by excluding the Jews. According to him, it was the Aryan race alone that represented the apex in racial development. He suggested that during a war it would only be fitting to send inferior members of the race to the front lines as cannon fodder. Furthermore, as an added measure to insure physical fitness, Plötz suggested that at a child's birth a consultation of doctors should judge its fitness to live or die. The ruthlessness inherent in this method of racial hygiene was due to the exaltation of human power, inevitable as long as it was maintained that human survival depended upon the cultivation of an elite and the eradication of the weak. It was especially pernicious in that nations were viewed as racially exclusive and judged according to biological superiority or inferiority.[27]

Another contestant, Ludwig Woltmann, failed to win a prize but won much greater influence instead. He wielded a double-edged sword, cutting at both a racial and a class protagonist. A convert from right-wing Marxism to Darwinism, Woltmann tried to effect a marriage of Marx, Darwin, and Kant in a system of thought that proposed mass struggle, a racial opponent, and metaphysical inspiration.[28] On the whole, his contribution was to transform the dialectics of class struggle into the philosophy of race struggle. However, it was his attachment to a bastardized Marxism that gave his thought a mass base. All his racial writings and theories were infused with an anti-bourgeois bias.

According to Woltmann, biological laws of nature, discovered by Darwin, directed the evolution of man as they did that of plants and animals. The laws even applied to human society in that they equated racial development with social progress. Using this as his "scientific" criterion, Woltmann went on to say that the Germans stood at the forefront of the species *Homo sapiens*.[29] But his evidence was aesthetic rather than scientific.

Woltmann claimed that the primary criteria of race were to be found in the proportions of the human body, facial geography, and other physical characteristics. In short, aesthetic qualities, subordinated to racial presuppositions, were introduced to substantiate theories that had pretended to be based in the natural sciences. Correspondingly, it was the Nordic, the Aryan, ideal of beauty that supported his claims for the primacy of the Germans. The proportioned torso and head of Nordic man, the alleged inner spirituality that glowed in his face and lent it a distinctive character, these were Woltmann's proofs of racial qualities. Studying the fine points of his Aryan ideal, he came to assert that the relationship of the legs to the buttocks of Nordic man duplicated the "absolute proportions of architectural beauty." [30] Nature, through the process of selection, had here produced a harmonious structure that mirrored not only an inner spirituality and outer grace, but the laws of absolute aesthetic values as well. Aryan beauty and a pseudo-science were, in the end, the twin proofs which furnished the backbone for Woltmann's influential work. A mixing of races, according to Woltmann, would result in the destruction of the physical proportions and harmony of the race. This would be accompanied by a degeneration of the spiritual faculties. The beauties of Germanic form under such conditions of decay would be submerged in what Lapouge had called the chaos of forms and colors of Central Europe.[31]

But race had another significance for Woltmann, a significance that appealed widely to his audiences. An inner racial force had to find a commensurate outer task: a race, if it is a master race, must physically conquer the countries it needs for its development. For proof he pointed to the example of the Germans who, by surviving, defeated the Ice Age, and their descendants who, millennia later, had endured the extensive migrations during the Dark Ages.[32] This point had already been made by Guido von List, but Woltmann went even further and asserted that the "Germanic race has been selected to dominate the earth." [33] From beauty and graceful proportions he passed on to world domination. Pan-Germanism was a fatefully logical extension of his racial precepts.

The Marxism to which Woltmann had subscribed earlier in his life acquired distinct racial overtones. The internationalism of the Marxian class struggle was transformed into a universal race struggle, class differences were embellished with racial overtones, and economic criteria took on a biological content. The Marxism that was retained (an interest in German workers) was overshadowed by racial and Germanic considerations. His advocacy of the admission of the Social Democratic party into the government, for instance, was based primarily on a desire to destroy its revolutionary doctrine and its internationalism by subjecting that party to national discipline.[34] On the whole, Woltmann took a negative attitude toward modern industrialism. He claimed that the change from an agrarian to an industrial society had hastened the decline of the race.[35] In contrast to nature, which engendered the harmonious forms of Germanism, there were the big cities, diabolical and inorganic, destroying the virtues of race.[36] And though this development was consistent with Darwin's theories, it likewise, according to the same theories, paved the way for the emergence of a more vital force yet: the racially fit German workers.

On this basis he rejected the rigid class structures, whether modern or medieval, as advocated by other racial and Volkish thinkers. Moreover, he claimed that they were deluded if they thought the present form of society was changeless. After all, according to the laws of nature life was an incessant struggle for survival whose end could not be foreseen. Class conflict was the most recent manifestation of this struggle. And German workers were battling for their freedom and independence in total conformity with its precepts, just as their overlords, the bourgeoisie, had once fought the nobility.[37] But even here Woltmann's sympathies were not with the socialist theories that aspired to the elimination of class differences and the growth of equality. Instead he championed what he claimed to be the genuine ambition of the German workers: a nation of racially pure members. A healthy race could be built not on a class structure dominated by the economically powerful but upon ability inherited through family, Volk, and race.[38]

Equality was not an issue for Woltmann. He believed that the bourgeoisie, by raising the cry of liberty, equality, and fraternity, had retained the privileges of the rich but at the same time had ignored the natural differences between the strong and the weak, the clever and the stupid—in short, the "natural" contrast between master and servant.[39] Woltmann desired to see all obstacles in the path of racial development removed, for they limited the natural superiority of the racially fit. No matter what his background, any German who demonstrated the requisite racial strength should automatically be advanced to the forefront of the Volk. He admitted that, in the beginning, capitalism had proved to be one of the best systems of social selection, but it had degenerated into economic domination by a shallow caste and carried within it the seeds of racial destruction.[40] Now it was imperative that new standards, embodying the proper racial criteria, should inspire and bring forth that individual talent, that man of genius who must always be allowed to lead society. Good racial stock, not economic expertise, was essential to the continual vitality of the German race.

Woltmann's espousal of revolutionary action was consistent with his analysis of the racially determined social structure. Again, it was not economic incentives that inspired radical deeds, but rather the fact that the social and intellectual superstructure no longer corresponded to the organic nature of the Volk, of the race.[41] The dynamics of Woltmann's political anthropology were applicable within the race itself as well as to its relations with other, lower races: revolutionary violence within and aggressive, imperialistic expansion outward.

While this concept of race had scientific and aesthetic pretensions, it also had historical aspects. Like other Volkish writers, Woltmann claimed that all the great deeds in Western history had been performed by men of the Nordic race: the great popes were Germanic (he cherished this fact though he hated what he called the international Catholic conspiracy) as were the leaders of the French Revolution. His appreciation of the Revolution was not generally shared by other Volkish thinkers, but he defended his ideas by means of racial arguments, claiming that the Revolution represented the rising of those Nordic elements within France who felt their potentialities stifled by the restrictions of the *ancien régime*.[42]

In his *Die Germanen und die Renaissance in Italien* (*Germans and the Renaissance*) (1905), Woltmann presented a history of the

German race based almost entirely upon visual evidence. External criteria of Nordic beauty dominated all else, and more than one hundred portraits appeared in the book. Its central theme was that the leaders of the Italian Renaissance had descended not from Romans but from Goths and Langobards.[43] Using portraits of Dante and Michelangelo, he rested his proof on facial characteristics, physical proportions, and the color or shade of the skin. Here again there is abundant evidence of irrational tendencies in the distortion of scientific evidence; a typical feature of all combinations of racial and New Romantic thought.

That National Socialism never really accepted all of Woltmann's ideas can be explained in several ways. For one thing, there was no anti-Semitism in his thought and writings. Interestingly enough, this was due to his belief that positive aspects of racial progress would manifest themselves without an internal adversary. In other words, the German race, according to Woltmann, carried within itself the seeds of eventual success or failure. Another factor that worked against the wholehearted reception of his thought by the Nazis was its over-dependence on Darwinism. Many Volkish and Nazi thinkers did not accept Darwin's theories and referred to them as the "English disease." Even during the Third Reich, when a collected edition of Woltmann's works was undertaken, the National Socialist editor felt constrained to remark that natural selection did not produce any new hereditary qualities.[44]

National Socialist editorial comment on Woltmann's work revealed the Nazis' attitude towards Darwinism. Evolution had to be denied since it postulated a primitive and elemental beginning for all races without exception. Moreover, evolution might negate any inherent racial virtues or superior distinctions. Consequently, the Nazis asserted that the stronger the racial roots, the less effect natural selection had upon them. As National Socialism and the Volkish movement claimed that the German race was perfection incarnate, that its greatness was immutable, the idea of racial evolution and progress had to be rejected. "The race now as a thousand years ago," read a caption in a National Socialist newspaper below a photograph of a bust of a Roman face next to that of a modern German.[45] In this context, Woltmann's Darwinism was only an irritant. Yet his idea of struggle, his concept of inner revolution and outer expansion, and his aesthetic criteria were all invoked in future racial and Volkish thought.

Woltmann's theories easily lent themselves to exaggeration. For example, Ludwig Wilser, a friend of Schemann, stressed the aesthetic criteria of race to a degree verging on the insane. In his two-volume

work *Germanen* (1914), as well as in his earlier *Rassentheorien*
(*Theories of Race*) (1908), Wilser criticized Chamberlain for stressing inner racial qualities to the detriment of external characteristics.[46]
He himself, like Woltmann, claimed that the pigmentation of the
skin was of the utmost significance and that there was a direct correspondence between the whiteness of the skin and intellectual bril-
liance.[47] With this equation, mysticism dominated racial anthropology. Lightness of hair and skin was connected with the sun mythos,
which considered the Nordic people to be the children of light.

The perfection of racial strains through racial hygiene was not
the exclusive concern of the Volkish elite. It was diffused among
German youth by an organization closely tied to the Youth Movement. In 1910 Hermann Popert founded Vortrupp (Advance Guard)
for the purpose of developing a more beautiful, stronger, and health-
ier German. His aim was immediate and practical; he was less interested in cosmic theories than in combating drunkenness and promiscuity, which were undermining the strength, beauty, and health of
the German race. The problem which Popert tried to deal with was
a real one. All over Europe the nineteenth century saw an alarming
increase of drunkenness, not just among the lower classes of the population but among all types of youth. In Germany the fraternities
had become drinking and dueling societies and were corrupting the
flower of the nation's youth. While in England evangelical movements took up the cause of moral reform, in Germany Popert sought
a solution in racial hygiene. This furnishes one more example of the
diffuse impact of Volkish thought and its ability to draw all sorts of
causes within its orbit.

Popert presented his views in one of the most widely read novels
of the time, *Helmut Harringa* (1910). It was written roughly at the
same time as *Wiltfeber,* but it lacked the cosmic overtones, the odor
of *Götterdämmerung,* that infused Burte's book. The hero of the
novel, Harringa, represented a prime specimen of the German race.
Possessing all the necessary virtues—blond hair, broad chest, energy
and determination, a glowing youthful face—the hero displayed a
corresponding moral purity. The connection between the external
and the internal is vividly depicted in a scene in which a judge, confronting Harringa, who has been wrongly accused of cheating, declares that he cannot believe that someone with the defendant's
looks could be a criminal.[48] The purity of stock mirrored an inherent
honesty.

Events, the fate of people close to him, and his own reactions made
Harringa an impassioned advocate of racial hygiene. He was a cru-
sader, a true idealist of deeds. Abstinence from alcohol, he felt, was

vital for mental and bodily health. The alien and poisonous nature of alcohol, which worked its effects on all levels, was brought to Harringa's attention with a vengeance when his brother drowned himself in remorse over a night of drink and illicit love. It was, however, a death of honor and penitence carried out under the family motto: "The tribe of Harringa cannot live with a deflowered body." At the same time he sadly contrasted the physical endurance of his ancestors, who had triumphed over the Ice Age (echoes of Guido von List again) and whose "marrow was strength and splendid their bodies," with another brother's wretched syphilitic frame.[49] Popert re-emphasized the basic struggle of the race against all impure elements in the character of Harringa. But here the enemy was not so much another race as it was the degeneration from within symbolized by drink and illicit love. His advocacy of racial hygiene was drenched with love for the Volk, and he extolled the potentials of the German race if it followed his prescriptions.

Popert did not rest content with opposing drink and extramarital love, but added further criticism on dress and mores with a view toward the improvement of the race. He was concerned with the problem of matching complementary couples in marriage. Since the quality of the race must be maintained, it was imperative that the partners be able to match each other's physical properties. For that it was necessary that they be able to appraise each other's physique and proportions and judge each other's merits and demerits. Consequently, one of his associates criticized the modern dress of his times because it hid the faults of the body, thus increasing the difficulty of choosing the right partner.[50] Popert devoted the cover of his journal, also called *Vortrupp*, to depicting a series of males with perfect bodies which accented the theme of Nordic ideals of beauty.

Popert realized that the Youth Movement represented the best receptacle for the dissemination of his views. It was ripe for conversion. He attended the convocation of the German youth on the Meissner Mountain and propagated his views.[51] It is rather hard to assess his direct influence, but it is immediately clear that his thesis bore the stamp of the times. The Meissner youth did reject alcohol and refrained from indulging in illicit love affairs. But their temperance cannot be directly credited to Popert. Rather, alcohol was frowned upon as a symbol of student fraternities and bourgeois life, while love, as we shall see shortly, was supplanted by Eros, based on Platonic ideas of the company of men—expressed in German by the word *Bund*.

Although Popert did contribute to the stock of racial ideas, his concept of race left something to be desired from the Volkish point of view. He was half Jewish himself and thus did not fit into the commonly accepted racial definitions. Moreover, his concept of race rested on territorial criteria; that is, anyone living in the German state should be able to become a true German by practicing the racial eugenics outlined in *Helmut Harringa*.[52] But his concept of race—and others similar to his—was ultimately rejected, and he became something of an outsider, even in the Youth Movement. Nevertheless, his romantic idealism did help to shape the adolescence of generations of German youth.

What, then, did the racial theories accomplish? By the end of the nineteenth century, racial thought had transformed the struggle for the survival of the fittest into a racial imperative. In uniting with tendencies in romantic thought, it presented the "whole" man as an alternative to the alienated and dislocated individuals who were drifting in the wake of industrial change. The presentation was visual. The Aryan was represented by certain definite external characteristics, supposedly reflecting the inner qualities of the race. The enemy too was stereotyped for easy identification. Whether because of a life of debauchery or because of non-Aryan origins, the enemy's appearance betrayed him. He was presented visually as either an example of degeneration or the exact opposite of the ideal Nordic type. The hostile attitude toward the Jews—there were individual exceptions—was a stock reaction to a correspondingly grotesque caricature. However irrational these racist ideas were, they sunk so deeply into the minds of many Germans that they were accepted even in the face of contrary visual evidence: for example, despite the evidence of photographs, in 1933 the periodical *Die Sonne* assured its readers that Hitler was blue-eyed and blond.[53]

Throughout this chapter we have attempted to trace the development of a component part of the Volkish ideology, which, for all its scientific pretensions, had a romantic and mystical basis, as did other parts of the ideology. Through a step-by-step examination of the ideas of various influential exponents, the racist ideology becomes more comprehensible. Taken by themselves, theosophy, sun worship, and the Nordic ideal of beauty seem outrageously irrational. But taken as a whole, they provided an explanation of the world and man's place in it. Combined, they crystallized the yearnings of those classes who were sinking in the social scale. To these it offered the hope of future power; to the lower classes it promised a better life. It provided a vision of eventual superiority, however bleak the present looked, however near bankruptcy the old structure might be. Moreover, science seemed to validate the illusion that a change to a new order would be possible without disrupting the class structure. Whatever change would come about, it would not abolish classes but would reconstitute them in a more congenial form—the concept of estates pleased those who were losing in the industrial struggle. From this point of view, despite its excesses, the ideology becomes historically more plausible and, indeed, understandable.

One of these excesses must now be discussed. There were impetuous members of the Volkish movement who wanted to actualize a racially pure society immediately. They attempted to build islands in what they considered to be a world that ignored the truth, a world in which the purity of the race was declining through admixture with degenerates. Just as utopian-minded socialists tried to establish socialist islands in a capitalist world, so they too tried to construct communities which would serve as models, as the hope for the future.

CHAPTER 6

Germanic Utopias

THERE ARE VALID REASONS why the Germanic utopias have not yet found their historian. Comparatively few politically conscious people in Germany removed themselves from society so drastically. Then, too, none of the colonies achieved its purpose, and except for the influence of individuals who came out of these environments, they left no heritage. But, viewed as a part of the Volkish movement and as an attempt to actualize a New Romantic and racial ideology, they take on some significance.

The utopias were effectively removed from the real world, rural islands in a sea of industrialization. Basic to the utopian movement was the urge to return to the land. It embodied an effort to root the Volk in the soil once more, to reconstruct surroundings that had a natural rhythm, that soothed the discord of urban life. The appeal was leveled at city dwellers, at disgruntled intellectuals and educators, people who had ideologically declined positive identification in urban life precisely because they rejected the values of modernity. It was spurred on by a double purpose: to escape the debilitating effects of city and industry and to reconstitute the Volk and the race. Not all the establishments at first devoted themselves to these tasks —some advocated natural education, others the advantage of co-operative living—but most of them developed into movements with a Volkish emphasis.

As agrarian communities founded on the soil, the utopian settlements were to be not only compelling examples for the Volk, but also living indictments of modern capitalism. To counteract the capitalist-encouraged migration from the land to the city, these utopias attempted to reverse the process, or, at least, to safeguard the remnants of rural life. To them the migration to the city and the commercial exploitation of the peasants represented the destruction of the organic base of the Volk. Above all, it was the land itself, the sacred German soil, that had become the object of exploitation. The peasant novel had already expressed this feeling: the old peasant in Polenz's *Büttnerbauer* hanged himself in sight of the farm he had lost, soon to be replaced by a factory.

The Germans did not stand alone in this concern, but shared in a world-wide anxiety. Some even looked for answers across the Atlantic. The influence of Henry George was significantly greater in Europe than in America. In Ireland he was courted and avidly listened to; in England he was a mighty force among the Fabians; while in Germany he seemed to reaffirm an ideology which endowed the native soil with intrinsically mystical qualities.

Capitalism makes false use of the land! Land speculation causes economic maladjustment! The soil must be demonopolized and made into common property! The "single tax" would effect just such a transfer! In this manner, Adolf Damaschke took up George's cry in Germany, and his *Die Bodenreform (Soil Reform)* (1902) marked the beginning of a lifetime of agitation. Damaschke thought that reform of landholdings currently associated with capitalists investment was the *sine qua non* for a society that wished to prevent domination by mammon or by communism.[1] Mammonism led to poverty, whereas communism abolished freedom. Land reform alone could bring about a society in which land would be owned in common for the common good while private property would be encouraged in other sectors of the economy. Only when the "unearned increment" of land had become the property of all would the conditions become ripe for the truly organic development of the Volk.[2]

A search for the middle way between capitalism and Marxism occupied the economic formulations of the Volkish movement. But it was imperative that the soil be the central source of both spiritual and economic sustenance. It was precisely in this respect that Damaschke's ideas were welcomed. During the First World War, H. S. Chamberlain wrote Damaschke that he felt himself drawn to the reformer's ideas and that caution and national considerations in time of war alone prevented him from outright public endorsement.[3] However, others in the Volkish movement considered Damaschke's analysis and prescriptions rather superficial. Their idealization of the soil and its transcendent significance pointed to more radically utopian measures than Damaschke, never Volkish himself, had envisaged. Franz Oppenheimer, a pioneer in the settlement movement, accused Damaschke of cheapening the great cause of soil reform by converting it into a mere bourgeois theory of taxation.[4] Here was the crux. George's single-tax concept was never as important to these men as freeing the land from a callous capitalist exploitation and restoring it as the home of Volkish cultivators—of agriculture as well as race. They felt that this would usher in the good society. Their slogan: "Make the land free!"

The attraction exercised by George through Damaschke was reinforced from another quarter. The demand for free money was added to that for free land. It was first raised by Sylvio Gesell and started him off on a career as a major figure in the free-land movement just before the First World War. He wanted to found a "natural" national economy. Land must be nationalized and mortgages abolished to enable "free" Germans once more to live on free land. Money, the medium of exchange, was not to be abolished; rather Gesell advocated the establishment of a central office to regulate the money already in circulation until the prices of all goods were stabilized. His measures would simultaneously lower interest rates until they disappeared entirely. The emphasis was on the free flow of money and its regulation in terms of supply and demand. The result would be to rid the country of debtors and the realization of a truly free Germany.[5] Gesell, like Damaschke, did not renounce economic competition, but wanted it removed from the land and deprived of its unearned increment. Gesell, of course, drew on a long history of opposition to usury in Europe which had found expression in Catholic encyclicals and had been the basis of many anti-Semitic riots. But he also had successors. Smashing the "slavery of interest charges" was far from being a unique point in the program of the National Socialist party, for it had long been part of the Volkish search for a national economy that transcended both capitalism and Marxism.

Damaschke's own movement attempted to establish colonies in Mexico, but they proved to be a failure. A rival and, at the time, more popular organization was the Free-Land movement, founded by the Viennese journalist Theodor Hertzka, who in a novel, *Freiland* (*Free Soil*) (1890), sketched a singularly elaborate utopia. There, all land was to be held in common and profits divided according to the amount of work done by each member. When his colonists reached Tanganyika in 1895, the British kept them waiting on the barren coast until the experiment had dissolved before it ever got started.[6] Hertzka's plan was known to a fellow journalist from Vienna, who worked on the same paper, and who at one point also looked to Africa as a place of settlement. Theodor Herzl's main inspiration came from other sources. Yet territorial Zionism partook of the same urge to return to the soil, free from capitalist entanglements, which captured so many in the German-speaking world. However, with one exception (Förster's experiment in Paraguay), the other utopias sprang up on German soil, in a German environment. For if the task was to revive the German race and its Volkish values, then going to Africa made little sense.

The colony of Eden, founded in 1893, was one of the more successful as well as one of the earliest settlements. It too combined the idea of free land with a modified plan of profit sharing. The latter element helped to make it more successful than those utopias which boasted total equality in sharing the fruits of labor. The land at Eden was common property and the inhabitants contributed a part of their labor for the benefit of the whole community. This work could be done either in the fields, in the Eden factories, which produced substitute meat dishes and vegetable-oil products such as "Eden butter" (which can still be purchased in the Germany of today), or in the co-operative buying and selling organizations. Money was de-emphasized as a meaningful means of exchange. Instead, the settlers conducted their transactions by means of barter arrangements. However, individual enterprise was allowed expression. Each settler or family had an allotted section of land which the owner cultivated in his own time and whose produce he sold on the open market.[7] This serious, though realistic, concession to private enterprise was quite successful as it avoided the pitfalls of instituting a complete social-ism within a capitalist economy over which the settlers could exercise no control.

Originally, there was little evidence of the Volkish impetus at Eden. Indeed, the founders were not disciples of the Volkish move-ment but vegetarians. Its originator, Bruno Wilhelmi, belonged to the circle of Moritz von Egidy and accepted his ideas on humanism and ethical culture. Moreover, as late as the early thirties Franz Oppen-heimer claimed that the settlement tolerated all shades of political opinion—from National Socialism to communism.[8] But the docu-ments belie such a claim. The colony increasingly developed a Volk-ish ethos. The first celebration of the "Free-Land Day" at Eden, in 1916, announced that for such a settlement "the Volkish ideology is a prerequisite. And for this only the Aryans are fitted." [9] The leader of Eden at the time, Carl Russwurm, substantiated this assertion philosophically in his book on the Germanic foundations of the con-cept of freedom. In it he traced the ideas we have so often dissected and mixed them with Sylvio Gesell's free-land and free-money theories.[10]

As the colony manifested increasingly Volkish tendencies, it also displayed a racist emphasis. It attempted to form an exclusively Aryan community that would cultivate and produce the virtues that were idealized by the Volkish ideologists. The utopia was to represent an identification with truly regenerated Germanic freedom and life. Rituals were practiced which would tend to enhance this identification; so, in addition to celebrating Christmas—with a Germanic touch, to be sure—they also paid homage to the changing of the sun and similar Germanic festivals.[11]

Moreover, Eden served as the training ground for the leaders of several smaller Volkish settlements which were to spring up after the First World War. Ernst Hunkel, who had once edited the official Eden paper, founded Donnershag, which will be discussed later, and another settlement, symbolically called Sigfried (1921), also originated with a member of the Eden colony. Sigfried was designed to further a "spiritual aristocracy of German blood" in order to protect the Volk from "Asiatic and Welsh [i.e., French] hordes, not just with the sword, but also with the spade and above all through the furthering of armanish [secret Indian-Aryan] wisdom."[12] There can be little doubt of the predominantly Volkish atmosphere of the Eden colony in which such men had lived and worked. This Volkish and racist quality was fully understood by a part of the Youth Movement and by the settlement's prewar leadership as well.

Theodor Fritsch, for one, grasped the truth as early as 1908. Fritsch was one of the most important early racist and violently anti-Semitic publicists. In 1887 he founded the "Hammer" publishing house whose first effort was *The Anti-Semitic Catechism* (later called *The Handbook on the Jewish Question*), which went through forty editions before 1936, a veritable arsenal of anti-Jewish opinion. The Nazis were to honor him (he died in 1933 at eighty-nine years of age) as *Altmeister*—the master teacher. Typically enough, Fritsch, from a petit bourgeois background, was interested in preserving the middle classes from being crushed by the new industrialism and urbanism. He therefore became interested in building garden cities which would be closer to nature (*Stadt der Zukunft—The Town of the Future*—1896). This led him into the settlement movement, bypassing urbanism altogether. It was then that he looked to Eden for inspiration in planning a settlement for his own organization, the Hammer Bund. He did assimilate two ideas from the older colony: economic matters were to be conducted as in Eden because its policy alone prevented the atomization of body and soul, while a common racial spirit would cement the sense of the community's identity.[13]

Though this colony never got started, its ideas and spirit were influenced by and extended through Fritsch's close friend and collaborator Willibald Hentschel. This remarkable figure was a pupil of Ernst Häckel, the popularizer of Darwinism in Germany, and also received training in chemistry, biology, and agriculture. Hentschel was an academic proletarian, a university person without any university position. Like his friend Fritsch, he witnessed the unification of Germany (he was born in 1858) and lived long enough to be honored by the Nazis, especially through *Der Stürmer* of Julius Streicher. Early in his life he had joined various anti-Semitic organizations and had been one of the founders of the extremist Deutschsoziale party in the last decade of the century. Above all he remained close to Fritsch, joining him in his propagandistic ventures and having his books published by the Hammer. The impetus to Germanic utopian thought and racial identification which Hentschel provided was as influential as it was extreme. Today it is forgotten, but in his time Hentschel's book *Varuna* (1907) was considered to be as influential as Spengler's work in the formation of a general, popular state of mind. Such a comparison is undoubtedly exaggerated, for Hentschel lacked Spengler's universality of mind.[14]

In his analysis of man's history, Hentschel affirmed the Germanic and racial world view. He thought that the process of history was integrated with spiritualistic elements. The course of man's development, Hentschel asserted, was similar to a release of energy potential: history was powered by energy which had been accumulated and stored from the abundant supply of racial dynamism in primeval times. Race was an electric charge, it was dynamic, and it had to be preserved and enhanced by increasing the degree of racial purity. Even within the race, the most promising stock was to be encouraged and the inferior left behind. The Aryans, who did not spring from an admixture of races, must affirm through themselves the quality of noble blood that runs through their veins. Aryan nobles and warriors were to be formed, as they had always been, by selection and selective propagation. Social division, a special class, indeed a caste system, was thus essential. To ensure the creation of such a racial and Volkish nobility, Hentschel proposed the establishment of a truly Germanic colony.[15]

The settlement was to be called Mittgart after the legendary place to which the Aryan race traces its origins. The colony was to constitute a new beginning for the race. Hentschel claimed that the racial stock must be isolated, or rather insulated, in this way, so that it would be protected from the corrupting effects of modernity. Only a German village could provide the incentive necessary for the development of the Volk. Consequently, Mittgart was to be founded on the land and would therefore breed a race firmly attached to the soil. Even the selection for membership reflected this attitude. In recruiting, Hentschel asserted that the non-fit should be shipped to the city, where the environment would destroy them, while the fit should leave the urban centers and join the settlement or stake out land for themselves. In this manner, the Volk, freed of its inferior stock, would be able to strike roots once more.[16]

What then was Mittgart—this generator of racial energy—like? The settlers were supposed to form one big family, a special brotherhood of men. No trade or money would be permitted, and the necessities of life and capital goods would be purchased by a sage and aged senate composed of friends of the settlement. Quarrels between members would be brought before a court of honor—or decided in individual combat, "still the best law, which gives its due to the strong." The whole spirit of Mittgart, and especially the institution of trial by combat was a revitalized adaptation of medieval customs. However, as Mittgart's purpose was to build for the future while attempting to evoke ancestral purity, selective racial breeding was considered. Hentschel, the pupil of Ernst Häckel, declared his intent to erect a model community to breed the fittest Aryan specimens, who would champion the survival of the race.[17]

Along these lines and in the service of his ideal, he made his most sensational suggestion: he advocated instituting polygamy. Hentschel regarded the current state of the race as desperate: it was rapidly waning in strength and endurance. Only a crash breeding program could recover lost ground and halt the degeneration. Constant production, continuous propagation of the race, was imperative, and the breeding capabilities of Aryan men and women must be used to the fullest. According to Hentschel's proposal, the leadership of the settlement would determine who would marry. A marriage would automatically terminate when the woman became pregnant. The man was to remarry immediately, while the woman was to devote herself to tending the child for two years. Thereupon she was to enter into a new union and again conceive for the glory of the Aryan race. The position of the woman was clearly defined: she was the breeding stock of the race who tended the children and the settlement gardens. In many ways this found a direct application under National Socialism.

The children of Mittgart were not supposed to breathe the "dust of the school" until they were sixteen. When they reached this age, they left the settlement for the bourgeois world, where the state was to provide them with the formal education they had missed. At Mittgart they had more important things to learn. The girls helped their mothers with the domestic chores; that was their place and calling. Meanwhile, the boys would be organized into groups of one hundred, inculcated with the Germanic spirit, and trained by the elders to bear arms. The use of group song and story sessions was a popular way of instilling in the youngsters a sense of their Germanic identity. Heroic songs praising ancient Germanic bravery were to be sung in the open air. A secondary purpose of these exercises was to stimulate the youths' memory and their sense of rhythm. The emphasis was clearly anti-intellectual, an aspect of the Germanic ideal that will confront us time and again. Not the power of reasoning, but an emotional state of mind and physical prowess were the chief objectives. Germanic man should again be fused with the cosmic forces, and it is small wonder that Hentschel regarded Paul de Lagarde as the last religious genius that Germany had produced.[18]

Hentschel calculated what he thought was the proper sex ratio for the breeding ground of the racial elite: one thousand women to one hundred men. And though this situation—in addition to the attraction of racial hygiene—might be expected to appeal to prospective male members, the Mittgart Bund was never able to sink permanent roots in German soil. This elaborate utopia remained enshrined in the pages of Hentschel's book. But Hentschel was not the only one with such themes. Others were working for the same ends in similar ways. The "German League for Regeneration," for instance, founded by Dr. Alfred Damm and Otto Hauser in 1902, proposed the establishment of a "Teutonic Foundation" with purposes similar to Hentschel's.[19] In Conservative party circles the Mittgart Bund was first received with approbation. The newspaper Die Kreuz Zeitung lavished high praise on Hentschel in 1892, but by 1912 it had toned down its own extremism and with it its outright support of the racial utopias. The interval had seen a change in editorial policy from an anti-Semitic position close to Adolf Stöcker's to a more moderate conservatism, and the paper now mockingly referred to Hentschel's breeding institution as the "chicken farm" and fulminated against Hentschel's "grotesque regression into the realm of zoology." [20] The Bund der Landwirte, omnipresent in the Volkish movement, took a more conciliatory position. It thought highly of Hentschel, stressed his anti-Semitism, and glossed over the sexual extremism of Mittgart. Warm praise came from sympathetic individuals who shared his racial aspirations and who were equally impatient in their desire to see his goals achieved promptly.[21] Erich Mathes, for instance, a publisher deeply involved in the Youth Movement, brought out a novel praising the institutions of Mittgart in poetic form.[22]

All of Hentschel's utopian schemes reflected the Volkish ideology. There was hardly an element that was not derivative. This was true, of course, of his racism. Mittgart was based on the racial theory that asserted the inherent beauty of the Aryan race and, like the majority of racial formulations, it equated inner qualities with external characteristics. The Aryan race was the blond, perfectly proportioned race. Consequently, the belief in external beauty as the mirror of the beauty of the soul led Hentschel to praise the Aryan body and encourage the cult of the body. He asserted that any manner of dress alienated man from his body, which was a divine gift, and thus destroyed his inner equilibrium. Aryan beauty, being genuine beauty, must be nude, said Hentschel, echoing Fidus.[23] The cult of the body grew and became so popular that just prior to the First World War the *Freibad*, nude bathing, was a more or less common phenomenon. The practice was encouraged by a journal significantly entitled *Volkish Nudism*.

In many respects this was not a new phenomenon. Physical culture, without the racial emphasis on nudity, had been identified with the Volkish movement ever since Father Jahn had encouraged it among his own disciples. Indeed, the German Gymnasts, founded by Jahn, became a part of the general movement. The emphasis on physique and the glorification of strength had been a distinct undercurrent in their philosophy as well. Gymnastic exercises steeled the Aryan body in the struggle against foreign as well as internal enemies. Physical culture found further encouragement within the utopian movement. In 1903, for example, Paul Zimmermann founded his settlement, Klingenberg, in Prussia, expressly as a place "for the furtherance of Nordic body culture." He also adapted Wachler's idea of the open-air theater. Meeting under the blue sky, his group would solemnly reaffirm a dedication to Germanic culture, race, and heritage.[24]

Modifying his earlier ideas, Hentschel reasserted himself in the period after the First World War to demand the creation of a "heroic guild of agricultural workers." In a pamphlet entitled *Was soll nun aus uns werden?* (*What Shall Become of Us?*) (1923) he called for a concerted effort to form a company of fighting knights to protect the German earth. It was the religious duty of youth to join such a group, to dedicate themselves to the preservation of a German Volk that had been created according to a God-given order. The deity of the Aryan race, asserted Hentschel, was to be the god Artam, and so he named the organization Artam, which was later changed to the collective, Artamanen.[25]

Willibald Hentschel gave the ideological impetus, but the organization was actually founded by a rightist-oriented section of the Youth Movement—under the leadership of Wilhelm Kotzde, the leader of the youth group Adler und Falken (Eagles and Falcons), and Bruno Tanzmann, a personally unstable agitator. Unlike Mittgart, the Artamanen were successful because they adopted a more realistic economic system. They did not settle in a utopian community but hired out as agricultural workers in order to obtain the funds necessary for later settlements. They first began to work on a Saxon estate in 1924. Here Hentschel's idealism was fused with a practical economy; the union was beneficial. More than any of the other utopias, it presented a plausible solution to modernity and the agrarian dislocation that faced Germany. The Artamanen set to their task with dedication. High on the list of their priorities were the following demands: foreign labor (mostly Polish) must be removed from the estates on Germany's eastern frontier; the eastern lands themselves must be colonized by Germans once more; and the border of the nation must be pushed ever further east.[26] These sound like military goals, almost a declaration of war, and the stakes were indeed high. *Lebensraum*, living space for the Volk, was considered a prime necessity, and any acceptance, on the part of national leaders, of foreigners appropriating or working on native soil was regarded as an act of treason. Opposition to the Versailles Treaty prompted this outcry, while modernity still provided the basis for identifying the internal foe. Ludwig Woltmann had complained earlier that the flight into the cities had permitted foreign and lesser races to usurp the German's station in the countryside and thus destroy his relation to the native soil. The conditions of the cities, on the other hand, doused the sacred fires of the race.[27] The Volkish condemnation was short and sharp. A people that allowed foreigners to till their native soil while they preferred to exist as the proletariat of the cities committed national suicide. Redress was needed for the Volk, the race, and the soil. The Artamanen were ready to take up the cause.

The Volkish ideal of the peasant was thrust into the foreground of the propaganda drive to recruit new members and to represent the character of the Artamanen. Hans Holfelder, the most important of the early leaders of the organization, stated that a nobility of blood was synonymous with a nobility of the peasantry. The perfection of the race was to be found in the perfection of the tiller of the land.[28] This image was projected everywhere. Advertisements placed by the Artamanen in the papers of the Youth Movement and the Volkish press depicted the radiant profile of a boy, with the caption: "The sun will brown your skin and cleanse your blood."[29]

The same emphasis dominated the activities of Bruno Tanzmann before he became associated with the Artamanen. In 1921 he launched a school for adult peasant education designed to revive the strength of the peasantry and to utilize it in the modern struggle. By promoting peasant culture—folk songs, dances, and tales—he sought to instill new life in the peasantry. The themes of these activities, in Tanzmann's view, contained an undercurrent of pure force. This elemental, primitive energy was indispensable, since, according to his formulation, true peasant culture required the awakening of a primitive imagery within the breast of the Aryan Germanic Volk.[30] It is significant that Heinrich Himmler in the 1920's had high praise for the adult peasant education (*Bauernhochschul*) movement, calling it vital for the development of peasant self-consciousness, for the peasant estate is "the foundation of the Volkish state." In this connection he stressed the importance of settlements as a bulwark against the Slavic workers, thus linking his thought with that of the whole settlement movement.[31] Such ideas became common among the Artamanen as well, interrelated as they were with romanticism and racism.

But the Artamanen had practical ideas as well. They managed their economy realistically; they worked hard at agriculture and regarded themselves as the instrument of transition from the city to the land. The members of the Artamanen resided in rural communities and worked as agricultural laborers earning wages according to the prevailing rate. Their goal was to accumulate enough capital to enable them to purchase land and settle down as independent peasants and farmers, but their movement collapsed before they were able to realize this goal. Despite its failure, the Artamanen scheme was superior to the self-contained community which was primarily interested in abstract ideals. In addition, the Artamanen discarded the essentially unworkable ideal of "free land." [32]

The emphasis on practicality, which distinguished the Artamanen from other utopias, was instrumental in attracting intellectual and financial support from various sources. Georg Schiele, the agricultural expert for the Deutschnationale party and minister-designate of agriculture during the Kapp putsch, was one of Artamanen's most avid supporters.[33] Even bigger forces aligned themselves with the agricultural settlement. The whole Volkish movement was sympathetic. The National Socialists were enthusiastic. From the very beginning, there were intimate ties between them and the Artamanen, at least between their leaders. Tanzmann was the publisher of the anti-Semitic *Swastika Calendar* and eventually joined the party; in 1933 Hitler honored him with a lifetime income.[34] Hans Holfelder became a party member in 1925 and was able to bring Himmler into the movement. Friedrich Schmidt, the chancellor of the Artamanen, joined the next year. But, at first, the Artamanen Bund as a whole resisted amalgamation with the Nazis.

Himmler did his best to convert them, telling them that without the transcendent *Weltanschauung* of the National Socialist party the whole movement made no sense and was futile.[35] But to no avail. The Artamanen's resistance was based on their racial ideology. Their objections to the Nazis were similar to those of the rest of the Volkish movement. The Nazis were too democratic (they appealed to the masses) and too political (they participated as a political party in the work of the Diet).[36] However, by 1929, when the international economic crisis was being felt in Germany, the Artamanen movement came to a standstill, and many defected to the Nazis with the conviction that only the National Socialists could deal efficiently with Germany's enemies. Most of the Artamanen finally joined the Nazis, although some held out longer than others. It was dissolved only when the National Socialist labor service was established, itself partly inspired by the Artamanen.

Hentschel's ideas and the Artamanen exerted a significant influence on several men who were to play important roles in German politics. Walther Darré, who eventually became minister of agriculture, was intimately involved. He asserted that Hentschel had truly grasped the necessity for a racial and Volkish peasant nobility.[37] The Nazi breeding institutions were anticipated by Mittgart, and the agricultural imperialism of the Artamanen Bund outlived Hentschel. But there was some disagreement. Even Darré disagreed with Hentschel on the issue of polygamy. In fact, Hentschel's advocacy of polygamy was mainly responsible for pushing the concept of Artam into the background of the Volkish movement, although it had at first been well received. The disruption of the family structure and the impermanence of marriage vows were anathema to the movement. Being fundamentally conservative, they regarded the family as the inalienable center of race and Volk. Though Himmler shared some of their racial and cultist views, he wanted above all to wean them from their independent position and bring them into association with the National Socialists. Holfelder served as a go-between, and in the process expanded his contacts to include Adolf Hitler himself.[38]

But in the end it was the relatively numerous membership and the success of the Artamanen that attracted the Nazis. It was the largest of the utopian groups. In contrast to the other utopias, whose membership ranged from 200 to 300, that of the Artamanen spiraled from 100 at the time of its inception in 1924 to 1500 four years later.[39] Again, in terms of the size of the politically conscious public, even those of the right alone, this was a pittance. But what they lacked in numbers they made up for in dedication. The importance of the whole Volkish movement never consisted in sheer strength of numbers. After all, the early National Socialists never had more than a few hundred members. Their importance consisted in the ideas which they propelled onto the national scene, the movements they were able to infiltrate, and the people whose imagination they were able to capture but who did not necessarily join in any organized effort. Those who were daring enough to spurn the mores and comforts of society were also more outspoken and less apt to be intimidated by an unreceptive or even hostile audience. In this respect, and because of their relative popularity, the Artamanen impinged upon the consciousness of the rapidly growing National Socialist party in a manner not equaled by other utopian groups.

While the Artamanen Bund was more successful than the earlier utopias, it itself was surrounded by settlements which aspired to the same popularity but with a different ideological emphasis. Many of these were founded in reaction to the economic and social disorganization, especially as it broke in upon Germany after the First World War. Even the left tried to found settlements that accorded with Marxist ideology. But it is significant that their membership amounted to only a tenth of that achieved by the Volkish utopias.[40] Unlike Marxism, the Volkish ideology lent itself readily to justifying the utopias. Some were directly inspired by Volkish thinkers. Using the ideas of Guido von List, tiny Briedhablik, near Danzig, which lasted from 1919 to 1924, styled itself as the "supernational Aryan union," adding vegetarianism, abstinence from alcohol, and nudism as pro-racial measures in order to supplement List's ideas.[41] Donnershag, founded by Ernst Hunckel in 1919 and lasting but a few years, went a step further by incorporating the precepts of two prophets of Volkish thought: the economic theories of Sylvio Gesell and the "Germanic faith" of Paul de Lagarde.[42]

Here we have to deal with a problem, both practical and ideological, that all these utopias faced. Regardless of its explicit political association, a community whose members live together, work together, and share the produce of toil is open to the charge that it entertains some communist tendencies. In the practical sphere the problem is easily answered, in that the economics of communalism were not sufficient to support the inhabitants of the utopias. Too many factors (the market, prices, inflation, credits, etc.) were beyond their control. Economically then, the utopias could not survive on a communal economy. The political charge, however, that they were atttempting to apply the economics of communalism, was more difficult to meet. Was not the establishment of these utopias precisely the socialism the Volkish theorists deplored?

There were many answers, some more sophisticated than others. Hunkel, the founder of Donnershag and chancellor of the Germanic Knights, who dedicated themselves to spreading Nordic beliefs, made it plain that only as much of the communist theory came into play as was necessary for self-preservation. In any case, this communism, it was asserted, was of a pure Germanic strain, practiced and perfected by the ancients. It was an emotional trait that came from the Volk soul and molded itself according to the needs of the Volk.[43] Then too, there was a distinct element of anti-capitalism both in Hunkel's argument and in that presented later in the famous book written by Ferdinand Fried (Friedrich Zimmermann), *Das Ende des Kapitalismus* (*The End of Capitalism*) (1931), and published by Eugen Diederichs. Avoiding the Marxist mechanism of class struggle, they decried capitalism in its modern form, labeling it "Manchesterism." It was condemned, however, not for perpetuating a hierarchical structure but for its role in destroying the Volk. In some instances, as in Fried's book, this argument culminated in the defense of socialist communal arrangements insofar as they facilitated the goal of complete nationalization of the land. But in all instances the utopians proclaimed their anti-Marxist intention—which was certainly reassuring in Volkish circles—of erecting not a classless society but one organized in estates, enjoying a hierarchical structure, and tolerating only the racially fit. The utopias were communal solely to enhance relationships between their members which would encourage the propagation of a healthy racial elite. If this was insufficient to dispel the doubts of anti-communists, there was always the mystical, religious aura, and the concrete activities of many right-wing utopias, to assure them they were in the proper company.

In several instances the need to propagandize and defend these Volkish utopias led to the establishment of publishing houses. Hunkel was well equipped to initiate such a venture at his settlement. Prior to and during the First World War, he had edited the journal of the Eden colony, in which he espoused racial ideas and connected them with Nordic beliefs of a mystical nature.[44] In this manner several organizations managed to exert an influence out of all proportion to the size of their membership (Donnershag numbered only 50 people) by disseminating ideas that were welcomed by many who were sympathetic but did not join.

As the Germanic utopias were in danger of being identified with communistic practices because of their communal philosophy, so some ethical and religious settlements, under the guise of a mystical humanism, actually veered toward the beliefs and practices of the Volkish settlements. The Vogelhof, established in 1920 at Hellerau in Saxony, was actually a pietistic foundation. However, its religious pietism advocated a spiritualized Christianity cleansed of foreign (meaning Jewish) influences and traits. The colony's program was based on re-creating the ancient Aryan unity between God and the world, between God and nature—a Lagardism which brought the settlement ideologically close to the orthodox Volkish colonies.[45] A romantic urge to return to the land permeated the Vogelhof program. The urge was so vivid and acute that the colonists were undeterred by the barrenness of the land they settled—indeed, they accepted it with delight. In a setting reminiscent of that in Byron's *Manfred*, the colony established itself among "wide vistas, sheer cliffs and wild gorges, deep woods, lonely heaths and a continuously blowing wind"[46]—a landscape that could evoke the consummation of Wiltfeber, the eternal German, and his bride by a bolt of Thor's lightning. Physical and racial culture was practiced. Mingled with the Germanic faith of Lagarde were such institutions as nude bathing, gymnastics, and vegetarianism.[47]

However, it was only after the dissolution of the first Vogelhof settlement that the program was consciously patterned after Volkish precepts. Unable to sustain itself on the unfertile soil of the romantic spot, the colony went bankrupt and, under the leadership of Friedrich Schöll, struck out in a new direction. Schöll, a teacher by profession, decided to found a country boarding school in order to supplement the income from the agricultural enterprise. In other words, the settlement was transformed into an annex of the school, supporting itself on the school's income and contributing to the children's education by supplying a conducive environment. The aim of the school was to enable the youngsters to conduct a totally Germanic life. Starting with the lowest grade of high school students, Schöll indoctrinated them in the virtues of Nordic man and a faith in "the sun as creator of life, the earth as mother of life, and the trees as its expression."[48] Under the symbol of the swastika, the settlers and the student boarders of the Vogelhof marched into a future molded by racial theories, Volkish interests, and a Germanic faith.

The school was successful enough to last until 1938, when the Nazis incorporated it into their educational system and Schöll joined the Nazi educational bureaucracy. He had prepared himself well as a publicist, having served as the editor of the important Volkish Hellerau publishing house. As a member of the national Volkish Sigfried Bund he attempted to expand the movement. By organizing, in the 1920's, the German Study Circle and the Days of Settlement, at which utopian leaders discussed mutual problems and plans, he attempted to create a forum for such pertinent questions as racial policies and the feasibility of using wheat as the basis of a German monetary system.[49] When he finally saw the dawn of Nazi Germany, he proudly declared that he had pushed the idea of the country boarding school to its logical culmination.[50]

In addition to the Vogelhof, there were other country boarding schools which followed the same pattern. The over-all contemporary emphasis on indoctrination of youth was taken up by other settlements and they too established training schools for the young. Hermann Harless founded a school of this type, with Volkish leanings, which indoctrinated the students in Germanic nature and folklore while teaching them practical arts, crafts and gardening. When his Hollsteig settlement, founded in 1920, was burned down two years later, he went to Hellerau, obtained new resources and inspiration, and started another school in 1928. His school at Marquartstein, on the Ammersee in Bavaria, was relatively successful until it was expropriated by the Nazis and merged with the Nazi educational system in 1933.[51]

Starting with the utopias and ending in the rural boarding schools, the movement we have been discussing was a direct expression of the growing sense of identity which coalesced around Volkish thought, from racism to Germanic faiths. They have been included in this study of the crisis of German ideology because they illuminate the pervading sense of urgency. The Germanic utopias catered to, and stimulated the yearning for, the actualization of the ideology; they wanted to accomplish their ends at once—here and now. They first arose during the last decades of the nineteenth century, subsided during the First World War, and burst forth with renewed vigor and determination afterward. They attempted to provide the anxious with the answers to the problems raised, first, by modernity, and then by the national defeat suffered in the war and the changes that came in its wake. The relatively small number of colonies and settlers did not prevent them from making a significant social and ideological contribution. Though they associated themselves largely with extremist elements in the Volkish movement and found themselves in greater agreement with various tenets of National Socialist thought, they did sharpen the image of the Volkish movement as a whole. On the whole, they made themselves known to the public at large. Whether through the publications of the National Socialists or through Diederichs' *Tat*, more people were familiar with and influenced by their existence than is indicated by the number of the hardy joiners. "In the beginning of a revolutionary movement, numbers do not matter. What matters is the strength gained by an ideology through living examples of it." Many must have echoed this defense of the settlements against their detractors.[52]

Ironically, the fullest realization of such peasant communities, based primarily on economic, religious, and social considerations, was to be a Jewish, not a German accomplishment. Aware that the Zionists also were attempting to establish agrarian utopias, the Germans soon conferred upon themselves the exclusive ideological privilege of doing so. For example, in 1922, a Volkish periodical asserted with contempt that Jewish settlements were a mockery and would fail since the Jews were not a Volk, had no peasants, and owned no land, but were only traders and parasites.[53] It was a typical attitude of the Volkish movement; judgments derived from ideological presuppositions were considered superior to objective evidence. When Jews did show an interest in, and a capacity for, agricultural occupations (which were always made difficult for them), the Volkish press proclaimed that young Jews who were training for agricultural tasks were doing so as part of a Jewish plot. It claimed that their ardor was indeed suspicious since it was common knowledge that Jews shied away from manual labor.[54]

But did the Germanic utopias and the underlying ideology have any influence on the development of the *Kibbutzim* movement? Did the general philosophical outlook of German Zionists contain elements similar to the land, nature, and Volk idealization of Volkish thought? The direct historical influence for the establishment of the *Kibbutzim* came not from Germany but from Eastern European and socialist sources. The only possible direct connection might be traced to the German Jewish *Habonim*. For this group, the Youth Movement provided the central rallying point. Their declaration asserted that the "immediacy of experience has been lost to us." The intimacy with nature, earth, the rhythm of the seasons, and the vitality of physical labor had been severed from the experiences of the young Jews. What was necessary, they declared, was to resume the struggle with nature, acquire the primitive strength of physical prowess, and live a life without intellectual trappings. "Our movement seen as a whole is romantic"; it is the Jewish longing for work, earth, and community.[55] These sentiments indeed mirrored the mood of New Romanticism. But they were not fully realized in the actual agrarian settlements in Palestine. Though for the historian there seems at first to be a tempting correlation, any significant connection between Germanic utopias and the *Kibbutzim* movement has not been established.[56]

So far anti-Semitism has entered our discussion only tangentially, though indeed it was central to the Volkish ideology. It identified the enemy and objectified him. If the German race had degenerated, then someone was responsible. To use a constantly recurring Volkish image: a snake gnawed at the roots of the racial tree, stunting its spontaneous, natural growth. That snake was the Jew, the obstacle to the realization of the Volk. He was to be swept away by mass terror and murder during the Nazi era.

CHAPTER 7

The Jew

FOR GERMAN JEWS in the nineteenth century, emancipation came sporadically, and their own fortunes seemed to rise and fall with those of the forces that sought political, social, and economic reform. Equality and political privileges were in all cases gifts of revolution—which the Jews supported but paid heavily for once reaction set in. In France the liberation of the Jews coincided with the general advance of progressive forces—which they joined and, at times, contributed to heavily. In Germany, however, they gained their rights in an entirely different setting. Here revolutionary fervor, defeated and chauvinistic, had settled into the emotional molds of romanticism. The affirmation of civil rights for Jews contrasted ominously with the victory of a romantic ethos.

This particular confluence of forces portended an unsettled and disquieting future for the emancipated Jews, and the prevalent cultural emphasis was to work in their disfavor. The Volkish movement in Germany, as we have come to know it, exposed the geography of the human soul. It defined the German—as well as the Jew—according to his inherent and integral traits. In contrasting these two mutually exclusive types, New Romantic thought made the following assertions: the Jew was an alien in the land of the Germanic peoples, which had been chartered in a spirit of pietistic Christianity and which was the native soil of the rooted Volk. During the middle of the nineteenth century, the contrasting images were promoted chiefly by popular literature. Writers such as Gustav Freytag had introduced a Jewish stereotype which was rapidly diffused in the period after emancipation. It held the Jew to be without a soul, without the humble German virtues, and consequently uprooted. The Jew, too, epitomized Riehl's troublesome, malevolent, and shiftless proletariat. The Jew, in short, was anathema to Volkish thought. In contrast to the German soul, which acted as a filter between man and cosmos, the soul of the Jew was an insensitive, materialistic thing.

How did the Volkish thinkers in particular, and many Germans in general, arrive at such conclusions? The historical image of the Jew never died in Germany. From the first, Jewish emancipation had been supported because it might enable Jews to shed their Judaism and with it their undesirable qualities. Johann Christian Dohm, the champion of emancipation, hoped that through it Jews would repudiate their past, become ethical persons, and settle down to "honest work." [1] When such men thought of Jews as Jews, they put them into the mysterious setting of the ghetto, and though its walls had fallen in Germany, the association continued to color the Jewish image, especially since the continued existence of the mass of East European Jewry within ghettos could be taken to typify Judaism and the Jews. To Germans this civilization on their border was both strange and soul-less. This view was enhanced by the exposure of ghetto conditions in the literary works of Jews who had left this environment and were now eager to repudiate it. In their novels, Leo Herzberg-Fränkel and Emil Franzos renounced their past, indeed, they claimed to despise it. Herzberg-Fränkel stressed the material and spiritual poverty of the ghettos, and used the dirty, crowded streets as his leitmotif; Franzos summed up his revulsion in the famous phrase "half Asia." [2] These condemnations fell upon receptive ears. The Germans along the eastern border who had dealt with ghetto traders and peddlers, and who, like Gustav Freytag himself, had supposedly been cheated by them, loudly agreed with Herzberg-Fränkel and Franzos.

The development of this feeling, along with the changing view of the nature of the Jew, was vividly presented in popular literature. Perhaps the most famous rendition of the stereotype appeared in Freytag's *Debit and Credit* (1855). Veitel Itzig typified all the qualities which Volkish thought was to associate with the Jew. He was ugly, grasping, and without any true humanity. A rootless being, he climbed to success through ruthlessness and false dealing. Itzig is contrasted to the German apprentice who retains his righteousness while making his way in the world and whose rootedness is demonstrated by his honesty and responsibility. [3] A similar theme runs through Wilhelm Raabe's immensely popular *Hungerpastor* (*The Pastor to the Hungry*) (1863). Here, however, the emphasis is on the religious element as a way of life. The German, satisfied with the ordered structure of the world and his place in it, is sharply contrasted with the Jew and his insatiable lust for aggrandizement. The plot of the novel well illustrates the theme. Two friends, one a Christian, the other a Jew, venture into the world to make their way. The Christian strives honestly and raises himself to become the benevolent pastor of a poor seaside parish. The Jew is dishonest, ruthless, and consumed by a lust for power, but in the end his ambitions are thwarted.[4] Raabe allows his Jew a cleaner end than that granted to Veitel Itzig by Freytag: literally drowning in a dirty river. But, in his novels, Freytag exonerated himself by introducing the good Jew who yearns for assimilation into Germanic rootedness and renounces his father's unscrupulous ways. There was still hope.

Stereotypes of this sort converted the Jewish question, in the words of Adolf Stöcker in the Prussian Diet, into an "ethical question." [5] Not race alone, nor nationality or religion, was at stake; a whole way of life was endangered by alien values. The everyday behavior of a people, the way they conducted their daily lives, reflected their nature and set them apart from others. Antecedents for the behavior of the Jews were found in various interpretations of the Old Testament. Judaism, it was asserted in true Volkish fashion, was a materialistic fossil devoid of any ethical impulse, which, unlike the Germanic elements of Christianity, could not produce the virtues of honesty, loyalty, and forthrightness present in the German soul. The barren stones of the ghetto streets epitomized the soul of Jewry. The mystical element in Volkish thought went on to elaborate the leitmotif. The ghetto, with its dark streets and mysterious caftaned inhabitants, excited the imagination of various writers, who further contributed to widening the gap between German and Jew.

Hermann Gödsche, who adopted the more romantic pen name of Sir John Redcliffe, wrote a novel popularizing the mysterious aspects of the Jew. The Jews were portrayed as conspirators against the Gentile world. In his famous *Biarritz* (1868), the Jewish conspirators met in the "mysterious" cemetery of the ghetto of Prague, where they plotted to take over the world. Gödsche remained popular and personally active, serving on the editorial staff of the ultra-conservative *Kreuz Zeitung* and contributing to its opposition to the liberal forces in post-1848 Germany. Through these efforts he acquired a special relevance to racist, Volkish, and National Socialist thought. His book was a forerunner of *Protokolle der Weisen von Zion* (*Protocols of the Elders of Zion*) and helped to pave the way for the acceptance of more extremist ideas. For the Nazis, Gödsche's fictional account served as documentary proof of the world conspiracy of Jewry. In the 1930's Johann von Leers reprinted the chapters dealing with the Jewish conspiracy as support and justification for an increased anti-Semitism.[6]

Religious preconceptions further consolidated the stereotype of the Jew. Christianity had its own anti-Semitic bias, which it had emphasized for centuries and still did not abandon in the century of enlightenment and its successor, the age of liberalism. To it the Lagardes and the Langbehns as well as a score of Volkish authors contributed the element of Germanic faith, of a de-Semiticized Christianity. Voltaire had maintained that Judaism was a fossilized religion; Lagarde viewed it as a skeleton lacking the life-giving immediacy of communion with God; and even Johann Christian Dohm made the liberation of Jews conditional upon the hope that Jews would now reject the dead corpus of Judaism.[7] The religious prejudice was of the greatest significance, since it provided the philosophical rationale for anti-Semitism prior to the introduction of the "scientific" racial theories. With the growth of the Volkish movement and the popularization of the images presented in the writings of Paul de Lagarde, this religious anti-Semitism was given further impetus when the various racial theories began to be advanced. In fact, it remained an indispensable part of racism. According to the prophets of Germanic Christianity, the Jew lacked a soul, all virtues, and the capacity for ethical behavior for the reason that Judaism was a fossilized legalism. What a striking contrast this made with the German soul, steeped as it was in communion with the cosmos, the recipient of nature's mysteries, striving to relate itself to the glorious deeds of its ancestors, and rooted in nature, the soil, and the landscape. Here Lagarde again set the tenor: Jews could never become Germans, precisely because they lacked spiritual depth, a shortcoming that had affected their secular disposition as well.[8]

Of course, the religious antagonism was not confined to dogma or fought solely with theological weapons. As we have pointed out, anti-Semitism pervaded all areas—ethics, culture, and everyday pursuits. But whether it was to accuse Jews of conspiracy to subjugate and destroy the Gentiles or to perpetrate ritual murders, anti-Semitic agitators always turned to an interpretation of the philosophical books of Jewish law for substantiation of their charges. By the 1860's, the Talmud had become the leading symbol of Judaism and Jewish nature. It was brought to the attention of the public through the efforts of a Catholic scholar, August Rohling, a professor at a church seminary in Prague, who published an edited section of the Talmud under the title of *Der Talmud Jude* (*The Talmud Jew*) (1871). His purpose was to reveal to the world that the Jews had no religion, properly speaking, but that their highest doctrine commanded them to engage in ritual murder.

More than any other attack, Rohling's work caused a panic among the Jews of Central Europe. It was indeed significant. Here a respected, supposedly erudite Catholic scholar had encouraged an attack which hitherto had preoccupied only marginally respectable figures. Moreover, the Catholic Church's dilatory behavior in repudiating Rohling seemed to abet the accusation. The Church moved only after a lawsuit had disgraced Rohling and proved his knowledge of the Talmud a sham. But even though Rohling was officially out of favor, his arguments continued to be used. His book was translated into French by Eduard Drumont and then retranslated into German along with Drumont's preface.[9]

These essentially religious accusations soon made their way into the secular world. In Germany, France, and the Austrian Empire, the ritual-murder legend was far from dead. It was revived periodically, especially encouraged by intellectuals, and grew to a popular clamor that took on the proportions of a movement. In the Austrian Empire alone, there were no less than twelve trials for ritual murder between 1867 and 1914. To be sure, eleven defendants were acquitted, but the one guilty verdict, in 1899, was considered vindication enough of the general accusation. These trials and the persistence with which the accusations were made revealed the popularity of "evidence" such as that provided by Rohling. To the public at large, the trials and the sensationalism that surrounded them demonstrated the Jewish conspiracy against all Gentiles.

In 1879 Wilhelm Marr, a journalist who had lost his job because of his efforts to increase popular hostility against Judaism, founded the first organization to bear an explicitly anti-Semitic name, the Antisemiten Liga (Anti-Semite League). Both Marr's league and Rohling's accusations, which paralleled Lagarde's alternative to Judaicized Christianity, had clear connections with the Volkish movement. Their campaign against modernity had found its ideal embodiment. Here was the real, tangible enemy of the Germanic faith; not a vague entity, but an actual historical people whose philosophy was inimical to German life. The supposedly fossilized Judaism was linked with materialism and thus to modernity. Correspondingly, to oppose the Jews meant to struggle against the champions of the materialistic world view as well as against the evils of modern society. The Jew, the incarnation of dishonesty, ruthless in his quest for power, egoism exemplified, was contrasted with the genial German, who longed for an end to the dissonances of modern, urban life.

Racial thought came to the support of religious anti-Semitism, even though the religious arguments themselves contained sufficient secular factors. Significantly, it appeared at first in the form of a historical argument. Christian Lasser's *Indische Altertumskunde* (*Indian Antiquities*) (1877) contrasted the Aryan and Semitic peoples, their history and culture, on purely racial grounds. Here too the German scholars seem to have found a vindication of their theological aversion to Judaism, for the historical "evidence" supported the view that the Semites, the Jews, were egotistical and stubborn, a people ingrained with a belief in their God-decreed, legalized superiority.[10] Another scholar, Eugen Dühring, in a book appropriately entitled *Die Judenfrage* (*The Jewish Question*) (1880), claimed that he was the first to consider the "Jewish question" in Germany in terms of racial categories. His book derived its influence from his respectable standing as a scholar. Applying his racial theories, he condemned the Jew as a whole, not just some of his characteristics. Dühring linked Jewish depravity in culture, morals, and manners to inherent racial traits possessed by all Jews. No tolerance was to be extended, for it would only play into the hands of the Jews. They would surely exploit such feelings and in the end create a more terrible intolerance.[11] The same restrictions applied against their joining the Christian faith and being assimilated into Gentile society; the outward adoption of Christianity, Dühring claimed, was in fact a sly Jewish device in furtherance of their ends. Only the Nordic gods could help the German people to victory, for only the Nordic religion was able to combat Jewish infiltration. According to Dühring, the battle lines were drawn between the forces of Jewish materialism and Old Germanism.[12] With their inherent racial strength the Germans would triumph over the alien intruders. In this manner, the formulations of Volkish thought began to be used as weapons in a widespread German anti-Semitism.

Aside from this emphasis on German gods and race, Dühring displayed another side to his anti-Semitism, which was more significant because it enjoyed a wider political reception. Dühring, though a professor at the staid and conservative University of Berlin, styled himself a radical, and his political affiliations, theories, and writings were deemed important enough by the Marxists for Friedrich Engels to level against him the well-known critique *Anti-Dühring*. Dühring had connections among the Social Democrats, in whose policies he saw a sensible approach toward creating a strong national state. He espoused a particular brand of socialism that envisaged a self-sufficient national economy and an idealized expression of the general will of the people. For our purposes it is important to note simply that he tied his anti-Semitism to a democratic urge. Although here his ideas ran counter to the Volkish aversion to mass politics, Dühring's saving grace, in their eyes, was his resistance to the established order and the mythical base of his "general will" theories. According to him, the Germanic Volk was an entity that possessed a unity of interests capable of expression in a general will. As such, in its best interests—that is, those of survival—it was engaged in a struggle against the Jews, who, by means of modernity, opposed the Germanic general will and common good.[13]

In this manner, anti-Semitism and the stereotype of the Jew was integrated into the dynamic of the Volkish struggle against a state that did not, so it seemed to them, represent the true will of the German Volk. We have discussed aspects of this in previous chapters. But this was the kind of anti-Semitism that came to the fore in the last decades of the nineteenth century. It was the wave of the future. Although the prejudices of a man like William II's royal court preacher, Adolf Stöcker, flared up ominously, they held little future promise. Stöcker had used anti-Semitism as a prop for the existing social order which was symbolized by the Protestant orthodoxy of the Prussian state.[14] He felt that Jewry was an enemy of order itself and that, particularly, assimilated Jews had been enabled to practice their subversion from within. Dühring, on the other hand, insisted that the Jews were not so much the enemies of order as they were obstacles in the path of progress. They blocked the fulfillment of the true dynamic manifestation of the Volk. The future struggle therefore would be to the death. This was the genre of anti-Semitism that enjoyed widespread and respectable support. Houston Stewart Chamberlain and indeed most of the men discussed in the last chapters, held to this doctrine of anti-Semitism. As a concept, such a war between the races was quite alien to Stöcker's brand of anti-Semitism, but those who stressed the inherently dynamic nature of the Volk considered such a course inevitable. The democratic will would express the interests of the Volk and resolve them victoriously in a test of racial strength.

One of the first concrete applications of this theory of racial struggle was found in the anti-Semitic movement launched by Otto Böckel in the years following 1885, after the fortunes of Stöcker's party had declined. While, in a sense, the movement attempted a partial resuscitation of the party structure, it renounced the policy of the party. Otto Böckel was a type which we will meet often in these pages. He was an educated man who held a doctorate and was a librarian by profession. In fact, most of the Volkish leaders, before and after Böckel, belonged to the professional classes. Böckel, unlike Stöcker, was no Conservative; indeed, he believed in extending the franchise to the whole population as well as in the progressive income tax. His was a "democratic movement," and it is in the combination of anti-Semitism and greater democracy that the importance of his movement lay.

Böckel was elected to the Reichstag as the first anti-Semitic deputy who was independent of the Conservative party. This was indeed an omen for the future. Böckel himself lost his seat in 1903 and after that retired to a village, a beaten and shy recluse. The Nazis were to erect a museum in his memory in Marburg, where he had practiced his profession. This honor was warranted, for his movement advocated a type of national socialism and for a time it was popular and swept the countryside of Westphalia and Hesse. Anti-Semitic measures formed the central plank in the platform and, in these rural regions, where many Jews were middlemen and cattle dealers, the racial theories were well received. Böckel adroitly played upon the Volkish and economic fears of the peasants by raising the specter of Jewish overlordship. He claimed that a Jewish conspiracy was in control of every facet of life, except, typically enough, work, from which the Jews shied as from a plague, and that they were in fact the kings of the present epoch—a slogan he adopted from de Toussenel's characterization of the house of Rothschild.[15] The conclusion was obvious: repossess the wealth siphoned off by the Jews, and German peasants will again be prosperous; get rid of the Jew, and speculation will end, and the peasant will be able to live well again. Once this battle had been won the Volk could march unhindered down the straight road to its destiny.

Böckel was an agitator, not an organizer. Unable to cope with division in the ranks, he presided over the collapse of his movement; but not before it had polled 263,861 votes in a parliamentary election in 1893, as part of a general anti-Semitic wave.[16] Earlier, Austria too had fostered the Antisemiten Bund (1889), which, though not nearly as successful, had engaged in similar agitation among the urban masses. Here the central theme was the protection of artisans from displacement by Jewish craftsmen. Combining racism with economics, the Antisemiten Bund raised the fearful cry that one Jew was capable of ruining one thousand native Viennese tailors.[17]

This variety of anti-Semitism was "democratic." It was geared for mass appeal, especially as it incorporated lower-class economic interests with a belief in the ideology of the Volk.[18] Here the elitism of the Volkish ideology broke down or, rather, incorporated the element which was to render it popular. In fact, anti-Semitism became the chief vehicle for the diffusion of the Volkish movement. Those who were attracted primarily by anti-Semitism had no difficulty in accepting the basic Volkish ideas, and those already in the movement took readily to the precepts of anti-Semitic racism. After Böckel's failure, there was a reversion in the higher echelons to an elitism which, although maintaining the incompatibility of German and Jew, still attempted to discuss the question in a less volatile manner. Exclusion of the Jews and cultural unity among the Germans were to be their weapons. But potentialities of the popular Böckel type of violence and democracy were not to be lost to future movements, especially not to the National Socialists. When, in opposition to the rest of the right, they began to build a mass movement after 1920, the Jew was singled out as the best anti-Volkish symbol, the most effective means of engaging the economic and national concerns of the masses. The respectable Volkish right deplored this method as "street-corner anti-Semitism." They decried it not because it was anti-Semitic, but because of its demagoguery. Like the elitist elements in the Volkish movement, they regarded more academic and social means as more appropriate vessels for anti-Semitism. And then, of course, there was their fear and resentment of the effective and potentially explosive mass organization—though they regarded it as a collection of rabble—that the Nazis could command.

A lull in the more violent anti-Semitic agitation in the first decade of the century coincided with the transference of the issues to a more academic, quiescent, and respectable forum. As in France after the Dreyfus affair, so in Germany after the failure of Stöcker and Böckel, there followed a general, though less satisfactory, reconciliation of public opinion. Anti-Semitic agitators sensitive to the changed atmosphere attempted to adjust themselves to it. Overt antagonisms were softened to "opinions." Theodor Fritsch, for example, who previously had demanded the outright extermination of the Jews, now maintained that he was only a "cultured anti-Semite" and would not stoop to the vulgar level of persecuting individual Jews. The individual Jew, he said, was relatively innocent of the damage done the German Volk, which must be blamed on Judaism as a whole. The individual Jew, claimed the "reformed" Fritsch, could not help himself. Correspondingly, the anti-Semitic struggle must be conducted on a plane commensurate with its goals. Since violent attacks do not solve the *whole* problem, stated Fritsch, the approach must be shifted onto a broader level, the task must become more abstract and general. Through education, a pragmatic rationality was to take the place of demagogic mass movements.[19]

Though Fritsch did not keep his promise, others did. The theoretical approach came into vogue. Works such as those of Chamberlain were singled out as representative of this scholarly school of anti-Semitic thought. The anti-Semitic outlook continued to represent the Volkish influence in Germany, but now it was couched in the language of racial anthropology and cultural differentiation. Racial antagonisms were cultivated and permitted to strike roots. In contrast to what happened in France, the reconciliation following the attacks on Jews went into effect only superficially. The hostility toward the individual Jew inherent in the ideology did not disappear, but was carried forward in much of the New Romanticism of Diederichs, in the Germanic utopias, in the stereotypes presented by Volkish painters, and in the Youth Movement. In actual practice, Jews were effectively isolated from Gentiles, to such an extent that by 1910 the *Korrespondenz (Bulletin)* of the central organization of German Jews announced: "Few outright anti-Semite attacks can be reported; but only a few correspondents tell us about private contacts between Jewish and Christian Germans." [20] This regrettable state of affairs had been affirmed earlier, in 1899, in a triumphal report of an anti-Semitic social reform party: "In the 1850's schoolboys still maintained social contacts with their Jewish fellow students and even with their parents. Now, a Jew sitting at the same table with a Gentile excites notoriety." [21] Such pronouncements were no doubt exaggerated, but the basic trend is borne out by historical evidence.

Especially significant is the effect that anti-Semitic thought had on the youth. Historical evidence proves that the younger generation was more vehement in its refusal to have contact with Jews than were their elders, who remembered a previous age. Among them, anti-Semitic agitation found a receptive and fruitful soil. Student fraternities expelled Jews and refused fraternal Jewish societies satisfaction in dueling—after all, Jews had no honor to defend. In 1878, the Viennese fraternity Libertas began to exclude Jews on racial grounds, and by 1890, both in Germany and in Austria, all fraternities declared themselves *Judenrein.*[22]

Various forces were instrumental in enhancing this susceptibility. Stöcker in Germany and Schönerer in Austria encouraged the separation of students on racial grounds. Stöcker's disciple, Friedrich Naumann, was deeply involved in the founding of the influential Volkish anti-Semitic Union of German Students—which, in turn, was closely associated with the Anti-Semitic Petition (1880), which asked the government to exclude Jews from German life.[23] In schools, pedagogues discussed and emphasized racial differences even if in as mild a form as the teachers in Theodor Fontane's novel *Frau Jenny Treibel.* The romantic ideology that glorified the Germanic heritage permeated educational circles and disseminated the stereotype of the Jew. And then there was the sphere of religion. Where in France teachers and students identified their radicalism with the anti-clerical movement, in Germany a comparable anti-clerical drive was cloaked in a mysticism and chauvinism that only deepened the already pervasive ideology of Volk, Germanic faith, and Aryan race.

But while racial anti-Semitism remained largely an academic argument manifesting itself in cultural and social but nonetheless real ways, it also contained a direct appeal to violence. Religious anti-Semitism showed a similar undercurrent. Here too, ideas of force and cruelty, which ran throughout the Volkish ideology, came to the fore. The whole Germanic heritage of fighting—for survival during the Ice Age, against the degenerate Romans, and to keep alive elements of mysticism in the face of doctrinaire Christianity—was considered a model for the future struggle of the races. Moreover, the speculation on the inevitability of a race war only brought the cruelty and ruthlessness into the foreground. At first, to be sure, only a minority of people were affected; but they constituted a vociferous group. However, it was not until after 1918 that it really took root as the necessary conclusion of Germanic and New Romantic thinking. And then, when it came, it was precisely that "street-corner anti-Semitism" which Fritsch had condemned and allegedly abandoned; it was a continuation of the volatile anti-Semitic outbursts of the 1880's and 1890's in which agitators had aroused the economic hostility of the lower-middle classes and the peasantry and enlisted them in the fight for the survival of the Volk.

The First World War helped to further such attitudes, at first toward Eastern European Jewry. As Germany occupied Poland, many Germans came into contact with the Jewish population of the country, men who may have known about the ghettos, if at all, only from literature. Franz Blei, for example, a writer for the avant-gardist *Die Weissen Blätter* (which could not be accused of anti-Semitism), pontificated that the only kind of relationship these Jews had to the rest of the world was that of "usurious trade." Even if such people were "civilized" and put into modern clothes, they would still remain two million trading Jews weaving a net of business and trade around the presumably innocent Germans. Moreover, René Shickele, the editor of the journal, claimed that he was swamped by contributions on the "Jewish question" sent from the Eastern Front. He even cites titles: "The Polish Jews and Ourselves"; "Under Foreign Brethren"; "Is a Solution Possible?" [24] The authors of these articles were not reactionaries, but young men who had been exposed to the newest in literature and art. This is surely a telling example of the extent to which the image of Eastern European Jewry as a foreign and immoral force permeated German attitudes toward the Jewish question.

The Eastern Jews did have a different cultural pattern, for they lived in a highly competitive society in which they were at an essential disadvantage but in which competition was the only way to survive. Eastern Jews began emigrating to Germany in increasing numbers during the 1880's, at a time when Germans themselves were disgruntled with the conditions around them and when Volkish voices became most strident. From the very start, Volkish agitators condemned the influx of Eastern Jewry as adverse to the interests of the Volk and predicted that they would eventually achieve domination over the Germans—unless something was done immediately.

At first they made a distinction between Eastern and native Jews. The German-born Jews could assimilate, even according to Freytag and some later writers, whereas the aliens could not. But from the end of the century on, the distinction became blurred in the minds of the Volkish thinkers. The Eastern Jew, and the ghetto life he represented, increasingly came to stand for the Jew in general and all Jews came under the same proscription. By 1918, the Volkish ideology's objectification of the Jewish evil, both in pictorial and literary propaganda, no longer permitted any distinction between the native and alien Jew.

The frustrations of a national defeat that had not been conclusively settled on the battlefield left the door open for rationalizations stressing the heroism and the invincibility of the soldiers on the front lines and blaming defeat on the desertion by cowardly elements on the home front. The contradictory orders on disbanding and disarming returning armies, the official toleration of the Free Corps' participation in the anti-Bolshevik fighting on the Eastern Front to contain the revolutionary overflow into the Baltic countries—all played up the heroism and physical trials of the German soldiers, who could withstand the *Stahlgewitter* (storm of steel) but not the servility of political compromise. The impossible had become the real, and the feasible and expedient the unreal. The German Volk had been denied satisfaction on the field of honor, where, had events been permitted to run their course, victory would have been achieved. Now the hostility as well as the idealized bravery was transferred to the struggle of the races, a mortal struggle that demanded a resolution. Expressions of violence coupled with the actual use of force against the Jews became more common under the Weimar Republic.

There were open cries for the use of physical force to settle the Jewish problem once and for all. Heinrich Pudor vociferously echoed this demand of the far right wing of the Volkish movement.[25] Pudor was an intimate acquaintance of Fritsch and the Artamanen leader Bruno Tanzmann. Tanzmann devoted part of the publishing facilities of the Germanic settlement of Hellerau to the dissemination of Pudor's racial ideas. These men formed an intimate circle and their ideas on this question transcended their differences on other

issues—whether they be Schöll's Vogelhof or Tanzmann's Artamanen. There were pockets advocating violence as a solution to the
racial issue even in respectable conservative circles. Count von Reventlow, for instance, also advised the use of force in dealing with the
Jewish problem, but he finally opted for legal means of exclusion.[26]

These ideas had broad repercussions. The doctrine of applying violent anti-Semitic methods took on its real pernicious character in the
hands of people who commanded greater political and popular attention. The notorious agitator Müller von Hausen advised that Jews
who transgressed the special laws for foreigners under which, in
his opinion, they were to live should at times be hanged.[27] The suggestion was supported by the powerful Pan-Germans, whose leader,
Heinrich Class, had earlier, in 1912, advocated a preliminary step: the
rigid isolation and double taxation of the Jews.[28] Economic and social
dislocation, as well as the untried system of democracy introduced in
the postwar era, increased the desperation of those classes which had
earlier supported the Germanic ideology. Correspondingly, agitators,
taking advantage of their receptive audience, provided new "proof"
of the increasing Jewish drive for power. It was Müller von Hausen
who translated and published the notorious *Protocols of the Elders
of Zion* immediately after the war.

However, the question remains whether, prior to the Nazis' implementation of their "final solution of the Jewish problem," the advocates of violence were really to be taken at face value; and if so,
whether they could have found popular support for their proposals.
There was a great difference between proclaiming the doctrine of
violent race struggle and extermination and actually putting it into
practice. Karl Paasch, involved in popularizing Rohling's *Talmud
Jew*, believed that killing off all Jews was the simplest and most practical solution to the Jewish question. But he thought that it would
probably be impossible to accomplish this in Germany and that therefore it might be best to intern the Jews and to ship them to New
Guinea. He did not stand alone in his desire for violence, in this
longing which he did not believe possible of fulfillment, or in his
resignation to a less cruel solution.[29]

The case of Hermann Ahlwardt, a teacher and more famous agitator, is still more illustrative: in 1890 he published *Der Verzweiflungskampf der arischen Völker mit den Judentum* (*The Desperate
Struggle Between the Aryan Peoples and Judaism*). Invoking the
precepts of the Germanic prophets, Ahlwardt stated that a people
who rid itself of Jews freed itself for the natural development of the
Volk, and thereby rose toward dominion over the world.[30] For him,

as for the romantic advocates of the Volk, Jewry was the Mephistopheles of world history. In dealing with the Jews, Christian mercy was decidedly out of place. Instead, Ahlwardt asserted, the nation must act with determination to combat the menace. He cited with approval a saying falsely applied to Prussia's Friedrich Wilhelm I, who, it was said, when he saw a Jew in the morning had the gallows erected by evening.[31] Was this a plea for violence? Certainly! But, when it came to concrete proposals to effect such measures, he displayed an ambivalence which was, as yet, typical. When he drew up an actual program, Ahlwardt could only advocate the imposition of stringent restrictions upon Jews, a decree proclaiming them foreigners on German soil and excluding them from all areas of German life and culture. He also proposed that eventually all Jews be deported from Europe and their surplus capital retained by the German nation.[32]

Curiously, this was almost exactly the same as the National Socialist program for dealing with the Jews. Aside from the popular and politically more violent demagoguery which marked the Nazis' rise to power and the concrete application of the Nuremberg Laws, Ahlwardt's program broadly foreshadowed that of the Nazis, for they also reflected an ambivalence. On the one hand, there were the fanatics who asserted that the "final solution" must bring about a correct correspondence between ideology and action and that the deportation of the Jews to distant places only evaded the issue. On the other hand, there were those functionaries and leaders in the party who wanted to encourage Jewish emigration at all costs. Of course, there were various obstacles to the latter course: first, the refusal to permit the Jews to retain the financial resources that would enable them to leave, not to mention the reluctance of nations to accept Jewish immigrants; and then, of course, the effective closing of all doors when the war began. It was then that the final solution, as history knows it, became a reality. At that stage the ultimate consequences of a glorification of merciless cruelty within Volkish ideology, and the Nazi extension of it, finally engulfed the minds of Germany's leaders. Extermination became the literal fact, not just a rhetorical device to arouse human passions.

If the agitation for violence in settling the Jewish problem did not achieve an immediate implementation, but rather had to wait for the appropriate juncture of events, it was not completely unproductive. It helped to prepare the nation for events that followed. In conjunction with the over-all depiction of the Jew as an inhuman, un-German intruder, it contributed to the shaping of a state of mind that either apathetically acquiesced in or actively supported the final verdict. The dehumanization of the Jew is perhaps one of the most significant single developments in the evolution of the Volkish ideology.

Slowly the stereotype had to take its effect. On the ethical and religious fronts, it was asked whether, if the Jew lacked a *proper* soul, he could be classed as human. On the economic and social front it was asserted that Jews had consorted in diabolical intrigues to seize power in order to dominate the Gentile world. For the average reader, the Jews in Freytag's and Raabe's novels were unforgettable embodiments of abhorrent qualities; for the anti-Semite, they only fortified entrenched convictions. Similarly, in a whole series of popular novels Jewish characters lacked all human qualities and met miserable fates, victims of their egotistical power drives.[33] The objectification of the Jew as evil by means of his inner drives was reinforced by an emphasis on his outward appearance. Race, after all, was a total criterion. The physical properties of the Jew were accordingly contrasted with the Germanic ideal of beauty; a contorted figure resting on short legs, a greedy and sensual corpulence, and, of course, the "Jewish nose" were unfavorably compared with the aesthetically proportioned figure of the Nordic man. To be sure, such stereotypes had been in existence since the sixteenth and seventeenth centuries, but they were not as critical then. The Jew at the early date was still pictured as a comic, though grotesque, figure.[34] In the image presented by Volkish thought, he became a menace; he held the Germans in actual bondage.

Racial criteria also prevented the consideration of "special cases," of maintaining a distinction between assimilated and immigrant Jew. As long as racial standards were invoked, the assimilated Jews were made to bear an increasingly difficult burden. They were singled out as arch-fiends, as infiltraters and polluters of the blond Germanic race. Though Freytag could still describe a "decent" Jew who longed for assimilation, such an apostate was considered the acme of all evil in the twentieth century. Racially it was decreed, and popularly believed, that all Jews bore the same marks of distinction: they were ugly, bearded, and wore caftans. If they diverged from the mean it was to disguise their conspiracy to dominate Germany and the world. If they exhibited passions and emotions which would normally be considered expressions of love and affection, they were really giving vent to their need for an immediate gratification of lustful senses. The infinite was not the object of their striving, since material goods limited their horizons. Power was their goal and that could be attained most easily by infiltration of the Aryan race and through subversion. Jewish lust for power, claimed Volkish anti-Semites, was conveniently

coupled with the gratification of the senses; and both could be gained
by corrupting the Aryan race with an admixture of Jewish blood. Although this was the special fear that plagued the Volkish tranquillity
of Theodor Fritsch,[35] it was also shared by most anti-Semitic writers.

The fear of racial defilement through intermarriage, with its associations of sex, love, and physical features, became an obsession with
Volkish thinkers. The image of the pure, blond, spiritual, feminine
German woman succumbing to the love of a Jew became a nightmare
to the prophets of the race. A flier distributed at the University of
Frankfurt in the early 1920's bears witness to an anti-Semitic fusion
of racial, sexual, aesthetic, and religious elements. It declared it a sin,
an unnatural act, for an Aryan girl to let herself become enamored
of a Jew. It was a transgression tantamount to Eve's succumbing to
the sophistry of the serpent.[36] The Nuremberg Laws elevated this
obsession to the level of a legal system and extended it even to the
point of forbidding Jews to hire Christian domestics. There were
countless stories about the affairs of rich Jews and Aryan servant girls,
delusions which cannot be ascribed merely to the sexual frustrations
of anti-Semites. Here, after all, was an image which could strike terror
into the heart of every German who loved a wife and daughter. The
identical appeal is used, after all, by those in the United States who
advocate the segregation of the Negro, and this with equal fear and
frustration. Then, too, the Germanic revival had idealized female
virginity and the woman's primary role as wife and mother—the
receptacle of the seed of the race. And though one of the Germanic
utopias, Hentschel's Mittgart, had envisaged the institution of multiple
marriages solely to secure pure, efficient racial propagation, it was
rejected primarily because of this view. On the whole, the anti-
bourgeois Volkish movement proved itself extremely bourgeois in its
sexual mores.

While playing on the social and individual prejudices of many Germans, the anti-Semitic stereotype did not omit the link between Jews
and money. Jewish lust for Aryan women was always connected with
lust for money. Economic prejudices were always prevalent in anti-
Semitism and they attained academic respectability with Werner
Sombart's treatise *Die Juden und das Wirtschaftsleben* (*Jews and
Capitalism*) (1910). This eminent economic historian linked the
growth of capitalism to the role played by the Jews. As usurers in
the Middle Ages and entrepreneurs in modern times, the Jews had
been a vital force in building the capitalist system. He asserted that
their restless character had made them the motive force of capitalism,
a role which Max Weber more astutely ascribed to the ethos of Protestantism. Actually, Sombart was not condemning Jews, but merely,

as he thought, providing a historical analysis of the evolution of capitalism. Volkish writers and propagandists, however, were quick to
use Sombart's treatise for their own purposes. Broadly, it agreed
with their image of the Jews as the shiftless, rootless, conniving
middleman and stock jobber, hoarding the gold coin and bleeding
Germany dry. But Volkish thought was not to accept all of Sombart's ideas. Instead, it took snippets and condemned the rest. When
Theodor Fritsch, for example, published his *Handbook on the Jewish Question*, which originally appeared under the title *The Anti-
Semitic Catechism* (1887), he turned in the later editions to Sombart
for a description of the Jew's economic role in modern society.[37]
However, he stopped short and turned on the scholar when it came
to the connection between capitalism, originating from Jewry, and
culture. Here he condemned Sombart for even daring to insinuate
that the Jews or their efforts could indeed create anything of beauty
or culture.[38]

The stock-exchange jobber, the corpulent banker, these were the
stereotypes of the Jew that were widely accepted and disseminated
through popular literature. The stock exchange in particular became
the symbol of the nightmarish capitalism that had been foisted upon
Germans by the Jews. It came to represent the hub of their control
system, and it was there, early Volkish thinkers proclaimed, that the
world revolution to oust the alien money lords would emanate. Adolf
Wahrmund stated this clearly in 1887.[39] But popular anti-Semitic
propaganda was to go one better: it fused the images of Jewish hunger for money with his lust for Aryan women. The resulting image
widely used as propaganda pictured a fat Jewish banker caressing a
blond woman on his knee. The same agent who milked Germans of
their wealth also depleted their racial strength; that was the Volkish
anti-Semitic theme. It was to become that for a multitude of Germans.

Novels depicted the debilitating effects of interracial intercourse.
Arthur Dinter's *Die Sünde wider das Blut* (*Sin Against the Blood*)
(1918) put across the typical message and sold in the hundred thousands. It told of the violation of a German woman's racial purity by a
rich Jew, and even though she left him and married an Aryan, her
offspring continued to resemble Jewish stereotypes. The book was
not pornographic (so its large sales figures cannot be attributed to
prurience); rather, it communicated the horror of racial defilement
by a figure that was simply inhuman. The vicious stereotype of the
Jew was sometimes projected to the public by state authorities. In
1915, for instance, and again in 1919, the Jewish community in Hamburg protested the captions on official police posters which described

a criminal's "special characteristics" as a "fat Jew" with a "Jewish nose."[40] In 1919 the police of northern Bavaria deplored the increase in overt anti-Semitism in their report to Berlin. However, the police too had reached the fatalistic conclusion that Volkish thought had always presented. Their report stated that no remedy existed since the agitation "has its roots in the difference of race which divides the Israelitic tribe from our Volk; this gap can never be entirely bridged."[41]

The pioneering work of Volkish racial thinkers played a central role in the creation of the anti-Semitic image. The stereotype of the Jew strove successfully to convey the image of a parasite. In Darwinian terms, the Jews were an arrested development in evolution, a fossil that lacked the strength or roots to nourish itself. The racial stereotype attributed so many grotesque qualities to the Jew that he was in essence dehumanized. Fritsch's work again demonstrates this ominous development, for in his *Leuchtkugeln (Fireballs)* (1881) he explicitly denied human status to Jews. Here he claimed that God had created the Jew as a buffer between man and ape.[42] The Nazis assimilated this thought in their own propaganda when, in 1931, one of their speakers asserted that non-Nordic man occupied an intermediary position between Nordic man and the animal world. The non-Nordic was not a whole man, for he still shared traits with the apes.[43] In 1932, another National Socialist speaker likened the Jews to bugs and called for their extermination. Interestingly, the speech was monitored by the secret police of the Republic, and their report pointed out that not the masses, but the "better bourgeoisie" of the Berlin upper-class district of Charlottenburg, had made up the gathering and joined in the "stormy applause."[44] The Jewish stereotype had indeed eaten deeply into the fabric of German bourgeois society. In their reasoning, whether out of fear or simple prejudice and hate, the bourgeoisie joined in accepting the dehumanization of the Jew.

That it was the "better bourgeoisie" who were passionately aroused can be attributed to the change in anti-Semitic tactics that followed the cease-fire of the post-Böckel era. As we have pointed out earlier, Fritsch, one of the exponents of vulgar racial hate, redirected his efforts to a more refined anti-Semitism. Fritsch's more spiritual anti-Semitism directly contributed to deepening anti-Jewish social attitudes. In fact, according to one reliable witness, it was only after Stöcker lost favor and violence fell into disrepute that anti-Semitism became an "epidemic" among the upper class.[45] From then on, Fritsch's writing was directed toward a literate Volkish elite rather than at the masses, at an elite who, he thought, would put his exhortations into practice. And this community responded, as can be judged from a directorate report of the Jewish community of Vienna in 1883 which stated this early that literary anti-Semitism had attracted not just the half-cultured elements of the population but even the highly cultured ones.[46] This claim was supported by other informants. A book dealer writing to the *Zentralverein* (Central Assembly) of the German Jews in 1900 stated that "the fact that every year tens of thousands of anti-Semitic pamphlets are sent free to all officials of the state and members of the upper ten thousand cannot but produce some effect." [47] His statement was made on the basis of the high percentage of anti-Semitic literature that he found in libraries offered to him for sale.

The issues of race, presented on a literary and theoretical level, enjoyed great popularity as subjects for discussion and debate on a wide intellectual front. At times both sides were presented. In 1912, the prestigious journal *Kunstwart* reviewed the question of anti-Semitism from both the Jewish and the New Romantic point of view. One year later, in 1913, the Jewish issue burst upon the Youth Movement with full force. There it became the source of long discussion over the next few years. In fact, the Jewish problem never ceased to provide mental and emotional exercise among teachers, self-styled educators, and students.

The effects of the basic strands of Volkish anti-Semitism described in this chapter are well summarized in a discussion of the issue by the Central Assembly of the Vienna Jewish community in 1882. The meeting indicated the gravity of the situation and the extent to which the accusations had stimulated the fears and concerns of the community. Though, on the one hand, the community resolved to defend itself, on the other it gave countenance to some of the charges by calling upon its members to reform. Clearly, the accusation of immorality, the lack of true, ethical roots, cut deepest. As a primary response to this attack, the community's respected leader, Wilhelm von Guttmann, moved to publish a popular summary of Jewish moral beliefs. The motion was passed and acted upon. Next, to correct the image of the Jew and destroy the stereotype, Guttmann moved that among themselves Jews should attempt to eliminate loans at high rates of interest. Furthermore, Jewish youth must be discouraged from entering trades; instead, they must be encouraged to become peasants and craftsmen.[48] A decade later, his last exhortation was implemented when the banker Moritz Simon founded a Jewish orphanage at Ahlem, near Hamburg, for the explicit purpose of cultivating the youth's interest in the soil and handicrafts.[49]

Thus the attacks against them, as well as, perhaps, a sharing in the effects of the Germanic ideology, led important segments of the Jewish community to make attempts at accommodation with the Volkish charges. We shall see more of this later in the chapter on German youth. Indeed, it is instructive to see the extent to which the victim attempted to remove the stain that, in fact, had never existed. It is also little short of tragic that many Jews came to believe in the reality of that "Jewishness" the Volkish movement proclaimed as true. Those who attempted to accommodate, or even assimilate, were, of course, especially affected. Thus, it is ironic that Moritz Simon founded the orphanage not only to rear rural-oriented children but also to make them strong and healthy defenders of the fatherland. He too claimed, as had the anthropological racist Otto Amon, and as Heinrich Class was to assert at a later date, that city youth make poor soldiers.[50] Along these same lines, in 1899, a Jewish *Turnerschaft* (gymnastic association) was founded in order to develop a healthy Jewish people, to counteract the concentration of Jews in the cities, to direct them into manual work and handicrafts, and to offset the image of the "over-intellectualized" Jew engaged in study and conniving in trade.[51] There were those, especially among young Jews, who reacted by declaring themselves proud to be Jews, striving at the same time to emulate the goals of their Volk. A discussion of the cultural Zionism paralleling some Volkish thought which resulted from this attitude is outside the scope of this chapter, but it is a topic to which we shall return. It must be clear, however, that the depth of the Volkish attitudes can be measured, in part, by the effect which they had even upon those toward whom their hatred was directed.

In 1913, when the first wave of violent anti-Semitism had passed and the second had not yet arrived, at a time just before Jews were to fight for Germany, Aby Warburg, the head of the Hamburg Jewish community, wrote to his brother: "Here, in Hamburg, there is no open anti-Semitism, but much latent anti-Semitic feeling."[52] There were many who kept the fires smoldering. Education played a crucial role. More than the elitist groups, which proclaimed a fierce but open anti-Semitic program, it laid the groundwork for the institutionalizing of the Germanic ideology, of which anti-Semitism was an integral part. Without its help, the flames might indeed have burnt low. In this context, we must also examine the radical turn to the right taken by the bourgeois German youth. To the evolution of this development, as well as to the propagation of the Volkish ideology, secondary and university education made a decisive contribution.

PART II

The Institutionalization
of the Ideology

1873-1918

CHAPTER 8

Education Comes to the Aid

By THE END of the nineteenth century the ideological foundations of Volkish thought were securely laid. During the preceding years they had been formulated and reformulated to accommodate new disciplines and answer to new conditions.

Volkish thought had always been "alienated" in the sense that its point of departure was a deep dissatisfaction with existing reality. At mid-century, after the frustrating Frankfurt Congress of 1849, men like Riehl had retreated into a nostalgia for the Volkish past. This nostalgia also translated itself into a longing for German unity, and consequently the creation of Bismarck's *Reich* in 1871 was greeted with tremendous enthusiasm.

But political unity was not good enough for many Germans. They had learned to think in cultural terms during the long period of frustration, and this habit of thought endured. For these thinkers Bismarck's unification of Germany was "merely" political, for he had not overcome that spiritual separateness which they considered to be at the heart of Germany's crisis. As if this were not enough, Germany's prophets were suddenly confronted with a new source of disruption and alienation—the industrialization of the nation. Disraeli had once called England the home of two nations, the rich and the poor. Germany suddenly found herself being similarly divided. Between 1850 and 1871 annual coal production increased from one and a half million tons to thirty million. And by 1906 the figure would reach over one hundred million tons.

This development not only produced a serious imbalance in the distribution of wealth—this had always existed—but it brought into being a socially conscious proletariat which suddenly found its political voice. That these developments were regarded as grave matters is clearly evidenced by the variety of anti-socialist legislation which

Bismarck demanded in an effort to silence, isolate, and ultimately destroy proletarian political activity.

Volkish thinkers attempted to heal the rupture in the national fabric by appealing to the organic *Volksstaat*, to the common roots of all Germans. To these people the tragedy of the new unity was symbolized by the quest for the material goods of the new industrial economy. They saw the growth of an enervating materialism all around them, as well as the rapid transformation of the traditional German landscape into dirty, smoke-clogged industrial cities. During the second Empire the Volkish thinkers found a receptive audience among several important groups.

The traditional right-wing radicalization of German bourgeois youth made it possible for the Volkish ideology to strike deep roots both in the Youth Movement and in educational institutions. Teachers and professors were imbued with a nationalism centered upon the creation of a common German culture. The traditional conservatism of the educational establishment, combined with the reactionary tendencies of the youth, produced an atmosphere that favored the Volkish cause. Furthermore, many of the Volkish intellectuals were what might be termed "academic proletarians"—men who had received their doctorates but who were compelled to teach below the university level because of the scarcity of professorial chairs. As we have seen, both Langbehn and Lagarde were in this position, and many other Volkish prophets had a similar background. Such men continued to expound the Volkish message. Over the years they found an increasingly eager audience. However, it is difficult to determine the size of the audience or the precise way in which it furthered the cause, since it did not organize itself politically. At all times, prior to the early twentieth century, the influence and importance of the movement was demonstrated through small gatherings, enterprises, and publications that were representative of the movement as a whole.

But we know that the ideology appealed to a widespread audience, one which identified with the character of Volkish literature and its message. As literature came to the support of Volkish thought, the influence of the movement radiated out to the literate and cultured segments of the population. We must always bear in mind that the prevalence of the Volkish attitude toward life cannot be gauged simply by the circulation figures of the books that advocated this outlook. To be sure, the workers largely ignored the message, while the semi-cultured preferred the sentimentalism of a Courts-Mahler to the novels of Freytag, Burte, or Löns. It was the literate bourgeoisie that was saturated with the ideology. This class came to comprise the largest single bloc in the movement, and at the turn of the century the anti-Semitic stereotype and the Aryan ideal came close to being commonplace bourgeois notions.

That Volkish thinking had been incorporated in works of literature and upheld in popular philosophical treatises was indeed a measure of success for the movement. Moreover, political parties and social movements drew up programs which actively attempted to transform society according to the Volkish image. Some mass organizations, like those of Stöcker and especially Böckel, were early manifestations of neo-Volkish drives for power; but they faded from the scene and left the field open to the elitism of contemporary Volkish thought. For better economic conditions prevailed at the beginning of this century, while the attempted mass movements, such as Böckel's, destroyed themselves through bitter infighting. Small groups of elitist-oriented initiates were more important for the continuation and propagation of the ideology. Educators, students, and a multitude of such groups attempted to implement the Volkish ideology as a part of the social and national character of the German nation. Through these channels, leadership and aristocratic ideals were exalted above the democracy of the masses; the initiates were called upon to actualize the Volkish "idealism of deeds," to help diffuse the spirit of the Germanic Volk.

The movement entertained several definitions of "aristocracy." In one sense the aristocracy could include a great many people, as when the term was applied to the Volk, the Aryan race, or the Youth Movement, which numbered in the tens of thousands. All true Germans ranked above other people, but within the Volk some formed a conscious aristocracy of leadership. This could be small, as with Diederichs' group or Theodor Fritsch's Hammer Bund. Suffice it to say that for all these elitist thinkers the Aryan race and the Germanic Volk subsumed all other criteria of aristocracy. In all cases, the elite, bound by a common ideology and purpose, regarded itself as setting an example for the nation. Internally it organized itself according to aristocratic theories, as when it concluded that the *Bund*, or union of men wedded together by a common Volkish impulse of creativity, should be the sole organization in a good society.[1]

Historically, such elitist organizations have usually become sectarian, withdrawn, isolated from society, and condemned to feed upon themselves. This did not happen in the case of the Volkish movement, a fact demonstrated by the movement's survival during a period when it seemed to have exhausted its reason for existence. For after the last decade of the nineteenth century it did seem as if Volkish thought had become out of joint with the demands of the times. The German bourgeoisie was enjoying what was to be its last great span of prosperity and tranquility, though none could foresee this. The Volkish movement, temporarily subdued, revived with new vigor. It was to be the true beginning and not the end of the Volkish age.

During the period of relative inactivity, the Volkish movement was busy planting the roots of its faith. The elitist groups were never isolated from important currents within the nation. There were all the academic and literary ties; there was the Youth Movement. which absorbed and became the vehicle for the young people's revolt against bourgeois mores, authoritarianism, and spiritual vacuity; and there were the vital connections with the Conservative party and with the important Bund der Landwirte, the association of farmers and landlords which had been especially receptive to Volkish ideas. Most important, however, was the intimate relationship between Volkish thought and German educational institutions. Here it identified with the widespread urge for school reform and was, in some cases, able to shift this desire into its own channels.

The ideology was to see its greatest triumph in this accomplishment. It became institutionalized where it mattered most: in the education of young and receptive minds. Schools were founded according to Volkish blueprints and principles. In the state schools the ideology infiltrated into the minds of the students through books, curricula, and teachers. Student organizations adopted Volkish principles; and teachers, as well as students, passed through the Youth Movement and entered adulthood to spread the ideas they had picked up. Volkish ideals, infused in German youth through education, prepared the soil for the shock of the war which abruptly ended the flowering of the German bourgeoisie. It was then that the Volkish movement transformed itself into a mass movement by becoming a most powerful embodiment of the reaction to the crisis of German defeat.

Education pre-eminently institutionalized the ideology. Prior to 1918, no political organization or group of like-minded people were as important as educators in anchoring the Germanic faith within the German nation. Fritz Stern writes quite correctly that "a thousand teachers in republican Germany who in their youth had worshipped Lagarde or Langbehn were just as important in the triumph of National Socialism as all the putative millions of marks that Hitler collected from the German tycoons." [2] These teachers were deeply affected by the crisis of modernity for the solution of which they accepted not only the dictates of the prophets of the Germanic faith but all the other aspects of the Germanic ideology as well.

The generation of teachers that came to fruition during the last decades of the nineteenth century, in their youth represented a segment of that phenomenon we have had occasion to mention so often, the turning of bourgeois German youth to the right rather than to the left. At the beginning of the nineteenth century these young people had, as university students, associated themselves with the aspirations of Father Jahn's fraternities. While the teachers of the 1880's and 1890's were growing up, anti-Semitic and racial thought expanded into the universities and came to dominate the fraternities to which most of them belonged. The Stöcker era had vitally influenced their youth and the youth or student organizations to which they belonged. These teachers handed down the Germanic tradition, in which they placed greater and greater faith, to the generation that was to wage the catastrophic war. They had shaped the next generation of bourgeois youth who, as we shall see, turned even further to the right. For in Germany bourgeois youth was to continue to turn to Volkish solutions in times of national crisis. That they did so seems closely related to the institutionalization of Volkish thought through the various facets of the educational system.

This picture contrasts sharply with the one that emerged in France, England, or, indeed, most of the world. Students in other countries favored social equality, economic betterment for the underprivileged, and social justice; they rioted against the established order and threw their support to liberal regimes. Not so in Germany. If the German students of the eighteenth century had cried "Down with tyrants!" they meant not the *ancien régime*, but Charlemagne, the slaughterer of their forebears, of the ancient Saxons. And so it was to remain. Not he who transgressed against humanity and social justice, but he who ignored the interests of the Volk was to be their adversary. Teachers and students, members of the same movement, reinforced one another in forging a great propaganda machine that spread Volkish thought among the population.

An investigation of the role of the Volkish movement in education, however, presents a difficult problem. Germany's federal structure did not allow for a national standardization of schools and curricula. Local variation was considerable; the tens of thousands of German schools were not patterned after a master plan. Therefore, we have chosen, as a practical course, to examine what seem to be representative cases according to the available evidence.

Some Germans, after reading the pages that follow, may say: "This was not my experience. My teachers were liberals [few will be able to say socialist] who condemned all racial and New Romantic ideas." But such men will be in the minority. To be sure, there were regions where schools were not bedeviled by Volkish thought or where schools had freed themselves of these ideas, but not many. The fact is that schools dominated by the Volkish ideology were so numerous as to constitute the center rather than the fringe of German education.

This is attested, in part, by Erich Weymar's recent analysis of nineteenth-century history textbooks. Weymar professed to be shocked at the results of his research. Rightly so, for within those high-school textbooks is to be found every feature of the Germanic ideology. From the beginning of the century, the books praised Volkish ideas, and the destiny of the Volk with its sense of German mission pervaded most of their content. Modernity was universally and irrevocably condemned; the spirit of the Germanic forebears, the primitive but heroic inhabitants of the Teutonic forests, were held up as examples to be emulated.[3] This trend persisted into the present century. It is indeed significant that an analysis of history textbooks used during the Weimar period uncovered a continuation of this trend. Even the authors who favored republican statesmen felt compelled through an inner conviction to praise Lagarde as the great German who had opposed a society dedicated solely to material and scientific progress.[4] The relative conformity of the texts in these respects, whether from 1816 or 1926, demonstrates dramatically the penetration of the anti-modern ideology.

However, in the earlier texts, the Germanic message was tempered in important respects. Protestant Christianity was still central to the historical context, though it increasingly took on a Germanic coloration. Moreover, the Old Testament, which so many after 1900 vehemently rejected, was highly regarded as the basis for the doctrine of election.[5] A Germanic faith was not yet the sole precondition for being a chosen people—though it was to be shortly. Nevertheless, throughout the nineteenth century, with or without the Germanic faith, Tacitus' descriptions of the ancient Germans formed the center of Germanic consciousness.[6] While the Christian and Germanic impetus existed side by side, it was the Germanic faith which increasingly made inroads upon the Christian, to finally overshadow it at the beginning of the new century. Then, in 1905, some 273 teachers from Bremen recommended that a doctrinaire religious orthodoxy not be taught in public schools. They especially condemned the Old Testament, since it allegedly acquainted the students with the ideas of Syrian-Arabic Bedouins instead of dealing with the more vital Germanic heritage. Moreover, they held that the Scripture was alien to the Germanic experience and was outdated by the new ideas of evolution—and they quoted Darwin against Moses to prove it.[7]

In the same vein, an incident occurred in 1909 which shows how far the trend away from orthodox Protestantism had gone. Ludwig Gurlitt, a leader in the school reform movement, after being charged with blasphemy, escaped serious harm. In fact, only a few years later, at a teachers' meeting, he again strongly denounced the effects of Christianity on the education and development of the German nation. He charged that Christianity had cheated the nation of its best inheritance and that the healthy body of the Volk was now reacting powerfully against its poison.[8] Since Weymar's examination of textbooks was confined to the years before the unification of Germany, it does not deal with the hostility that had developed against orthodox Christianity and the Old Testament. Briefly, we might account for this by referring to the influence of Lagarde's religious views and the rise of anti-Semitic attitudes during the 1880's and after, which go far in explaining the hostility toward a "Jewish document."

Further evidence of the developing institutionalization of Volkish ideas in the schools was the growing demand by teachers and parents during the last decades of the nineteenth century for the introduction of *Heimatkunde* into the curriculum. *Heimatkunde*, literally rendered as "lore of the homeland," is another one of those terms that cannot really be translated. It may best be understood, however, in terms of the aims of Heinrich Wilhelm Riehl, who, as we have seen, at mid-century advocated the teaching of the integral relationship of the German people with their landscape and the customs in which they are rooted. This demand was elaborated and supplemented by Volkish pressure, and, in general, the educational institutions complied. In 1889, at a teachers' conference, one faculty member urged that the academic curriculum of the *Volkschulen* include the study of Germanic hero legends and fairy tales to enable students to appreciate more fully the accomplishments of the Volk. (The *Volkschulen* were the primary schools, which all children were required to attend.[9]) In the primary schools, as well as in the high schools, where the indoctrination in *Heimatkunde* was continued, the minds of the young were filled with the teacher's dreams of a frustrated German glory.

It can, of course, be argued that *Heimatkunde* was not necessarily Volkish, but in practice it tended to prove otherwise. The approach was often chauvinistic and the subject matter was characteristically Volkish. An incident in Posen, in 1907, is illustrative. A director of a school, addressing his fellow staff members, held that Jewish students should be dismissed from instruction in *Heimatkunde* because they could not be expected to have sufficiently deep or sacred feelings about it to appreciate the message.[10] This attitude spread into other fields. In 1931, the German Jewish community was much agitated by an article in a respectable philological journal which claimed that Jewish students could never be expected to grasp the import or spirit of classical German writers. Kleist, for example, was held to be too "intimately" German to be understood by Jews.[11]

While schoolteachers made these charges in defense of the German Volk, they themselves reflected the attitude they were defending. They were the most outspoken advocates of the Volkish ideology, particularly in connection with the racial question. There was ample justification for the complaint, lodged with the Austrian chancellor in 1889, that teachers were the most frequent contributors to anti-Semitic journals.[12] The situation was to continue until the Nazi seizure of power. Not satisfied with verbal anti-Semitic attacks, educational institutions at times acted upon their convictions. The most effective procedure was to bar Jews from faculties and gradually to force out those who already had tenure. Similar measures were carried out against students. University fraternities refused to accept Jews and alumni associations, such as that of the famous Leipzig gymnasium, denied admittance to its Jewish graduates (1908).[13]

Perhaps the most notorious case occurred in 1880, in what has become known as the "horse-tramway affair" of Berlin. Through this incident the public, and especially the Jews, were given a glimpse of how far the Volkish ideology had penetrated the teaching profession. Two teachers, passengers on the tramcar, voiced loud anti-Semitic remarks. An outraged Jewish passenger struck one of them. In the controversy that followed, the teacher who had been hit, Ernst Siecke, identified himself as a member of the staff of a prestigious Berlin high school. He maintained that his deportment did not indicate a prejudicial attitude toward Jewish students in his class; he claimed that his resistance to the unwarranted Jewish influence on German life did not impair the fairness of his relationship with Jewish students. The struggle he engaged in, he asserted, was part of the historical enmity between the German people and the Jews, a struggle which he, as a teacher, could not shirk.[14] Siecke was, in all probability, an adherent of the Stöcker movement.[15]

Siecke's companion, however, is more interesting. Bernhard Förster taught at Berlin's famed Friedrich Gymnasium, where his students regarded him as a sensitive romantic. He seems to have been a versatile man, for, in the year of the tramway incident, he became one of the chief architects of the Anti-Semitic Petition, which attempted to circumscribe the influence of Jews in Germany.[16] Despairing of immediate action in his native land, he emigrated to Paraguay in order to establish a pure Germanic utopia.[17] However, he was to have a deeper influence than this. As the brother-in-law of Nietzsche, he exercised a powerful influence upon his wife, Elizabeth Förster-Nietzsche, in her highly questionable editing of her brother's works. As we have already seen, and shall note again, in the hands of Volkish thinkers Nietzsche became a prophet of a new Germanism.

In addition to influencing teachers and changing school curricula, the Volkish movement profited from the late-nineteenth-century cause of school reform. This agitation originated outside the Volkish movement. Objectively, the need for such reform was great and so recognized by various liberals who gave the movement a humanitarian and free-thinking direction. The enmity between authoritarian teachers and students and the crowded curriculum produced a reaction against the system. Distinguished men, such as Franz Wedekind, protested that sensitive youth was being destroyed by an antiquated scholasticism. The charges could indeed be supported. Literally. In Prussia alone, between 1883 and 1888, 289 students committed suicide, 110 of whom were high school boys.[18] But the suppression of the students' creative and inquisitive spirit cannot be documented by statistics. The response was twofold: the state educational functionaries took notice of the evidence and charges, convened teachers' conferences, held interminable debates, and made minor adjustments; and there was a movement to establish private schools that would differ from urban public schools in their philosophy of education, their curriculum, and their setting.

The appropriation of school reform by the Volkish movement as its own sacred charge is best mirrored in the thinking and actions of one of its leading exponents. Ludwig Gurlitt, a teacher at Steglitz at the turn of the century, served his cause both as an educator and as a force within the German Youth Movement, in which he was the first to occupy the position of chairman of the advisory council to the Youth Movement, the Wandervögel. Gurlitt's philosophy of education provided the guidelines for a group that diverged from the catholic trend of the original reform movement. Although impressed with the Expressionists' critique of the educational system, Gurlitt rejected their solution. The Expressionists, at the beginning of the century, were in revolt against rationalism and interested in the development of creativity within the individual through his inner self, his soul. Like the Volkish thinkers, they decried the bourgeois age, and as young people they saw this age typified by the strait jacket of the school. They wanted freedom to develop and this led them, at times, to advocate sexual license as well as social and political revolution. Gurlitt termed their revolt anarchic and denied that the remedy lay in either leftist revolution or in granting youth unrestricted freedom. Instead, the ideal and the practical, the supreme and the immediate solution lay in "giving oneself to the Volk." [19]

What this meant and how it was to be achieved was revealed in Gurlitt's philosophy of education. Like other school reformers, Gurlitt gave priority to man's natural rather than his intellectual make-up and similarly regarded direct experience as superior to secondary knowledge—that is, wisdom derived from books. He insisted, first of all, that a child be allowed to develop naturally—a familiar enough cry in his day. Interpreting this literally, he stated that each human should be permitted to grow within the limits set by nature, limits which could not be surmounted.[20] Men would be able to find their role in life by identifying with the environment, the traditions and the values of the Volk. Similarly, love of the fatherland could not be acquired through formal education, but only through a love of the *Heimat*.[21] Gurlitt exhorted students to learn their higher religious sense from nature rather than spending their time dissecting some "dark saying" from the Bible.[22] The same would apply in practical education. Instead of drilling their minds with abstract scholastic matters, the students should occupy themselves in perfecting traditional skills in workshops and learn to know nature and the soil. To be revived, the Volk needed not rootless laborers but people who lovingly cared for the soil or carried on the artisan traditions.[23]

However, education was not to exclude all "academic" subjects. Such fields (revamped, to be sure, for the correct emphasis) as history, literature, and philosophy were to enhance the identity of the individual with the Volk. They were to forge the bonds which connected man with his national and racial peers through identity with the natural environment, with heroic tradition, and with a pantheistic Germanic faith that stressed the idealism of deeds in the interest of the Volk. In this vein Gurlitt criticized those textbooks which could not draw the proper distinction between the grandeur of Charlemagne and the heroic stature of the old Saxons—though they were defeated by the Carolingian monarch. Such books, he claimed, demoted the Volk to second place.[24] If the current system of education were continued, it would only support Lagarde's charge that German youth had lost, and was continuing to lose, its idealism.[25]

This lost virtue was to be recaptured through the Germanic faith as called for by Lagarde and Langbehn. Like these prophets, Gurlitt considered religious feeling to be an inner manifestation of a man's whole personality. Therefore it was essential that the youth be enabled to find their own inner strength and feeling without being stifled by inflexible doctrines and obsolete traditions.[26] Christianity, of course, was obsolescent, as it stifled the vigor of youth, offering only a consolation, a "something for those tired of life." Indeed, for Gurlitt, all traditions unaffiliated with Germanism were archaic. Both the Catholic Church, that centuries-old suppressor of the Germanic spirit, and the culture of classical Greece as well, with its contributions to literature and the arts, were inconsequential to the flowering of the Volk, past or future. Only the artistry of the ancient Germanic peoples from the Bronze Age onward, their elemental sense of creativity, was sufficient to produce a culture superior to those of other nations. It was a unique expression, totally unrelated to the heritage of the Assyrian-Semitic nations or to the Roman and Greek civilizations, indeed, it was one of the founts of these cultures. Consequently, he argued in prime Volkish fashion, the vitality, the spiritual richness and naturalness of the ancients would have to be regained before the German Volk could again assert itself. German youth were ripe for the task. And in rediscovering the Germanic context they would automatically strengthen the Volk and increase their own idealism.[27]

Gurlitt was convinced that the New Romanticism and the Germanic faith would be accepted by a freely developing youth. He was to base this belief on his own statement that "Young Germany understands [Langbehn's] *Rembrandt* book, understands Lagarde, and is delighted with Chamberlain." [28] Was it really so? Although wishful thinking and reality may have overlapped, Gurlitt, unlike most of his colleagues, was in personal touch with developments among the youth both in schools and in the Youth Movement. His influence was extensive. Thus, for example, the graduating class of the Graz Gymnasium in Austria quoted Gurlitt to justify their bitter criticism of the school. Students should indeed criticize their school, Gurlitt had said, but "cool rationality" should not be demanded of them. Instead youth should be a whole, living personality.[29] This is just one example of the appeal and influence of this educator whose direct personal involvement put him in touch with many thousands of students who wanted to throw off the shackles which an oppressive society had fastened on them. Consequently, we may take him as a relatively reliable source, at least as regards the dissatisfied students. It was they who were especially affected by Gurlitt's philosophy as well as by the religious content of contemporary Volkish thought. An admixture of these complementary trends was embodied in the principles of the Youth Movement, with Gurlitt as the chairman of its advisory council. Their revolution was Gurlitt's brand, not that of Gustav Wyneken, who also prescribed independence for youth but along more democratic and free-thinking lines. There is, consequently, no doubt that Gurlitt sincerely looked to Young Germany to usher in a second Reformation—"for so our century will be known"—a task, he thought, commensurate with their abilities.[30]

Where Gurlitt philosophized about education, Hermann Lietz, Gurlitt's contemporary, went directly to work. Gurlitt, who beheld the flowering of the boarding-school movement around him, saw in Lietz's work the fruition of his own ideas of school reform. Indeed, in the hands of Hermann Lietz, who in 1898 transferred the English public-school idea to a German setting and gave it the task of transmitting the Germanic ideology, school reform became for Gurlitt the fulfillment of his own educational theories.[31] Lietz, by his very example, influenced many German educators who were not actually involved with his boarding-school movement. Moreover, his schools were imitated both before and after the First World War. By the 1920's there were at least forty such boarding schools, which for all their variety traced their origins back to Hermann Lietz. To be sure, only a small number of students actually passed through these schools, but they made their presence felt in society, as they came to occupy positions of influence in government, business, and education. These, then, are the reasons why we must devote so much attention to Lietz: because of his imitators, who formed the German boarding-school movement, and because of the discussion he aroused throughout the educational establishment.

Lietz had a great advantage in that he could experiment outside the rules of the established educational bureaucracy. The public schools had been subject to Volkish pressure, and in many of them a Volkish spirit prevailed, but in Lietz's schools the whole range of Volkish attitudes could be applied in a more thoroughgoing way. It is thus to Lietz and his experiment that we must now turn to see Volkish educational ideas in action.

Although Lietz was to deny it, it is quite certain that he was influenced by the example of the English public schools, especially by the radical new innovations at Abbotsholme. There, while a guest teacher, Lietz observed the work of Dr. Reddie as he directed his educational institution under the motto: "Education spells Empire." The school had a nationalistic spirit, an identity with Britain's martial and "civilizing" powers, which Reddie attributed to the nation's fidelity to her ancient traditions. Lietz was particularly impressed with three of Reddie's procedures. First, there was a concentration on an English history that stressed the greatness of England throughout the ages and paid relatively little attention to other nations. Second, there was an observance of the Anglican service which was embellished with and made flexible by readings from Carlyle and Ruskin. And third, Lietz admired the heavy emphasis placed on

physical fitness and excellence in sports.[32] Lietz transposed these procedures to the German scene and applied them in such a way that it
did seem as if he had introduced something unique. Indeed, he implemented a revolutionary program in terms of content; it was a
skillful adaptation of the British public-school system.

Lietz's ideas came to fruition in 1898 with his first school, founded
in Ilsenburg, Saxony. The school and the housing for the lower grades
were strategically located in the countryside—in close proximity to
a small village, fields, and simple peasant folk. Lietz thought that
this environment would be beneficial to the students, whom he
wanted to become familiar both with the native soil and with the
rhythm of the people who lived on it.[33] The success of the first establishment led to the founding, in 1901, of a second school, at Haubinda, which housed only the middle grades. Finally Lietz crowned
the whole enterprise by the purchase of the ancient castle at Bieberstein to accommodate the upper-high-school classes. This complex
of educational facilities, to which an orphanage was later added, represented a most concerted effort to spread the cause of school reform.
The principles of boarding-school life applied here were to start, in
Lietz's estimation, a new trend in education that would be oriented
to encompass more of the child than could be done through books,
scholarship, and one-sided intellectual development. As one disciple
summed it up: the strong personality was important for the school,
not the strongest intelligence.[34]

As we have noted, Lietz, in transferring Reddie's ideas to a German setting, made some changes. These were of crucial importance.
Whereas Reddie groomed his students to enter the active service
of the Empire, Lietz aspired to inculcate his charges with the pantheistic belief in nature—which increasingly took on a Germanic slant
—and an abiding dedication to the welfare of the Volk. Both were
to be acquired through a curriculum centered on residence in the
country, growing familiarity with nature and the soil, and a knowledge of the simple ways of peasants and the trades of unpresumptuous
artisans. As we shall see later, this was merely a bare outline, for some
selected classes and students were to reach beyond these modest
goals. But these goals were nonetheless effective. To a large extent
they arose out of the romantic identity with rural tradition that Lietz
himself inherited and continued to foster. In later years, his wife asserted that his peasant heritage had vitally influenced his whole perspective on the world.[35] Even when he instituted sports for physical
exercise, he considered manual labor on the soil a more fitting form
of physical conditioning. Working at reforestation and other land
improvements was the best way to build a well-developed German

physique and mind;[36] even as a sick man, on the verge of death, Lietz would help his boys plant trees.

Lietz's schools, however, did not represent a mere back-to-nature movement, though in later years it was falsely described as such. At times he was pictured as a simple peasant and his agricultural and rural interests were equated with an uncomplicated mind. One of his early collaborators even depicted him as an elemental and primitive personality, while another, Gustav Wyneken, then a staff teacher, later a figure in the Youth Movement, attributed to his superior an anti-intellectual disposition that regarded all acts of cerebration with deep suspicion.[37] Lietz did, of course, hold that the intellectual development fostered in urban surroundings and placed in the service of modern technology was inimical to the quintessence of the Germanic mind, but it would be erroneous to see in him a genial nature addict and an outright anti-intellectual.

Lietz was neither as pragmatic nor as primitive as some of his associates depicted him. In fact, one might almost call him an idealist primarily concerned with the spiritual destitution of the nation and with the resuscitation of the Germanic base for the Volk. From the first, he combined his views of nature and the role of the German peasantry in the national culture with the immediate and long-range interests of the German people. Deeply immersed in the Germanic ideology, he claimed that his schools were established on the principle that education presupposed national feelings and national deeds, for *Heimat* and Volk were the pillars upon which all culture rested.[38] It was education's task to counteract the damage done by modernity, a task best fulfilled through loving care for the soil of the fatherland and a cultivation of the historical German inheritance. Such education, he claimed, would lead to an ethical idealism commensurate with the needs of the Volk.[39]

This concept of education covered a large area; to quote Lietz, it was education for living. One of its most significant vehicles was to be religion, but a religion that was more a religious feeling, a veneration of nature and the soil that slowly fused with a Germanic faith.[40] Lietz was especially fond of the works of Lagarde, as Lagarde too defined culture in terms of man's relationship to his *Heimat* and Volk, and Lietz made liberal use of his ideas.[41] Whereas in early life Lietz could say that religion and the Bible were among the source materials for the education of youth, in his last years these were supplemented by the Germanic faith.[42]

In their curricula, the schools spread the Germanic ideology and their courses were designed to create in the students a fervent identity with the nation. The core of their curricula was the study of the

German language and German history. Lietz was always most anxious to teach the history courses himself, and it was in this field that he pioneered in the use of source materials.

During the first few years, Lietz made use of Biblical sources, but gradually the Biblical studies were displaced by ancient and medieval history. This change was complete by 1909, when he declared the books of the Old Testament to be inferior to German medieval histories and chronicles.[43] Later he asserted that the Bible had no religious value either. Christ, freed from Pauline-Jewish fetters, was either Germanized as a heroic figure or transformed into a repository of those virtues associated with the Germans.[44] The religious spirit of a Christ-centered faith took on a Germanic personality. In combining historical narration with the appropriate religious feeling of the times, Lietz came to idealize Ulrich von Hutten, the early companion of Martin Luther, who, he held, had combined an appeal to the German nation with a plan for religious reform.[45]

For the heritage of German culture outside the field of history Lietz turned to the literature of his native land. Instruction in this subject was combined, as in the history courses, with a sense of religious dedication, surrounded with an aura of veneration. In Lietz's hands Abottsholme's Anglican chapel was transformed into something not very dissimilar to Wachler's open-air theater, and literature, mostly with a Germanic and patriotic content, was read nightly under the stars to the students. These readings were from Volkish books we have already discussed. The secondary-form pupils, for example, were introduced to such books as the emotionally "moving" *Büttnerbauer*, Freytag's *Debit and Credit*, and Popert's *Helmut Harringa*, while the upper-high-school students read a combination of history, philosophy, and literature in Treitschke's *German History of the Nineteenth Century*. Supplementary reading was to be found in the literature of the Volkish press. After 1900, Theodor Fritsch's paper *Der Hammer*, the journal of the Pan-Germans, Damaschke's book *Soil Reform*, and the material of New Romanticism were all recommended reading for the students.[46]

While German literature, especially that of national geniuses like Goethe, Schiller, and Kleist, was heavily emphasized, foreign authors were almost totally neglected. When members of the teaching staff, Gustav Wyneken and Paul Geheeb, introduced such foreign works as the new psychological literature from Russia, Lietz violently disapproved. He condemned the literature as un-German and berated its intellectual content for cultivating the kind of critical turn of mind which was anathema to the national Germanic ethos, for it introduced a spirit of irreverence.[47] If foreign literature was banned, foreign languages fared equally poorly. Foreign languages—with the exception of English, which was deemed necessary in the developing competition with Britain for economic markets—and mathematics occupied an auxiliary role in the curriculum.[48]

The social organization of these schools provides further evidence that German youth were being educated in accordance with definite goals. While the new institutions had at first drastically moved away from the authoritarianism of the state schools and instituted the English prefect system of student self-government, they just as quickly abandoned it. Instead, they organized the students into "families" in which the teacher was the mentor of a small group of students. In the abolition of student self-government after so short a try, Lietz reflected the patriarchal attitudes inherent in the Germanic faith. In this context Lietz recognized the importance of leadership, a quality he later deemed indispensable for the Germanic revival. Accordingly, he demanded that his own educators possess harmonious as well as powerful personalities that were capable of leading and inspiring youth. Gustav Wyneken called Lietz's system an "enlightened patriarchal despotism." [49] The teachers' task was to train young people who would easily assimilate into the social and political organizations envisaged by Volkish thought: a society based upon hierarchical principles.

Lietz's view of the state was consistent with his ideas of school organization; he thought that the state should be like a well-run farm with everything in its proper place.[50] He felt that amorphous mass parties, drawing their legal sanction from majority-rule principles, had destroyed the just order of things. To correct the imbalance it was necessary for the leadership of the nation to revert to those who were capable of leading and could envision a national greatness. The rest of society, structured according to hierarchical principles, was to be composed of the masses, graded according to occupations and intelligence.[51] It is important to note that Lietz shared this outlook with the Volkish movement as a whole, a world view which persisted into the age of mass parliamentary parties as an instrument for advancing elitist concepts. And typically enough, he too held to a social differentiation based upon class and economic criteria. In his educational establishment, for example, he cut short the school attendance of the poorer students, students from his orphanage over whom he could exercise absolute control. In place of intellectual tasks, they were assigned manual work. Of them he said philosophically: "The children of the broad masses should not get half-cultured; otherwise they will make demands for the satisfaction of which there is neither the strength nor the money available." [52]

The increasing accentuation of the Volkish theme in Lietz's educational institution was also reflected in its growing anti-Semitism. At first Jews were readily received at the school and contributions from Jews substantially helped to finance the operation. The number of Jewish students was not inconsiderable; in fact at one time they comprised the majority of the upper class at Haubinda.[53] The reasons for this high degree of Jewish interest can only be guessed at. Perhaps these Jews were reacting against their urban stereotyping, or perhaps it was just that they were able to afford this means of getting their children out of the strait jacket of the state schools. However, from the beginning, but for one exception, the Jewish students were not Lietz's favorites. And even he, Erich von Mendelssohn, was to disappoint him when he wrote a novel in which he bitterly portrayed the social relationships at the school.[54] On the whole, the Jewish students were apt to be too intellectually precocious, urban, and irreverent for Lietz's Germanic tastes.[55]

Quite suddenly, Lietz attempted to restrict the admission of Jews. He failed in his first attempt, being outvoted at a teachers' meeting at which Wyneken and Geheeb spearheaded the opposition.[56] The issue, however, was further aggravated when Theodor Lessing, a Jew, became a member of the teaching staff. The case of Lessing is interesting in itself, as it reflected an attitude that goes far in explaining the attraction of Lietz's establishment to many Jews. Lessing believed Lietz to be a fellow idealist. Indeed, to Lessing the headmaster was a "hero" and his school gave to the German fatherland—with which he identified—"heroes of deeds." Lessing also subscribed to the Germanic ideals of beauty; however, his image included not only the beautiful male figure, but intellectual excellence as well.[57] In these respects he was in harmony with Lietz—indeed, with the whole of New Romanticism.

But Lessing was a humanist and his Germanic faith drew extensive inspiration from classical models. It was in this direction that he misread Lietz. He set forth his ideas in a newspaper article which showed him clearly at odds with his headmaster. First, he asserted that all religions, in view of their essential equality, should have equal standing in the curriculum. Lietz must have taken exception to this, for even though he had rejected doctrinaire Christianity, the revitalized Germanic faith was still a necessary belief for him. Though Lessing was a fervent patriot at that time of his life, even then he diluted this feeling with a spirit of humanist education "which should not be drowned within the merely practical." Here was another potential area of conflict with the headmaster.[58]

Lessing was dismissed. The actual grounds for dismissal show

Lietz's increasing anti-Semitism, for he accused Lessing of conspiring with the other Jewish students against his leadership of the school.[59] For Lietz the Jewish conspiracy, in which so many of the Volkish thinkers believed, had invaded his schools. Moreover, he must have seen in Lessing's humanism an "intellectualizing" and a critical mind which was typically Jewish in its lack of veneration for the genuine. Lietz's action came as a shock to Lessing and led him back to a greater affirmation of his Jewishness. He went on to become a distinguished philosopher, only to be brutally murdered by the Nazis in the end.

When Wyneken and Geheeb, who also quarreled with Lietz, departed in 1903, discrimination against Jewish students became a conscientiously applied policy. In 1910 a teachers' conference decided that all children of non-German descent would have to have special recommendations for admission and must pay higher fees. The questionnaire for admission asked if children were of "Indo-Germanic" or "Semitic" descent.[60] This special ruling went into effect at a time when Volkish agitators were advocating double taxation of all non-Aryans. It may not be irrelevant to note that before 1903 Lietz was in debt to a Jewish contractor as well as to Jewish-controlled banks. This certainly must have added to his growing anti-Semitism.[61] In spite of the obstacles, some Jewish parents still sent their children to the schools. Yet, to the end, Lietz considered them foreign elements unable to lose their uniqueness, too critical, too contentious—in short, too intellectual. In the end, he too succumbed to viewing the Jew according to the prevalent stereotype.

Lietz's anti-Semitic attitudes developed alongside his ever more ecstatic patriotism. In 1913 he bypassed attendance at the Youth Movement's rally on the Meissner Mountain in favor of participating in the centennial celebration of the Battle of Leipzig which had contributed to the defeat of Napoleon. The following year, at the outbreak of the First World War, the overaged Lietz volunteered for the army and was accepted. During the war and especially toward the end of it, his writings showed a greater racial orientation and an ever deeper identity with the Germanic faith. This change represented a logical fruition of his earlier outlook, but the drastic manner in which it came about has been attributed by some largely to the fatal illness he contracted during the war and to the shock of watching Germany succumb to defeat.[62]

Lietz's work during the war represents a more concrete orientation toward race, nation, and Volk. What is newly accented in these last writings is the importance of racial purity for the Volk. The Jews were condemned for their materialism and stigmatized as having sold themselves to the "demon capitalism." In terms of the economy, he recommended nationalizing the land and distributing it to the peasants. Those industries which affected the national and common good were likewise to be nationalized. He still adhered to his "German idealism," which he defined in terms of nature, simplicity, and Germanic Christianity.[63] In his last years, the desperate years filled with dark forebodings of Germany's future, these views were printed in Dietrich Eckart's *Auf Gut Deutsch*, where they appeared side by side with articles of what was soon to be the early National Socialist movement.[64] Lietz died in 1919, before the Nazi party was founded.

In reviewing Lietz's life, a writer in Diederich's *Tat* posed the question: How could such a revolutionary educational innovation spring from such a conservative person?[65] The answer is that obviously such an innovation could come only from a conservative person, for it was symptomatic of the desire for a conservative revolution, imbued with the New Romanticism and a rejection of modernity. Through it Lietz harnessed school reform to the Volkish cause and transformed education into an engine for its dissemination. His students were thought of as an elite which would renew Germany. Given the importance of education in the institutionalization of an ideology, Lietz is certainly an important figure in any history of the Volkish movement.

Lietz's work at the schools was continued by his apostle, Alfred Andreesen, who had joined him in 1908. By 1919 he was ready to fill his master's place. When he assumed his new position he immediately declared that the future of the nation depended upon the successful completion of the struggle against a materialistic and skeptical Judaism. The harshness of the declaration was "mitigated" only by the concession that some select Jews might themselves overcome their failings.[66] From these views he later went on to join the educational organization of the National Socialists, a step which some have attributed to his desire to save the schools after 1933.[67] But Andreesen was more than just a fellow traveler. His edition of Lagarde's writings was accompanied by a carefully expurgated edition of Lietz's *Memoirs*—which is still the only printed edition—which was slanted in a National Socialist direction much more than the original warrants. Furthermore, he was the representative of the boarding schools in the National Socialist teachers' organization, where he praised the Adolf Hitler Schools as the culmination of Lietz's work.[68] In all this, Andreesen only fulfilled the ideological presuppositions upon which the country-boarding-school movement was founded.

Of course, one has to take into account the general direction in which school reform moved, which to a large extent was beneficial for urban youth. Even in Lietz's establishment, it was good for city boys to be able to enjoy the natural surroundings, to become acquainted with agricultural life, and to learn the blessings of physical labor. When implemented in a humanist vein it represented the best in school reform. Wyneken and Geheeb, who had broken with Lietz, founded schools which attempted this very combination. In Wyneken's Wickersdorf, true to its title "School Community," students and teachers were granted an equal voice in administering the school. Intellectualism was encouraged and art was practiced for its own sake instead of being used as a doctrinaire vehicle for the improvement of the Volk. Geheeb, in founding his Odenwald School, stressed the free development of the individual in a humanist society. His romantic humanism was accompanied by the concept of the democratic school community. He too permitted all the members of the school to participate equally in discussions of school problems.

Where Lietz's schools, like Hentschel's Mittgart, surrounded themselves with real or figurative fences to prevent alien factors from interacting with the purity of the Germans, Geheeb located his school in the vicinity of a large city and encouraged a constant interchange. With Geheeb and Wyneken, narrow nationalism and Volk interests had no place in school reform.

But to view Lietz's program stripped of its ideology is not to see it in its full meaning; nor should one think that Geheeb's and Wyneken's experiments represented the dominant trend. On the contrary, most of the schools that adopted a boarding-school format and a revolutionary educational methodology were accompanied by a Volkish emphasis.

While Lietz's schools can serve as the classical case in point, a few other examples, out of many similar developments, show the proliferation of his educational ideas. In fact, some of Lietz's staff members themselves became founders of new institutions. One of them, Martin Luserke, became the director of the school on the island of Sylt. Dedicated to the rearing of a Germanic soul that encompassed all of nature's depth and intensity, he located the school by the ocean so as to provide the most conducive setting. The rhythm of the sea in its grandiose simplicity was to provide the soul with the required beneficial stimulus.[69] Furthermore, Luserke's stress on inculcating his students with the "will to perform deeds" led him through an easy transition into National Socialist thought, where he came to connect his own belief with the natural heroism of Nordic man.[70]

The years after the First World War saw the growth of several new educational establishments which exhibited a concentrated drive to better the Volk—especially as it had emerged from the terrible strains of the war. These schools endorsed a new effort to infuse in the students that "idealism of deeds" which would assist the emergence of a strong and spiritually united nation, a reconstituted Volk. In this effort, Kurt Hahn, the director of the school in Salem endowed by Prince Max von Baden in 1920, emphasized "giving oneself with all one's soul" to an effort and an idealism which would overcome the spiritual vacuum of postwar Germany. Aside from the spiritual tasks, there was of course the old emphasis on physical fitness, now of particular significance after the defeat in the war. But along with this concern for the physical well-being of the German Volk, there was also a commensurate stress on the development of a strong, purposeful, and dedicated will. Hahn's students were educated with these goals in mind, but without any racist prejudices. His students, a few among many similarly trained youth, formed a disciplined and hardened elite prepared to face all challenges and to resolve them successfully.[71]

The Heimat Schools, which also flourished in the 1920's, had similar goals. In addition to their stress on nature and the steeling of the character for action in the interest of the nation,[72] they emphasized studies of race, *Volkstum*, and the origin of the German character. These schools were usually special adult-education centers along the lines of Bruno Tanzmann's Peasants' School, established in 1917. Like the latter, they were largely inspired by Lietz's schools and their emphasis on Germanism, nature, and ancient peasant customs. What they added was an appropriate emphasis on race.

We have dwelt at length upon these schools, for they and their staffs, along with the curricula in many of the state schools and individual teachers with Volkish leanings, effectively institutionalized the Volkish ideology. But not only did a multitude of young people pass through them on their way to an active participation in the life of the nation; these schools also gave encouragement to the German Youth Movement.

While the connection between the schools and the Youth Movement may have been close in certain areas (for example, when joined in the persons of Gustav Wyneken and Ludwig Gurlitt), by and large the Youth Movement and the boarding-school movement existed side by side rather than wedded together. Though Lietz had little direct ideological influence on the Youth Movement, he did, late in life, write an article for the movement's periodical. In it he discussed the necessity of physical development—in defense of which he invoked the classical beauty of the Greeks and their attainment of perfection of physical proportions—as well as intensive knowledge of Volk and fatherland. The movement in turn paid its respects to Lietz for his work in the cause of the Volk, their common interest.[73] There was, therefore, between the founder of the country boarding schools and the Youth Movement a definite rapport based upon similarity of ideology rather than upon personal involvement and direct exchange. It is to the Youth Movement that we must now turn.

CHAPTER 9

The Youth Movement

THE DEVELOPMENT and growth of the organized German Youth
Movement was a unique phenomenon in German history. No other
movement produced such spontaneity, filled the young people with
such enthusiasm, or enrolled so many in its ranks. Founded in 1901
as a hiking association for schoolboys in the Berlin suburb of Steglitz,
it soon spread over most of northern Germany. The organizational
framework was a loose one from the beginning. Each leader recruited his own followers within a school and led them both on their
excursions and in their singing and talking sessions in their "den."
At first there actually was an over-all organization, and Karl Fischer
became the leader of all the Wandervögel (as the members of the
Youth Movement were called). Yet largely because of the strong
leadership concept which Fischer developed, the movement soon
split into several groups, each with its own leadership structure.
These groupings and regroupings need not concern us, for all shared,
to a greater or lesser degree, the basic ideological presuppositions
which were essential for the success of the movement as a whole.[1]
From a handful of students at Steglitz the Wandervögel could claim,
by 1911, 15,000 German youths and the movement continued to
grow at an even faster rate. For what was new and revolutionary
about the Wandervögel was the absence of adult tutelage. The excursions had begun under the slogan "Youth among itself" and in this
way had become symbolic of the revolt of youth against their elders.

The movement was a conscious effort on the part of the youth to
organize themselves for the purpose of appropriating certain intellectual, cultural, artistic, social, and political ideals opposed to the
manners and outlook of their parents. Or so they thought. This potential explosiveness of the youth, their inner dynamism—though it

might well have been rooted in disillusionment—was a tempting target for exploitation by both the left and the right.

Tradition, however, did play a central role in the German Youth Movement. The young people remained faithful to a conservative attitude shared by most German youth throughout the previous century. The movement represented a further turning toward the right on the part of the bourgeois German youth on a scale not equaled until the Nazi harvest of a whole new generation. It is not easy to document at what point it first acquired a definite Volkish allegiance. Nor is it simple to determine to what degree the movement was actually aware of the direction it desired to take and the means to pursue it. During its first, developing years the organization was flexible, and revised its own original declaration of intentions to meet the pragmatic needs of the moment or to follow an especially influential and commanding leader.

But it was firm in its loyalty to the concept of the Volk, myth or reality. Its allegiance to the Volk, Germanic faith, tradition, heroism, nature lore, and its identity with the aesthetic qualities of Nordic man were varied but concrete. Here, among the youth, essentially Volkish aesthetic and ethical values were received with enthusiasm. By 1904, the wave of the Wandervögel had swept Germany with such force that not even Karl Fischer could adequately explain it. Surely we can regard this phenomenon as a radical expression of New Romanticism penetrating the younger generation. It too was a part of the attempt to resolve the crisis in German ideology.

After the inroads made by Volkish thought, a large segment of German youth associated hikes through the countryside with revolution, and identifying with nature was thought equivalent to subverting the existing order. And here alone it functioned as a vital part of an ideology that was conservative as contrasted with the progress of the times. Hans Blüher, the movement's first historian, stated that the upsurge was a "protest of youth against the stifling of its spirit." [2] Indeed, it did attempt to liberate itself from the strictures of modernity in the form of school, parents, authoritarianism, and the whole order of bourgeois mores, prejudices, and hypocrisies. But the direction it took immersed youth in a romanticism based upon the native landscape, elemental vitality, and awareness of the German past. The first Wandervögel called themselves "Bachanten," a name which does not derive from the Greek God Bacchus but from the wandering scholars of the German Middle Ages.[3]

Karl Fischer, the founder of the Wandervögel, regarded the movement as a romantic expression of a vital German character. In view of its sources of inspiration, he was justified in this view. He and his early followers had drawn extensive inspiration from the writings of Lagarde and Langbehn. They also turned to Ludwig Gurlitt for ideological support. Riehl inspired their sense of veneration for the landscape, teaching them how to appropriate the landscape into their souls.[4] And in aesthetics and art Fidus provided them with their favorite depictions of youthful idealism, physical beauty, and the inspiration of nature. Not the least important influence, however, was that of Father Jahn and the patriotism that had been channeled into the youth of his own day remained as a symbol for the youth of modern Germany.[5] The Wandervögel lived up to it, with less patriotism as such, but with a deeper sense of identity with the Volk. "Because the landscape which inspires [the Wandervögel] is the landscape of the German *Heimat,* such love awakens love for Volk and fatherland . . . a national-Germanic background for all their culture and style of life." [6] In these respects, in the context of Wilhelmine society, the movement was radical and viewed itself accordingly.

To dismiss the romanticism of the youth as essentially "unpolitical," as many historians have done, is a grave error. Though it did not present a clear political program or engage in practical politics, its peculiar approach to the nature of the German character clearly presented an alternative way of pursuing the nation's policies and interests. If the political identity of the youth is not recognized, their essential desire to reach a working unity with the Volk through nature and custom is badly misinterpreted. Moreover, their contempt for contemporary politics as "superficial" is mistakenly accepted at its face value.

In defining their patriotism as loyalty to the interests of the Volk, these young people contrasted markedly with their chauvinistic parents and with bourgeois society as a whole. They felt much closer to the ideals of Langbehn than to those of Bismarck. However, during the growth of the movement, its patriotic feeling fluctuated in intensity. As we shall see, its original radical enthusiasm was gradually dissipated, supplanted for a time by an intense patriotism, only to be revived shortly before the war. But this vacillation will be examined in detail in connection with other interrelated issues.

The deep love of fatherland that rises above social class and politics which was stressed in the Wandervögel's manifesto of 1904[7] presented some difficulty to Hans Blüher, the organization's first historian. He tried to resolve the conflict between the superficially nonpolitical posture of the movement and certain actions which reflected a deep-seated attachment to the fatherland. For example, while the German state did not seem to concern itself with such problems as the morale and aspirations of German nationals in neighboring countries, the Wandervögel took it upon themselves to display an appropriate interest. In his history Blüher describes the journey undertaken by Fischer and his troop in 1902 to visit the German communities in Poland. It was to impress upon their fellow countrymen, settlers in that country, that the youth of Germany were interested in their fate, their aspirations and complaints, and they vowed to communicate their impressions to the people back home.[8] This excursion was supplemented by subsequent trips to other hard-pressed German minorities in the Austrian Empire. How markedly this contrasts with the rest of Blüher's history, which describes the supposedly simple attempt by the organization to join itself with nature and to engage in activities solely on the basis of spontaneity.[9]

The disdain for the patently patriotic, on the one hand, and identity with the Volk, on the other, continued to be exemplified in other practices as well. Instead of celebrating the pompous and popular Wilhelmine festivals, such as the anniversary of the Battle of Sedan, the Wandervögel held rites of Germanic origin. The celebration of the Summer Solstice was especially popular. Here was a ritual that brought forth the aura of heroism, of group participation, of conforming to a natural sublimation in the Volk.[10] A typical celebration began with the lighting of a bonfire in a selected romantic spot. A speaker then would invoke the true spirit of the German people, praise the virtues of Germanic ancestry, and exhort the youth to emulate this great heritage. This was followed by singing, after which each youth, as an act of rededication to Germanic values, jumped through the fire. Their motto, "To maintain oneself in spite of all the powers that be," clearly expressed a revolutionary dynamism which directed itself against the modernity of the bourgeois world and which held forth a vision of a vital union with romantic Germanism.[11]

The identity with the Volk was continued in other fields as well, though in a less spectacular way. Fischer fused the influence of several Volkish thinkers, among them Riehl and Langbehn, with the spirit of adventure found in the fiction of Karl May, a famous German author who concocted tales of American Indians. From these stories Fischer derived a sense of romantic and simultaneously idealistic action, for May's heroes, scouts like "Old Schatterhand" and noble Indians like "Winnetou," were the epitome of vitality, chivalry, and endurance; they were imbued with a sense of exploration and possessed an individuality that was virile as well as virtuous.[12] Here, perhaps naïvely, Fischer saw his "idealism of deeds" at work. He aspired to more than adventure; he wanted to create an identity that would lead to deeds,[13] an idealism that would arise spontaneously out of the contact between youth and the landscape. Roaming, wandering through the countryside, was to provide the substructure of such an idealism. It would familiarize the youth with what Riehl had preached so avidly: an intimate knowledge of one's native land, an acquaintance with the customs and aspirations of the simple peasant folk, and the perception of the intimate relationship between the present and tradition. Fischer thought that this would produce a "living contact" with the Volk heritage that would go deeper than anything to be gained from merely looking at national monuments.[14] Here his Wandervögel would find that context in which their idealism of deeds would become operative.

Interestingly enough, the Wandervögel's love of nature sharply contrasted with that depicted in the idyllic scenes which, as children, they must have seen in their homes. For them it was not a pastoral union with a benign force in nature. Rather it was a conquest of, as well as a fusion with, a vital and elemental essence. Only where two comparable energies were at work could a fair merger take place, could the appropriate fusion of individual into the whole be manifest. Georg Götsch, an early Wandervögel leader, aptly described the idea behind this submergence when he stated, in his description of the Siberian landscape, that after his journey there he beheld the "great unities and encompassing elements" of nature everywhere he looked.[15] He was not speaking of the sentimental aspects of a sitting-room nature scene, but of the harshness and independence of an elemental nature. Both Frank Fischer, one of the movement's most important theoreticians, and Götsch stressed the idea that hardiness and nature went hand in hand,[16] a concept that was in many ways similar to Fontane's description of the Prussian landscape and its role in the shaping of a stalwart character. This note of physical and emotional toughness permeated the ideals of the Youth Movement and helped shape the concepts of physical beauty which, in turn, were given functional roles in the ideal of German youth.

A further reflection of the young people's desire to achieve unity in a common cause was their love of polyphonic music. The immense popularity of Frank Fischer's collection of German folk songs, first published in 1905, demonstrated that the group function was regarded as more meaningful than the self-awareness of the isolated individual. With their traditional themes, the folk songs enabled the youth to share emotions and values. They described events from the point of view of a group that worked in harmony toward common goals. For their songs the Wandervögel went back to earlier centuries, rejecting contemporary and romantic tunes, which were generally scored for one voice only.[17] As in the fusion of the individual with nature, here too there was a subordination to the virtues of a greater good. The individual was circumscribed by forces that gave him identity—not in the abstract, but in a living community of tradition. Folk songs, like roaming through the countryside, were not merely romantic forms of expression; both stimulated a community of purpose and, through a merging with nature and tradition, a community of the soul.

Though these methods of achieving group identity seem simple and innocent, there was another aspect which became problematical and controversial. Again it was Blüher who pointed to it. In his book *Wandervögel as an Erotic Phenomenon* (1912), which gained notoriety because some thought he was accusing the Youth Movement of encouraging homosexual relations in its ranks, Blüher described the role played in the movement by what he called Eros. While for him Eros certainly meant a sexual attraction between men, these drives did not necessarily lead to an overt display of affection, nor did they culminate in physical sexual relations. Instead, the Eros impulse worked, socially and culturally, to deepen friendships between males and to increase the cohesion of a male group. Basing his argument on his own observations and somewhat influenced by the theories of Freud, Blüher claimed that men who stand in close relationship to one another inevitably display homosexual impulses which, however, are sublimated in the form of surplus energy. This vital force, not finding a physical or organic release, eventually finds expression in true creativity which centers on the *Männerbund*, the society of men.[18] As evidence, Blüher listed several factors he observed among the Wandervögel. First, there was the *charisma* of the leaders, that captivating quality possessed by the exceptional few, the most imaginative, creative, and attractive personalities. Second, there was the ideal of male beauty, which found expression in the admiration for the muscular and lithe Germanic types. And third, there was the exclusion of women (who nonetheless founded their own organizations).

How serious were Blüher's findings and what connection did they have with the Volkish ideology? In terms of the ideal of male beauty the connection was obvious, as may be seen from our analysis in previous chapters. The Wandervögel journals were filled with descriptions of the ideal Germanic man; that given by Carl Bösch, another leader of the movement, may stand as typical. It defined a true Germanic personality as one which possesses an "instinctive" quality linking his soul to nature and the Volk. In addition, he must have that instinct for beauty and form through which he will want to steel his body and make it beautiful.[19] Though this concentration on the physically strong and beautiful was a protest against the bourgeoisie's artificiality and hypocrisy in sexual matters, as indicated by their deep-seated shame of the naked body, it had both an aesthetic and a functional place in the lives of the individual Wandervögel. It became a conscious ideal of male beauty among the youth as portrayed in the paintings of Fidus, which were reproduced in most of the movement's journals. Moreover, this concept of beauty was associated with strength and activism, with the "idealism of deeds." In the hands of Blüher and others, the idea of the *Bund*, the male society, was elevated to a general principle not only of life but of government as well. As such it will play an important role in our story. The *Bund* was one of the ideals of the Youth Movement, but, in all probability, for the majority of the Wandervögel it was largely devoid of the purely sexual meaning which Blüher alone had superimposed upon it. To be sure, Wilhelm Jansen, who succeeded Fischer as leader, sought to encourage the development of an ideal type through gymnastics and nude bathing ("light and air baths").[20] He was accused of homosexuality by rival leaders in the movement and expelled. But the physical ideal described by Bösch remained. As late as 1924, a highly respectable Volkish paper praised the love of nudity as the core of the Youth Movement and as a paramount expression of their genuine closeness to nature and the Volk.[21] However, this love of physical form, centered, as it was, upon the male body, in conjunction with the Eros of male membership reflected a negative attitude toward the role of women in society and in the Volk. Even when girls formed their own branch of the Wandervögel they were not readily accepted as an authentic expression of the ideals of youth. Only after the First World War did mixed groups come into existence.

But there was a more significant aspect of the emphasis on male membership and beauty, and that was the effect it had on Volkish principles of organization. The Volkish movement was especially impressed with the Wandervögel's *Bund* formation. Here they saw their own elitist ideas in operation. The *Bund* structure, by means of which the youth were able to organize their members on the basis of strong leadership, while holding them together by ties of Eros and common ideology, appeared as an alternative to both Marxism and capitalist class society. To one leader, writing after the First World War amidst the ruins of the shattered nation, the *Bund* structure seemed to be the only remaining true German form of political organization. It transcended the dichotomy between individualistically oriented capitalist society and the collective emphasis of socialism in that it incorporated the best of both by basing itself on leadership, Volk, and community.[22] The Youth Movement's concept of the

Bund was to remain a constant inspiration in the Volkish search for a means of organizing society according their views, a society which was neither capitalist nor socialist.

To be sure, the movement was largely made up of boys between the ages of fourteen and eighteen, and they could hardly be expected to give deep thought to the formulation of a coherent ideology. For them membership in the Wandervögel meant rough adventure, escape from school and home, and status among their classmates. Yet the many talks given by their leaders and the many publications which ascribed a definite purpose to their actions must have had some effect on even the younger members. The ideology was formulated by the young men who led the movement and for them the ideology had far greater meaning than it had for the younger members. Indeed, many came to think that the movement, instead of representing the aspirations, interests, and values of the youth, actually was serving the ideological and personal purposes of the adult leadership. By the First World War a large part of the leadership was composed of adult, mature men whose tutelage and direction dominated the organization to such an extent that many asked whether the movement was still representative of "youth among itself." Indeed, changes of such magnitude had taken place that Blüher accused them of having turned the early romanticism of the movement into a sham artificiality.[23]

But to some extent Blüher's attitude was an unwarranted oversimplification. The New Romantic vision of the Volk was central and remained so. Youth had expressed their love for the fatherland with a fervor and, in their minds, a "genuine" idealism which was far removed from the saber-rattling patriotism of their elders. The German woods and dales, the small towns and villages which nestled within them, and the songs of old made for a union of the individual with the Volk. This was the goal of youth's search for identity and commitment, linked as it was with a shared feeling of Eros springing from such soul experiences, putting before them the "ideal type" of Wandervögel. But, as the movement entered its second decade of existence, much of this had changed. A high school student, writing a speech for a summer-solstice festival in 1914, contrasted the fervor of the movement at its inception with the staid atmosphere of his own time. At the start the Wandervögel had been distinguished by a "flaming romanticism, infinite longing and burning love"; now the soul was dead and even the folk songs had become conventional.[24] The youngster called for a revival of the ideals, but the means were not at hand.

It seems no coincidence that the cooling of the movement's earlier revolutionary ardor paralleled the increasing importance assumed by young teachers in the leadership. They attempted to quell the rebellion of the youth against the society of their elders. One such teacher asserted, in 1913, that a rebellion could not have taken place since the German soul is in complete harmony with order, that it despairs at anarchy and bursting the bounds of discipline. In the same speech he characterized Gurlitt, for his attack on school and religion, as "un-German."[25] The following year another teacher denied that the Wandervögel had ever revolted against the authoritarianism of the schools.[26] The increasingly strident note of conventional patriotism, however, had a longer past. As early as 1906, one of the Wandervögel leaders had exhorted the youth to reformulate their ideas and to direct them toward the interests of the fatherland and the state. He called upon his charges to prepare themselves emotionally and physically to take up arms and fight for their native land.[27]

But the Youth Movement had traditionally been opposed to this kind of saber-rattling patriotism. Their love for the Volk sought a cultural identity, a deepening of true love of fatherland through an understanding of the landscape and the customs and history of the Volk. To them the state was an outward, superficial manifestation of the Volk. The cult of the military, the parades, the outward trappings of what they regarded as bourgeois patriotism, they abhorred. Their allegiance to the Volk, based on a shared culture, tended to be peaceful, and they recognized the validity of other nations' peoplehood. The Youth Movement itself took two steps to reaffirm its own love of fatherland in contrast to that of the "professional and aggressive patriots." By 1913 it was able to go on record for a policy that placed the cultural expression of their allegiance to the Volk above the defense of purely state interests. In that year before the war, the German Youth Movement, meeting on the Meissner Mountain, politely rejected the saber-rattling appeal of their Austrian namesakes to join them in calling for an all-out battle against the encroaching flood of Slavs. Likewise, it dismissed as mere artificial words the exhortation by Gottfried Traub, a young former clergyman and now a member of the Pan-Germans, for youth to enroll themselves as warriors of the German Empire. The movement felt secure in taking such steps because of what it considered to be its own more profound identification with the Volk. To both appeals they replied, in effect, that the patriotism manifest in their "idealism of deeds" was more genuine than any other.[28]

Instead of adopting the state patriotism which men like Traub advocated, the movement deepened its attachment to the nation by building upon its own traditions. Hans Breuer, the principal leader just before the war, did most to propel the ideology in this direction, and with significant results. In 1913, in a famous article, he asserted that the Youth Movement was the only agency capable of restoring Germany to health. The age of science and reason which had done Germany serious injury had to be transformed into an age of culture, which under present conditions could be found only in the precepts of Germanism. Langbehn's prescription for a nation of artists found its echo here. Omitting reference to either Bismarck or Frederick the Great, Breuer cited Kant instead in his appeal for a Volkish commitment. The philosopher's principles of civic duty were read as Volkish cultural imperatives. The Volk was an organic growth basic to any society. The Wandervögel should recognize their duty and become the conscience of the Volk.[29] And this was the Wandervögel's conception of their task when they gave a cool reception to the ultra-patriotic proposals in the debates leading up to the Meissner meeting. It also formed the basis for their attitude toward Jews, and explains as well their soul-searching vacillation with respect to the humanist proposals of Gustav Wyneken.

Though the Meissner resolution of 1913 was vague in all respects, calling only for truth and responsibility, the underlying ideological currents of the Youth Movement became more explicit when faced with questions of immediate relevance. Such an opportunity arose in the framing of the policy on admitting Jews into the Wandervögel and in defining the role of the Jews relative to Germans. It was precisely in this area, in the confrontation with the Jewish question, that the Wandervögel gave expression to the Volkish substance which had underlain their ideological presumptions from the very start.

The exclusion of a Jewish girl from membership in the female branch of the Wandervögel in 1913 thrust the Jewish question into the open. This incident, however, was not the first of its kind. Rather, it served as a catalyst in opening up formal discussions of the issue after a long history of such incidents that had colored the approach of many of the Wandervögel groups. Now all of the Wandervögel chapters were compelled to formulate a definite policy. Essentially four positions were brought forward in the national and local debates that followed in the next few years. Some opted for allowing assimilated Jews to participate in the movement; another faction, vociferous and increasingly popular after 1918 and supported by the Austrians, held that Jews were racially inferior and therefore pariahs; a third point of view, endorsed by many of the leaders, favored recognizing the Jews as an autonomous and separate Volk that had merits similar to those of the German Volk; finally, a smaller group favored granting the Jews essentially unrestricted admittance.

But, however the final judgment was rendered, for the many local chapters the confrontation with the Jewish question sharpened the Wandervögel's consciousness of the Volk.

Those who would accept the assimilated Jew nevertheless regarded Jews as a whole as culturally and racially different from Germans. But they granted the possibility that the exceptional Jew might change. One writer emphasized this point when he stated that those Jews who could count several generations in the country could not be excluded *if*, in their appearance and soul, they had shed their "Jewishness." [30] Obviously, the physical qualification here shows that the Germanic criteria were very much in force. This was, indeed, far removed from the liberal idea of a German-Jewish symbiosis. In this respect the Youth Movement clearly reflected the closing of the doors on the Jew as a Jew in Germany. There remained only a slight crack through which Jews who had acclimatized and transformed themselves, who had grasped the uniqueness of the German character, its landscape and tradition, could enter to participate in the revolt of German youth.

The exception made for the Germanized Jew was, however, of some moment, for it meant that a Volkish ideology could exist without a racist outlook that automatically barred Jews from membership in the youth organization or the nation. Along with several local chapters and Wandervögel groups, the Neue Pfadfinder (New Pathfinders), a Volkish youth group established in 1920, adopted the policy of accepting assimilated Jews. Its South German branch admitted Jews on this basis. Nevertheless, it was not all that simple. As a pro-assimilationist Jewish periodical contended, the acceptance of Jews on the basis of Germanization affected "only those Jews . . . who are more Nordic than the Nordic Aryans. Secretly they are made fun of all the same." [31] Since the Neue Pfadfinder also entertained the cult of beautiful Nordic man, Jews who looked "Jewish" were not likely to be accepted. This attitude strongly indicates that the ideology was always determinant in defining the limits of toleration even among those groups that rejected total exclusion of Jews.

The idea that the Jew was racially distinguishable from the German Volk was first presented to the Wandervögel in the years before the First World War. Supported by only a small segment of the movement's leadership, the *Wandervogel Führerzeitung* discussed the Volk and the youth organization in racial terms. This paper was dominated by two of the faction's theoreticians, Friedrich Ludwig Fulda, a young teacher, and Dankwart Gerlach. Gerlach exhorted the youth to become familiar with the work and thought of the racist Lanz von Liebenfels, an intimate member of the Guido von List circle, which maintained the existence of a mystical Aryan race.[32] These racists advocated that the racially different and inferior Jews be refused membership in the Wandervögel, that their own organizations be denied equal status with the German groups, and, in fact, that the Jews be ostracized from the company of youth and the Volk. They based the correctness of their attitude on an instinctively Germanic anti-Jewish prejudice; as one writer put it: "A Jew is an impossibility at the festival of the changing sun." [33] Fulda's and Gerlach's arguments differed little from the general anti-Semitic arguments of the racist element of the Volkish movement and they need not be reiterated here. Suffice it to say, though, that at that time most of the Wandervögel rejected the extremism of their approach. By and large, the Wandervögel settled for a seemingly more harmonious coexistence which they thought would be fair to both peoples.

The third view on the Jewish question had its origins in the social thought of the founder of the Wandervögel, Karl Fischer, who conceived of the Jews as a separate but equal Volk. Consequently, he argued, they had the right and obligation to stand by their nature, heritage, and tradition—in short their peoplehood—just as the Germans did. On these terms he showed respect for the Jews—but not as Germans, as a separate Volk.[34] This point of view prevailed throughout a large section of the Youth Movement and was reflected in the more comprehensive theory which held that humanity consisted of separate Volks, each possessing unique traits.

It was this section of the Youth Movement that for a time displayed a certain sympathy with Zionism, which it recognized as the peculiar expression of the Jews' longing for their own Volk. This attitude was not unique or radical, for it enjoyed some following in Volkish circles at large. For example, Karl Bückmann, a Volkish writer, approvingly cited Martin Buber's *Three Speeches on Judaism*. For Bückmann, Buber's discourse on the Volk and blood ties was sufficient evidence that the Jewish ethos, like that of the Germans, was rooted in the Volk.[35] Within such a conceptual framework the usual anti-Semitic agitation became irrelevant, since the Jewish problem had found its logical solution in Zionism. Jews should be encouraged to draw together around their traditions and beliefs; this would naturally produce a separation of the two peoples. These views do stand in direct and sharp contrast with the low opinion of the Jews held by racial theorists such as Chamberlain. But Bückmann was not alone in his opinion and the question continued to be raised as to whether a clean break between the Germans and the Jews would not put everything in order for both.

Interestingly enough, the argument had its adherents not only among German youth but among Jewish youth as well. Among the latter, Moses Calvary, one of the Jewish Youth Movement's most able spokesmen, asserted in 1916 that Jews would indeed sever themselves from their roots if they adopted a German identity and outlook.[36] To encourage the cultivation of closer ties with the Jewish traditions, which they wanted to transform into national traits, Blau Weiss (Blue and White), the Jewish Youth Movement, was established. It was dedicated to the creation of a Jewish nation, but, singularly enough, not dissimilar to what the German Youth Movement desired for its Volk. Calvary, believing the individual to be inseparably and profoundly tied to the Volk, exhorted the Jews to learn from the German Youth Movement the ways of achieving close identity with the landscape, traditions, and beliefs of the Volk.[37] But it was the German landscape they learned to know and identify with—a development that was bound to produce conflicts within those who believed Palestine to be the proper environment for Jews. Moses Calvary drew attention to this ambivalence when he stated, in a remark to a leading Zionist, that his dreams "ripened under pine trees and not under palms." [38] Yet Calvary was a thorough Zionist, and he left Germany for Palestine in the early 1920's. Nonetheless, many Jewish youth experienced similar inner conflicts regardless of their deep Zionist faith, conflicts which arose from an identity with the real and immediate instead of a distant landscape.

Undoubtedly, certain concepts of Jewish nationhood were greatly indebted to the Germanic ideals; what was true for Buber's *Speeches* was equally valid for the Blau Weiss. One former member, reminiscing about his days in the Blau Weiss, recalled that it was the ideal of the heroic rather than Jewish confraternity that made the Jewish Youth Movement appealing to him. Moreover, the Jewish counterpart of the Wandervögel not only accepted the heroic ideal; its members were also influenced by works such as Conrad Ferdinand Meyer's *Jürg Jenatsch* and even Schulze-Naumburg's works on Nordic beauty.[39] Organizationally the group constituted itself as an *Orden*, a *Bund*, and replaced its earlier ideas of democracy with the "more efficient and natural" concepts of leadership. Thus, this important movement of Jewish youth, attempting to evolve a deep-seated Zionist identity, assimilated certain aspects of the ideology of the German Youth Movement into its theoretical framework. Here we have another instance of German-Jewish symbiosis, but the Zionist solution was rejected by the vast assimilationist liberal Jewish majority.

Admittance without regard to race or creed was the official attitude of the Wandervögel. This policy, however, was supported by only the more liberal faction of the national leadership and a small percentage of the local chapters. The integrationists first presented their arguments in 1916 in a debate on the Jewish question that was carried on in the organ of the Freideutsche Jugend, the university organization which united all former Wandervögel. All points of view received a hearing. Articles opposing anti-Semitism were printed alongside a reprint of Lagarde's views and articles which attacked Jews. In this debate the position of the liberals took shape, especially in the articles of the movement's highly respected Knud Alhorn. He asserted that a healthy and well-run organization with a Volkish emphasis could best be secured by the maintenance of strict standards of selection within the individual groups. These standards were to be defined by the needs of the group and judged by how well they performed; not through the indiscriminate application of racial criteria. Accordingly, these practical standards would be able to provide the best guarantees against infiltration by foreign and divisive influences.[40] Alhorn's argument, in the end, became the basis for the leadership's refusal to demand the outright exclusion of Jews.

Ample evidence exists to show that this debate was essentially a review of decisions which had been implemented locally throughout the early years of the Wandervögel—decisions which were to pursue their set course in the future. Within the individual chapters the picture was not very bright. In fact, according to an inquiry made in 1913-14, 92 per cent of the local chapters reported no Jewish members. Even more revealing was the fact that 84 per cent had specifically adopted resolutions excluding Jews from membership.[41] In the light of this, the leaders' decision not to prevent Jewish membership had little meaning, since they also refused to interfere in the affairs of the local groups.[42] And these local groups, whatever their basis for discrimination—race, autonomy for different Volk identities, or assimilation—set the pattern for future development. Meanwhile, the pressure from the racist-oriented Austrian Youth Movement had steadily increased. The Austrian organization had officially adopted the Aryan paragraph (admitting Aryans only) as early as 1911, and even as late as 1918 they castigated their German brothers for having "foreign blood in their midst." [43]

As the basic Volkish tendencies were reflected in the resolutions of the Jewish question, so they also found expression in the refusal by the Wandervögel to rewrite their ideological creed in a humanist direction. The rebuff received by Gustav Wyneken in his attempt to influence the movement is significant in that it exemplified the integrity of the movement's Volkish roots. After breaking with Lietz and founding his own school at Wickersdorf, Wyneken became interested in the Youth Movement through reading Blüher's books. He believed that his own ideas essentially paralleled those of the youth and that where there were differences they could be resolved in his favor. He too entertained the concept of Eros, of male companionship expressing itself culturally and creatively, and held that the only means of regaining an authentic culture was to break with the contemporary mechanization of life and return to an emphasis on nature.[44] Here the similarity between Wyneken and the movement ceased, for Wyneken had in mind different goals—and different means.

Wyneken spoke at the Meissner meeting. He carefully avoided the blatantly patriotic exhortations employed by other speakers, but, and more significantly, he also rejected the context of the Volk as a frame of reference for deeds, values, and guidance. Calling upon the German youth to refrain from commiting themselves to either nation or Volk, he presented them with a different alternative. He asked them instead to keep their eyes and ideals focused on the concept of freedom, the highest of human values. Freedom, however, was meant here as freedom in an individualistic sense: the development of each person's individuality toward the highest plane of creativity that the human spirit could attain and that the absolute spirit made available.[45] Wyneken thus presented a Hegelian alternative to the ideology of the Volk, an alternative that rejected the Volk not only on its own terms but also as the repository of the *Geist*. As a Hegelian, Wyneken saw the *Geist*, both human and absolute, in terms of a never-ending development, furthered through a critical spirit (a point over which he had broken with Lietz) and a creative and artistic education. The movement of a collectivity of individuals toward higher aspirations would develop an ever more profound sense of community in which absolute values and not narrow patriotic considerations centering on the Volk would play central roles.[46]

In his effort to draw the youth into his own ideological camp, Wyneken aligned himself with the editorial policies of the gymnasium student newspaper *Der Anfang (The Beginning)*. Here he found like-minded youth who agreed on the humanist direction and on discarding the Volkish frame of reference. In its pages, the critic Walter Benjamin, who later in his life moved closer to a Marxist position, called upon youth, under the pseudonym Ardor, to view the present critically and engage themselves in creating a culture commensurate with future needs.[47] Wyneken and the students further supported the development of a truly free community in which Eros could emerge out of the confining darkness. The pages of *Der Anfang* were filled with views reminiscent of the rebellious and idealistic attitude of the early Youth Movement while they also reflected a Nietzschean influence in articles that stressed human effort, will, and aspirations beyond supernatural and irrational forces. In combining Hegelian and Nietzschean ideas, and in pieces like Otto Braun's poem "Why Should There Be Gods?" the paper reflected an emphasis on the heroic and willful in man.[48] To a certain degree, these themes were shared by the Wandervögel, but among them they were employed in a different service: in the interest of the Volk, not merely of the individual.

Wyneken and the staff of Der Anfang differed with the Youth Movement in another important area—the role of art in expressing the human spirit. Whereas the Youth Movement idealized their stereotypes of the Nordic man, Der Anfang welcomed Expressionism from the very start and favorably contrasted it with the crude colors and vulgarity of the Youth Movement's "primitives," as they referred to Volkish art.[49] Art for Wyneken and Der Anfang was subject to the Hegelian idea of a necessary development which must not be blocked by tradition-bound concepts. For Wyneken, Fidus and his saccharine, sentimental art spoiled the artistic sensibilities of youth. Even the rejection of realism inherent in Fidus' and the rest of Volkish art, and the mystical attempt to express nature's soul, did not satisfy Wyneken. Consequently, he argued, not the existing Youth Movement, but a reformed one could be linked out of inner necessity with the revolutionary ethos of Expressionism.[50]

But it was not to be. Regardless of the revolutionary appeal, the depiction of the ideal landscape and not the portrayal of the Expressionist search for the essence and chaos of soul, was the ultimate goal of the Youth Movement.[51] Wyneken had linked his affinity for Expressionism with his hopes for the movement. He appealed to youth on the basis of a truly revolutionary dynamic. He demanded that youth align itself in support of a freely developing "living community" that was beyond the Volk and that it pursue individual development through spiritual affinity with the Geist, which, as a force beyond nature, pointed to growth in uncharted seas. Wyneken summed up his ideas in the slogan "Youth for itself alone," symbolizing the rejection of bourgeois traditions, parents, and school for the free development of the unfettered Geist of youth.[52]

At first the movement reacted favorably to his message, but ultimately it rejected it. Several factors accounted for the initially favorable reception of his ideas. There was, first of all, his own charismatic quality. In addition, the movement was eager to retrieve its antibourgeois origins, as reflected in its vacillation over whether or not to endorse Expressionism. Wyneken's emphasis on the revolutionary aspects of the new art form and the freshness of the style itself did sink into the aesthetic consciousness of the nation. It is interesting to note that after the First World War extreme racists—such as the Geusen, a youth group—regarded Expressionism as a religious experience that penetrated to the depths of the soul.[53] Furthermore, in the 1920's the Volkish movement's emphasis on the mysticism of the soul seemed to provide a congenial climate for Expressionism, while the Nazis, both before and after attaining power, flirted with the idea of endorsing Expressionism as a valid means of depicting the "essence" of Germanic subjects—until Hitler summarily declared that the only authentic art was that based on the Volkish tradition.

The attraction that Expressionism exerted on the Volkish movement was based upon a misunderstanding. The attempt to plumb the depths of the soul seemed to link them together. But that which divided them proved to be more important. Volkish thought could not accept the chaotic individualism which characterized so much of Expressionist art and literature. The soul was tamed and integrated into the Volk. No wonder that Volkish thought only "flirted" with Expressionism, that it always ended up by rejecting it, just as the Youth Movement had rejected Wyneken's dynamic world view which seemed to be beyond the Volk's control.

Wyneken, however, did not fully succumb when the Wandervögel leadership broke off relations in 1914. In 1918 he thought his day had come. In that year he entered the Prussian Ministry of Education as an adviser. He made an attempt to reform the school system and thereby influence the sensibilities of the youth through a series of executive orders which gave students a major voice in the administration of the schools. His most important orders were directed against compulsory religious instruction and called for the creation of school forums where students and teachers could discuss educational problems as equals. Both directives raised a storm of protest, especially among the teachers, and their opposition was instrumental in his dismissal from his post. Looking for support, he appealed to the Freideutsche Jugend. But once more he was repudiated by the Youth Movement. Misfortune now dogged his steps. Charged with sexual offenses against his students, he faced trial (at which, singularly enough, among many others, Eugen Diederichs came to his defense), was found guilty, and left public life altogether.[54] Ironically, Wyneken, who had concentrated upon developing his native land, was finally appreciated in the newly constituted Soviet Union, where his work was studied and commented upon. Now, some thirty-seven years later, Wyneken, in looking back on the events and tracing them through recent history, holds conclusions similar to ours. In retrospect, he sees his failure in terms of the triumph of

Volkish ideas. Indeed, the ideals of Hermann Lietz, who had dismissed the young Wyneken for differing with him, had triumphed.[55] They proved to be closer to the mainstream of the ideology of the youth than the revolutionary concepts of Wyneken.

This is not surprising. Two thirds of those involved in the Youth Movement came from a middle-class background, at the very least, and the interests of such youth had always been channeled toward national concerns. Throughout the First World War, the youth had wholeheartedly supported the struggle led and rationalized by their elders, whom they had tried to repudiate two decades earlier. Then they failed to rally to the revolution that ushered in prospects of democracy. As one high school student explained to Wyneken, they were merely boys, unfamiliar with freedom, its responsibilities and its application, and therefore unreceptive to his ideas.[56] The older bourgeois youth were outrightly hostile. Like the Volkish movement, these youths did want a revolution, but one oriented toward roots and Germanism, not toward the upheaval of the existing order, not even toward the uncharted seas of the human spirit. They wanted to end their alienation by finding roots, not through a flight forward such as Wyneken advocated.

In short then, the Youth Movement was a bourgeois phenomenon that could not discard its class interests and fears.[57] Though the youth rebelled, theirs was a futile attempt to cast off their essential limitations. Their achievements in the cultural field amounted to only a minor victory that did not alter the alignment of political or economic forces. Their radical turn toward the right only reinforced their anti-modernist position, and in the particular juncture of events and circumstances that made up the Weimar Republic, it placed them in the camp of anti-democratic thought. Thus it is erroneous to absolve the Youth Movement of all and every guilt for the Nazi catastrophe. This has been done, however, by historians who have essentially exonerated the movement. Yet hundreds of thousands of youngsters passed through the Youth Movement, and many of them found it not very difficult to accommodate themselves to the ideological propositions of the Nazis. Their youthful experience, it seems, had not accustomed them to a form of government which was incompatible with the new faith.

That is not to say that the officials of the Wandervögel were on amicable terms with the Nazis, at least not during the 1920's. In fact, during the years of the Republic, most members of the Youth Movement were openly hostile toward National Socialism. The majority of the Wandervögel did not share the racism of the Nazi youth, and the National Socialists, once they geared their drive for power and mass support, frowned upon the *Bund* concept and its Eros and exclusiveness.[58]

Whatever its later relations with National Socialism, there can be little doubt of the Youth Movement's Volkish orientation of thought, which was combined with a rejection of the parliamentary process. Indeed, the youth looked beyond bourgeois representative government, which they considered artificial and lacking the genuineness that their own movement supposedly possessed. Whole generations of German youth regarded the *Bund* of males as a genuine form of political and social organization, in tune with their New Romanticism and Germanic faith, and held the parliamentary process in utter contempt. This was an ominous sign for the Republic and its institutions. For the Volkish movement, however, the ideas were familiar and welcome.

The picture we have sketched of the influence of the Volkish ideology on German youth is significant. Teachers, high school students, school reformers, and the Youth Movement institutionalized the New Romanticism and directed it at a most vulnerable target. Whole generations thought that reidentification with the Volk as expressed in the Germanic ideology was the solution to the German crisis. Now the further question arises as to how the older, the immediate generation of the war and postwar eras received the same ideological outlook. What of the university students and professors? Did they, as custodians of a long humanist tradition, remain immune to the historical trends we have described so far?

CHAPTER 10

University Students and Professors on the March

WHILE A PERCENTAGE of the students involved in the Youth Movement continued on to higher education in the universities, they were unable to effectively transmit their ideology. The atmosphere was unreceptive; it had a tradition of its own. The differences in outlook and goals between the former members of the Youth Movement and the rest of the students also seemed to protrude more forcefully, and the Youth Movement's ideology was ably contested by the existing fraternities, corps (another kind of fraternity system), and similar university organizations. The variances between the two finally reached a point of polarization where the Youth Movement's influence exerted itself in a liberal direction while the established organizations defined themselves more conservatively. On the university scene, the former members of the Youth Movement were confronted with institutions which seemed to have fossilized. But the movement had, from the beginning, fought against existing institutions because they seemed unresponsive to the deeper longings of the Volk. The Youth Movement was liberal in this context, because it wanted reforms which would abolish such conservative strongholds as the fraternities. Moreover, they were used to the endless discussions within the movement, and demanded the abolition of all restrictions on the free exchange of ideas. This did not mean the abolition of their own basic attitudes, which we have discussed in the previous chapter, but the opportunity to debate them freely.

Generally speaking, the older university organizations were able to parry the challenge of the youthful, romantic, and rebellious intruders. They effectively limited the functioning of the Deutsche Akademische Freischaar, founded in 1907 by Knud Alhorn, and of

the Akademische Vereinigung, founded in 1912 by former members
of the Youth Movement.[1] And though the ideals of the Youth Movement attracted some support, especially after it instituted a free exchange of ideas and open discussions, neither the Wandervögel's
attempt to penetrate the existing order nor the post-1913 effort by
the Free German Youth, the Wandervögel's university organization,
was really successful. The competition was too rough and the challenge to greater liberal action found an unfavorable reception, because it was untimely, because it was followed up in a halfhearted
manner, and, above all, because many university students considered themselves in possession of a more effective, direct, and un-
equivocal Volkish identity.

The history of the university students' development of Volkish
consciousness is clear, though uneven. In the early years of the past
century, the students were among the first to perceive that the country was disunited, preyed upon by overzealous foreign influences,
and in sore need of committed and dedicated nationalistic leadership.
They beheld their true mentor in Father Jahn and followed him in
celebrating the Wartburg Festival, and even in the burning of un-
Germanic books. The uniting factors of the *Turnerschaften* (gymnastic organizations), the *Burschenschaften* (fraternities), the uniforms,
the Germanic exclusiveness of the organizations—all combined with
the growing sense of romanticism and the Volk ideal to launch the
students on a radical turning to the right.

During the 1840's, this movement toward the right received a temporary setback. Under a reactionary regime that failed to fulfil any
of the students' national aspirations and actually hindered progress
in the direction of unification and national strength, a majority of the
students became receptive to democratic ideas, combined as they
were in 1848 with advocacy of German unity. Many of them became
outspoken leaders in the Revolution of 1848. In addition, there was,
however, an over-all relaxation of tensions as reflected in the admission of Jews into fraternities and the greater freedom of intellectual
intercourse. On the whole, the students became more broad-minded
and the enthusiasm aroused by the Revolution of 1848 remained with
some of them despite the betrayal of the cause and the subsequent
reaction that took control. During the next three decades, new
forces, vital and politically successful, commanded the allegiance of
a new body of students disillusioned with the ineptitude of the older
liberals.[2] German unification and control of its own politics, internal
and external, had been gained through the efforts of a few men; and
only an army acting on Bismarck's orders had accomplished the feat.
Now it was for the students, as well as other forces, to provide the

framework for the true interests of the German people which would bring about a new change, this time for the benefit of the whole Volk, not merely the state.

Their minds devoted to the new order, their hearts and souls committed to the Volk, the generations of students attending universities in the 1880's had resumed the radical movement toward the right. The reason for this reversion lies partly in the disillusionment with the 1848 liberals who had not accomplished the task of unity. But the equally strong disillusionment with the newly found unity was also of the greatest importance. The students now looked to Volkish thought, which advocated true unity as a solution to Germany's problems. We have seen earlier how such attitudes informed the whole Volkish movement; now they began to influence the students as well. By 1881, one student could write that "experienced politicians are surprised by the change in the new generation; 1848 is already a mere legend." [3] Students had not remained immune to the events of the day, which were producing a turmoil of aspirations and complaints in the contemporary literature and among groups with growing influence and increasingly vocal spokesmen. Lagarde and Langbehn gave them fresh inspiration and new goals; Diederichs provided the idealism and a revitalized romanticism; while writers from Freytag to Chamberlain provided the vision of the enemy in his multiple forms.

Here, then, in the universities, among students and teachers alike, the spearhead for the more radical profession of Volkish longings took shape. The development was not surprising, in view of the students' class background and aspirations. Around 90 per cent of the students came from the bourgeois class, a group whose youth was most anxious to support the Germanic ideology and who saw in it a solution to the crisis which beset Germany as well as a vehicle for attaining a meaningful identification with the nation. They saw this crisis in their own, personal terms. For these students were in competition with the scions of the nobility, especially with those of Prussia, for the prestigious and influential posts in government and civil service, as well as for the top positions in commerce and industry. Here, in the field of private enterprise, the bourgeois students met double competition. There were a substantial number of industries and commercial enterprises controlled by the newly rich and the aristocracy and in addition a number that had come under Jewish ownership. In their competition with the Jews, which was of course considered easier, they descended to the level of using anti-Semitism to achieve their ends.

On the whole then, the university youth saw itself in a fight to preserve and enhance its economic position and to acquire the means of establishing the criteria of social and political power and mobility. There were, of course, more direct stimuli for action against a frustration which this youth identified with modernity. Here, the *bon mot* among students that "a few more semesters and we shall be unemployed" was fully warranted. Any student who aspired to an intellectual position stood a good chance of joining the ranks of the intellectual proletariat, thus sharing Langbehn's fate. Academic advancement was slow and a whole generation of aspiring university professors spent their time teaching high school students. It was highly frustrating, and the Volkish framework seemed to provide the appropriate outlet.

An instructive comparison can be made with the youth of other nations. In France, for example, the young people rallied to the cause of the left, whether it was in the social, economic, or political realm. They championed their cause in class terms, not in those of a Volkish nationalism. The contrary was true in Germany; here Volkish nationalism defined the issues. National concerns were uppermost and with them came an ideology which advocated a revolutionary dynamic that was tied to the Volk. Its triumph would create the good society automatically; details were not spelled out. Only the strength and penetration of the Germanic ideology as it had developed from the start of the century can account for this difference between Germany and France. In Germany, the early nineteenth century had seen the first wave of the students' radical turn to the right, a wave that swelled to major proportions in the 1880's and 1890's and reached its crest in the postwar years of the twentieth century. Bourgeois youth was lost to the Weimar Republic even before the Republic got properly started. This is a fact worth pondering by those who still believe that National Socialism was a mere accident of history.

One of the first concerted efforts on the part of the youth to move in a Volkish direction was the founding of the Verein Deutscher Studenten–Kyffhäuser Bund (Association of German Students) in 1881. This organization, marching hand in hand with the university fraternities and the corps, played an important part in subsequent developments. Their banners were inscribed with the ideals of the Volk and their members consecrated themselves to the fight against materialism and liberalism and against the Jews, who spread the spirit of rationalism.[4] Both the young Friedrich Naumann and the elder Stöcker were instrumental in getting the organization started and involved in immediate issues. Stöcker addressed the initial convocation of a thousand students in Leipzig.[5] Both, however, had miscalculated the essential impetus underlying the youth's desire to join. Whereas

Stöcker and Naumann had envisioned both a pro-Protestant and Volkish ethos for the organization, shortly after it was established the organization perceptibly gravitated in a more exclusive Germanic direction. The Volkish momentum gained the upper hand and the Protestant orthodoxy was soon discarded and largely replaced by Germanic Christianity. The general Volkish aspirations also fused with a mystical outlook, and this was reflected in the emblem of the organization, which showed a young man stretching his arms from the earth upward to heaven. This symbolized man; man as he was rooted in the soil with the power of his will linking him to the cosmos.[6]

Along with the fraternities, the Verein placed its Volkish aspirations in an anti-Jewish framework. For them anti-Semitism in its various forms provided them with the weapons to combat the enemy "within" the nation and at the same time objectified the foe in the form of different, racially inferior people. A unique view of this interlocking theme is found in a play performed by the Verein in 1889. This depicted the rejuvenation of the German nation and the expulsion of her enemies. A character in the play is a Polish Jew who is revealed as Ahasuerus, the eternal Jew, who narrates the rise and fall of many peoples and prophesies the eventual decline of Germany. But Ahasuerus is proven wrong in his hasty forecast and expelled from Germany to wander the desert, rootless, nomadic—the historical fate of Jews. The play ended with a *tableau vivant* which depicted the power of "Young Germany" as the wave of the future.[7]

Anti-Semitism was strong and central to the Verein and the fraternities. In fact, the impetus for a program of anti-Jewish prejudice, as in petitions, ostracizing of fellow Jewish students, and even violent expressions of hate, was provided by student organizations. They kept the issues alive for ideological reasons long after Stöcker and Böckel had lost their popular support. And though under the National Socialists the Verein was to criticize its earlier years as lacking the correct and proper amount of anti-Semitic feeling, the *mea culpa* seems quite unwarranted.[8] On the contrary, the Verein had been zealous in implementing its beliefs. From the very first, it exhorted fraternities to adopt similarly strict measures against Jews and to make anti-Semitism an integral part of their programs.[9]

The fraternities also should have been among the last to be criticized for slackness. Though exclusion of Jews had not been a central point of discussion at the fraternity conventions of 1882 and 1886, the decade witnessed the admission of singularly few Jews to membership. Austrian German fraternities, who were in close contact with their German counterparts, had acted more quickly in refusing to pledge Jews. And their action there was to affect the subsequent history of anti-Semitic measures in Germany. They provided the impetus for a more accelerated program, though their singular role should not be exaggerated, both north and south, since the soil was fertile for the seeds of anti-Semitism.[10]

However, it will be instructive to take a brief glance at this southern neighbor of Germany. There the racial outlook assumed greater proportions and significance in the light of the minority status held by the Germans. Of the population of Austria-Hungary, the Germans constituted only a small percentage, with Slavs, Magyars, and other Central European peoples comprising the majority. Even the Jews made up a sizable portion of the population, especially in Vienna, where there were more Eastern European immigrants than in all of Germany. Vienna, Guido von List's "Holy City" and the place where Hitler first received his anti-Jewish impressions, together with Linz, Hitler's birthplace, stood in the center of the strife—with Linz, perhaps accidentally, chosen as the location where fraternities met to pass their racist and Germanic resolutions.

The role played by Stöcker in Germany was performed in Austria by Georg Ritter von Schönerer. He also applied himself to student affairs and drove them in a Volkish direction. Prior to the 1870's, Austrian universities had been relatively free of anti-Semitism, but this tranquillity was shattered by 1889, when the fraternities adopted the Aryan paragraph as a criterion for membership.[11] The move had other ramifications as the racial attitude spread and engulfed the whole gamut of student relationships. Near the end of the century, when the question was posed whether a Jew could render satisfaction in dueling, many students contended that the Jew could not be a partner in a duel since he had no honor to defend. Though it might seem absurd and insignificant in our own day, at that time dueling was a major symbol of status and those who could not engage in it found themselves excluded from the proper society. The fact that in 1896 the general assembly of Austrian fraternities at Waidhof officially endorsed the view forbidding Jews the honor of challenge is startling proof of the extent to which the anti-Semitic stereotype had penetrated the social elite among Austrian German students.[12] Yet the actual application of the Waidhofer resolution was slow, for by 1914 it had been accepted completely by only 29 out of 44 fraternities.[13] But P. G. J. Pulzer is correct when he states that for many of the young Austrians of the 1930's Nazism seemed merely a logical application of the slogans which their fathers had been mouthing since their fraternity days.[14] Much the same would hold true for Germany.

The Austrian pace, once started, was duplicated in Germany during the 1890's. By 1894, Jews had been so effectively barred from fraternities that at the general convention of the university organizations they were no longer counted as constituent members.[15] Yet the exclusion in Germany differed from that in Austria in one respect: while the south applied its restrictions even in the case of baptized Jews, the north still allowed Jewish converts to Christianity into its ranks. This clemency, however, was of short duration. In 1919 the German fraternities subscribed to the Eisenach Resolution, whose racist basis decreed that baptism and spiritual conversion could not mitigate the inherited racial divisions. Then, in 1920, the German fraternities also denied the Jew the honor of dueling.[16] It was not long thereafter that the fraternities could pride themselves on being *Judenrein*, and the corps followed suit.

In Germany the students were not content with setting their own house in order; they wanted to do the same for the nation as a whole; they wanted to take up the Volkish revolution. Not to be outdone by the anti-Semites of the Volkish movement, in 1880 they drew up a supplementary petition to the Anti-Semitic Petition which had gathered 290,000 signatures in support of excluding Jews from government jobs, public life, and the professions. The role of the students was the more insidious in that it was conducted under the banner of impartiality and objectivity. They declared themselves better judges of the Jewish question since they had no axes to grind and no economic competitors to eliminate, or, as they put it, they had no special interests and "jealousy of Jewish competition [did] not apply to us." [17] Surely this was a strange claim considering the close competition waged by the bourgeoisie for professional posts and economic advancement in all areas. The success of the student petition was especially great in northern Germany, where, relative to the population, it gathered a large number of signatures—400 in Göttingen alone.[18]

Liberal students, of course, contested the propriety of these petitions and circulated their own disclaimers. Their petition, asking for no favored treatment of Jews and calling for moderation on the issues, did less well in Göttingen, finishing with 180 signatures. But it is typical that even these liberal students (as they called themselves), opposing the Anti-Semitic Petition, denounced "pushy" Jewish students who demonstrated the Jewish question "ad oculos." Moreover, they conceded the existence of racial differences between the Jews and themselves.[19] Can there be a clearer indication of the deep penetration of the Volkish ideology among students?

Manifestations of anti-Semitic feeling increased with the years.

From 1907 onward, *Die Mitteilungsblätter,* the chief Jewish journal devoted to fighting anti-Semitism, became increasingly concerned with student affairs. There was much to report. For example, in 1907, when Walter Kohler, the distinguished legal theorist, suggested his class read the commentary by Willamovsky and Levy, both Jews, he was greeted with derisive remarks from the students. When, annoyed by the response, he mentioned that Levy had been murdered, the students broke into thunderous applause.[20] By the 1920's, this spirit had bloomed into an antagonism that transcended the bounds of schoolroom differences. It had been enlisted in the service of the national crisis. In 1922 the threat of a student riot carried enough force to compel the University of Berlin to cancel its proposed memorial service for the murdered Walther Rathenau.[21] Were these sporadic and isolated events that had no thread of development? The Jewish reaction to the measures taken by Gentiles documents the seriousness of the situation.

From the beginning, Jews reacted to their exclusion from Gentile fraternities by founding their own organizations. The first was established in 1886 at the University of Breslau. Its appeal for membership read like an indictment, and its validity persisted into the twentieth century. The Jewish students eloquently stated: "Depressed by the prevailing conditions [at the University], embittered by the fanatical hatred of the adversary, all those [Jews] who still have a feeling of independence and personal honor have retired from student life. In their isolation they despair of improving conditions." [22] It was a moving document, mirroring the feeling of what Theodor Lessing, fifty years later, called a helpless minority delivered to the hatred of the majority. Though under the Nazis their despair was final, under the previous regimes it was just as intense and tragic. The Jewish fraternity was a reply to the despair felt in the universities and in academic circles; it was an attempt to accommodate to the prevailing attitudes and to work hopefully for the better. For, as a community of men at once German and Jewish, it aspired to symbolize the fact that union, after all, was possible with a little toleration and effort.

Their path, however, was beset with difficulties. Socially the Jewish fraternities were ostracized, denied the satisfaction of defending their honor in dueling, and omitted from formal or informal gatherings of the rest of the university community. Moreover, the university administrations repeatedly dissolved the Jewish organizations. By 1901 the faculty of the University of Heidelberg decreed that "the very existence of a Jewish fraternity is sufficient to endanger peace among the students." Though this was a faculty decision, it was the students themselves who pressured for such restrictions.[23] The Jewish fraternities, however, persevered and eventually, approximately twenty-five years after their inception, attained official recognition. But the prolonged struggle should be sufficient to prove the difficulty of a German-Jewish symbiosis among students.

The first decade and a half of the twentieth century saw a general relaxation of tensions in Germany as a whole. Yet this did not indicate a progressive step, as at the same time the social isolation of Jews became increasingly effective. For example, the Kyffhäuser Bund stated in 1910 that while the Jewish question seemed to have receded into the background, socially directed anti-Semitism was by now the common property of all academic circles.[24] On the whole, anti-Semitic feelings, especially those emanating from the Volkish section, were intellectualized and transferred to elitist frameworks for implementation. Jewish fraternities, however, were eventually recognized and between 1904 and 1918 an increasing number of Jewish fraternities were able to find dueling partners.[25] That this was an expression of toleration, even of acceptance, is undeniable. But it was acceptance on a segregationist basis. In other words, it signified the "clean separation" between Jews and Germans which had long been a Volkish ideal. It was, by no means, an acceptance of a German-Jewish symbiosis.

The favorable trend was abruptly ended after 1918, when the war and the resulting defeat once more produced a deep crisis. The students especially suffered under the stigma of defeat, and, as was indicated by the Rathenau affair at the University of Berlin, they found an appropriate means of expression. In the face of this serious and growing antagonism, sections of the intellectual community launched idealistic ventures to bridge the gap. The Reform Fraternity Movement repudiated anti-Semitism and engaged in halfhearted efforts to bring Jews and Gentiles together. The Freie Wissenschaftliche Vereinigung (Independent Academic Association), founded on the principle of parity between Jew and non-Jew, attempted to bring students of Jewish and German descent into closer relationships with each other. But it was doomed, as the organization became predominantly Jewish.[26]

At this point it may be instructive to turn to an analysis of the different degrees of intensity of student anti-Semitism under the monarchy and the Republic respectively. It must be remembered that under both forms of government, at least among students, anti-Semitism was the most direct expression of Volkish beliefs. For the younger generation, bent on acting in the cause of the Volk, the Jew presented the perfect foil. In line with their bourgeois sensibilities, these students shied away from socialist ideas. They were not going to wage a struggle against the Wilhelmine state, nor were they honest enough to follow their emotions and join the Youth Movement in the university in the revolt against the bourgeois style of life. And though they sincerely believed the Volk to be an institution above the state, yet, because of their opposition to popular democracy, they could hardly be expected to attack the Emperor—whom, in any case, they believed to be in their own camp. But the Volkish revolution remained in the forefront of possibilities—not, to be sure, under the monarchy, but during the hapless attempts at democracy under the Weimar regime. Consequently, frustrated under the monarchy, the Volkish movement, student and non-student, concentrated on the Jew, a concentration which was continued under the Republic, where it met with greater success. Under democratic rule, a complete turn to the right as well as in a Volkish direction became possible. The regime, more liberal in nature, permitted a great range of opposition, and all sorts of Volkish, anti-republican agitation retained a mantle of respectability. Yet, even here, where discontent could be resolved in a true social revolution, the students kept their Volkish identity and supported agitation against a regime that, to them, symbolized Jewish control.

The revolt against the Jews rather than against social injustices or economic and political forces was an element in the Volkish thinking which Adolf Hitler was to exploit to the fullest. As a sham revolution, it promised much; above all, it precluded a genuine social upheaval. Thus the Jews were crucial foils. In this context the Volkish movement was bound to become popular: smash the Jewish conspiracy and the Volk will bloom forth unhindered. In fact, the elimination of Jews would be accepted as a deed of liberation. Hitler plumbed all possibilities, and with devoted, pliable, and acquiescent accomplices even carried out the "anti-Jewish revolution" beyond the belief of those who accepted his promises in *Mein Kampf* at face value.

While the students can be called into account as instigators of many Volkish policies at the universities, they were not alone. The faculty also played its part. In Germany professors tended to be either scholars who withdrew into their own specialty, taking scant notice of the world around them, or men who attempted to play the role of prophets. The first kind of academic wanted only to be left in peace and could hardly be expected to defend freedom or to take stands on issues of the day. The professor as prophet, with very few exceptions indeed, was to be found on the side of the nationalists. After all, they were state employees who had to be confirmed directly by the government. Like the schoolteachers, they almost naturally drifted into the Volkish camp.

For many, the public image of the professor was set by the historian Heinrich von Treitschke, professor at the University of Berlin, who used the lecture platform for patriotic purposes. He was active prior to unification, but his influence was especially notable during the years after unity had been achieved. It reached its climax in the last decades of the century—precisely the years which witnessed the developments among the students which have been our concern. Standing before packed audiences, Treitschke eloquently proclaimed his faith in a Germanic morality and his deep feeling for the Volk. A note of militancy pervaded his lectures, as if he were attempting to transcend his deafness and in his lectures accomplish the feats of courage that were denied him on the battlefield. And, typically enough, he too turned to the Jewish question to resolve certain problems in Germany's history and in current developments.

Treitschke's article "A Word about Our Jews" (1879) placed his prestige at the disposal of the anti-Semitic movement at large. He also recognized the existence of the problem and thought it of considerable importance, especially as Germany was newly unified, a young nation; it needed a consensus of total support and was searching for its own self-consciousness. There was an ambivalence in his work on the Jewish problem which derived from his national considerations as well as his rejection of the total racial context. Like Gustav Freytag, he favored the possibility of assimilating the Jews. He believed that native German Jews, at least the best and most willing among them, could become Germans in the full sense of the word if they discarded their "Jewishness" completely. However, there were dangers inherent in this solution. For, if assimilation should fail, it would produce a bastard German-Jewish culture that would destroy the purity of the thousand-year Germanic heritage.[27]

Germany could not afford such a setback; the Jews should recognize that, said Treitschke, Germany was a young nation, emerging from years of weakness, just beginning to exercise its strength. And it was searching for national self-awareness. If, then, in this complicated and delicate development some Jew should be injured or his beliefs restricted, it was all part of the risks one should expect when residing in a vitally changing state. Youth knows no restrictions; it must try things out and adapt itself to the new reality. Treitschke's was a vital "idealism" that found influential spokesmen and became a popular point of view. Eugen Diederichs was to restate it and the conservative theorist Möller van den Bruck picked up the thread in contrasting young Germany with the old nations, the vigor and "expansiveness" of youth with the decline and "shrinking" of old age.[28] All of them, Treitschke, Diederichs, and van den Bruck, believing in the youth and vigor of Germany and trusting that the Volk had finally begun to assert itself, cried woe to the stranger in their midst.

Treitschke's advocacy of the possibility of the German-Jewish symbiosis became more halfhearted as the times changed and he lost his faith in the ability of the Jew, even if he so desired, to discard all of his heritage. In this regression he reflected the progressive increase all around him of an ingrained anti-Semitism. Historical, religious, and anthropological studies had helped him formulate these new doubts. Contradicting his earlier statements, Treitschke remarked that assimilation could go only as far as religion, tradition, and tribal nature would allow. But how much would they allow? Treitschke equivocated. Sometimes he would favorably contrast the German Jew, who could become a German, with the undesirable alien Jew of Eastern Europe. At other times, such as in his *History of Germany in the Nineteenth Century*, he would even attack the Germanized Jew, as when he criticized the novelist Berthold Auerbach for creating "phony" peasants who, in reality, were "disguised Jews," asserting that the author's "Jewishness" prevented a genuine empathy with German peasantry.[29] Compared with the anti-Semitism of Böckel or even that of the students, Treitschke's antagonism toward the Jews was neither racial nor all-inclusive. He refrained from condemning all of Jewry as the enemy of Germanism and, at times, even deplored the effort wasted on anti-Semitic action when it could have been better employed in pressing the direct cause of the Volk.

Treitschke's modified anti-Semitism was only one indication of his adherence to Volkish views. He also looked back to the earlier Germans with a nostalgia for their ordered social and economic life. These olden days had been times of rootedness, when the nation, composed of craftsmen and nobles, warriors and tillers of the soil, enjoyed its labors and prospered under the benefits of a settled hierarchy. Modern urbanism had destroyed the harmony of this Germanic heritage. Modernity, unless stopped, would continue on its course of destruction. Here again he brought in the Jew and accused him of ruining thousands of German villages and farms through usury and the introduction of modernity.[30]

Treitschke's intellectual contribution was of great value to the cause of the Volk. Here his *History of Germany in the Nineteenth Century* assumed special significance. The work successfully linked literature, art, and politics and presented itself, quite rightly, as a pioneering work in cultural history. But not only did the work argue for a unique culture and nationality (in that it implicitly compared German cultural development to a many-branched tree which rooted all events in a common and basic ideology); [31] it also provided a full synthesis from the point of view of the Volk. Indeed, in Treitschke's hands, cultural history purposefully deepened the ethos of the Volk.

Not all professors agreed with Treitschke and what he stood for. The great historian of Rome, Theodor Mommsen, and the famous surgeon Rudolf Virchow, castigated him for his nationalistic views. Both men were liberals in whom the spirit of 1848 lived on. They were of an earlier generation than the students. Our analysis does not deny the obvious, that there were liberal students as well as men such as Mommsen and Virchow. But the point is that they were in the minority. And they became a still smaller minority as, from the 1880's on, the faculties did little or nothing to discourage the growing wave of anti-Semitism.

Faculty attitudes can easily be explained; they are not very mysterious and should be apparent to all, even today. Academicians rarely oppose the regime in power; in Germany they were directly connected with it, and consequently tended to support the *status quo*. And here we come to the most often invoked reason for their behavior; faculties desire only peace and quiet to conduct their "impartial" researches. This attitude was in evidence before the First World War and found its culmination under the Nazi regime. When, as one of the first official invasions of the academic preserve, the National Socialist government of Thuringia forced the University of Jena to accept the racial writer Hans F. K. Günther as a professor on the staff, protests were at best feeble even though a faculty commission officially disapproved of the appointment. The commission, instead of citing principle, argued that the chair would drain funds from other departments.[32] Günther, of course, received the appointment and the Nazis faced no shortage of willing teachers.

From our discussion of students and professors it is clear that a large and important segment of the German bourgeoisie entered the Weimar Republic unfit to participate in the experiment in parliamentary democracy. In this they were not alone, nor outcasts or in disrepute; rather they were established and respected members of society. This group expressed an open hostility to the Republic's toleration of political parties which tended to divide a Volk which could be saved only by being unified. It did its best to obstruct the smooth functioning of the system. This was a handicap the Republic faced from the start; it was not just a by-product of economic depression. The rapid increase in the bourgeois youth's radical turn to the right also affected the Republic adversely. This too was not merely an accidental development, initiated by war and various economic crises; it had a historical development behind it. It was produced by the thorough indoctrination of important segments of the bourgeoisie in New Romantic and Germanic ideology. Above all, faith in the Volk was the source of strength in any national crisis. Both young and old found it difficult to resist an appeal that promised to solve the nation's problems in Volkish terms, by a return to German hands of all property, powers, and abilities now allegedly possessed by foreign and anti-Volkish interests.

Believing themselves involved in a permanent crisis of nationhood and ideology, many Germans came to regard themselves as knights riding bravely between death and the devil. Dürer's famous picture "The Knight, Death, and the Devil" came to stand as a symbol for the situation of the Volk. It was an exhortation to heroic action. A study of these feelings, especially as they expressed themselves in poetic visions, will aid us in further illuminating important aspects of the ideology, for, in the end, the knight, the heroic German, would triumph.

CHAPTER 11

Leadership, *Bund,* and Eros

To MANY PEOPLE, both inside and outside the Volkish movement, the prospects for a vital spiritual assertion on the part of the German nation seemed dim as the nineteenth century drew to a close. Culturally there seemed to be a lack of idealistic fervor. The arts and society seemed imprisoned by conformity to the functions of a bureaucratic state. In neighboring France a multitude of changes had taken place—at least there was frequent turmoil and a broad range of public controversy. Revolutionary ideas in art and literature had found a similarly fertile soil in France, while the new art forms were only borrowed by Germany afterward and enjoyed only a weak flourishing. Shortly before the end of the nineteenth century and into the first decade of the twentieth, the German intellectual community was unable to find a cause to identify with. The bourgeoisie seemed too philistine, disinclined to inspire or encourage diversity of thought, to tolerate new artistic forms, and to moderate their moral and social codes. For intellectuals and exponents of Volkish thought alike—and the two categories are not mutually exclusive—it was a time of frustration, without ideals or heroism or leadership. Many thought it a period of trial in which the German people walked between death and the devil, striding ever onward, the knight in search of the Holy Grail.[1]

To be sure, various forces were at work trying to create meaningful spheres of individual identity. The Volkish movement had done well in forging broader perspectives of Volk, nature, Germanic faith, and the Aryan race. Diederichs declared the century of New Romanticism, encouraged the formation of groups of initiates, and called for the implementation of an "idealism of deeds." And the Youth Movement combined the two in its own peculiarly pragmatic brand of Volkish identity. Aesthetically, Fidus depicted an idealized Nordic manliness that emanated from the Volk, surrounded by its natural habitat, sublimating its religious feelings in cosmic forces, and striving toward a new spiritual future. But others, sympathetic to the cause of the Volk or merely concerned with the alienating tendencies in the nation's development, also asked how a change could be effected, and beyond that, who was to bring it about. Still others thought in terms of organizations and theorized about the means required to lead the nation out of stagnation. It is to these latter groups and to the answers they provided that we must now turn.

What seemed to be lacking, according to these men—Volkish adepts, New Romantics, and admirers of Stefan George—was a mythos that embodied the longings of the German people. We have seen earlier how this concept of mythos lay at the heart of the world's problems as those influenced by Eugen Diederichs' New Romanticism came to see them. Now we must return to this mythos to see how such men infused it with Nietzschean ideas and thus brought it to full flower. To them, the German soul seemed to be dead, unable to enter into intercourse with the cosmos, and lacking a spiritual character that reflected its values, aspirations, and abilities. Certainly it had a history to identify with, a tradition of heroism that was alive, though subdued, in the Volkish heart. But what of the future? What did the German soul want of the future, what did it have to offer? Here the generation that learned from Diederichs and, above all, from Nietzsche stepped in and provided an answer.

The philosophers Arthur Bonus and Ernst Bertram, the racist Hans F. K. Günther, and the poet Stefan George, all heavily influenced by Nietzsche, considered that the new mythos had to be gained in man's, Germanic man's, transcendence of his limited historical framework. Though the past was not to be rejected *in toto*, its merits—such as its heroism, the free and genuine life of the ancient Germans, and a society ordered according to estates—were to be transvaluated. The new mythos, correspondingly, was removed from the continuum of history and elevated as the product of man's will, his imagination, and his artistic creativity. The spirit of the times—the real spirit, not just the mirrored reflection—was to be embodied in man's constant aspiration toward perfection, his striving to merge with the cosmos. In this respect, the mythos had a double identity. On the one hand, it was limited by the perspectives of the times, of history, of the collective national aspirations; and on the other, it was absolute in its efforts to transvaluate known values through the power of the will—which, in effect, meant scrapping the nineteenth century for the sake of the Volkish revolution.[2]

The establishment of such a mythos was no mean task. Men of exceptional qualities were needed. The consensus, not collectively or consciously arrived at, among these disciples of Nietzsche was to look to an exceptional personality, a leader. In a sense, these longings can be explained by the times. Frustration, an extreme sense of disappointment, a deep discontent at a situation where change was necessary but no forces capable of implementing it seemed at hand, all led to solace in illusions. It was a time of prophets, of poetic seers; it was a time when only a charismatic leader seemed capable of ending the malaise of the intellectuals. Thus the intelligentsia looked to a heroic leader for release. The most vivid image of this leader was that exemplified by Willibald Hentschel, who saw the Germanic hero in Dürer's knight, who, in the forbidding company of death and the devil, nonetheless, tranquil and full of hope, rides toward the Holy Grail of Germany's future.[3]

Arthur Bonus and Ernst Bertram likewise endorsed the idea of a new heroic personality who would embody the new mythos of Germany. For Bonus the hero had to possess a strong autonomous will, a sense of heroic determination that would replace the old Christian mythos, which had stressed the good and the bad, guilt and repentance.[4] Bertram went a step further. He had discovered in Nietzsche the heroic personality capable of combining the new mythos with the aspirations of the nation. In his book on Nietzsche, Bertram claimed that a legend of the great man, imbued with his thoughts and goals, would be sufficient to serve as the basis of the new mythos. Great and heroic men, he claimed, generated a spiritual substance that persisted in the strivings of every man. To create this identity, however, it was necessary that the model be made intelligible to every man, that it be embodied in the forms most easily appreciated by people at large. He claimed that this could be achieved through legends, relegating to the realm of spiritual experience the task of communicating the "quintessence" of the great man.[5]

For Bertram's purpose, it was essential that Nietzsche be removed from his historical context. He had to be detached from the body of German philosophical thought and placed above its limitations. Thus Nietzsche was to be depicted as a philosopher who had transcended the pettiness of his people's thinking and raised himself to the stature of an *Überdeutscher*, a climactic German. Moreover, certain of Nietzsche's pronouncements as well as his very person were to be construed in a manner favorable to this interpretation. Nietzsche was the knight who bravely traveled along his path of necessary horrors, oblivious of the surrounding dangers, in pursuit of his ends; while his anti-Germanism was read as a transcendence of the pettiness of Germany and the grandiose fulfillment of a new German mythos.[6] "Evidence" for this interpretation was taken from the philosopher himself. Had not the great man stated that all people had to pass through grave dangers before achieving the climax to which they were destined by the intensity of their despair and the courage of their suffering? This was read to apply to the contemporary situation in Germany, and Nietzsche was regarded as embodying leadership qualities that were to lead the nation to the greatness it deserved.

For Bertram, Nietzsche's prophecy was the grand gesture of a Germanism that aspired to rise "beyond itself," and, for the legend Bertram concocted to depict the new mythos, the philosopher himself represented the "lightning breakthrough of the self-knowledge of the Volk at the moment of its greatest inner danger—while, simultaneously, he also represented an awakening and development through the saving will and the saving instincts." [7] According to the legend, Nietzsche had posited a new mythos and with it had created the youthful Elysian century.[8]

Thus Nietzsche was declared to be a Nordic prophet. Bertram's interpretation was echoed by writers of more explicitly Volkish leanings. Alfred Bäumler, a popular philosopher, transmitted it to the Nazis directly.[9] Today we recognize the error of this interpretation. Yet, to use Bertram's terms the right and wrong of "shameless historicism" [10] are beside the point, for, like a mythos, the image acclaimed by generations as the correct one, even though erroneous, transcends reason as it does good and evil. It mattered little that Nietzsche had ridiculed and rejected the intellectual material of Lagarde's works.[11] In spite of it, he became a living mythos of the Volk. His rejection of things as they are, his statement of Germany's plight, were taken as a projection of a power of will which facilitated his transcendence of historical limitations. The Nietzschean mythos was finally fused, as noted earlier, with the image of Dürer's knight. This combination of the extraordinary will power of the philosopher with the endurance and courage of the knight produced the idealized version of the German leader. In addition, it appealed to those who, like Guido von List, expected the leader to "come from above." This had a considerable impact. Later on, Hitler was to give it additional currency when he had himself portrayed by Hubert Lanzinger as a medieval knight, astride a horse, wearing a look of determination as his gaze penetrated into the future. When beholding the picture of the knight, any initiate of the National Socialists who believed in the lavish promises of future grandeur for the nation, drew the appropriate moral: courage in the face of danger and a steeled suppression of doubt.[12] To a leader of the Artamanen, the knight inspired a similar vision that stressed the imperatives of action and courage as the impetus driving the hero ever onward.[13] And though the Volkish emphasis was slow in coalescing, by 1938 a consensus had been fully achieved. It was then that Bertram, writing in the *Völkische Beobachter*, identified the knight as a peasant figure, close to the soil and secure in his actions. He was a Faustian man, active and of flesh and blood, fighting merely intellectualized (*geistige*) power.[14]

Where Bertram's knight attempted to set the mythos of the age while remaining above temporal and historical ties, the hero envisioned by Hans F. K. Günther was circumscribed by ties to the Volk. He was the servant of the Volk, his actions and ideas confined by the immediate interests of the people and soil from which he stemmed. Here was an explicitly Volkish hero, one who could assume leadership over those disciples who had formulated the correct ideas but lacked the resources and guidance to implement them. The vision was promulgated in Günther's book *Ritter, Tod und Teufel: Der heldische Gedanke* (*The Knight, Death and the Devil: A Heroic Thought*). Written in 1924, the work brought the author to the attention of Walther Darré, the future agricultural specialist of the Third Reich, and gained him entrance to the social and intellectual circles of the National Socialists.[15] It was a favorable beginning, and Günther eventually became one of the principal racial experts under the Nazi regime.

In the book itself, Günther reduced Nietzsche to a few ideas concerning the powers of will and the germination of a superman through an inherent consciousness of election. The knight represented the hero, standing at the beginning of the world, who grasped man's fate and, through his inner strength, molded it according to his own criteria. The knight's values, however, emanated from the Volk, whose racial virtues were inalienable and eternal. So it was only a question of reapplying them. The knight, the modern superman representing qualities usually ascribed to the ancient Germans —heroism, loyalty, honesty, racial purity—was dedicated precisely to reclaiming the greatness of the Volk. Here Günther fused the Nietzschean ideals with Germanic vision. He tamed his hero, who was at one and the same time a unique leader and bound by the spirit of the Volk.[16] This was a step, a reduction of the will to power, which Bertram never countenanced; and as we shall see, it was also at variance with other visions of heroic German leadership.

But this image gained great popularity under the Nazis. More so then Bertram's knight, Günther's Germanic hero was endowed with all the right Volkish virtues. It was this doctrine of leadership which was propagated by subsequent writers. Walther Darré was to use Günther's knight extensively as a model figure in his exhortations to the farmers to give their wholehearted support to the new Germany. The National Socialist writer Eberhardt Wolfgang Möller even incorporated the theme of "the knight, death, and the devil" into some of his poetry. Here, in poetic form, the knight was presented in the person of Adolf Hitler.[17] The motif, without Hitler, has survived, and years after the Second World War, the Volkish poet Wilhelm Pleyer repeated the same theme. This time, to be sure, the knight is confronted by a new adversary, presumably the Russians. But his victory is again assured.[18]

Although the image of the knight, hero, leader, had its particular relevance to the Volkish context, the same image, in poetic form, was successfully presented to a great number of other literate people. Characteristically, the image had always lent itself best to poetic devices and statements. Bertram, too, claimed that the comprehension of the mythos stood outside rational and scholarly analysis; that, moreover, the poet alone could appreciate all the subtleties and, sometimes, provide the solution. Bertram, interestingly enough, had been an early follower of Stefan George, and it is to that poet we must now turn.

It has been generally accepted that George was fairly intoxicated with his own prophetic function as a poet. He seriously believed in his role as a poet-seer, as a herald of change. To him it seemed that poetry was the most suitable vehicle for describing the tragic conditions of the times, which, he thought, could be alleviated only through the strength and determination of a leader. Poetry struck at the heart of the matter, and was, at the same time, impartial and uncommitted to any particular political solution. Above all, a poet was not limited by the seeming fatalism of materialistic, historicist, or realistic considerations. He was above them. He was in direct touch with the pulse of the nation. In this framework, it was logical that the poet should stride forth as the new prophet. The idea had enjoyed the support of romantics as early as the start of the nineteenth century, when Chauteaubriand had stated that a few lines of poetry greatly surpassed the value of all discovered mathematics.[19] The Germanic ideology had likewise stressed Volkish creativity as the highest good, as a measure of how close man's inner senses were to the genuine forces of life.

George, in a sense, represented the ultimate development in the urge toward a Germanic creativity. Indeed, he absolutely rejected the value of science and the supremacy of man's rational faculties.

He assured his disciples that in his person or work one will find "no path that leads to science." [20] Instead, Hölderlin, the Greeks, and some of Nietzsche's writings spurred him on in his poetic identity. He joined Hölderlin in being a poet of a truly creative Volkhood, while Nietzsche provided him with the hero's antagonism to modernity. The Greeks gave him their classical heritage and, significantly enough, a Dionysian context of companionship, especially as it was reflected in the Munich circle, where George joined his disciples Alfred Schuler, Ludwig Klages, and others in celebrating heathen festivals as a means of capturing the feeling of genuine primeval culture. [21]

But where Bertram and Günther had turned to individual leaders, George concentrated on defining the need for an elite leadership—which did not preclude the emergence of a single leader. Instead of the image of the knight, it was the concept of the "order," such as the Knights Templar of the Crusades, that George promoted. The eschatological urge was strong in him, for he sincerely believed that solutions would eventually be found. The coming century was to be the age of the elite, not of the masses. It would be an era in which great personalities would impress their image, creativity, and accomplishments upon the face of society and culture. George saw these new personalities as representing both godliness and manliness and possessing extraordinary powers of will. [22]

But what of the *Orden* or *Bund* of the elite from whose ranks the leaders would emerge? Here George's ideas were similar to those of the Youth Movement. Like them, he denied that conventional organizational ties could bind a group together in a common purpose, thought, or deed. Instead, he too invoked the power of Eros, of dedicated love between men, as the mortar of the elite. Eros, as we defined it earlier, was regarded by George as a function of beauty, of physical male beauty, a quality which was supposedly an indispensable basis for any appreciation, much less creation, of cultural phenomena. "Nothing is so purely external that it could not be [for George] a symbol of inward man." [23] Cultural rebirth, which would take place among the elite, would be attained only through the sharing of Eros, through the manifestation of the beauty of both the body and the soul.

George not only expressed his longings for leadership and the elite in his poetry, but tried to give them reality in his own life. In 1902 he thought he had found a person who possessed all the beauties he longed for: a young friend of his named Maximin, who, in the words of one of George's disciples, "transformed magic into reality." [24] For George, the young man, who died in his youth, possessed a godlike quality which was not to be found in any of his other disciples.

Here, among his disciples, all with dispositions similar to his own, was the core of the elite. George himself selected the members and judged them by the beauty of their carriage, by the quality of their bearing, and by the fire burning in their eyes. The group was linked by a shared Eros inspired by the "master," George, on whom all their group rituals centered. George surrounded his movements with secrecy and held his meetings in the back rooms of a friend's residence.[25] Discussion would revolve around the problem of reviving a feeling for the beauty of primeval forces in a modern world which was indifferent to the culture of classical times. On occasions, such as around 1912 but also at other times, the circle approached the Volkish outlook and the Germanic faith. At times like these, George would be particularly despondent regarding the future of Germany. He was afraid that within fifty years the essence of Germanism, the German soul, would vanish and be obliterated by the encroaching disease of urbanism. In this respect, he expressed a loathing for the influence America was exerting on Europe and characterized the United States as a world of ants.[26]

George personally was not a man of action, and it was left to others to apply his ideas in an area where they inflamed the passions: in politics, and especially in the kind disdained by George, mass politics. George disagreed with them and had nothing but contempt for their intellectualism. Moreover, he rejected the blatant Volkish ideology and looked with sadness upon certain events conducted in the name of the German Volk. He deplored the anti-Semitism of rabid Germanists like Alfred Schuler and Ludwig Klages, men whom he had befriended in his youth. In later years he rejected the proffered presidency of the Nazi Poets' Academy—electing to die in exile, in Switzerland. While he presided over his own circle of initiates he refused to deny membership to anyone on the basis of race or creed. Jews, just as young romantic German Gentiles, felt themselves drawn by his appeal and there were many who idealized his thoughts. Aside from the esthetes and the intellectually precocious, many people who were not necessarily of a Volkish persuasion accepted his prophetic insights as a reflection of their own concern for the nation.

But many of George's disciples developed overtly Volkish attitudes. For example, Alfred Schuler and Ludwig Klages, two Volkish fanatics who had been close to George for some time, broke with him in 1904 and proceeded to lay a greater stress on the denunciations of modernity which fit into a Volkish and Germanic category of thought. Both men elevated their hate of the Judeo-Christian conspiracy into a position of priority totally unacceptable to George. In their hands the emphasis on primeval forces became a recapturing of the blood of their Germanic forebears. And, like Bertram, both found their belief incarnated in the person and what they believed to be the philosophy of Nietzsche. Klages de-emphasized the will to power as embodying the virtues of capitalism, which he rejected, because it left no room for the functioning of the inherited and genuine soul of the Volk.[27]

Though there was direct antagonism between George and Klages on the relevance of the Volkish thesis, on other levels they shared a number of ideas, the most important of which concerned the structure and nature of organization. Both were elitist in outlook and both adhered to the principles of the *Orden* and the *Bund*. The former had more formal connotations, since it tended to refer to groups of men organized to perform a specific service or task. The *Bund* comprised a more flexible association and simply referred to a social organization regarded by its members as the true community of man with a common soul. Moreover, it was claimed that the *Bund* did away with the artificiality of bourgeois society and its hypocritical relationships, morality, and culture. But though we have already examined the *Bund* in connection with the Wandervögel and Stefan George, we must now take a closer look at this important phenomenon. For the *Bund* became an important and lasting ideal for many Volkish thinkers, a new means by which an elitist society could be organized. Our best source of information on the subject is Hans Blüher, who must be recognized as the theorist *par excellence* of the *Bund*.

The great experience in Blüher's life was his association with the Wandervögel at the beginning of the century. But he had gone on to study philosophy and German philology and had become increasingly interested in defining a philosophy of nature. However, Blüher did not teach, but instead became a publicist, writer, and private scholar. His restless mind was always fertile with ideas and ready to do combat. Small wonder that he despised the mass movement of National Socialism and during the Hitler period retired into the private world of his own study. His fervid dislike of the Nazis was, no doubt, due in large part to the ideal of the *Bund*, the community of a male elite, in which he had believed ever since his Youth Movement days, for the Nazi mass movement seemed hostile to elitist ideas.

It needs to be stated at the outset that the idea of a male community, based as it was on sexual affinities and similarity of ideological dispositions, was not unique to Germany. Only the application of the concept and its service in political and social causes were peculiarly German. The ideas of Eros and the tendency toward homosexuality, were known not only in Germany but also, and concurrently, in France and England. In France, André Gide and Marcel Proust shared Blüher's concepts and we e attracted to both Eros and homosexuality. But they regarded such inclinations as personal matters. Neither they nor their contemporary in England, Oscar Wilde, thought of using sexual inversion or sublimation as a basis for a cosmic theory which attempted to provide alternatives to present social and political organization. The *Bund*, in Germany, took the latter course and it is to its application there that we must now turn.

Blüher's theory of the functioning of Eros presented in his book *Die Rolle der Erotik in der männlichen Gesellschaft* (*The Role of the Erotic in the Male Community*) (1917) was an offshoot of Freudian analysis on the origins of culture. Both Freud and Blüher asserted that culture was a product of sexual sublimation. The refining of sexual urges that accompanied social restrictions was seen as the impetus to transferring the energy used in sexual attraction to a new object of passion. The simply personal "pleasure principle" gave way to longings of more noble dimensions. It was thought that once man's sensual gratifications were sublimated his energy could be directed into the realm of cosmos and metaphysics.[28] Blüher, however, did not deny the merits, function, or necessity of sexual life. Instead the cosmic identity as it was forged in a *Bund* atmosphere had to be accompanied by a satisfying sex life; in fact, the author held sexual health and gratification as synonymous with the forces of Eros. Eros had to be engaged in a situation where human relationships produced not children, whose survival would demand the total concentration of the parents at the expense of their spiritual lives, but works of lasting cultural and social value. In other words, Eros was to be a catalyst in fostering cultural creativity, not simply used up in biological propagation.[29]

Within such a scheme, the homosexually inclined came to be regarded as the most socially creative individual. Because the normal male directs his total sexual energy and affection toward his family, toward providing them with the material essentials of life, Eros here is essentially captured, circumscribed, and dissipated. This does not hold true for a homosexual, who is able to direct his surplus energy toward cosmic concerns and, above all, toward cementing the ties of the true *Bund*.[30] Unfettered by common everyday worries of home, family, and children, he can direct his sexual energies into creative occupations and sublimate them in cultural activities. Within the *Bund*, which was laid out according to leadership principles, those members who were the most attractive, spiritually as well as physically, would gravitate toward leadership positions. For Blüher the homosexual experience was common to all males to one degree or another.[31] It was these men, infused with the true Eros, who through their surplus energies would guide the *Bund* toward genuine goals, giving all of themselves to the cause. Such leaders were to be the heroes, the sources of brave and courageous deeds as well as the inspiration for other men to join the group.[32]

Blüher, however, did not restrict the concept of Eros to the *Bund* structure or to leadership. He also applied it to the state. In dealing with the nature of the state, its organization and purpose, Blüher claimed that the concept of the *Bund* was elemental in the origin of the nation.[33] A state was more than just a utilitarian framework; it was an integral aspect of human organization. Those who traced the origins of the state to various forms of social contract, he quickly dismissed as theorists who reduced the essence of human organization to calculations of political power. The state, as an organism in the service of the Volk, had a greater purpose than merely the protection of its members; it represented greater and more mysterious forces which united the citizens of a nation around a common point of identity. Blüher delegated this function to Eros.[34] It was the subliminal force that provided the state with an elite and culture. Accordingly, he measured the strength of the state in terms of the Eros that bound its people together. The *Bund* infused with Eros was a social organization that derived its *raison d'être* from the elemental sexual and erotic urges that underlie the relationships between men. That is not to say that sexual values displaced all others. On the contrary, factors such as proper physical proportions, common cultural affinities, and similar heritage, history, and race were all seen as interconnected with Eros in producing that entity peculiar to one country and alien to all others. Here also the revival of the correct and most conducive organization of men was a part of the longing for a new mythos.[35]

Freudian psychology was obviously influential in making explicit the theory of the *Bund*, but the disillusionment with bourgeois society and the contemporary forms of social organization was basic to its popularity. Moreover, Volkish thought had always been conservative with respect to the role of women in society, relegating them to the home as their Germanic ancestors would presumably have wished. In addition, the women's rights movement had been active and vocal ever since the end of the nineteenth century and the Volkish thinkers regarded it as a threat to the Volk. The modern woman, the suffragette, was a symbol of hated modernity. This upsurge in the demand for women's rights contributed to the fact that a significant number of men came to consider their own emotional and sexual urges as ultimately creative, while relegating those of the female to a lower and more biological order. In one case Eros led to cultural, artistic, and political creation, while in the other it was circumscribed by biological needs which allowed no time or energy for the pursuit of truly creative ends.

A considerable literature grew up around this theme, based upon the presuppositions which Blüher was, later, to formulate so strikingly. The popular work of Otto Weininger, an apostate Jew, *Geschlecht und Charakter (Sex and Character)* (1903), elevated the female-male dichotomy into a cosmic principle. The masculine-centered theory of Eros relegated women to a position ancillary to that of men. Women, Weininger claimed, lacked the Eros peculiar to men; they were preoccupied with marriage, with reproduction, and with providing for the needs of the offspring. Consequently, they could not responsibly possess the cultural Eros. Weininger, attempting to lend a touch of objectivity to his thesis, paid tribute to the "feminine-motherly" as an elemental force, but he eulogized the "masculine-creative" as the superior force typifying the spiritual capacities of man. And he developed his argument even further— only to grow increasingly more absurd and irrational. He not only accorded the female an inferior role but introduced a racial argument as well. As the female was opposed by the male, so the Jew was contrasted with the Aryan. The traits of the Jews were equated with those of women: both were preoccupied with material goods at the expense of spiritual interests and similarly transformed love into lust. However, whereas the female was only secondary to the male in a racial context, the Jew, both male and female, was lower than the whole Aryan race. Women were simply inferior; Jews were antithetical to the soul and to spiritual life.[36]

Where Weininger's argument left off, others stepped in and completed the cosmology of racial dichotomy. Georg Lomer, for instance, an advocate of Germanic sun worship, saw the Aryan male symbolized by the sun, while the Jew, like the female, represented only reflected light in the form of the moon.[37] Just as the moon parasitically reflected the sun's light, so the Jews, lacking an original creativity, were compelled to merely imitate their betters. Judging by the number of anti-Semitic pamphlets which referred to the Jew as a "moon creature," Lomer's idea seems to have had some currency. Lomer may have been more *outré* than Weininger, but these increasingly irrational elaborations of the theme only indicated that the wellsprings of the ideology were already contaminated.

Whereas Weininger had attempted to identify the cosmological distinctions between male and female, Aryan and Jew, others went on to apply them in broad racial terms. This process was manifest in the manner in which elitism was reduced to signify election through the blood. The theory was presented by Lothar Helbing, whose work *Der dritte Humanismus* (*The Third Humanism*) (1928) stated that the genuine Eros of the state depended, in the first place, on the purity of blood inheritance. Earlier Blüher had denied Jews participation in Eros for fear that they would improve their own racial and spiritual strain and thus drag humanity down to a level of materialism and utilitarianism.[38] Significantly enough, this was consistent with the Volkish charge that Judaism was implicated in an anti-Germanic conspiracy.

Though many people did not endorse the whole body of Volkish or Germanic ideology, it attracted enough adherents to constitute an issue of considerable importance. And even if a large number of these adherents did not subscribe to the whole gamut of the theories, they accepted the basic ideas and were active in disseminating them. Thus, though only a relatively small part of the total population accepted the concepts of Eros and *Bund*, it was a vociferous group, sincerely believing that the *Bund* of males provided the cell "from which all states have their origin."[39] The Youth Movement had found the new principles of organization congenial to its needs, and had high hopes for applying them in other areas. Looking to the future, the members of the Youth Movement exclaimed that "the *Bund* is our state, the state of youth, and is our guide to the state of the future."[40] They felt that they had discovered a radically new organization in total opposition to the contemporary social structures, which had been erected on the basis of a spiritually shallow rationality and a crass materialism. In contrast, their organization was the true reality which must be the basis of the future state if the nation was to be saved from extinction. By the 1920's Volkish thought had come to grips with this trend and had accepted many aspects of it. For all the prudery of the National Socialists, the idea of leadership structured on Eros was continuously alive in the feudal groupings around the standard bearers of the New Reich. Enemies were to cry homosexuality and the accusation struck home in the youth circles, among the elite gatherings of sensitive poets and literati, and especially in the ranks of the early National Socialists. But the charge, with its suggestion of moral depravity, was beside the point. Whether or not a sexual experience was involved, the concepts of

Eros and *Bund* nourished many Volkish theories of elitism and leadership.

We must now look at the organizations which further institutionalized Volkish ideology and which functioned according to *bündisch* principles. These *Bünde* were of the utmost significance. The early Nazi party was a typical *Bund*, though Hitler changed this in his drive for power. However, within the Strasser wing of the party the ideal of the *Bund* remained alive and relevant throughout the 1920's.[41] Other organizations, more orthodox in their Volkish commitments, also abided by *bündisch* concepts. These groups tried to put across their views on national affairs and the crisis of the German ideology. What is of interest to us is the nature of the solution they prescribed for that crisis.

CHAPTER 12

Organizations Carry On

THE IDEA of the *Bund* did not remain in the realm of theory. A number of organizations took it up and shaped themselves according to its precepts: principles of leadership and the close cohesion of male interests. Obviously, the idea had an appeal and it seemed to meet some of the problems of the times. But however noble an ideal the *Bund* actually proved to be, its effectiveness was limited by the extent to which it could be fitted into an actually existing situation.

What were the limits imposed by the actual situation in Germany during the last part of the nineteenth century and to what extent was it amenable to the Volkish plan for the reorganization of German society? From the 1890's onward, various organizations had tried to implement what, in 1924, Max Wundt, a professor of philosophy at Jena, summarized as the essence of Volkish ideology. The concepts he brought forward were somewhat more polished, but they were the same that had aroused the passions of earlier groups. Both strove to realize a unity of the German people by transcending the limitations of the temporal political regimes, whether monarchy or republic. Both adhered to the conviction that blood and soil gave the elemental form to the community of the Volk and that this community must be lifted into conscious peoplehood.[1]

But, while both agreed on a number of points, there were also significant differences. For one, the audiences of the 1920's were considerably larger and more receptive. On the whole, it is correct to say that whereas Wundt could appeal to an expanding Volkish spirit, the earlier organizations only held their own, with two significant exceptions: the Youth Movement and the Pan-German Association. We have already discussed the role and nature of the Youth Movement's organizational concepts. Now we must turn to the Pan-

Germans as representative of a Volkish organization which made itself and its message felt in the community at large.

The organization of the Pan-Germans deserves special emphasis because it was a relatively well-known, influential, and respectable society. Before the First World War it was the most important of the organizations that advocated a program based on various Volkish precepts. Only after the war, when numerous *Bünde* contested for dominance and splintered the following of the Pan-Germans, did the organization lose its commanding position.

The Pan-German Association was organized in 1890 as a patriotic group protesting the prospective release of the island of Helgoland to the English. The Pan-Germans almost immediately became sponsors of a German imperialism based on a Volkish rationale and formed themselves into a permanent body. They endorsed an expansionist foreign policy, advocating an enlargement of German territory in Europe as well as in the colonies. They subscribed to Volkish ideas to the extent that they demanded that a true racial and cultural unification be achieved in Germany which would give the German *Geist* a vital role in culture, social organization, and politics.[2] Moreover, they showed typical Volkish prejudices in selecting their areas of operations; for example, rather than forging a strong link with industry, they preferred to devote themselves to agricultural issues. This position, however, was soon recognized as untenable in a Germany where a part of industry stood ready to contribute members and money to the Pan-Germans, largely because of their rabidly expansionist foreign policy.

The change came mostly after the war, due to the ever increasing influence of one member of the organization: Alfred Hugenberg, the former director of Krupp's industrial empire,[3] who forged a connection between industry and the Pan-Germans. Hugenberg's early affiliation with the organization and its leadership might well have rested, to a large extent, on their vociferous advocacy of a war to prevent the encroachment of militarily stronger neighbors. For the Krupp director this belligerent attitude might have translated itself into orders for rearmament, at a time when industry faced several exceptionally severe depressions. However, there were many concepts which Hugenberg and the Pan-Germans had in common, among which their anti-leftism, anti-socialism, and more rabid anti-communism were high in priority.[4]

We have said that the Pan-Germans were highly respectable. Prior to and especially during the war, the organization's list of members was graced with the names of such prestigious men as the sociolo-

gist Max Weber, the politician Gustav Stresemann, and the historian
Karl Lamprecht. Although Weber and Stresemann, supporters of a
strong, imperialistic German foreign policy, soon left the organization—largely because they disagreed with the emphasis on agricultural issues—the Pan-Germans flourished and grew.[5] Further prestige, appealing to more directly Volkish audiences, was supplied by
members such as the Social Darwinist Ernst Häckel and the romantic writer Friedrich Ratzel. Ludwig Schemann, the popularizer
of Gobineau, became an important member of the executive board.

From the beginning the Pan-Germans enjoyed a competent and
strong leadership. The first president, Ernst Hasse, set the tone with
a call for an aggressive foreign policy and the cessation of further
immigration of Jews into Germany.[6] Eighteen years later, in 1908, he
was succeeded by the even more able Heinrich Class. Class became
the organization's moving spirit and ruled it with an iron hand until
1939, when it was disbanded. Among the Pan-Germans he drew
his support from the more extremist members, such as the racist
Schemann, while he was highly respected outside the organization,
in conservative political and social circles. Of special significance
was his influence among powerful military and political groups.
He had frequent access to these circles and he made unstint-
ing use of it, not, of course, without leaving behind the mark of
his own ideology.[7] This respectability stood him in good stead.
Dressed in top hat and frock coat, Class attracted the devotion of
the upward-striving petite bourgeoisie. Teachers, retail merchants,
white-collar workers, and others flocked to the organization and
comprised the bulk of its membership.[8] All of them liked respectability, especially if it seemed to be useful to their Volkish cause.

Not long after he took office, Class made his ideological position
clear in a popular book entitled *Wenn ich der Kaiser wär (If I Were
Emperor)* (1912). One of his principal points was the advocacy of
a German dictatorship which would actualize the ideal society embodying the "eternal Volk." The only limits on the discretion of the
dictator were to be those imposed by an elitist parliament composed
of and elected by an aristocracy of birth, those with extensive land
holdings and those who had rendered signal service to the state. He
termed this aristocratic component of government the "organic"
element basic to all Volkish sovereignty.[9] In the book he also showed
some indecision about whether to espouse the cause of land or that
of industry—with a growing tendency to support the latter. His
concern with the emphasis upon agrarian interests led him to advocate extensive efforts to colonize and resettle the eastern territories
of the German nation.[10] Small wonder that such concerns led the

Pan-Germans into qualified support for a Germanic utopia such as Willibald Hentschel's Mittgart.[11] However, he opened a gap in the Volkish resistance to modernization and industry. Class's book paid tribute to the contributions that industry had made to the cause of the nation and the Volk. Some of the industrial enterprises, in the words of the Pan-Germans' *Alldeutsche Blätter*, "contained healthy Germanic elements within them." [12] Class had kind words for the Krupp enterprise, which was singled out as an example of a nationally valuable industrial complex (for all we know, this might have been part of the attempt to play up to Hugenberg). But he extended no such good will to the department stores and the banks. He viewed these with the venom typical of the Volkish movement, which had always denounced them as the overt agents of exploitation and the embodiment of the Jewish conspiracy.[13]

Whatever Class had endorsed in his book he was also willing to implement himself—above all, if he were made dictator. He did not rule out that possibility. Many years later, in the 1930's, when the organization had lost much of its support, the Pan-Germans still fervently believed that Class might yet take his place as the "born leader" of the nation.[14] Class's disappointment at the failure of his aspirations, which had no real basis, was so intense that he never reconciled himself to the facts. The hope had been ridiculous. Hitler, after all, had a mass following, while Class had only the support of a dwindling organization. Instead, it was his close friend Hugenberg, who, having built on the earlier support of the Pan-Germans and become the leader of the conservative political party the DNVP, associated himself with Hitler's regime as a cabinet member with the vague hopes of collecting the pieces if the regime lost the confidence of the nation.

Class led the Pan-Germans from a moderate attitude on the Jewish question toward vehement hostility against Jews. Anti-Semitism, as we have documented it, had always been a principal ingredient of a Volkish outlook; this case was no exception. From 1908 on, Class launched a determined campaign against the Jews, declaring them to be carriers of modern materialism and, consequently, enemies of the Germanic spiritual substance.[15] Along with his predecessor and other members of the organization, he advocated that the state limit the immigration of Jews; but Class would also restrict the cultural and professional activities of native German Jews. The Jews were to be excluded from teaching, banking, and public office and forbidden to own landed property. Moreover, their persons and possessions were to be subject to double taxation. Their activity in the theater and in the literary journals, which had increased considerably in the last two decades of the nineteenth century, was similarly proscribed, and newspapers which employed Jewish writers were to display a Star of David on their masthead.[16] Class went on to support, by 1928, the so-called "Juden Ordnung," a foreshadowing of the Nazis' Nuremberg Laws, proposed in 1919 by Müller von Hausen and his "Society against Jewish Domination," which had been the first to publish a German translation of the *Protocols of the Elders of Zion*. For most of the Pan-Germans, Müller von Hausen went too far. The "Juden Ordnung" systematically excluded Jews from all professions, indeed from German society. It threatened punishment by hanging for those who disobeyed. For all their dislike of Jews, the Pan-Germans considered this excessive, but not their leader, Heinrich Class. It is highly probable that Class supported a "Juden Ordnung" all along, for Müller von Hausen's proposal merely repeated the points which Class himself had proposed in his book. Class's organization had earlier found the "Juden Ordnung" ridiculous.[17] It is a measure of Class's success that in 1919 the Pan-Germans adopted a declaration which linked national rebirth to the removal of Jewish influence. The Pan-Germans stated flatly that "the idea that everything with a human face should have equal rights is a doctrine which is contradicted by daily life." [18]

Class, therefore, was most effective in spreading racial doctrines among the Pan-Germans themselves. It is, however, not surprising that the organization proved receptive. It had a continuous record of anti-Semitism which dated back to its first official proclamation, which called for national unity based on race and culture. With Class's accession to the presidency, the drive was intensified and outright exponents of racial doctrines were admitted as members. Class himself served as defense attorney for H. S. Chamberlain in a lawsuit charging him with racist libel and encouraged the work of the racial expert Professor L. Kuhlenbeck, whom he recruited for the organization. Kuhlenbeck was to be an invaluable addition, for he provided the Pan-Germans with the latest information on the developments in racial theory. His lectures, usually bearing "spiritualized" titles such as "The Gospel of Race," were listened to with attention by the members. Class's endorsement of Kuhlenbeck's ideas enabled them to penetrate more deeply. Both men praised the Bund der Landwirte (Farmers' Union) as the shock troops of a racially pure Germany.[19] Kuhlenbeck, moreover, succeeded in making the Pan-Germans aware of the value and function of political anthropology by stressing Woltmann's works on racial hygiene. Like Woltmann, he viewed history in racial terms and rewrote the great events of the past from a Germanic or Aryan perspective, as when he declared to the Pan-Germans that the blond Aryan was the real transmitter of all European culture.[20] What Kuhlenbeck and the Pan-Germans discussed did not, however, remain within the organization. Kuhlenbeck, for example, wrote on the Renaissance in the publisher's catalogue of Eugen Diederichs' publishing house. He followed Woltmann by linking Germanism to the Renaissance. Yet here, curiously enough, he toned down the usual emphasis on the desirability of racial purity by advising that Aryan blood could do well with a small dose of dark blood to enhance its artistic creativity. For this statement he claimed a respectable source which had been honored by the Pan-Germans: Gobineau.[21]

The organization's other attempts to make itself felt in German life and government extended into the realm of politics. Here it initiated a minor revolt against the Volkish abhorrence of all political maneuvering: it established ties with a political party. Of course, it did not go so far as to constitute itself as a political party seeking office, but it considered it opportune and advantageous to link itself with the policies of a like-minded organization. Immediately after 1918, the Pan-Germans entered into close relations with the reconstituted German conservative party, the Deutschnationale Volkspartei.[22] To the distress of the Pan-Germans, it was not really to their advantage. The direct benefit of the connection went not to them, but to the DNVP. However, in the beginning it held some promise.

The Pan-Germans came to the political scene with a reputation that stood well with the conservatives, especially with those who saw the system of politics itself as degenerate and inoperative and hopefully endorsed the ideology of the Volk, which held out the promise of a regime that would rise above parliamentary politics. From the beginning of the war, the Pan-Germans had stood for a determined drive for German victory, and in the last stages of the war they spearheaded the attack against Chancellor Bethmann-Hollweg and his peace proposals because they regarded them as too compromising. Their super-patriotism paid off. Conservatives in the highest military and government posts were especially grateful to Class and the Pan-Germans for their ideological support and for the considerable sums they helped to raise for the prewar expansion of the German fleet. As a token of gratitude, or in recognition of services rendered, they granted Class entrance to their councils.

In forging the alliance with the DNVP, the Pan-Germans simply extended their policies into a new, expanded field. Their main efforts were concentrated on attacking the Republic. Opposition to the Republic had always been eminently respectable and it came naturally to Class and his followers. But in addition to directing overt hostility toward the parliamentary state, the Pan-Germans forged intimate contacts with the military and government establishment which enhanced the effectiveness of their ideological propaganda. Their ideology had remained uncontaminated. Its Volkish elements had been cultivated and strengthened through intimate connections with other Volkish organizations that had sprung up since the war. In fact, in spite of the direct relations with the DNVP, Class still attempted, though unsuccessfully, to bring about a coalescence of all radical Volkish groups into one representative organization. The venture foundered over differences in ideological emphasis. However, Class was able to gain for the Pan-Germans the total commitment of the violently anti-Semitic Völkisch Schutz- und Trutzbund (League for Protection and Defiance),[23] which, among other things, financed many of the racial works of Hans F. K. Günther. In this respect, the Pan-Germans reaped a harvest in two fields: in political respectability and among the less respectable organizations that provided them with their ideological impetus and strength.

The double aspect of the Pan-Germans—their respectability, on the one hand, and their extreme Volkish outlook, on the other—was best illustrated in their propaganda efforts. Through close personal connections, the organization was able to aid the most important organ of Volkish thought, the newspaper *Deutschlands Erneuerung* (*Germany's Rebirth*).[24] It was published in Munich under the editorship of J. F. Lehmann, an early and close associate of Hitler. The paper attained such distinction that every important theorist in the Volkish movement, regardless of his particular emphasis, contributed to it—among them Class, a deputy editor who published numerous articles; Dr. Paul Bang, the economic expert of the DNVP, who formulated the economic policies of his party; Alfred Rosenberg and Wilhelm Frick, who joined in representing the Nazi viewpoint; and Georg Schiele, who added his voice to the Volkish chorus as a supporter of the Artamanen.

For a time, before the fateful years 1932 and 1933, the Pan-Germans worked compatibly with the political organizations of the right, from the DNVP to the National Socialists. In these relationships the organization hoped to further its ideological position, and Class worked to enhance his own political aspirations. The progress of his cause was reported in his own newspaper, *Deutsche Zeitung*. The early issues, which reported the rise of Hitler, wrote of the new political force in a sympathetic light. Class strongly condemned the efforts to expel Hitler from Germany after the failure of his putsch. He declared that it would be scandalous to keep

Hitler out of Germany while undesirable foreigners—that is, Eastern European Jews—were constantly being admitted.[25] As the union with the DNVP became more intimate and the contest between Hitler and Hugenberg seemed imminent, Class slowly gravitated away from Nazi sympathies. Furthermore, he began to share Hugenberg's misgivings about the leader of the National Socialists and finally severed all ties with him. Thus, while in 1920 Hitler could kiss Class's hand and honor him as the author of *If I Were Emperor*, by 1932 the Pan-German leader publicly condemned Hitler as an upstart.[26]

The history of the Pan-Germans drew to a close when Hitler came to power. The membership, as apart from the leadership, had turned toward the more viable National Socialists by the early 1930's. The change-over was perceptible in the depletion of the ranks of the Pan-Germans—40,000 in 1922 to 8,000 in 1933.[27] Most of them first shifted their allegiance to the DNVP and only from there went over to Hitler, but, at the time, Class blamed and resented only the Nazis. We should not be surprised at the shift. To many the policies of the Nazis merely represented the logical consummation of their own Volkish ideas. This fact has been emphasized by several historians who have called the Hitler regime a child of the Pan-Germans.[28] But this conclusion is a vast exaggeration, for while Hitler's ideas may have coincided with those of Class, these ideas were not original with the Pan-German leader. They developed from and belonged to the whole Volkish movement. The importance of the Pan-Germans lies in their success as the strongest and most respectable of the Volkish organizations until their decline in the 1920's. Through it, Volkish ideas found firm footing within the establishment itself; and thus this organization must be ranked with the Youth Movement and the educational system as the chief transmitters of the Germanic ideology from the prewar to the postwar world.

With the slow dissolution of the Pan-Germans after 1933, Class retired into semi-obscurity and proclaimed his love for a newly found "freedom." [29] This reaction was duplicated by other Volkish leaders, who realized that Hitler had beaten them to the draw and usurped their aspirations to form a dictatorship of the Volkish movement.

The efforts of the Pan-Germans to become representative of the Volkish movement were emulated by other organizations. Most of them never gained great renown, distinction, or influence; but they left their mark nonetheless. Just prior to the war, which formed a watershed in the activity of the Volkish organizations, Ottger Gräff made a futile attempt to create a united Volkish front under his own leadership. His group, Die Greifen (the Hawks), representing a radical segment of the Youth Movement which disseminated extremist racial views, had gained great strength in Austria, where, incidentally, it was the group Adolf Eichmann passed through as a youth. But its views proved too extreme and violent for the German movement as a whole. Though endorsed by Fidus, H. S. Chamberlain, and the head of the largest white-collar union, the Deutschnationale Handelsgehilfen Verband (DHV), Gräff failed in his attempt. The Fichte Bund, the result of his efforts, remained only one among the many Volkish splinter groups.[30]

Though there were no more significant attempts to forge a united Volkish front, the *Bünde* themselves rapidly increased in number in the immediate postwar years. The fighting, it seemed, had failed to instill a pacific spirit, despite the horrible killing and mutilation that had gone on; instead, it had only whetted the appetites of the younger generation. Perhaps the young people were driven by guilt for having failed the nation, for having lost the battle and the nation's honor; perhaps by the fact that the cessation of hostilities had come by surrender, not from a decisive contest in the field; or, most likely, the young soldiers were really looking for something to identify with, to fight for, now that the state they had fought for had ceased to exist. To a large extent, all of these factors coalesced to create the new martial and heroic feeling of the soldiers returning home. The war and the events resulting from it had infused both the *Bünde* and the Youth Movement with a renewed spirit of national consciousness.

The soldiers' experience at the front line had strengthened the idea that the *Bund* of men, bound together by a common spirit, spilling their blood together, was the only valid form of social organization which remained after the catastrophe. The experience of the war and what it meant readily found its way into literature and as such shaped that image of the conflict which influenced the younger generation's thinking on the subject. Two of the most distinguished literary contributions to this mood were made by Franz Schauwecker and Ernst Jünger. Schauwecker, who later became one of the Nazis' favorite writers, best summed up the feeling of communion instilled by the war as "experiencing the nation." He wrote: "We saw our blood drench the living earth in which we had buried two million brethren. We came back and had experienced the nation. Only where there is destruction can there be such a mighty revelation."[31] The same phenomena of blood, cruelty, and destruction also inspired the works of Ernst Jünger, to whom we owe the description of the hostilities as a trial of endurance, character, and national heritage. His book *Stahlgewitter* (*Thunder of Steel*) (1919) exalted the storm troopers, the men who braved the baptism of fire, and called them the true aristocracy of the nation. Both writers, glorifying the contest between men, had done their work: they had inspired a youth dislocated by the war and the ensuing events to believe that only by recapturing the war spirit would they restore their self-identity within the greater, revived glory of the Volk.

Some youth acted immediately. Soon after the armistice seventy-three *Bünde* came into being. As time went by, each maintained an independent position, but their memberships tended to overlap. The most volatile and distinctive of these groups were the Free Corps, voluntary army units that continued to fight on Germany's eastern frontier in defiance of Allied demands. Realizing that the war was lost on the western frontier, they still were determined to halt the spread of communism, to keep the enemy in the east, the Poles and Lithuanians, from taking more German soil. The Free Corps were not a part of the regular army but real *Bünde*, united by a common spiritual bond and led by a single heroic figure. One of their members, Ernst von Salomon, later wrote that these *Bünde* were effective only when they centered on real leaders.[32] Whatever Volkish inspiration these units possessed was only heightened once they returned home from the east. Most of the members streamed into other *Bünde*, concentrating upon the nation's internal problems as well as on the French occupation of the Ruhr. To both problems they brought a determination to have them resolved in the interests of the German Volk.

When the existing organizations did not suit their fancy or did not measure up to their standards of toughness and purpose, former Free Corps members formed their own *Bünde*. Beppo Römer, for instance, and his *Bund* Oberland returned from fighting against Polish encroachment in Silesia to help defeat the leftist government of Bavaria.[33] Many groups, like the Organization Escherich, believed that they were defending an idealistic concept of life against the inroads of materialism, which they translated in practical terms to mean supporting the Volkish ideology and defeating all leftist movements.[34] The *Bund* Wherwolf, for instance, which concentrated first on fighting the socialists and then the French in the Ruhr, depicted itself as representative of the revitalized "new generation" which opposed all socialism, plutocracy, and liberalism.[35] When they realized that they were too divided to constitute a viable force within the nation, many members of the various *Bünde*, as soon as a larger movement with an impetus similar to their own came along, elected to participate in larger *Bünde* or political organizations so as to be more effective.

One such possibility was the rapidly growing Jungdeutsche Orden, founded in 1920. Under the leadership of Artur Mahraun, this organization consciously attempted to translate the ideology of the Volk and of the youth into an effective political force. As we will return to the specifics of the Jungdeutsche ideology in a later chapter, it should be sufficient here to mention that it dedicated itself to the cause of the Volk and limited its membership to Aryans. A common purpose united with the concept of Eros to provide the cohesive elements of the organization. It was structured along the lines of a medieval order of Germanic knights and sought to perpetuate itself as *the* future German nation, founded on principles of community and leadership.[36] The prospects of the group looked bright; its appeal was compelling and, by the mid-1920's, it had considerably more than 130,000 members, not counting the marginal adherents.[37]

But the large membership of the Jungdeutsche Orden failed to translate itself into electoral strength. Many members, reflecting a basic Volkish attitude, may have been opposed to involvement in Republican politics. The elitist structure of the *Bund* made it singularly ill equipped to pursue truly mass support. Mahraun never resorted to the mass-appeal techniques employed by the National Socialists, nor did he fully exploit the emotional dynamite of anti-Semitism.[38] In fact, realizing that there were significant differences between his program and that of the National Socialists, he joined in an alliance with the Democrats, a liberal party, a move that was at variance with the Volkish emphasis of his organization. Without doubt, this sophisticated political maneuver cost him the support of many who wanted their Volkish state *now*, regardless of the means, and, as a result, opted for the DNVP or, more likely, the National Socialists.

Whereas the Jungdeutsche Orden remained true to Volkish and elitist principles of organization, calling for a close and idealistic *bündisch* relationship, the National Socialists went out to organize the masses and achieved their goal: ultimate power.

Interestingly enough, some of the origins of the National Socialists themselves are to be found in circles that attempted to form a united Volkish front before the war. The first manifestations of this intent were incorporated in the establishment, in 1912, of the Germanen Orden. Unable to muster enough strength, the *Orden* dissolved and reconstituted itself as the Thule Bund in 1918, which considered itself a secret lodge dedicated to combat the alleged conspiracy of secret Jewish organizations. Harking back to ancient Germanic mythology, it adopted the swastika and the spokes of the sun's rays as its symbols.[39] The context of this organization, its principles and goals, formed the background for the development of the National Socialist drive to power, but not before Hitler had placed his indelible mark on the group by radically changing its tactics.

Franz-Willing, possibly at one time close to the National Socialists and now one of their historians, correctly emphasizes the early *bündisch* nature of the party. The National Socialists considered themselves an *Orden* of men under the guidance of Karl Harrer, now largely forgotten. When Hitler became a member and eventually took over the leadership, the *bündisch* character was consciously sacrificed to the principles of a mass party.[40] Hitler had found the structure too confining. His accomplishment of leading the party away from the *Bund* structure was his greatest innovation. But in certain respects the mass movement retained traces of its *bündisch* origins: the leadership principle; the Eros that played a significant role in providing the cohesion of the SA, until it too was destroyed by Hitler; and the male exclusiveness of the elite structure of the party.

Although the *Bünde* and the Volkish organizations did not distinguish themselves as viable individual groupings, they still gained some renown due to the competent figures that emerged from their ranks. Two such men, in addition to Heinrich Class, who has to be viewed in conjunction with the Pan-Germans, were Reinhold Wulle and Gräfe-Goldebee. Both emerged from the Deutschnationale Volkspartei and both were active in founding, in 1922, the Deutsch-Völkische Freiheitspartei. Both flirted with the idea of uniting with Hitler but found themselves at odds with his emphasis on the priority of gaining power instead of solving the cultural, social, and ideological crisis of the German Volk. In these respects, they clearly mirrored the evolution and eventual dissipation of the purely Volkish movement. An examination of these men will give us a clear picture of this process.

Throughout his career Wulle remained faithful to Volkish precepts. As late as 1931 he still devotedly acknowledged the inspiration of Lagarde and Langbehn, when, in his principal theoretical contribution, *Die Sendung des Nordens* (*Mission of the North*), he paraphrased them in saying that "the unspoiled German is an aristocrat; his ancestors were peasants." [41] He closely adhered to the Volkish principles that the peasant was the most vital organism of the Volk and that the whole nation had to be rededicated to a

spiritual intercourse with earth and cosmos.[42] This mystically religious emphasis highlighted his opposition—reflecting a similar
thinking in the whole Volkish movement—to the later Hitler and to
Catholicism, the foreign theology.

At first Wulle had courted Hitler, and he claimed later that they
had even come to an agreement in 1923, in which Hitler had
promised to lead the northern wing of the Deutsch-Volkische Freiheitspartei. But this agreement came to nothing[43] and shortly thereafter Wulle became a highly vocal opponent of Hitler and the Nazi
party. His antagonism stemmed from a combination of disillusionment with the mass politics practiced by Hitler and a growing fear
that a pro-Catholic Fascism, such as seemed to have grown up in
Italy, would endanger the Germanic heritage. Of particular anxiety
to Wulle was Hitler's political maneuverability; he was able to nego-
tiate even with the Catholic Center party—when it was to his advantage. Wulle later condemned Hitler as the "Bavarian cross-breed
between Mussolini and Louis XIV." [44]

As we have already noted, the rationale for Wulle's opposition to
the Nazis is to be found in his devotion to the Volkish mysticism, in
the light of which he considered the power politics of Hitler immoral and heretical. Before the state could be reformed, he proclaimed, the soul of the German nation had to be purified. Only after
that was accomplished could the Third Reich blossom forth. Simply destroying the existing state structure was by no means sufficient.
Political parties alone could not achieve the Volkish goal; a whole
new Germany must first be created![45]

By 1932, left without an orthodox Volkish alternative, Wulle supported the cabinets of both von Papen and Schleicher. He was not
fully satisfied with either—in his eyes they were too lenient on the
Jewish question[46]—but they were the last competent representatives
of conservative authoritarianism, and might serve to prevent a take-
over by Hitler. After the Nazis assumed power, Wulle was considered dangerous enough—in spite of his explicit support of Hitler's
anti-Marxism and anti Semitism[47]—to be incarcerated in a concentration camp. He was eventually released through the intercession
of the Nazi minister of interior, Wilhelm Frick, the National Socialist
closest to the Volkish leaders.[48]

Gräfe-Goldebee, a close associate of Wulle, was another significant
figure who emerged from the Volkish organizations. He too was devoted to Volkish principles, but he was a man of greater personal
force and had better social connections. Originally he had also
been a member of the DNVP, but, like Wulle, he became dissatisfied
with its slow progress in fostering Volkish interests and left the

party to join the Freiheitspartei. However, he retained intimate ties with the DNVP and for all intents and purposes continued to be regarded as a member. The DNVP, in turn, and perhaps to its advantage, regarded Gräfe-Goldebee as a close ally.

During the 1920's Gräfe-Goldebee at first maintained a cordial attitude toward Hitler. Along with General Ludendorff and Gregor Strasser, he signed the petition for Hitler's release from prison after his abortive putsch.[49] This friendliness, however, soon turned to outright hostility. For reasons similar to Wulle's, Gräfe-Goldebee decided that the leader of the National Socialists had equivocated in identifying irrevocably with the Volkish cause. For instance, in 1929 he thought that Hitler had betrayed the sacred interests of the Volk by hushing up the plight of the Germans in the southern Tyrol, which the Versailles Treaty had placed under Italian rule. Moreover, Gräfe-Goldebee charged, Hitler had done so for purely mercenary and political reasons, having been paid off by Mussolini. With this accusation, Gräfe-Goldebee, like Wulle, linked Hitler with Italian Fascism and thus to the international Catholic conspiracy.[50]

Gräfe-Goldebee pursued this line of thought even up to 1932. In that year, in a letter to a friend, he maintained that the National Socialist party, although an excellent instrument for arousing in the people an awareness of nationhood and the Volk, could not save Germany. Its leaders were concerned with self-glorification, whereas the true, creative leader puts the cause above himself and recognizes the imperfection of all that is human. Here Gräfe-Goldebee injected a note of sectional and religious prejudice by stating that the Catholic German South, the seat of the early Nazi strength, lacked all talent for statesmanship. Only the Protestant North could provide the saving forces. The leader had to come from the North, for, just as it was "inconceivable that a Bismarck could have come, let us say, from Munich, or a Luther from Baden," so, under present circumstances, the South would be unable to provide the necessary caliber of leadership. Moreover, the National Socialists (and Gräfe-Goldebee wrote this before the purge of Röhm) engaged in a demagogic flirtation with socialism which might conceivably result in National Bolshevism. Gräfe-Goldebee feared that their dependence on the undisciplined and rowdy masses was an added danger that could lead to the destruction of the disciplined, authoritarian structure of the nation.[51]

Gräfe-Goldebee and Wulle were not alone in these fears. The DNVP, where they had first received their political indoctrination, shared their views. Moreover, the party's strength lay mainly in the Protestant North and it was strongly anti-Catholic. It is obvious that these tendencies would greatly restrict the effectiveness of such a Volkish movement and its affiliates. It is difficult to see how they could attain national power if the whole of the South was written off as politically sterile. Hitler, as we know, did not make this mistake. His anti-Catholicism was subordinated to the business at hand. He negotiated with any group if it was to his advantage. When it suited him, he even dealt with the Catholic Center party. And the fact that he himself came originally from the South effectively discredited the regional prejudices of his Volkish adversaries.

In addition to the individual *Bünde* and the outstanding personalities who emerged from them, the Volkish organizations made another contribution to the furtherance of the Germanic ideology. The newspapers that the various organizations published proved to be the most effective means of communicating the ideas of the movement. The Volkish journals provided a forum through which everyone, from Class to Wulle, from the Deutschnationale Volkspartei to the National Socialists, could be heard. Among them *Deutschlands Erneuerung* and Wulle's *Deutsche Tageblatt* were the most important. Other papers, representing a narrower spectrum of the movement, such as Eckart's *Auf Gut Deutsch*, published the works of such men as the Nazi Alfred Rosenberg, the educator Hermann Lietz, the dramatist Ernst Wachler, and the ubiquitous racist Theodor Fritsch.

We must now turn to a significant question, which has already been partly answered: Why, if the *Bünde* were so widespread and, at least temporarily, popular, did they not prove to be a more durable political force? For one thing, the membership of these organizations, including the early National Socialists, was very unstable.[52] Their size at any given moment depended on a variety of factors: the immediate situation, the needs of the members, politics, education, and so forth. For another, the constant turnover in many of the smaller organizations prevented the development of a dedicated, stable cadre. But the most important reason is that the *Bünde* were essentially elitist. They scorned to proselytize, to appeal to the masses, to organize themselves into political parties. Above all, they failed to unite. As we know, Hitler did not make the same mistakes. By instituting a social program, making skillful use of propaganda, and training a dynamic leadership, Hitler solved the problem for the Nazis.

However, the Volkish organizations were not entirely ineffective. Despite their divisive tendencies and their inability to resolve differences of opinion, they continued to agitate and to produce important political figures—a reflection of their tenacity and widespread support. Ideologically, there was not much to choose between them, and they shared basic concepts with the National Socialists; politically, they were deadly enemies. But this antagonism should be interpreted as clashes between personalities in the struggle for power. For most of the figures we have discussed here thought of themselves as charismatic leaders. Class believed himself to be the "great man from above," and Hugenberg, Wulle, Gräfe-Goldebee, and even Mahraun had similar ideas.

In evaluating the contributions of these men we must not read history backwards. In 1932 it was not at all obvious that Hitler would triumph over the rest of the Volkish leaders. At that date, Hugenberg still held fast to his ambitions, while others hoped their turn would come after von Papen and Schleicher, the God-sent intermediaries, had squashed the upstart. But, at the risk of repetition, we must again emphasize that these were political antagonisms and that fundamentally all these men shared a common ideology. Basically their solutions for the crisis of the German ideology were the same. But some were more successful in accommodating themselves to the realities.

From this analysis, the claim of Volkish survivors of the Nazi regime that they opposed the rise of Hitler would seem to be exaggerated.[53] These men helped to spread the Volkish ideology, tried to destroy the Republic, assisted the rise of Hitler, and turned on him only when he became the principal threat to their aspirations, when he had become a rival personality. There was little ideological basis for their opposition; nor, in fact, did they claim serious ideological differences. That Hitler, after his assumption of power, silenced them was only logical; they had done their work and were only divisive influences at a time when a more powerful force was attempting to consolidate its power. Only a few organizations, not essentially National Socialist, escorted Hitler to power and shared it with him, however insignificantly, for a time. It is to two of these groups, the DNVP and the Stahlhelm that we must turn to see the very roots of the alliance between the German right and the Germanic ideology.

PART III

Toward National Socialism
1918–1933

CHAPTER 13

Bedeviled Conservatives

In PREVIOUS CHAPTERS our investigation was of necessity carried forward beyond 1918, for the ideas and the careers of men with whom we have been concerned developed, to a certain extent, independently of the events of the war. But though in many cases these men were not in close touch with reality, the war nonetheless marks a crucial period in the history of Volkish thought. The ideology, of course, had been widely disseminated before the war, but afterward it was suddenly transformed into a politically effective system of thought. It was after the war that the ideology acquired a mass base. And it was after the war that National Socialism emerged to translate what had been a utopian vision into a ruthless reality.

The year 1918 brought with it the kind of development which justified the fears of the Volkish thinkers. A war had been lost, and the prestige of the nation had been undermined. In 1918 revolution broke out in both the North and the South of Germany. While the revolution in the North, which resulted in the abdication of the Emperor, was brought under control by the new government of the Republic, that in the South threatened to get out of hand. In Munich, first a left-wing republic was established (1918) and then a soviet republic (1919) patterned after the Russian model. The Volkish thinkers reacted strongly to these developments in Bavaria: their worst fears of a communist Germany seemed to be coming true. The birth of Nazism was greatly facilitated by these developments in Munich. Not only did the leaders of this Bavarian Republic adhere to anti-nationalist (indeed pacifist) doctrines, but many of them were Jews besides. The Bavarian Republic was crushed in 1919 with the help of the Free Corps, troops who had refused to demobilize after the war and who became attracted to Volkish ideals. The Bavarian danger was removed, and the German Republic endured. Though it was "middle of the road" politically, those of Volkish leanings regarded it as the product of a left-wing revolution and thought that its true nature was symbolized by radical uprisings like the one that occurred in Munich.

Had the Republic found a more lasting stability, the history of Volkish thought might well have ended in 1918. But the middle classes found themselves increasingly threatened by inflation, and even during the few so-called "good years" of the Republic their status was in grave jeopardy. Increasingly they turned toward radical political solutions. And while the middle classes turned primarily toward the right, unemployment—rising toward six million within the first decade of the Weimar period—produced a strong left-wing movement among the working classes.

Haunted by the specter of a floundering nation, Germans of both political extremes sought alternatives to a parliamentary republic. With the failure of so many German hopes and dreams, the political thinking of those opposed to the Republic became increasingly utopian and unrealistic. Indeed, as we shall see, Volkish strength continued to increase even during the "good years" of the Republic; nor was it fundamentally affected by the various economic crises of the 1920's. The German right was rapidly becoming a Volkish right.

Apart from the National Socialist party (NSDAP), the political party which benefited most from the Volkish atmosphere, yet one which was also bedeviled by it, was the reconstituted Conservative party, now known as the Deutschnationale Volkspartei (DNVP). In 1918 leading members of the Conservative party proclaimed a new party which promised to pay greater attention to the masses. The party adopted the name German National Peoples' party in order to symbolize this new spirit. In reality the members of the party continued to be known popularly as the Conservatives, and we shall use both terms interchangeably. Unlike the Volkish groups which we have discussed thus far, the DNVP was a major political party, polling some six million votes at its peak. An analysis of the influence of Volkish thought upon the DNVP is thus of the utmost importance, for it goes far toward revealing the extent to which this ideology penetrated the "respectable" right. This was not a party of poets, philosophers, or the uprooted; it was composed primarily of those who believed in the sanctity of private property, the Church, and the state. Moreover, consistent with the prewar conservative tradition, the DNVP advocated loyalty to the house of Hohenzollern, and continued to do so as late as 1928.

The DNVP always attempted to give priority to the traditional conservative allegiances, and yet these principles were constantly challenged by Volkish agitators within the party itself. As a result of this tension, Volkish precepts, mixed with traditional conservative concerns, became ever stronger during the period of the Weimar Republic.

While the postwar era saw the conservative elements draw dangerously close to the Volkish movement, the trend had already been initiated in the 1880's and 1890's. During these years, which were marked by economic dislocation and recession, the conservatives entered into several alliances with Volkish organizations. In the field of agriculture, confronted with the painful process of shifting from a rural to an urban economy, the conservatives identified with the Bund der Landwirte, which had been founded on the Germanic principles of blood and soil. In the sphere of foreign policy, an alliance was quickly formed with the recently founded Pan-Germans, and it was strengthened and consolidated under the Weimar Republic. Most significantly, on the Jewish question the conservatives of the 1880's and 1890's had come to support most of Adolf Stöcker's programs to exclude Jews from German economic life. At that time, the Conservative party's Tivoli program stated that "Jews were the uncompromising opponents of conservative principles." [1]

These anti-Semitic attitudes, which were of Volkish origin, continued as undercurrents throughout the history of the Conservative party. The newly founded DNVP was Janus-faced, with one side looking back in the direction of Adolf Stöcker, who had believed that anti-Semitism does not apply to baptized Jews, and the other looking toward more radically racist Volkish notions. The latter trend came to the surface during the war, when leading members of the Conservative party allied themselves more closely with the Pan-Germans and the Vaterlandspartei (Patriotic party). Within the Conservative party itself, the tradition of the eighties and nineties was carried on by men like Gräfe-Goldebee and Richard Kunze, who became the party's propaganda chief in 1913. Kunze was popularly referred to as Knüppel Kunze (Kunze with the stick) because of his virulent attacks on the Jews. After Germany's defeat in the war, when the Conservative party had reconstituted itself as the DNVP, the Volkish impetus gained new vigor and continued to increase steadily.[2]

The Kapp putsch of 1920, in which right-wing elements attempted to overthrow the Republic, was important in the relationship of the Conservatives to the Volkish ideology. Wolfgang Kapp succeeded for a very brief time in establishing his regime in Berlin and momentarily drove the Republican government out of the city. He was overthrown by a workers' general strike—a testament to the fact that a conspiratorial group could no longer hope to effect an elitist takeover of a state in which the working class was politically aroused. To succeed, the lesson went, it was imperative that a large section of the populace lend at least its tacit support. The failure of the putsch, however, provided the Conservatives with several alternatives. On the one hand, the debacle encouraged those who thought that greater participation in the parliamentary system was the best way to achieve power. On the other hand, it similarly added fuel to the arguments of those who leaned in a Volkish direction. The latter, regardless of their small numbers, seemed to have gained strength, for their agitation, their accession to positions of leadership, and their advocacy of a revolution of the Volk constituted a stumbling block to the orthodox Conservatives. The strength of the Volkish influence within the DNVP was attested by Kapp's own secretary, who wrote that "within our circle [that is, the Kapp group] there is no enthusiasm left for anything, except for anti-Semitic agitation." [3]

The leadership of the putsch reflected the traditionalist-Volkish division, which influenced the course of events in the spring of 1920. Kapp himself was a member of the Prussian aristocracy, a high Prussian official, and a wartime member of the Pan-Germans and the Vaterlandspartei, and he vehemently opposed the efforts of Germany's wartime chancellor, Bethmann-Hollweg, to bring the hostilities to an end. As a member of the Imperial Diet, however undistinguished, he had connections with the old Conservatives as well as the Volkish camp. Among the Volkish group, Kapp played an important role in the founding of Lehmann's newspaper, *Deutschlands Erneuerung,* and was one of the first supporters of Eckart's *Auf Gut Deutsch.* [4] These connections with the Volkish ideologists brought him active supporters in his putsch. Paul Bedereck, his influential press secretary, for instance, came from the Verein Deutscher Studenten, the Volkish student movement founded by Stöcker and Naumann, while his agricultural minister-designate, Georg Wilhelm Schiele, went on to become a sponsor of the Artamanen. Kapp hesitated once he was in control of Berlin. The Volkish element among his supporters pressed for action against those who opposed the regime. Members of one of the most famous of the Free Corps, the Ehrhardt Brigade, wanted to use force against Kapp's enemies and to start a pogrom against the Jews. Kapp restrained them. In the last resort, his traditional conservatism, which valued law and order, won out. He did not want to involve the nation in a blood bath. [5] But how else was the putsch to succeed? The venture ended in a welter of endless talk and indecision in the face of the general strike. Kapp gave up and fled to Sweden—his rule had lasted all of five days. It is important for our purposes because it reveals the two sides of the Conservatives: the Volkish and that of the party tradition, the party of law and order, of the *status quo*. Indeed, officially, as an organization, the DNVP had kept out of the putsch, though many of its members were involved.

The diagnosis of the Volkish adherents in the DNVP, however, was that the putsch had failed because of insufficient Volkish direction, and they now vigorously applied the doctrines of anti-Semitism in an attempt to take over the leadership of the DNVP. They were largely responsible for the eventual elimination of the moderate Oskar Hergt (one of the founders of the DNVP) from his position as party leader in the early 1920's. The career of his successor, Count Kuno von Westarp, demonstrates well the increasing pressure to orient the party in a Volkish direction. In 1908 Westarp, already influential among the Conservatives, had advocated tolerance and equality between Jews and Germans.[6] By 1919 a Jewish journal, which had earlier praised his tolerance, castigated him for "anti-Semitic ravings." [7] When, in 1922, Wulle and Gräfe-Goldebee broke away from the DNVP, Westarp, impatient with the pace of Volkish penetration, exhorted the party to tolerate the "perhaps one-sided attitude" of the group which they had formed.[8] Volkish pressures were becoming a cardinal factor in the maneuvering for leadership of the DNVP.

The Volkish faction had, in 1921, succeeded in having the party officially designate "German-Volkish principles" as the foundation of its philosophy.[9] Local chapters of the party, closer to the grassroots sentiment, instituted discriminatory requirements and, by 1923, at least six key locals had purged themselves of Jews.[10] One year later, such attitudes had attained national dimensions. In the crisis created by the resignation of Hergt, extremist agitators erupted with diatribes against Jewish dominance of the nation, against French influence, against parliamentarianism, and against oppression by "democratic capitalists." [11] No wonder that Westarp's period of leadership, which followed, was characterized as a time of "great anti-Semitic radicalization." [12] That this development was in accord with the wishes of an influential faction of the party was attested to by Walther Graefe. He wrote proudly in an official party publication that the "flames of anti-Semitism had flared high in the work of clarification which the DNVP had undertaken." [13]

While the Volkish contingent rose rapidly in the ranks of the party, and exerted a special influence on the leadership, their contribution to the conservative ideology was all the more serious in that it influenced people outside the party, the body of German conservatives at large. Again we must reiterate that although the Volkish proponents in this, as in so many similar situations, did not gain outright control of the organization, still their participation and the public image they projected were sufficient to inculcate in a great many people a political and ideological alternative which reflected a Volkish mood. Within the DNVP, this showed itself most successfully through the propaganda department. Here they worked to boil their views of the party's program and policy toward the Jews down to the essentials. In the DNVP's drive for popular support at the polls, its attitude on the Jewish question had always been an acceptance of the Jewish stereotype. Although at first this anti-Semitic propaganda was merely an undercurrent and optional for local party chapters, in time it attained official stature and support.

Anti-Semitic propaganda was used to castigate the Republic. The fear of revolution and the fear of Jewish dominance were linked—as when radical socialists such as Eisner and Leviné (leaders of the left-wing Bavarian Republic, both of whom were killed by right-wing fanatics) were compared with respectable middle-class personalities such as the Minister-President of Prussia, Paul Hirsch. The fear of a Jewish conspiracy—capitalist or communist, depending on the situation—was also used extensively. As early as 1919, the party circulated a flier depicting Jewish stereotypes, the *Kohn Sorten* (the Kohn types), which, along with other pamphlets, warned the electorate that if it failed to vote the DNVP ticket Germany would become a slave of Judah.[14] As time went on and the DNVP mustered greater electoral strength, the anti-Semitic appeal also grew in intensity and the fear of the Jewish conspiracy was used for all it was worth. The fliers of 1920 had asked the rhetorical question: "What has become of Berlin?"—to be answered: "A playground for the Jews!" By 1924 the party had declared that its efforts had been expanded to battle the "Jewish influence on all fronts." It exhorted the public to do likewise.[15] The use of portraits (or, rather, caricatures) of various Jewish public figures, making them scapegoats for the economic and political crisis in Germany, became popular, culminating in the DNVP poster of 1932, which depicted a series of Jewish faces with the caption: "Such men have guarded the beauty and dignity of the Republic."[16] But this crude campaign propaganda had a sophisticated side, in its visual restatement of a commonplace of Volkish thought. The public was told that the unpleasant and repulsive external features of the Jew did in fact correspond to an equally distasteful, egotistical, and alien internal nature, and that the two races, the Jews and the Aryans, were inherently incompatible and that any admixture would be to the detriment of the purity of Germanic culture, society, and ideals.

Thus, the Conservatives bear great responsibility for transmitting a central tenet of the Volkish and Germanic ideology to the masses. Side by side with the racist propaganda of the NSDAP, whose anti-Semitic fliers were virtually duplicated by the Conservatives, the DNVP made such anti-Semitism a central ingredient of political success. Oskar Hergt, for all his lack of Volkish zeal, which cost him his leadership, admitted in 1919 that the "wave of anti-Semitism will facilitate in an extraordinary manner the electioneering of the DNVP." [17] A decade later a Jewish journal stated that the DNVP welcomed anti-Semitism as a means of gathering votes. This statement was based on an analysis of DNVP newspapers,[18] but the propaganda posters had never left any doubt that, throughout the history of the party, whatever the leadership might claim, it was committed to the Volkish Jewish stereotype.

While respectable DNVP personalities in top hats and frock coats moved in the best social circles and played at parliamentary politics, their aides were on the street corners disseminating racist propaganda. The volume of anti-Jewish literature that flowed from both Conservative and extremist sources shows once again the central function of the Jew in the Volkish ideology. It is wrong to believe that the Jews were but a side issue and that a Hottentot minority in Germany would have served the purpose equally well.

By the 1920's the Jew had become a principal figure in Volkish and in much of conservative thought both inside and outside the DNVP, and was absolutely essential to the endurance of the ideology. Years of Volkish development of the stereotyped image had culminated in projecting the Jews as the only real obstacle to the attainment of the ideal society. The Volkish revolution, and the causes aligned with it, became an anti-Jewish revolution. Indeed, the clever Goebbels and the pragmatic DNVP would hardly have used such propaganda unless they were sure that it was a most effective popular objectification of their respective ideologies.

By 1929, the DNVP had officially gone on record as closed to Jews,[19] and yet there were some Jews and half Jews who belonged to the organization until the victory of the Nazis. Some of them, such as R. G. Quaatz, the floor leader of the party in the Diet, who committed suicide after Hitler's accession to power, even shaped policy. Yet Quaatz was only half Jewish and was an exception. Many Jews were not aware of the party's change in policy, and as late as 1928 Jewish members of certain locals wrote to the national office requesting information on the party's position on the Jews. As a matter of expediency—for this was just before an election to the Diet—headquarters sidestepped the issues and either replied after the election or ignored the questions entirely. A prime example of this occurred in 1932, when the question was of some importance in deciding the allegiance of many Jewish election districts.[20]

Why Jews continued to be interested in the DNVP has been debated innumerable times, but we do not have a really satisfactory answer. Two explanations, by no means mutually exclusive, may be suggested. Many Jews misunderstood the profundity of anti-Semitism in Germany and underestimated its effectiveness as a political weapon. They regarded the Germanic ideology as part of a nationalistic movement within which Jews might be accepted if they submerged themselves deeply and inextricably in the cause and the Volk. There was precedent for such thinking. Had not many early advocates of the Volkish outlook—such as Kapp, among the more recent—distinguished between the native and the immigrant East European Jew? The DNVP itself fostered the illusion when it harped on the dangers of further Jewish immigration from the East.[21]

The second reason for the Jews' continued adherence was more tactical and therefore more rational. They simply chose the lesser evil. From the point of view of the Jews, if a movement advocating the most radical brand of Volkish anti-Semitism was about to triumph, as the 1932 Nazi victory at the polls portended, then supporting the DNVP seemed a logical move. What were they hoping for from the DNVP? What was it in the party that provided them with some hope that the choice would be a correct one and to their advantage? It was the traditional element that had been bedeviled by the Volkish extremism, but which still defined the party's objective as the retention of order and property under a revived monarchism bolstered by Christian ethics. Thus what the Jews identified with was the core of traditional conservatism which still seemed to reflect the aspirations of the movement.

What were these elements which, although they had been surrounded by Volkish ideas and pressures, had not completely succumbed to the popular appeal of fanaticism and could still maintain the party's image as a champion of traditional conservatism? There was, as we have said, a considerable devotion to the idea of monarchy in the Wilhelmine tradition of Protestant Christianity. One of the party's favorite election appeals, for instance, depicted a mother and daughter reading the Bible, with the caption: "We cling to the word of God, vote DNVP!" [22] And even where it identified with anti-Semitism, it did permit the Jews the alternatives of conversion and spiritualization. Their anti-Semitism differed from the street-corner variety in that it derived from the ideas of Stöcker, whose antagonism toward the Jews, though volatile at times, was religious and served the interests of an ordered society and government. Consequently, it had a built-in safeguard that prevented the DNVP from resorting to anything approximating the "final solution." As late as March 1933, the central office of the party wrote that however much the soul of the Volk boils over at the mention of the Jew, the party opposes as a matter of principle any terrorization of groups.[23] The Nazis, devoid of such scruples, omitted Stöcker from their list of honorary antecedents and instead referred back to Otto Böckel and his mass-oriented anti-Semitism.[24]

This rejection of force represented a fundamental outlook of the party which was endorsed by many people, among them the vast majority of the DNVP's leaders. One such leader was Gottfried Traub. Traub represented the Protestant influence in the party and guided a whole section of ministers, one of the party's major assets, who formed a special subgroup that included the future bishop Otto Dibelius. The ministers rationalized their membership in the party as participation in the fight against leftist and anti-clerical forces, and at the same time an opportunity to further the ties of family, Volk, and German culture. No doubt they felt that the party's attitudes would also encourage church attendance. Moreover, a report to the Reichs Chancellery before Hitler's seizure of power emphasized that these Protestant ministers saw in the Volkish movement an ally against ultramontane Catholicism.[25] Many a German pulpit utilized the captive Sunday audience to disseminate Volkish ideas, and enveloped them in the respectability of Protestant orthodoxy rather than in Germanic sun symbolism.

In 1928 Gottfried Traub ruefully exclaimed that it was indeed a great "misfortune that Stöcker had failed." [26] At that time, this philosophy of conservatism looked like a godsend, for it seemed to provide something for everybody without involving extremism. But as a matter of fact Traub, early in life, had repudiated the Protestant orthodoxy of this conservatism. He had been converted to Jatho's liberal religious movement early in the century and had even joined the prewar Social Democratic party. However, the war changed all this and "introduced" Traub to the greater problems of the age. He joined the imperialistic Vaterlandspartei and returned to the orthodox Lutheran Church. Traub now devoted himself to the social and political problems of the day. Outraged by the "ineptitude" of the Republic, he participated in the Kapp putsch—in which he did his best to subdue the volatile extremism of the Ehrhardt Brigade—and joined the inner circle of the DNVP. Up to this point in his life, his radical political development reflected the pattern of the Conservative party; he even shared its qualified endorsement of Hitler. Traub appreciated and supported what he considered Hitler's "pure" nationalism but felt that it was too circumscribed and restricted by the leader's fanatical personality. He even went so far as to endorse the Hitler-Ludendorff putsch, and hearing of its failure—which he ascribed to Hitler's extremism—exclaimed that it was the "worst hour in my life." [27]

Though Traub had severed official connections with the Jatho movement, he still retained the imprint of his past associations. He conceived of Lutheranism in somewhat mystical terms and thought of it as the spiritual ingredient within the broad concept of the state as well as the religion of the personal and individual soul. Like Diederichs, he stressed the importance of the *Geist*, but he was an even more thoroughgoing Hegelian. He believed that the *Geist* saw the present as a mirror of the future, a future which would bring freedom through the instrumentality of the state viewed as an expression of the Volk. [28]

In this context, he inveighed against the supposed domination of the Jews as reflecting the supremacy of a materialism which prevented the Volk from attaining its due greatness. To him, Jewish and proletarian materialism, along with the vulgar desires of the masses, were elements hostile to the Germanic ideology. [29] And since he feared the use of radical and violent methods of eliminating the Jewish problem more than the materialism of the Jews, Traub fell out of sympathy with the National Socialists after Hitler came to power. The battle against Jewish influence was important for Traub, but it was not the central task. He believed that obsession with Jews endangered Germany's military potential. For if the anti-Jewish emphasis became the primary concern, as in National Socialism, the German soldier would not fight France with a "holy hate," but rather with the feeling that the French soldier was also a dupe of the Jewish conspiracy. Thus his will to fight would be weakened as enmity toward that conspiracy united the two "dupes" more than it divided them. [30] However, this rather odd rationalization must not obscure the fact that Traub's point of view was similar to that of several other Volkish figures. Men such as the Volkish writer Wilhelm Stapel also played down the Jewish question (while fully accepting the Volkish stereotype) because the salvation of the Volk must come through its own inner strength and not merely through war against the principal adversary.

When Traub rejected the policies of Hitler during the Third Reich he was sincere. He was one of the few former Volkish leaders who, in their isolation under Hitler, watched the culmination of their former Volkish policies with undisguised abhorrence. Traub, who frankly states that he was aware of the utter horror of the "final solution," has also blamed himself for cowardice in not helping those marked for extermination.[31] Eventually he embraced the theological precepts of Karl Barth, in contending that all religion, and especially Protestantism, must be totally disengaged from worldly power, that authority must not be allowed to rape the soul.[32]

If Gottfried Traub can stand for the more traditional conservatism within the party, Paul Bang, the party's economic expert, represented the extreme Volkish element among the leadership. He placed the Jews in the center of things. Under the name of Wilhelm Meister he authored one of the most unrestrained Volkish attacks upon the Jews: *Judas Schuldbuch* (*The Jewish Book of Crimes*). He condemned the Jews as being responsible for all crimes, and especially economic ones. To him international trade was nothing more than a form of Jewish nationalism.[33] Because Bang's economic theory was characteristic of economic thought within the DNVP, we must analyze it further. In typical Volkish manner he believed economic questions to be ethical questions, and by that he meant that they were related to the longing for the community of the Volk.[34] The Germans, he held, revered spiritual freedom as essential, but regarded it as limited if it were tied to merely material considerations, as was done by the French and the Jews. Spiritual freedom existed only within the Volk; thus, for Bang, anything that diminished the role of the Volk must be identified with materialism. Therefore free trade was the materialistic opposite of freedom.

Bang believed that a self-sufficient economy would solve Germany's problems, and he demanded a return to the mercantilist ideas of Friedrich List. Within the nation, he visualized a *Bund* of employers and workers forming a true community, with the employer assuming the role of genuine leadership. Here the ideal of the *Bund* again appeared, now transposed to the industrial scene. However, the emphasis was no longer solely upon agriculture. Bang linked industry to the land, because he recognized that the peasants constituted the greatest market for industrial products.[35] His theory of self-sufficiency entailed the expansion of Germany's frontiers so that the nation would be large enough to sustain a growing internal market. In his prescription for the ailing German economy Bang called for spaciousness of territory and fullness of blood.[36] Because blood meant race, only the Aryans could make this mercantilism work. The Jews were free traders, and thus could only oppose the true spirituality of the Volk. Against this backdrop, it is not surprising that, for Bang, the social question was an ethical question rather than an economic one. The official DNVP party publication endorsed this: "Mammonism does not reside in the purse but in the heart. . . . Man must accept the task which God and destiny have given him and swear a holy loyalty to the Volk." [37]

Nothing, except for their mass propaganda techniques, could better demonstrate the Volkish orientation of the DNVP than this economic theory, for it was shared by the entire movement. Bang wrote as economic expert not only for the journals of his party but for most other Volkish papers as well. Besides collaborating with the Volkish press, Bang was a member of the Pan-Germans and sat on the editorial board of Wulle's *Deutsche Zeitung*. When, in 1933, Hugenberg entered the NSDAP-DNVP coalition government (which prepared the way for Hitler's sole assumption of power that same year), he brought Bang with him into the Ministry of Economics. making him his secretary of state. With Hugenberg's resignation Bang vanished into obscurity, remaining, however, as a "guest" of the NSDAP in the rigged German Diet.

Alfred Hugenberg has been mentioned before in these pages. He now comes to the forefront of Volkish politics, for in 1928 he became the undisputed leader of the DNVP. However, Hugenberg had had a long history of involvement in conservative politics, a history that shows the growing influence of Volkish ideas in his thinking. He helped found the Pan-Germans at the end of the nineteenth century and from the very beginning of the DNVP was one of its leading figures. While he was gaining prominence in politics, Hugenberg had done well in private life, in a field that not only brought him wealth and connections in the business community, but also controlled certain propaganda machinery. For a long period of time he had been director of the Krupp enterprises and by 1918, through speculation and behind-the-scenes activities, had succeeded in assembling one of the largest publishing empires in Germany. Shortly thereafter, he climaxed his business career by gaining control of Germany's most important film company, the UFA.

While Hugenberg was successful in applying his economic leverage to gain domination of the DNVP in 1928, his subsequent hopes of directing the future of Germany came to naught. But he tried, and his years as party leader must be seen as preparation for the final attempt. On the basis of the idea that the German right alone could provide for future prosperity, internal security, and the cultural well-being of the nation, Hugenberg was determined to bring about a unity of the entire right. For this he sought and received support from both industry and agriculture. Through his connections with manufacturers he persuaded many influential men to join the party who had previously kept their distance. Representatives of agricultural interests hardly needed any encouragement, since they had extended heavy support to the conservative and Volkish organizations for years. Then too, Hugenberg's ideas on land and agricultural production were received favorably by landed interests. For him, as for his Volkish brethren, agriculture provided the real bulwark for the whole national structure.[38]

Hugenberg was essentially a technician of power, and Volkish newspapers often accused him of lacking firm ideological foundations. Yet Hugenberg shared Volkish attitudes, from regarding agriculture as the primeval trade to nostalgia for ancient "Indo-Germanic freedoms." He inveighed against "urbanism," as well as against what he called "sophisticated intellectualizing," as attitudes which dimmed the vision of Germanic eyes.[39] Nevertheless, there is one great gap in Hugenberg's ideology: anti-Semitism is missing. This has puzzled historians. Why should he have departed from Volkish thought on this issue? Hugenberg's opponents within the movement accused him of harboring Jews in his Scherl publishing house (there were eight Jews among the six thousand employees).[40] Still, he published at least one book which, following Bang's line of thought, linked the universal Jewish conspiracy with liberal economics.[41] Nevertheless, compared with Westarp, Bang, or even Traub, Hugenberg was certainly moderate on the Jewish question, or, as one Volkish periodical reported, his views were "veiled." [42]

They were veiled for a significant reason: his one-track mind was totally obsessed with the Marxist danger. Just as Traub had feared that an undue stress upon the Jews would make the DNVP forget the French, so Hugenberg believed that nothing should distract the Germans from the fight against Bolshevism. At the same 1931 party congress at which even Traub condemned the Jews and upheld racial thought, Hugenberg, ignoring the Jewish problem, pleaded for a healing of the "urban-Marxist" paralysis of the brain which was the source of all un-German theories.[43]

Hugenberg's obsessive fear of the left, of the Marxist parties, was the culmination of the fears of the older conservatives, who throughout the Wilhelmine period had regarded the existence of the Social Democratic party as the "great problem" [44] whose destruction was their principal task. During the Weimar Republic, opposition to the socialist parties, including the Communist party, was the DNVP's single most important reason for participating in coalition governments even though they stood opposed to the constitution they swore to uphold. From this point of view, Hugenberg considered that any concentration on the Jews as the prime agents of un-Germanic thought would only serve to distract the party from smashing the real enemy, the left. Yet, under his leadership popular anti-Semitic propaganda went on unchecked and among his close associates were men like Paul Bang and the Pan-German Heinrich Class. As far as we know, Hugenberg never protested against the party's anti-Jewish policy. He concentrated on other issues but he may well have shared the usual Volkish attitude toward the Jews.

Still pursuing the ends which had eluded the older conservatives, Hugenberg turned to the Nazis and the Stahlhelm (Steel Helmet) Veterans' Organization as allies in the destruction of the Marxist parties. They too had no scruples and were willing to try constitutional as well as non-constitutional means. In this area Hugenberg could count on the history of collaboration between the Nazis and the DNVP. Prior to the Hitler putsch of 1924, local chapters of the two groups had occasionally worked together harmoniously. A Catholic paper had earlier attested to the sympathy that the parties had for each other, at least in Württemberg, and we have documents which detail how the DNVP encouraged the National Socialists in Bavaria in the struggle against their common foe: Marxism and the Republic.[45] And while in later years Hugenberg turned away from Hitler—only to come back in the end—and called him "too fanatical," his mass movement's flirtation with socialism "too dangerous," by 1931 he was ready to include the Nazis in the Harzburger Front, a coalition designed to unify the right-wing elements. (This coalition takes its name from the "watering place" which was the scene of a mass meeting of members of the DNVP, the NSDAP, and the Stahlhelm Veterans' Organization in 1931.)

In his effort to consolidate this coalition, Hugenberg, according to a close political friend, believed that while Bolshevism brought death, National Socialism merely endangered life. Germans must attempt by every means to transform danger to life into a saving of life.[46] Thus, he set out to accomplish both of his ends: first to save the nation and the Volk, and second to disarm the National Socialists and raise himself to power.

To accomplish the first task Hugenberg went to great lengths to appease Hitler and enlist the aid of his forces. In 1932, for instance, he protested against the government's order prohibiting the SA, claiming that the order represented a Marxist plot to disarm the guardians of the nation.[47] Similarly, when Hindenburg, who believed the NSDAP to be more socialist than nationalist, criticized Hugenberg for his collaboration with the Nazis, Hugenberg replied that his collaboration was aimed at strengthening the sincerely national forces within the NSDAP.[48] At that time, he still justified his actions as attempts to prevent the National Socialists from developing into a variant of the deadly enemy, socialism.

In pursuit of the second goal, eliminating Hitler as a contender for power, Hugenberg used the Harzburger Front as a wedge to separate the various wings of the NSDAP. We must recall that at that time the National Socialists had not yet become a monolithic organization. In fact, throughout these years Hitler was deeply involved in a power struggle with Gregor Strasser. Hugenberg's attempt to form a united front did serve to produce a crisis in the leadership of the NSDAP which, if pursued correctly, might indeed have weakened and tamed the party. Just as he reassured Hindenburg that he was encouraging the nationalist and not the socialist elements of the NSDAP, so Hugenberg acted in the meetings held to organize the front. But here, strangely enough, it was Hitler who was the main adversary—in all probability as potentially the most powerful political foe—rather than persons like Strasser and Frick, who were ironically considered to be moderate men with whom one could make a compromise.[49] Hugenberg's efforts, as we know, failed. Like the later attempts of Schleicher, who attempted to work through Strasser, his efforts shattered on the fundamental misconception of both the nature of the NSDAP and the tenacity of Hitler.

Unsuccessful on this level, Hugenberg thought it would be easier to curb Hitler and even discard him after the National Socialists had discovered for themselves how thorny Germany's problems actually were. At this point Hugenberg and his party became the victims of the conservative ideology which believed in elitism and was deeply suspicious of mass movements—a trend reinforced by the elitism of Volkish thought. Hugenberg called universal suffrage a "crime." [50] The DNVP held essentially the same elitist ideas as the Volkish thinkers. But an espousal of a feudal order of society was out of touch with a democratically oriented Volkish movement. Although the DNVP, with the help of Volkish propaganda, did succeed in indoctrinating large sections of the masses, it could not arouse the enthusiasm which Hitler inspired in his followers.

It took Hugenberg almost a year to realize that his post in the Nazi-DNVP coalition government gave him little strength and that, far from playing the lion tamer, he had collaborated on Hitler's terms. But disillusionment did not turn into hostility. Subsequent events disclosed the essential sympathies between the two parties, which, in spite of differences on who should rule and the relative importance of the Jewish problem, allowed for a continuation of close relations. When Hugenberg left the government he still assured Hitler that he would not oppose the Third Reich in any way. His reasons reflected the policy that had led many conservatives to countenance Hitler's assumption of total power. He stated: "For us [the DNVP] there can never be a common ground with Marxists and Communists," who were opposing the Third Reich.[51] The anti-Communist obsession persisted, and in 1941 he prayed for the success of Hitler's Russian campaign. Victory, he argued, would not only destroy Bolshevism but would also open new agricultural, industrial, and economic vistas for Germany. The imperialist dreams of his Pan-German youth had been revived,[52] now with a greater likelihood of success. Unlike Traub, Hugenberg apparently did not regret his past, did not undergo a spiritual conversion. To the end he regretted only that he had not been the one to have had the chance to lead his beloved Volk into a Volkish, conservative, anti-Marxist future.

The question then remains whether the DNVP would have been greatly different from the NSDAP had it gained power instead. To many people their program was substantially the same as that of the Nazis. A Jewish journal, for instance, stated that, next to the NSDAP, the DNVP was the strongest factor in political anti-Semitism.[53] This was correct. Throughout the 1920's, as we have seen, they employed a similar propaganda. We can speculate that had they won, they would have instituted "cold" instead of "hot" pogroms. Nevertheless, they would have ensured complete exclusion of Jews from public office as well as from all cultural activities in Germany. They would have pushed the Jews back into a ghetto-like isolation, perhaps allowing a greater number to become honorary Aryans than did the Nazis. In short, both parties, the NSDAP and the DNVP, had agreed that the time had come to end the century of Jewish emancipation.

From our point of view, the DNVP must stand as one of the most important transmitters of Volkish thought and the Germanic ideology. Due to its greater resources, it influenced many more people than did the *Bünde,* and it appealed to many voters because it was respectable. If one was a member of the DNVP, one was not considered a Nazi rowdy or a Volkish fanatic. The underlying Germanic ideology of the party was clothed in such respectable garb that the "better" classes dismissed the party's election propaganda as being intended solely for the mob. As a result, the DNVP drew to its ranks, or enjoyed the sympathy of, wealthy bankers, industrialists, and professional people who would not have considered dining with Hitler but did so with Westarp, Traub, Bang, and Hugenberg. Then too, its image was made respectable by its sympathy for the deposed imperial family, and there were many rumors that the party would endorse the Crown Prince as the nation's future emperor. In short, the role the DNVP played was insidious precisely because it was covert. Whereas the Nazis openly proclaimed their intentions, giving the people sufficient time to find another alternative, even if only at the expense of a civil war, the party of Hugenberg hid behind a mantle of respectability which escorted Hitler into power and came out empty-handed itself. In this, however, the DNVP was not alone. Closely allied with the Stahlhelm Veterans' Organization and the Deutschnationale Handelsgehilfen Verband (the largest white-collar workers' union), the DNVP involved many people in Volkish activity who were outside the Nazi movement. It is to these organizations that we now must turn.

CHAPTER 14

Veterans and Workers

THROUGHOUT HISTORY and in every nation, veterans' organizations tend to become rightist pressure groups. This holds true both in countries victorious in war and, especially, in defeated ones. The war experience seems to unite the former combatants in an aggressive devotion to the fatherland in whose name, after all, they risked their lives. Any proposal to change their nation's policies is looked upon with suspicion. At times, especially those on the losing side, veterans will regard new ideas as a betrayal of their trust and as a sign of a lack of patriotism on the part of those who support them. Veterans want their nation to remain that for which their brothers died and for which they themselves suffered.

In Germany, not only was there a built-in resistance to change, but it took a most active form. German soldiers returned from the front to a land that had undergone hectic, but by no means thorough, transformation. The monarchy had been replaced by a republic. The disorder, dislocation, and disillusion they experienced engendered a strong desire for order and stability. Moreover, the first shock was only reinforced when it seemed that the Republic would endure. Consequently, veterans' organizations, like the Free Corps, aligned themselves with Volkish organizations or created their own rightist groups. For the same reason some veterans formed themselves into *Bünde* and occasionally gained sufficient power to be able to influence political events.

The largest and most famous veterans' organization, the Stahlhelm, was founded in 1919. It was immediately regarded as a success—though its membership figures vary depending on their source (the organization itself claimed a million members, whereas its enemies contended it had only half that number).[1] The Stahlhelm did not assert for itself any outright political role or consider itself a partisan body—if being for one's country right or wrong, as you have fought for it, does not in itself constitute partiality. To be sure, in the beginning at least, they abided by their declaration of political neutrality—except against the left—and attempted to raise themselves above the existing political framework.[2] Their goal was to represent the interests of the fatherland, not merely to attain political power. Their devotion found perfect expression in a statement made by the national leadership in 1924. In that year, after the Ruhr crisis, after the failure of Hitler's putsch, after the Communists had shown their strength in several German states, the Stahlhelm directorate asserted: "The Stahlhelm fights for the German Volk and therefore for the renewal of the Germanic race; it fights to strengthen German self-consciousness so that foreign racial influences will be eliminated from the nation."[3] This typically Volkish statement illuminates the organization's alleged political neutrality or, better, its rejection of political parties.

However, the racial impetus which was becoming important to the ideological vitality of the Stahlhelm was ambivalent. For instance, the Stahlhelm accepted racial distinctions between the Aryans and the Jews. It considered the Jews a foreign race that could not claim total German citizenship, an alien people that could never submerge themselves in a broader identity with the genuine German culture.[4] Yet there were exceptions. There were good people among the Jews, people who had made their home in Germany for several generations—three generations was the minimum requirement for any pretension to being a German resident—and some who, accepting "their place" and acting accordingly, had made appreciable contributions to the nation.[5] And, though grudgingly and with some qualifications, the Stahlhelm answered a request by the Jewish C. V. Zeitung for clarification on its stand on the Jewish question by agreeing that Jews had indeed fought for Germany on the battlefield. But the answer was qualified, for the Stahlhelm leadership minimized Jewish casualties and claimed that most Jews had remained behind the battle lines.[6] Hitler, as we know, was to go even further on this point.

Taking the admitted Jewish virtues into account, the Stahlhelm, in 1924 and 1925, went on record in favor of a division of labor between the Jewish and German veterans. Acting on the suggestion of the organization's leader, Franz Seldte, the veterans decided that there should be a clear-cut division in all activities between the two races.[7] This policy was eventually implemented when the Stahlhelm gradually barred Jews from membership in its chapters. This action was defended as late as 1932. At that time, the Stahlhelm referred to the Volkish spirit that had provided them with a "clear-cut solution" to such a vexing problem.[8]

But the racial thought of the Stahlhelm was not limited to anti-Semitism. In 1924, a year that in many respects seems to have been a time of great stock taking within the Stahlhelm, the organization's official journal, *Der Stahlhelm*, emphasized the importance of dealing with the rapidly waning physical and spiritual powers of the Nordics. It prescribed a course of racial revival and exhorted the German Volk to a program of racial hygiene.[9] The Stahlhelm advocated a better acquaintance with Germany's past, with the heroic deeds of the ancient Germans, and with the manifest Germanism in certain forms of contemporary culture. Adult education courses were organized for members, and a curriculum of the Brunswick chapter (1925), for example, included studies in the racial foundation of the German Volk, the virtues of the peasantry as opposed to the alienation of urban living, and even the precepts of the Artamanen.[10] The racial emphasis, however, did not persist at the same intensity throughout the organization's history, and this might account for the view that it was not as racist-oriented as has been suggested here. But the periods of relaxation in the late 1920's and early 1930's are readily explainable as a revulsion against the racial fanaticism of the Nazis, which the Stahlhelm, like many other Volkish groups, considered inappropriate and too dangerous. At such times the veterans would draw a distinction between a racism of blood and a racism of the spirit, advocating and endorsing the latter.[11]

Besides racism, the Stahlhelm adopted other elements of Volkish thought. It tended to further emphasize the racial division of peoples and to stress the concepts of the German Volk and the Aryan race. For their proposed social reorganization of the nation the veterans went back to medieval times and advocated government by an aristocratic elite, elected by indirect vote (modeled on the ancient Germanic ducal elections), as a means of achieving a "Germanic democracy." [12] They also stressed Germany's agricultural base and declared it endangered by the growing forces of industry and materialism.[13] Materialism, especially the Marxist variety, was singled out as a particularly dangerous enemy, for it subverted the principal unifying force of Germanism: the camaraderie of the *Bund*.

Politically, the Stahlhelm stood close to the DNVP. Alongside the Conservatives, the veterans' organization marched from the Harzburger Front, which it had joined in 1931, into the coalition DNVP-NSDAP government of 1933. Here it reached the peak of its power in that its leader, Franz Seldte, entered the Hitler government.

Originally, around the time of the Hitler-Ludendorff putsch, Seldte considered Hitler too fanatical. His objections—to a large extent similar to those of the DNVP—were shared by others in his own organization. The Protestant wing of the Stahlhelm, as late as 1931, attempted to tar Hitler with the same brush used by Wulle and Gräfe-Goldebee. At that time, Major Stephani, the Stahlhelm leader of Berlin, declared that National Socialism was an alien, "Catholic-Fascist" conspiracy.[14] At times, such as in 1928, Seldte went further than this and publicly differed with Hitler on the anti-Semitic emphasis. He was of the opinion that Nazi racism was too negative; pro-Germanic propaganda, he claimed, would have been more effective than Julius Streicher's campaign based on alleged Jewish sexual excesses.[15] But the members of the Stahlhelm slowly dissociated themselves from this moderate position and pressured him into reconciling his differences with the Nazis. By the mid-1920's, in some localities at least, extremist Volkish ideas seemed to have penetrated rather deeply: a result of the constant spreading of a Volkish mood.[16]

However, the Stahlhelm continued to disagree with the National Socialists on several important points. Within the Harzburger Front they battled openly. At one point the SA became so incensed that it refused to march in the streets with the Stahlhelm veterans, while the veterans in turn, to the chagrin of the National Socialists, entered their own nominee to oppose Hitler and the other candidates in the 1932 presidential elections. But it amounted to nothing. Düsterberg, the veterans' standard bearer, did not direct his campaign against Hitler; in fact, he even defended Hitler's right to run in a German election while holding Austrian citizenship. Interestingly enough, Düsterberg's argument was typically Volkish in that he maintained that Hitler had earned the privilege while thousands of Jewish immigrants presumed to enjoy the rights of Germans without having made a single contribution to Germany's well-being.[17] In the presidential election that same year, Seldte released his members to vote for either the NSDAP or the DNVP candidate.[18]

In January of 1933, Seldte joined the NSDAP-DNVP coalition cabinet. His differences with the Nazis on anti-Semitism had disappeared.[19] The more Volkish Düsterberg, ironically enough, was dropped because one of his great-grandparents was Jewish. Seldte, who over the last few years had succumbed to the increasingly strong Volkish pressure, supervised the merger of the Stahlhelm into the Nazi party and served throughout the Third Reich as Minister of Labor. As such, he exemplified the essentially moderate man who, intensely concerned with the German crisis and taken by the Volkish solution to it, drifted into the arms of the National Socialists.

Germany's largest white-collar union, the Deutschnationale Handelsgehilfen Verband (DHV), also drifted toward the Volkish solution. To a large extent it followed the socio-economic views of Stöcker. Stöcker had opposed the concentration of economic power in the hands of the few, which he equated with a supposed Jewish domination of the economic forces in Germany. The removal of the Jews would restore economic well-being to the classes which had lost it. Stöcker also advocated a corporate state in which estates made up of professions would replace parliamentary government. The DHV admitted its debt to Stöcker as late as 1929, when a union leader asserted that "we felt ourselves to be Stöcker's successors." [20] The union was founded in 1895 to organize commercial employees. It attained rapid success and was soon able to boast a large membership as well as considerable financial resources. The membership increased at a tremendous rate, practically tripling from 50,216 in 1903 to 148,079 on the eve of the war. Under the Republic its size doubled twice over, reaching 254,032 in 1924 and 409,022 in 1931.[21] Its coffers increased at a similar rate, and its income was supplemented by careful investment in banks, industries, and small loans to members or organizations. Competently managed, the DHV's annual income had reached the impressive figure of thirty million marks by 1926.[22] But these tangible successes only provided the background to the ideological impetus, dear to the heart of this Volkish labor union. This is illustrated by the way it used its resources.

The DHV, like the Stahlhelm, considered itself politically neutral, unaligned with any party, and welcomed all within its ranks. It thought itself above politics, motivated only by a sincere concern for the state of the nation's moral fiber. This did not mean, however, that it had no broad national goals, or ideas for improving the nation's culture, or an alertness to the dangers which threatened the German Volk. Prior to the war, the DHV had established close relations with the Pan-Germans, for both organizations were in favor of a more militant and imperialistic foreign policy. On the issue of nationalization of the land, it found itself on common ground with Damaschke's land reform movement.[23] But, above all, it still entertained Stöcker's aversion to the Jews—an aversion it had brought up to date in the intervening years in the form of outright anti-Semitism —and approached national and Jewish questions from the racist point of view. The DHV was not simply a naïve participant in racist issues. Its bookstores promoted Theodor Fritsch's *Handbook of the Jewish Question*, and its members listened to lectures of men like the Austrian racist Liebermann von Sonnenberg.[24]

Volkish anti-Semitism was central to the organizational structure and existence of the DHV. Within its ranks the issue served to unite the members of several parties, such as the Catholic Center party and even the Democratic party, and provided them with a common denominator for action. All elements endorsed an anti-Semitic domestic policy that claimed to solve not only the problems of the nation at large but also those of the working man. And what the union endorsed, it implemented. Jews were barred from membership, and in labor disputes employers that happened to be Jewish were fought with special vehemence. Jewish employers were charged with conspiring against the Aryan employees' welfare, with thwarting the employees' desire to better their conditions, with infringing on the employees' commitment to Christianity. One of the union's great attractions was its militant fight for a shorter work week, a struggle which was directed principally at Jewish businessmen who conducted transactions on Sundays.[25]

But the DHV had other Volkish tendencies, in addition to its anti-Semitism. As we have noted, the organization, though many of its members came from a working-class milieu, had more exalted aspirations. None of these were very clearly defined and no particular trend dominated. While the organization fought to obtain for its workers better wages and working conditions, greater and more equitable insurance and welfare funds, it looked beyond this struggle for its real identity. The members of the DHV wanted to be considered bourgeois, not proletarian. They were commercial workers and therefore properly believed that they were not members of the "classic" working class. Their outlook was petit bourgeois, and they were obsessed with preserving their status and not slipping into the proletariat. It is significant, as we have mentioned before, that this union represented the deepest penetration of the Volkish movement among the lower classes and that even here it remained essentially bourgeois. In this light, it is easy to understand why the union looked beyond its economic function to the cultural life of the nation,[26] to which it brought a Volkish emphasis.

With its ample resources, the DHV was able to provide many Volkish causes with financial support. In the 1920's it obtained control of leading Volkish publishing firms, the most famous of which was the Hanseatische Verlags-Anstalt of Hamburg.[27] The various issues of its *Jahrbuch* are filled with articles praising "German loyalty and German heroism," and they contain information on Guido von List, Felix Dahn, and a whole series on Volkish writers.[28] The Volkish ideology was important precisely because of the union's desire to be more than a mere working man's organization.

The effort to bring culture to the membership had the result of romanticizing the workers' view of themselves. Not only did they consider themselves bourgeois rather than working-class, but many had the romantic notion that they were artisans and longed for a return to past conditions and institutions. They thought of themselves as constituting an "estate" [29] which had been cruelly disregarded by contemporary society with its emphasis on materialism and industrialization. They yearned for a revival of a society based on guild relationships. At times, the idea of estates paralleled the concept of the *Bund*. For example, one leader equated the corporate, estate structure of the nation with the true community of the spirit, the *Bund*, as represented by the Youth Movement.[30] This romanticism was stretched further in connection with the role of women in modern life. The DHV, probably as a practical measure to insure enough jobs for men, opposed the employment of women outside the home. Wilhelm Sollmann, a one-time minister of the interior under the Republic, was correct when he called the union a "stranger to reality." [31]

But the DHV's connections with the Volkish movement were even more intimate. Many who belonged to the union also occupied positions of leadership in other organizations of a Volkish character. This was especially true of the DHV's youth branch, the Fahrende Gesellen (Wandering Apprentices). Founded in 1909, it set itself the task of rediscovering for youth the beauties of nature, of the German landscape, and of the peasant culture of the Volk. Its members participated in Germanic festivals similar to those of the Youth Movement and depicted the life history of their people in heroic songs and folk poems.[32] Of course, it was not completely idyllic. Many of its leaders were well aware of the political questions that faced the nation—or the Volk, as they chose to put it—and attempted to solve them. During the war many of them fought for the fatherland, and on the battlefield, as well as after the war, they developed a close identity with the society they had served. As a result, many of them wished to continue defending it, in a different way of course, and joined the soldiers' organizations, or *Bünde*, which mushroomed after 1918. The Gesellen supported and met in the rooms of such organizations as the Thule Society, which had been organized in Munich and was to provide the framework for the rise of the National Socialist party.[33]

The DHV, however, encountered difficulty when it attempted to form close relations with political parties. As an organization representing the interests of working men, regardless of how they viewed their position in society, it had to guard itself against charges of collaboration with the employers. Consequently, it was unable to enter into an intimate relationship with the DNVP, whose national views it had endorsed for some time. During the early 1920's, Blechly and Lambach, the leaders of the DHV, moved in DNVP circles, but not for very long. The two union men were gradually repelled by the increasingly reactionary labor policies of that party,[34] and the DHV was forced to search for political support and identity elsewhere. But where, outside the left and right, could it go, other than to Hitler? The question posed many problems during the years of the Weimar Republic.

The contacts between the union and the NSDAP were involved and interesting. Blechly and Lambach disliked the mass organization and violent methods of the NSDAP. Moreover, the Nazis were dangerous rivals to other Volkish groups. Significantly enough, it was the Nazis who took the initiative in establishing close contacts with the DHV, but their purpose was to take it over. They did make substantial inroads in the union and could, at one point (in 1930), claim the allegiance of three quarters of the Fahrende Gesellen. But the Nazis did not take advantage of their opportunity—a failure that has been ascribed to the uncompromising attitude of the Nazi leaders. By 1930 Alfred Krebs, the most prominent National Socialist among the DHV leaders, complained to Hitler that the Gesellen had turned to the other Volkish leaders, principally because of Nazi rowdyism.[35] Hitler ignored Krebs's pleas for an end to violent agitation, and Alfred Rosenberg continued his attacks upon the non-Nazis in the union. At that point, especially when the Nazis criticized the DHV leadership and its contacts with other political groups, the union chiefs condemned the Nazi demagoguery and drew away from the NSDAP.[36] While the Nazis eventually captured some local centers, such as those of Dresden and Chemnitz,[37] they could never, prior to 1933, dominate the union leadership. The antagonism between the DHV and NSDAP grew to such an extent that Habermann, the most important DHV leader, turned to the Conservatives and in 1932 endorsed Hindenburg rather than Hitler for president.[38] To the end, the DHV remained relatively independent and only after the victory of the Nazis did it merge with them in the National Socialist labor front. Like all the other Volkish organizations, it held out until the last moment, never effectively opposing Hitler but hoping for stronger, more orthodox forces to supplant him. When salvation failed to appear,[39] when the would-be giant killers lost their lives or positions before they could take any concerted action, they too were swept away with relative ease.

While the German DHV remained more or less unaffiliated with any particular party and did not itself assume a directly political function, its Bohemian-Austrian branch did. This branch of the DHV had been established independently in 1885 in Bohemia, on the frontiers of Germany. It had come into existence in the Sudetenland as a reaction to the preferential treatment Czech workers were receiving from their employers. By 1898 the union had spread to Austria, where eventually it came to be known as the Gau Ostmark branch of the DHV.[40] The conditions peculiar to the frontier region —the minority status of the Germans, their resentment of Jewish and Slav competition in their own preserve, and the longing for a closer identity with a romanticized concept of Germany—contributed to giving the labor union a directly political emphasis. More radical in outlook, it helped found and supported the Deutsche Arbeiterpartei (German Workers' party). By 1918 the aspirations of the party had grown to such an extent that it changed its specifically working-class outlook and welcomed other classes of the population as well. Correspondingly, it also changed its name to the Deutsche Nationalsozialistische Partei. With its outlook and emphasis broadened, the party entered into various discussions with the German Nazis to decide on some basis for action. To this end, in 1920, its leaders met with Hitler and Drexler, setting the stage for amicable relations that culminated in the party's merger with the Nazis.[41]

German historians have attempted to show that this Bohemian party was the real forerunner of the National Socialists. This would, of course, shift the burden of guilt away from Germany proper to the frontier regions under Austrian rule. While the Volkish movement certainly received a constant impetus from Austria and the Sudetenland, its roots were undeniably in Germany and it was in the center that it achieved its greatest success. The Volkish extremism that arose in the frontier regions was duplicated in Germany itself. The Sudetenland party can properly be viewed only as a concomitant development, springing from similar sources of anxiety, of identification with the Volk and its heroic past. The radical turn taken by the Volkish movement must therefore be kept within proper perspective. The border Germans, who felt the pressure of the Slavic populations, resolved their problems into a political framework. However, both they and their German confrères developed the same ideological attitude toward life and the problems besetting them.

In summing up the identification of the German working class with the philosophy of the Volk, we must repeat that the movement never penetrated below the ranks of the white-collar employees. Except for those who joined the Nazis at an early date (and these came largely from among the unemployed), the industrial workers were not attracted to the Volkish movement, for it had little to offer them that was not at variance with their dependence on the smooth functioning of an industrial society. A reversion to the idyllic estates system had little appeal for them. However, among the commercial union, representing the interests of workers who considered themselves artisans, the Volkish appeal of a romanticized social order was favorably received. From the end of the war onward, this Volkish social order was popularized by August Winnig. In his theorizing on the movement's attitude toward the workers themselves, he did not confine himself to the members of the DHV, but attempted to present a Volkish view of the working class as a whole. Winnig was not affiliated with any one Volkish group, but he published in Volkish periodicals and wrote books which were widely read and commented upon. He himself had a working-class background, something unique among Volkish thinkers. Winnig worked his way through the Social Democratic party organization and became head of the East Prussian government after the revolution of 1918. By this time his ideas had already shifted in a conservative-Volkish direction. In line with this he participated in Kapp's abortive putsch against the Republic and consequently lost his position in the party and the state. He then became the Volkish theoretician of the working classes, maintaining close connections with the DHV and other similar groups.

Winnig believed that in modern times the worker had been denied his inherent right to be free.[42] But it is significant that he did not equate freedom with equality. "Nature is a many-splendored thing, but one aspect will not be found in nature: equality." Only those estranged from nature could possibly believe in equality.[43] Such estrangement was a serious matter. Modern concepts of progress and democracy were wrong precisely because they tried to improve upon nature.

Volkish opposition to modernity, hatred of urban life, and a love of nature found echoes in Winnig's thought. Freedom meant partaking of nature, and an understanding of the landscape and thus of the Volk. Therefore, not as an urban proletarian, but only as a full-fledged member of the Volk could the worker achieve his freedom.[44] In practice this meant decent living conditions on a plot of land and adequate pay for one's work. It did not mean equality or a working-class internationalism which the socialists presumably advocated. Winnig saw the German state as an organic community in which all could work together at their appointed tasks, with some, of course, laboring under the direction of others. He regarded the worker as an artisan, and thus, like the DHV, viewed employer-worker relationships within the framework of the medieval guild. "The worker is destined to continue the task of the old estates in a new form." [45] Here also it is possible that the concept of the *Bund* was to be the modern formulation of harmonious employer-worker relationships.[46] As a member of the Volk, the worker attained a status of dignity. Thus it was the Volk which must claim the worker's primary allegiance.

Winnig developed a view of labor which was common to Volkish thought. Small wonder that he also advocated other Volkish theories which have occupied us in previous chapters. For example, he used the term "blood and soil," and even after the Second World War he continued to pay tribute to Germanic Christianity. "The great miracle of God become man, an annoyance to the Jews and folly to the Greeks, has found its true meaning in the Germanic soul." [47] In the 1920's he had seen the Volk not as a mere mass of voters, but as a segment of eternity.[48] From this point of view a socialist revolution was the very opposite of the Volkish way of life. To Winnig, such revolutions were the product of Jewish intellectualism, and he inveighed against the "foreign influence" in the labor movements.[49]

Such was the man who became the principal Volkish labor theoretician. Although some of the Nazi appeals to the industrial worker based themselves upon similar premises, the working classes paid scant attention to Winnig's works. He himself refused to cooperate with the Nazi movement, seeing in it a reduction of the people to mere masses of voters, and in its supposed socialism, a destruction of the Volk.[50] During the Third Reich he withdrew from all public activity and even engaged in minor underground activities.

Because August Winnig formulated many of the ideas which the DHV had already put into practice, both must be considered together. Thus, although he professed to concern himself with the whole of the working class rather than with a certain segment, he really transformed all workers into the kind of men who had found their home in the DHV.

These last chapters have attempted to demonstrate the penetration of the Volkish ideology among respectable conservatives, veterans, and workers, where it not only found sustenance but emerged stronger and more flexible in its relations to the rising Nazi party. Most of these groups co-operated with the Republic while conspiring to replace it with either a monarchy or an order that would be responsive to the best interests of the Volk. Many of them built on the Stöcker tradition, opposing the racist extremism of the Nazis, but were ready to elaborate and expand it with the changing times. They abetted the rise of the Nazis, and at first even welcomed them as contributing to the anti-Republican, anti-Marxist front. When they turned against them, they did so mostly for political reasons, as groups or parties opposing a threat to their own aspirations to power.

We must now turn again to German youth and their espousal of radical Volkish ideas. Here we will be concerned with the generation that had entered the war either as former members of the Youth Movement or the Fahrende Gesellen, or simply as patriotic citizens, but which, regardless of its previous affiliations and Volkish convictions, emerged from the conflict deeply affected by the changes which had come about on the home front. Interested in direct action and the achievement of goals, this bourgeois youth turned in a rightward direction and once again renounced their parents' institutions. Indeed, it seemed as if bourgeois youth might finally burst the confines of that bourgeois society which it had always professed to condemn.

CHAPTER 15

From Bourgeois to Anti-Bourgeois Youth

AFTER THE FIRST WORLD WAR, the urge to act continued to inspire the young men who had fought in the trenches. All over the West activism was the order of the day. Not only youth but many of their elders equated such activism with a spirit of youth as against the degeneracy of old age. For the activists the existing, traditional institutions which (so they held) could no longer cope with new conditions were symbolic of old age, and those who attacked them were animated by a spirit of youth. In this way the defeated nations could restore their self-respect: the victor nations were the old nations whose day was done in spite of their victory; the defeated nations were young, for they were actively engaged in an attack upon traditional institutions which might well carry the day. Much of the post-war Fascist movement was built upon the ideals of youth and activism, even among those who were no longer young in age.

In Germany, above all, youth itself followed the path of activism, but against the background of the specific tradition which we have already analyzed, a continued turn toward the radical right. Thus it has been estimated that the Kapp putsch had the support of some 50,000 students and youth.[1] Aware of the danger and conscious of the power of the youth, liberal reformers like Wyneken attempted to swing youth over to themselves and the Republic. But it was all in vain. Youth stuck to its own concept of "revolutionary" change—in favor of the Volk and a society in which both the traditional and the modern virtues of the nation would merge with the heroic deeds of the ancient Germans. Youth remained loyal to these spiritual values and continued to draw further inspiration in support of its ideology from schools, textbooks, and student organizations that were tinged with Volkish ideals.

Instead of lessening, the Volkish trend grew stronger, for it was fed by the unresolved problems and crises that faced the nation during the years of the Republic. Much of German youth rejected the democratic process, denounced all political parties, were intolerant of the opinions of others, and denied that a good government could be built on popular franchise. At every level bourgeois youth increasingly turned to Volkish solutions to the crisis of German ideology. Thus, from their point of view, it seems clear that the Republic was doomed from the start. The prewar tradition continued to provide the building blocks for the Volkish structure; the events of the postwar era facilitated its completion.

Here once more, the intensity of anti-Semitism can be used to gauge the depth of the penetration of the Volkish ideology. That it was widespread, touching even grade-school youth, there can be no doubt. High-school students were especially subject to Volkish influence, and their intellectual development was turned in an anti-Semitic direction. Swastikas, for instance, were popular with students of all ages just after the war. The fad reached such dimensions and carried with it such Volkish anti-Semitic connotations that the Prussian ministry of education, in 1919, had to take official steps to prohibit it.[2] But the pressures on the children persisted nonetheless. As early as 1919, and again in 1926, *Mitteilungen* (the Jewish anti-defamation journal) and a deputy in the Prussian Diet in turn attacked the schools as the chief breeding ground of the Volkish danger. The journal even declared that the "high school is the bulwark of the German nationalistic spirit." [3]

Despite the frequency of protests the Volkish anti-Semitic agitation among youth continued unabated. Its role was most pernicious in that it provided the children with a clearly defined object to vent their frustrations on, an identifiable obstacle to their aspirations which could be blamed for all their failures in later life.

How then did this deep-seated anti-Semitism develop within the postwar younger generation? In the schools and on the streets at home, children romanticized and acted out the ideas of their elders. Instead of cops and robbers or cowboys and Indians, some played the game of "Aryans and Jews." [4] As early as 1920, Müller-Claudius, a perceptive journalist, commented that the phenomenon of anti-Semitism represented a process of isolating the Jewish child which carried with it greater ideological overtones. In the future, Müller-Claudius asserted, isolation of the Jew would be transformed into considering him an absolute foreigner and would lead to a total rejection of him as a member of the community.[5] And indeed many Gentile school children did come to regard the Jew as a stranger, isolated for the good of the community and removed from intercourse with Aryans for the benefit of the German Volk.

What had started in the primary and high schools continued in the universities on a broader basis. Jews were excluded from fraternities and other student associations and were not allowed to participate in school functions. The Aryan clause, excluding non-Aryans, was applied by the fraternities, while agitation for the *numerus clausus* (quota for Jews) attempted to extend the same function on a wider level throughout the whole university system. Meanwhile, the Nazis, through the 1920's and early 1930's, found devoted adherents among the teaching profession and put them to excellent service in the field of propaganda. They were so effective that by 1932 Jewish parents were asking in the *C. V. Zeitung* to publish a list of schools free of anti-Semitism.[6] By 1931 the National Socialists had captured the national organization of university students, and it was estimated that same year that, proportionately, there were as many Nazi teachers in the universities as in the high schools.[7] That the danger was acute can be seen in the crumbling of the hopes that assimilationist-minded Jews had harbored for so long. No longer believing that Jewish children could safely live side by side with the German majority, the principal newspaper of the assimilationist Jews exhorted its readers to develop their bodies and to learn the art of self-defense in order to protect themselves against "bloodless pogroms."[8] It did so twice, for example, within the span of two months in 1926.

While anti-Semitism constituted the most conspicuous display of the Volkish ideology, other ideas also played significant roles in producing a younger generation dedicated to a revolution of the right rather than of the left. In addition to anti-Semitism, the schools continued to inculcate their charges with anti-modern, anti-Republican, and anti-progressive thinking. Many school textbooks, such as Hermann Pinnow's *History*, decried the transformation of the pastoral, agrarian past into the modern, mechanized present. According to Pinnow, the spiritual, mystical unity of the earlier German society and culture had given way to the cold, inanimate "externalization of life," as he called the scientific and technological developments of the 1890–1914 era.[9] Another popular history textbook spelled out this view in detail, saying that, "in the long run, this forced civilization cannot disguise the inner emptiness which it produced." [10] How reminiscent of Löns' picture of the elemental forces of the Volk finally bursting through the thin, superficial crust of civilization!

Even those textbook writers who identified themselves with the Republic collaborated in the end with its enemies by undermining confidence in its institutions and by confusing the problems that confronted modern man. Wilmann's strongly pro-Weimar history of Germany could not refrain from lauding Lagarde and Langbehn as Germanic prophets who wanted to "free man from the rot of the big city and have him live only for the genuine, the truly German, without any thought of monetary gain." [11] Wilmann himself did not elaborate on the characteristics of the "truly German," leaving the task to the classroom teacher. Walther Gehl, a history teacher, is an even more interesting case in point. Indifferent to the Republic, neither praising its virtues nor condemning its faults, Gehl strongly opposed the increased mechanization, the scientific emphasis, and the materialistic values that had supposedly become dominant in German society. According to him, these phenomena were only external riches gained at the expense of inner spirituality. Paeans to Lagarde and Langbehn also adorned his textbooks, but, singularly enough, they were free of anti-Semitic diatribes. [12] Not until a year after the Nazis had assumed power did Gehl condemn the Jews as well as the defunct Republic. In the process he became a leading Nazi educator. In their own ways, all these men influenced the youth in their turn toward the Volkish movement. The problems they described, the emphases and lessons they selected, and their nostalgia for the past succeeded in leaving the younger generation with only the tools of irrationality for solving their problems.

The German ideological crisis was more apparent and significant to the students in the universities. Competition with Jewish intellectuals for jobs was more intense. This was the initial battlefield where the Aryan, Volkish, and Germanic ideas mustered great force and eventually triumphed. The existing traditional institutions, rules, and over-all attitude of the universities were conducive to this course. Earlier we discussed the intense racial feelings that permeated most of the fraternity and social life of the students. Not only did the German fraternities exclude students of direct Jewish descent, but in 1919, at the general convention at Eisenach, this policy of exclusion was extended to include those Aryans who had married Jewish or non-white partners. Thereafter the racial theme resounded more often and with greater significance, until in 1928 the *Burschenschaftliche Blätter*, the fraternities' paper, could declare that racial composition was decisive in determining the Volk's intellectual and physical stature; and the fraternities felt free to state: "Not economics but race is our fate!" [13]

Before the postwar era, university students had found it relatively easy to set their own ideological requirements for membership without any real opposition on the part of the school administrations. In other words, things had gone their way and nothing had really tested their commitment to the racial philosophy, nothing had driven them to choose between dissolving their organizations and abandoning racial discrimination. The issue was now, for the first time, joined in the clash between the student body and the Prussian minister of culture, the liberal C. H. Becker. The minister, a member of the Social Democratic government of Prussia, threatened to withdraw recognition, and therefore subsidies, from the German students' organization if it did not change its policy of discrimination. Citizenship was to be the only valid criterion for membership. The incident grew out of the request, in 1925, of the newly organized Deutsche Studentenschaft (German Students' Organization) that it be permitted to merge with its Austrian counterpart, which for a long time had rigorously applied the Aryan clause. Since, if the merger were allowed, the official student organization would be condoning a policy of racial exclusion, the Prussian minister, supported by the Social Democratic Diet, refused to grant the request. Two years later, in 1927, Becker asked the Deutsche Studentenschaft to hold a vote among its members on the question whether to reject the Aryan clause as a condition for receiving official recognition and financial support, or to accept non-recognition and retain the policy of exclusion.[14] The students overwhelmingly rejected Becker's request. Sure of themselves and not wanting to split the organization wide open, the student leadership decided to remain as they were and hence to endorse racial discrimination.

The Studentenschaft had opted for what it considered basic to German existence and culture, and spurned the appeal of material benefits and official recognition. Pan-Germanism played some part in this choice—the desire to accept the Austrians into the organization and in this way to achieve some measure of unity with them, in the face of the Versailles Treaty, which forbade political union between Germans and Austrians. But the episode also shows a Volkish commitment on the part of the German students themselves, the harvest of a development which we have earlier traced to the last decades of the nineteenth century. How deeply Volkish attitudes had influenced these young people becomes luminously clear if we remember that this decision did *not* come during the economic depression, but rather during the "good times" of the Republic. It was not a specific response to an imminent crisis, but rather the expression of a deep and lasting commitment.

The newly found solidarity of the students on the issue of racial differences was also reflected in other fields of life and thought. They had found a basis for action that opposed existing authority yet remained independent of any political movement directed by their elders. Bourgeois youth made their protests obvious. Organization after organization, fraternity after fraternity, succumbed to the pressure of anti-Semitic agitation and advocated the anti-Jewish *numerus clausus* for their university charters. They protested the employment of professors that were either "leftist" or Jewish, and when more subtle means were exhausted they engaged in overt demonstrations to press their demands. In 1931, for example, anti-Semitic student riots erupted in Vienna, Berlin, Cologne, Greifswald, Halle, Hamburg, Breslau, Kiel, Königsberg, and Munich. No region was immune.

In these areas, as in the past, the faculties failed to provide any opposition, failed to use their administrative powers, and failed to organize effective alternative groups of students. At best they displayed a detached passivity, lending their ears to the racist harangues of fellow professors but never supporting either side. At worst they joined in the harassment of fellow Jewish or leftist educators. In 1932, at Breslau and Heidelberg, institutions which were internationally respected, the faculties dismissed Jewish professors accused of being Marxists. The Gentile academicians themselves made the basic decision.[15]

Whereas under Hitler all the student groups went over to the new Nazi youth order either out of conviction or by compulsion, prior to 1933 the rightist non-Nazi organizations still provided a Volkish alternative to the problems of the day. Beginning rather late, in 1929, the fraternities and corps first took the competition of the Nazi youth movement seriously. They marshaled their forces and attempted to stave off the rapid encroachment of their territory. As the pressure increased they rested their last hope with the conservatives, above all with von Papen. But to little effect. Although they attempted to steal the Nazi thunder and mercilessly purged their membership of Jews, they were unable to prevent the triumph of the National Socialist program. In 1931, even before their strong showing at the polls, the Nazis scored a signal victory in winning over the 140,000-member Studentenschaft at its meeting in the Austrian city of Graz.[16] They were assisted by the all-Aryan Austrian student organization. The Nazi expert in student affairs, Gerhard Krüger, assumed the role of president of the organization and henceforth signed his communications with the salutation "Heil Hitler." A total take-over followed, with hard-core Nazi agitators and organizers replacing the old guard.[17]

The students represented a more select group of bourgeois youth, for they had precise ambitions, for themselves and for the nation, which were all-important to them. But in their rightist, Volkish, and racial radicalization they were in tune with non-university bourgeois youth as well. General Gröner commented upon this development among all youth when he declared in 1933 that this radicalization of youth presented a real and serious danger to the Republic.[18] This danger was exemplified by the Youth Movement even more than by the students. Its aspirations were more revolutionary, and it addressed itself to the great, overriding questions. The social order, the economic and political establishment were the targets of the Youth Movement, as for the students, but the Youth Movement wanted to see a revolution, a transformation of modern society into something that directly represented the will and spirit of the German Volk. By comparison, the Jewish question took second place.

The Youth Movement was in search of the "third way," an alternative route that would liquidate the inadequate existing organizations and penetrate directly to the core of the Volk's desires. This "third way" is so important to the study of the German revolution as implemented by the Nazis that we will have to deal with it more fully in the next chapter. Let it be noted here that its basic component was a messianic message that had spiritual as well as practical roots in the evolution of German society and the Youth Movement. The messianism demanded an immediate and deeply spiritual catharsis, to be provided by the resolution of the crisis of German ideology. The Youth Movement, in response to the national predicament, thought itself in possession of this messianic dynamism and for one fleeting moment its revolutionary and romantic impetus seemed to have established a connection with the tradition of the sixteenth-century "enthusiasts."

To bring about this spiritual impetus in their own circles and pave the way for its acceptance among the population at large, the Youth Movement after the war turned to the *Bünde*. These organizations provided them with two essential aspects of their mission: a spiritual unity among the members, an Eros; and a framework for action, for implementing their "idealism of deeds." Among these newly organized *Bünde*, the Freischaar (Free Group) came to represent the most important attempt at consolidating and realizing the ideology of the movement. This group of young people regarded their organization and their principles as the "new community" that was to serve as a model for the reorganization of *all* society. Within it, it was possible to live one's life according to Volkish values. Here the individual was not alienated, here he neither transcended society nor subordinated himself to its inanimate and fortuitous demands. Here he was at one with the Volk, sharing in the most genuine freedom that man could attain. Ernst Buske, the leader of the Freischaar, summed it all up when he declared that the *Bund* reflected the essence of the Volk: a spiritual community cemented by a common *Geist*.[19] And it was the search for this kind of community, rather than a concern with the explicitly political struggles of the age, that set the Youth Movement now, as before the war, into motion.[20] An inner revolution, followed by a change in the institutions of society, was the only way left for the German Volk to regain its integrity, genuineness, and proximity with the cosmic spirituality that underlies all of life.

The emphasis on revolutionary change was significant. Having overcome the initial fear of revolutionary change, the German youth took a second look at the Bolshevik upheaval and, in part, liked what they saw. There was a strong state, a central system of power, directed by a single, capable leader; there was a society that worked in unison, expressing its own peculiar national fervor.[21] These German youth saw in the Russian Revolution not merely the beginning of an international movement but also the manifestations of an inner nationalism, a transformation that could be duplicated in Germany according to German needs and circumstances.

This revolutionary messianism came to the fore in other youth organizations besides the Freischaar. The Neue Pfadfinder, for instance, under the tutelage of Martin Völkel, developed similar ideas about a new Reich and a Germanic leader. Völkel, an able spokesman for the group, equated the Reich with the Volk, declaring that all national activities—such as commerce, politics, and jurisprudence —had to be integrated in it. Turning to Stefan George and his ideas, Völkel presented these to his troop as the alternative to the prevalent forms of social organization, capitalistic or socialistic. Within a *Bund*, held together by a spiritual magnet, were to be found the inspiration of heroic deeds and the origin of all states. Youth, according to Völkel, was determined to destroy the false gods of the state —commerce and industry—and to integrate them as new institutions in a new society serving the interests of the Volk.[22]

Some youth groups exaggerated the importance of the spiritual component and came to be regarded as merely eccentric. In Thuringia, for example, Muck Lamberty and his small, short-lived Neue

Schaar (New Band), organized in 1920, represented such a loss of perspective. Preaching to audiences in Thuringian churches, Lamberty lectured on the "Revolution of the Soul." He condemned all manifestations of modernity, all materialism and intellectualism, including medicine and the natural sciences, and advocated a direct contact with nature as the sole remedy for all modern ills. Lamberty exhorted his audience to make their souls "swing" in tune with nature, with their own subliminal desires, and in rhythm with the ancestral spirits of the past. Before and after the lectures he would lead his own group, about twenty-five in number, and such townspeople as were willing in a free-form dance that would start in the market place and wind through the village streets. They would abandon themselves in their dancing in an attempt to recapture that "enthusiasm" known by their ancestors in the far-distant sixteenth century, when their prophets had preached the Second Coming of Christ.

For a time Lamberty's cultism spread. This Pied Piper of the Youth Movement, followed by his small band of initiates, moved from village to village leading the people in dance and lecturing them on the salvation of their Volkish souls. In addition to the dancing, which was intended to liberate the body and bring it closer to the rhythm of the cosmos, the Neue Schaar also practiced vegetarianism and abstention from alcohol and observed such ancient Germanic festivals as that of the summer solstice. But the group's popularity was short-lived. Its eccentricity blossomed forth as sexual promiscuity and under heavy criticism the Neue Schaar disbanded.[23]

In contrast to the university youth, the Youth Movement refrained from heavy concentration on anti-Semitism. They made little use of it as a tool and still less as an end. Not that they were tolerant or advocated the integration of Jews into German culture, for they also held that Jews were an alien people, an alien Volk, which had its own peculiar cosmic reference. However, on the whole they disregarded the racial argument and formulated a policy that allowed for integration of Germanized Jewry. They believed that any peoples who strongly and decisively transcended their origins were capable of immersing themselves in a pure Germanism. In conformity with this notion, various groups of the movement accepted Jews as members. The Neue Pfadfinder, for instance, accepted Jews in Bavaria, but were less liberal in the North, in Berlin, whereas the Nerother Bund, the Altwandervögel, and the Freischaar had an open policy toward Jews.[24] The over-all situation was so favorable that Ernst Michael Jovy, after examining the problem thoroughly, concluded that anti-

Semitism actually decreased in the Youth Movement *Bünde* shortly before 1933.

This leniency was due in part to the Youth Movement's hostility to the Nazis. The leadership of the larger groups, such as the Freischaar, maintained a fine level of discrimination between their ideology and the seemingly similar ideological precepts of the National Socialists. Emphasizing a clear-cut Volkish commitment, they fought for their independence until the end, and when they were finally forcibly disbanded, they were still an autonomous group. Of course, some Volkish-oriented youth groups went over to the Nazis rather early—and with increasing frequency as time went by. Those organizations which shifted their allegiance did so because they were in general agreement with the program, strategy, and tactics of the Nazis or because they saw in Hitler the culmination of their own drives. But what drew them most strongly, and always chagrined the non-Nazi Volkish youth organizations, was the appeal to revolutionary action that the Nazis had writ large across their banner.

The question of revolutionary commitment played a large role in the compatibilities as well as in the antagonisms between the two movements. Both had endorsed the "German revolution." Both the Youth Movement and the Nazis praised the Volk and invoked its name as a sacred call to action; both demanded a primary renunciation of personality and individuality on the part of their members and required that they submerge themselves in the group, its ideology and discipline. Above all, both groups looked to a leader to accomplish the unification of the Volk under one banner. What, then, were the points of disagreement? First, there was the problem of Hitler, whom the Youth Movement rejected because of his vulgar tastes, his fanaticism, and his "proletarianization" of the party. Second, they disagreed with the Nazis' practice of appealing for the votes of the masses during elections as well as the opportunism of power politics.[25] The Nazis, on the other hand, also had their complaints and disagreed just as vigorously. Their first line of defense was to criticize the effeteness of the Youth Movement and its ineffectiveness in promoting the revolution. While the patriotic and devoted SA men were having their skulls cracked wide open, the Nazis asserted, the romantic youth were taking pleasant strolls through the countryside.[26] The youth retorted that they were the sole champions of a true Volkish program: they claimed that the most important task was to indoctrinate the Volk in a cultural, ideological, and activist revolution. But this could only be accomplished through the elitist leadership of a *Bund* and not through a mass party such as the NSDAP.[27] The Youth Movement built upon the elitist tradition which was such a vital component of the Volkish movement.

The youth thought of themselves as an *Orden*, like the Knights Templar, but they did not want to revive the medieval hierarchical system. The ideal of revolution kept them from being merely reactionary, and, more important still, the search for a common unity of and with the Volk meant that "estates are mere classes under a different name." [28] We have seen repeatedly that classes and political parties were rejected, that the *Bund* was to be the first step toward an "absolute unity." Indeed, some leaders even saw the Volk as only one more step toward the ultimate world state.[29]. Clearly all of this contrasted with the ideals of the Nazis, who rejected a structuring of society which began with the *Bund* and might even end in world unity. The Youth Movement understood this well when it accused Hitler of having made his decision in favor of a "political party" and not of the nation.[30] But while the ideology of the Youth Movement was consistent, its programs were too abstract to compete with the concrete program of the Nazis. The "experience of a living community," [31] as one youth leader put it, was too vague and the rejection of economic means as the keystone in building the new society bogged down their ideology in a morass of "feeling." The Nazis, in line with the Volkish tradition, also rejected "materialistic approaches," but they avoided the dilemmas of the youth groups by building a mass movement by means of a very astute, concrete political program. The Youth Movement countered this threat by taking steps to revolutionize themselves, and consequently they drifted away from their close relationship with the "respectable" DNVP and the patriotic Stahlhelm. Furthermore, even these moves were not sufficient to stem the gradual flow of members into the Nazi party. And when the National Socialists assumed total power, the Youth Movement, having nothing left to offer, disintegrated rather easily, without much resistance.

What motivated the increased defection to the Nazi youth groups? Part of the answer may be gained from an analysis of those marginal groups which, though in some ways representative of the Volkish resistance to the National Socialists, still flirted with them and attempted to attain a *modus vivendi* on a new, but Nazi-oriented program. Many of these groups had always been on good terms with the Nazis and had found in them emphases similar to their own— such as a thorough racism, a more rabid and militant attitude toward the alien elements in the nation, and a greater fanaticism. It might be said that in terms of numbers their contribution to the Volkish cause was trifling, but they do give some insight into the feeling of those on the edge of the movement.

Of these pro-Nazi organizations, the Adler und Falken and the Geusen can be singled out as the most popular and representative. They were small organizations, together consisting of only some 5,600 members, and they prided themselves on the fact, claiming that it was consistent with their elitist and exclusivist outlook. They believed themselves to be of the Volkish nobility, the shock troops of the cause. Ideologically, they fully supported the Volkish precepts: opposition to all things un-Germanic, from the Roman alphabet to the Jews, from orthodox religion to modernity.[32] They accented the "religious" nature of their organization. Radicalism in the Youth Movement meant a further heightening of the mystical component. Thus the Geusen rejected the idea of the *Bund* as too "practical" and materialistic, and regarded themselves as an *Orden* instead.[33] Moreover, they dwelt upon the past: "All great spirits are rooted in the past," the history of a people is nothing less than the unfolding of its soul.[34] Small wonder that these groups joined with the extremist elements of the Volkish movement in worshipping the sun.[35] Eugen Dühring and L. F. Clauss's *Die nordische Seele* formed their approach to the racial issue. Yet there was a more practical side to their activity, more so indeed than that of most of the other Youth Movement groups. The Adler und Falken and the Geusen functioned according to the immediate needs of their geographic stronghold: the frontier regions of the Sudetenland. Here they became the bulwark against the Czech pressure upon the German minority. Like the Deutsche Nationalsozialistische Partei of the same region, they concentrated on defending the rights of the German workers, citizens, and merchants against the pressure from the Czechs. In this situation the conditions were ripe for the development of a sense of community, a sense of "German socialism" that was manifest in certain forms of communal life. In the town of Troppau, for example, the youth *Orden* maintained common dining facilities and established a workshop under common ownership, the profits being used to encourage the cultural activity of the German community and to subsidize German artisans who—the weavers, for example— were most vulnerable to Czech competition.[36] Thus, the youth "experienced life through living" in the genuine *bündisch* nature of an ideal community. That whatever success they achieved was due to the tense and aggressive state of mind of the German minority in the frontier communities dawned on them only later, when the political situation had become increasingly strained. Then, in 1928, unable to stand alone, the Geusen threw in their lot with the German National Socialists as the most capable and dedicated defenders of their particular outlook.

But even here the Geusen, and later, under similar conditions, the other groups, were discriminating in their allegiance to the Nazis. They gravitated toward the Strasser wing of the party. Hitler was not sufficiently Volkish for them; he had compromised himself too deeply with the interests of the capitalist class, the class of modernity that had betrayed the Volk for silver. In Gregor Strasser they, as many other Volkish groups, found a more congenial leader. They hoped that he would establish a "German socialism" which would satisfy the needs of the Volk. For a time these distinctions were tenaciously defended by both sides. The Geusen, for instance, engaged in ideological disputes with the pro-Hitler youth, and both groups were hostile toward each other. Then, too, the Geusen came to occupy influential positions in the DHV's Fahrende Gesellen, where they threw their ideological support to the pro-Strasser Alfred Krebs.[87] But in the end, when Hitler himself abrogated all alternatives, these organizations, joined by the whole Youth Movement, declared their loyalty to the Third Reich, its leader, and the newly awakened Germanic Volk.

In this study of the postwar Youth Movement we have come upon the younger generation's greater concentration upon a "German revolution." This militant attitude reflected the profound tensions that racked Germany throughout the period of the Weimar Republic. Postwar youth thirsted for activism, and not just in Germany. But here this drive was channeled into Volkish longings and traditions, and the Bünde became the representative form through which these youth expressed their longings. But they became bogged down in a mystical ideology and lost their chance for political power. Here they were in the mainstream of the Volkish movement, with its emphasis upon the "idea" rather than upon practical alternatives, which they tended to equate with materialism. The bündisch youth were more overtly political than the members of the earlier prewar Youth Movement, but they carried on the "idealism of deeds" upon the same foundation. Indeed these antibourgeois youth of bourgeois origin had the same goal as their predecessors: to transcend their origins through a "spiritual revolution." The defeat in war and the difficulties of the Weimar Republic merely heightened this quest and gave it a sharper focus toward the building of a new society.

The Nazis also used the appeal of the "third way," the opposition to bourgeois society, but they combined this with the building of a mass political party. Moreover the "German revolution" which they advocated did not become the captive of vague "experiences" and mystical ecstasies. Instead it was made concrete and brought down to earth—for in their hands the "German revolution" became an "anti-Jewish revolution." The social aims of the Youth Movement were modified by directing the revolution against the "enemy within," rather than against the existing class structure. Contrary to the hopes of the Youth Movement, the success of the "German revolution" increased in direct proportion to its diversion into an anti-Jewish revolution. Hitler skillfully used the Volkish anti-Semitic tradition to achieve his ends. After all, the anti-Jewish element had become the spearhead of Volkish thought long before Hitler, and he made skillful use of this situation—which the Youth Movement refused to do. Most of the youth themselves eventually flocked to his banner. The Volkish content of their movement proved more important than their longing for social change.

CHAPTER 16

A German Revolution

THE SEARCH for a "third way," as an alternative to capitalism or Marxism, occupied much of German thought during the Weimar Republic. Even earlier, toward the end of the post-unification period, men had raised similar questions—in a more theoretical manner, but just as seriously. Indeed, the search for a viable "third way" was an integral part of the Volkish concern. This study, so far, has discussed the various Volkish attempts to transcend the limitations of the contemporary order of things, to penetrate into regions beyond the immediate reality. Disenchanted with the world as they found it, German thinkers attempted to find some way to raise the Volk above its temporal restrictions. They were determined to liberate it from the shackles of a materialistic civilization imposed by a state that callously disregarded the essentially spiritual needs of the Volk. The postwar era thrust the "third-way" alternative again into the foreground. Pressures were brought to bear on the nation by circumstances beyond the control of the state machinery or the national economy. Fascism and communism were gaining staunch adherents in adjoining countries and were making deep inroads in German society as well. Everywhere in Europe, fascism was based upon the urge toward a "third way," and Volkish thought here intersected with the mainstream of an international movement. What had Germany to offer that was uniquely fitted to her own requirements, that stemmed from her own historical and cultural heritage? There was the heritage of the abortive popular movement of 1848. There was the impetus that had moved generations of German thinkers to seek limited reform. Above all, there were the prophets of Germanism: Langbehn, who had proposed transforming Germans into artists, and Lagarde, who had urged the revival of the Germanic faith.

Whatever the alternatives presented by the advocates of the "third way," the underlying basis was always metaphysical. During the 1920's, intellectuals continued to view the coming German revolution primarily in spiritual terms. That the soil was prepared for a metaphysical ideal of action we have already seen. The "idealism of deeds" about which men like Eugen Diederichs and Hermann Lietz spoke constituted just such a spiritual revolution. A change in the people's attitude toward the Volk was more important than any concrete social reforms. While such men talked about socialism, it was not the Marxian version which they had in mind. For Möller van den Bruck, the prophet of the "third way," German socialism was a social order forged from the union of a medieval corporatism and the cultural peculiarities of the German Volk. As he emphatically asserted, in condemning Marxist internationalism, "every people has its own socialism." [1] But was it not a contradiction to believe simultaneously in a revolutionary yet conservative change? By no means, as long as there was a metaphysical foundation, as long as one's doctrine of revolution did not call for *new* and *radical* social and economic reforms. Man did not advance progressively, discarding his traditions as they became useless; rather he was bound by eternal laws that had been established in the past and embodied in tradition. Or, as van den Bruck stated it, "under a German socialism we understand a corporate concept of the state and economy that might have to be instituted through revolutionary means, but which, once established, must be bound by conservative principles." [2]

How then was this revolution to come about and what were to be the fruits of its success? Möller van den Bruck, in his famous work *The Third Reich* (1923), which he first called *The Third Way*, considered Germany to be a "new nation," as distinguished from the overripe "old nations" of the West, a nation with a mission. It was a country of the future that had not yet developed its inherent peculiarities and greatness. What it had lacked until now, a shortcoming that accounted for the failure of the recent past, van den Bruck declared, was a chiliastic ideal. The "new" Germany, he asserted, had to be fired by the *idea* of the Germanic past and of Germany's potential future greatness; it had to revive and make operative in a new age the traditions of medieval messianism.[3] Contemporary materialism, contemporary society and science, had to be discarded and the German soul must take wing and follow the unrestrained course of the *Geist*. Van den Bruck even subordinated anti-Semitism to this ideal. Nothing must stand in the way of the development of the ideal, not even the problem of race: "Racism must not lead to a new German problem by excluding, for biological reasons, men who spiritually belong to the race" [4]—an argument that rested on the undisputed primacy of metaphysical considerations. In a spiritual revolution all differences should be dealt with on this level; intellectual and cultural affinities were more important than biological and material differences. Van den Bruck was advocating a truly spiritual revolution.

But what would it accomplish? How would it transform the present society in accordance with the requirements of the Volk? First, the bourgeois social and economic order would be dissolved. The nation would revert to the corporatism of the Middle Ages, with allowance for certain requirements of the modern age—such as international trade, tariffs, taxes, and a relatively large amount of public spending—factors, van den Bruck asserted, which had long ago been taken into account in the protectionist ideas of Friedrich List.[5] The corporatist reorganization was to reap for the nation the benefits of a communal society, benefits which the bourgeoisie had not been able to provide. Embodying some aspects of socialism, the new organization would uphold the sanctity of special groupings such as guilds, estates, and orders, all of which were to be subordinated to the requirements of the Volk as a whole. Socially and politically, the new order was to complete the democratic changes of the nineteenth century. The citizen of the "new" Germany would participate to a greater extent in the political life of the nation and would be granted a "greater" role as an integral part of the *volonté général*. Who was to lead, who to govern? Van den Bruck was vague and ambiguous on this question, asserting only that the spiritual revolution would provide the answers.[6]

Other Volkish theorists elaborated on the theme initiated and expounded by van den Bruck. The circle around Diederichs' *Die Tat* took up the cause and propounded its own variation in the form of the New Romanticism. After Diederichs' death in 1927, Eugen Rosenstock assumed the ideological leadership of this group and advocated a German revolution in terms similar to van den Bruck's. He too asserted that it was not to be a political revolution, that its essence as well as the means used to bring it about must be spiritual. It would be Germany's third great revolutionary upheaval, the first being the Lutheran schism and the second the creation of the Romantic creed. Like the others, it would be a purely spiritual phenomenon.[7] Later on, in 1929, Hans Zehrer, the editor of *Die Tat*, reinterpreted Rosenstock's thoughts to meet new conditions. Speaking of the revived nationalistic anti-Weimar front, he identified the German revolution with a renewal of Lutheranism and said that it might even be equated with a second Lutheran revolution.[8]

The German revolution would be democratic but not parliamentary. Volkish thought had always been concerned with having all the people participate in the Volkish destiny and at the same time preventing the Volk from being atomized into political parties. Opposition to parliamentary democracy fused with the condemnation of the bourgeoisie as a class which prevented the true revolution of the Volk. For example, Carl Schmitt and Oswald Spengler, each in his own way, claimed that bourgeois parliamentary government had become a limited class institution that conducted private business by "other means." Both writers expressed the feelings of the times. Carl Schmitt especially was an able spokesman for the general consensus of "German revolutionaries." Himself a constitutional lawyer, he declared the existing parliamentary institutions insufficient as a means of providing for genuine democratic expression and demanded that a new political forum be created which would answer the needs of a mass industrial democracy. Parliaments were declared outdated organizations of nineteenth-century bourgeois liberalism; they were more pernicious than helpful, for in their tolerance of political parties they prevented the true unity of the Volk.[9] Möller van den Bruck reflected a similar disenchantment when he attributed "the whole political misery of Germany" to political parties.[10]

In answer, they all advocated a modified form of Rousseau's *volonté général*. However, they limited human endeavor, denied that the masses were capable of bettering their situation, and thought of them only in terms of traditional concepts of group identity. Correspondingly, the individual members of the nation were not seen as having uniquely personal desires, but as reflecting feelings common to the whole corporate membership. Individuals were only integral parts of a fictitious "personality," the corporation, which spoke in one voice representing the interests of all.

There were many Volkish precedents for this corporate view of society, as well as the romantics' awakened consciousness of the needs of the amorphous populace. Nineteenth-century German legal theory, dating from Hegel, had placed a corporate structure midway between society and the state, thus freeing the latter from direct involvement in personal and special interests. The corporation, basic to the organic state, permitted the uninhibited flow of life and ideas from the popular substrata to the government above. As the corporate structure, if it were to speak for the interests of all, had to settle all disagreements among its members, it left the state to exercise only spiritual guidance. Thus there was no need for representative bodies. Since the corporate bodies of the various interests and occupations of the population could be their own spokesmen, no other organ was necessary; parties could be dispensed with and parliaments became superfluous.[11]

But before the revolutionaries of "the third way" could fully accept the notion of the corporate structure, an improvement had to be made in the theory to bring the several corporations into line with the needs of Volkish unity. Grouping around special occupational interests was good so long as an internal unity could be provided that transcended the limitations of the various interests. A mythos and a national leader were required. The youth groups and the *Bünde* led the way in pressing this demand. At the same time, they offered the ideological solution in the form of the principles of their own organizations: Eros and concepts of leadership. Here was a concrete effort to resolve the problem. The *Bund*, as we have described it, was thought to represent a living form, a true forerunner of the organic community. It transcended the corporate structure without really abolishing it by providing an over-all unity through its Volkish precepts and the concept of Eros. Through these unifying factors, in addition to its concepts of leadership, it claimed to facilitate the ideological consensus of the corporate, or *bündisch*, organization by uniting body, soul, and the spirit of all in the service of the Volk. In the interest of leadership, the corporate unity envisaged by the advocates of the *Bünde* system would not tolerate equality among individuals. Instead, individuals occupied places in hierarchical orders according to merit. In this manner, the corporate aspects of the *bündisch* plan merged special occupational interests with the principles of local leadership by means of charismatic leaders as they would arise in each corporate organization. Confident of their destiny, the several *Bünde*, the Freischaar, the Neue Pfadfinder, and the Jungdeutsche Orden could declare: "Where a *Bund* exists, a new Germany starts!" [12]

The *bündisch* version of "the third way" was favorably received. It did indeed provide a middle course between capitalism and Marxism, for, as the German revolutionaries exclaimed, "true socialism is the community of the Volk." [13] That the theory contained ambiguities about how it could actually be put into practice, and that it had not been thoroughly analyzed, did not seem to matter. They were satisfied with the broad, over-all skeleton of the theory as it steered between capitalism (denying the metaphysical sanctity of private property) and Marxism (refuting the primacy of the proletariat and class needs in the coming revolution). The aim was to rejuvenate the spiritual orientation of Germans along the lines of nature, the German heritage, and the Volk. Or, as such men asserted, the order of creation demanded "first a new human being and then a new state," [14] first the spiritual transformation and then its material implementation.

Although the Volkish movement as a whole received the *bündisch* proposals favorably, there were men who looked at them with a more critical eye. For these, the concept of a strong leadership conflicted with the general idea of corporate interests. While, on the one hand, the corporate structure served the purpose of expressing the true democracy of the Volk, a strong national leadership would effectively demolish any such pretensions. The individual corporations and *Bünde* might, within the total structure, ably accommodate a leader without forgoing their democratic prerogatives, but a strong national leader would be at variance with such an arrangement. For, if the leadership ideal were made operative on the national scene, the whole corporate structure would become meaningless. Accordingly, these people claimed, there was a division of power inherent in the *bündisch* concept that required resolution.

Again, Carl Schmitt must be regarded as the most representative in his suggestions for resolving that division. Interestingly enough, he turned to the Italian example for inspiration and incorporated the two conflicting forces in a system of compatible responsibility and exercise of power. The corporations were to function in such a way as to make their own special contributions to a national mythos. A common bond, uniting all the various corporations regardless of their diversity, was similarly to join all the parts of the nation. This common bond was to be race: the Aryan race. The *Führer-prinzip*, which would direct the united forces of the nation, crowned the whole edifice. The *Führer* would be a representative member of the race of the Volk, and would be greater only by virtue of his charismatic leadership. Accordingly, his concern for the nation's welfare would necessarily be greater than that of the individual corporation, which would be primarily concerned with its own interests. In this capacity he would bridge the diversity of the corporations and draw them together in a concerted national effort.[15] Thus, the leader, the corporations, and, indeed, the whole Volk participated in a mystical racial unity that engendered identical attitudes and values. The common denominator was found: the Aryan race.

Here again we return to the crux of the Volkish argument, of the alternative it presented: rather than stating Germany's problem in economic or social terms, the proponents of the Volkish solution thought in racial and ideological terms. We recall that they had never regarded economics as a crucial social element, and the chief place was assigned, at all times, to the spiritual disposition of the German

Volk. Volkish economic theory, in its aversion to anything materialistic and concrete, had never advanced beyond opposition to the international (bourgeois or Jewish) capitalist conspiracy, on the one hand, and the international Bolshevik conspiracy, on the other. Its most sophisticated economic achievement was to define productivity as the work of skilled artisans and to condemn money and interest charges as unproductive. And this attitude, this slighting of the economic sector, was typical of all Volkish thought. The problems were never posed in real, concrete terms, but as conflicts of ideology, of identity, of spiritual values.

Though the door was closed to economic considerations, they came in by the window and in a converted ideological form played a major role in Volkish and National Socialist agitation. Many revolutionaries of "the third way" fused primitive economics with the omnipresent Germanic faith in order to direct the attack not so much against the bourgeoisie, whose capitalist inclinations it condemned, as against the Jews. In this manner the Jews were identifiable not only as a separate and alien people racially inferior to the Aryans, but also as the source of the imbalanced, pernicious capitalism that was plaguing Germany. Anti-Semitism could conveniently encompass the charges of racial adulteration, economic sabotage, and absolute enmity to the German Volk. It could also, just as conveniently, picture the Jews as the incarnation of the inferior race, as capitalism, or as Bolshevism. In short, Jewry was the corrupting force of materialism, or as Paul Krannhals, a Volkish philosopher, declared: "With Jewry stands or falls the mechanistic and mechanical concept of the economic system." [16]

Directed into the channels of anti-Semitism, the Volkish alternative of "the third way" became increasingly popular. As race became an indispensable ingredient, various individuals and organizations spurned those who lacked the proper racial emphasis. For this reason, Alfred Krebs of the DHV rejected Italian fascism, claiming that neither Mussolini nor his party appreciated the value and centrality of race. Similarly, the National Bolsheviks, those who combined their German nationalism with admiration for the Soviet Union, were accused of ignoring or minimizing the merits of race and Volk.[17] The clearest example of the implications and problems of the German revolution are found in the National Socialist camp. Here the brothers Otto and Gregor Strasser attempted to fight the anti-bourgeois, anti-capitalist, and anti-Marxist struggle.

The Strasser brothers had been early followers of Hitler and they made it their special concern to proselytize northern Germany. By the mid-twenties Gregor was the second most powerful man in the party. Otto, the theoretician, broke with Hitler as early as 1928. Gregor remained in the party and in 1929 attempted to rally the local party leaders around his standard in opposition to Hitler and the "Munich group" in the South. His nerve failed at the crucial moment (he did not show up at the decisive meeting) and Hitler won an easy victory. Nevertheless, Gregor remained in the party, albeit stripped of his power. Hitler's revenge came in 1934, when Gregor Strasser was murdered. Oriented toward the northern industrial regions and, especially, Berlin, the Strassers attempted to make meaningful not only the "National" but also the "Socialist" in the title of their party: to be Volkish and at the same time to present a German socialist alternative. Yet, in the end, we are back to a "spiritual revolution." On the Volkish side, they emphasized German spiritual and historical needs as well as race; on the socialist side, the communal approach to the solution of economic and social problems. The more they stressed the latter, the material implementation of socialist programs, the less emphasis was placed on Volkish ideas. Conversely, the greater the stress on the racial and spiritual aspects of the German revolution, the less attention devoted to the real issues. The two alternatives inherent in the Strassers' program were precariously balanced. But there was a subtle prejudice in favor of the spiritual even when a more concrete socialist alternative was put forward. For, upon closer analysis of the Strasser brothers' economic and social program, we find that anti-Semitism occupied a central position. This is consistent with the extent to which their proposed social and economic changes were to affect the real division of wealth and power. After all, even though they claimed to be revolutionaries, the Strasser brothers' reforms did not aim at abolishing private ownership of the means of production or at effecting an equitable distribution of the profits derived from the capitalist system. Their program was more "anti-capitalist"—in that it maintained that capitalist exploitation (that is, Jewish usury) had reduced Germany to economic and financial destitution—than it was pro-socialistic.

In his private utterances, in his public statements, and, above all, in the *Fourteen Theses of the German Revolution* (1929), which, after his break with Hitler, served as the manifesto and program of the factionalist Black Front, Otto Strasser clearly delineated the extent of his commitment to *socialist* social change. Here he summarized in three main points the program of his group: nationalist, against the enslavement of Germany; socialist, against the tyranny of money; Volkish, against the destruction of the German soul.[18] His first point placed him in the company of Möller van den Bruck, for he advocated a foreign policy oriented toward the East, toward what van den Bruck had described as the territory of the "young" Russian nation. His second point demanded two basic steps: nationalization of all land and the abolition of all unearned income, a socialist policy that left intact the core of modern industrial capitalism. And the third point was directed against the "foreign" elements that supposedly festered with the German nation: Freemasons, Catholics, and especially Jews. In the summary of his program he re-emphasized the third commitment, to "clean out" Germany, by asserting that the "fight for the German revolution is especially directed against Judaism." [19]

Since Strasser's group did effectively represent one of the more plausible alternatives to Hitler, an alternative that was seriously weighed by such people as Chancellor Schleicher in 1932, it will be fruitful to look more closely at the group's proposals. We will notice that whereas the first two proposals are rather vague and were pursued in a halfhearted mai nc , the third bears all the marks of dedication and conviction.

During the early 1920's, German social scientists had observed a shift in Soviet Russia away from an internationalist policy toward a concentration on national concerns. To them, and especially to some German nationalists, Russian Bolshevism had successfully combined the essential aspects of a fervent nationalism and a utilitarian socialism. The Strassers maintained close contact with the group that evolved out of such sympathies, the National Bolsheviks, many of whom were also members of the NSDAP.[20] Intrigued by the developments in the Soviet Union, the Strasser group, including, by the mid-twenties, Joseph Goebbels, considered a foreign policy that would attempt to reach a *modus vivendi* with the eastern neighbor as in the best interests of Germany's own future national socialism. But since this policy could not be implemented until the National Socialists assumed power, many aspects were left vague.[21]

The economic proposals, as they struck close to home, were subjected to a closer scrutiny and, consequently, were more detailed. Here the Strasser brothers concretized the anti-bourgeois element in the revolutionary drive and translated its anti-capitalist longing into a demand for a semi-corporatist, semi-socialist society. The former insofar as society would be organized according to skills and interests: and the latter, as it pertained to the division of property and profits.

After his break with Hitler, Otto Strasser continued to spell out the direction of thought both he and his brother had voiced within the party. Gregor, remaining a party leader, failed in his bid to depose Hitler the following year, but he still refused to join his brother, who had by then founded a new group, the Black Front. Otto Strasser denied the sanctity of private property and even advocated the complete nationalization of land, though the farmer would retain the right to sell his produce on the free market. Yet he did not call for a greater nationalization in industry, transportation, and banking. We must remember that nationalization of land had been a common Volkish demand and that utopian groups had tried to put communal ownership into practice. In connection with the division of property and profits, Strasser's proposals were as follows: capital property was to be apportioned in such a way that the workers would hold the rights to 10 per cent, the state 41 per cent, and the private owners the remaining 49 per cent; profits, meanwhile, were to go 49 per cent to the workers and 51 per cent to the owners.[22] On the whole, these were halfway measures, more in line with reform than revolution. Private property, after all, was not drastically affected, at least not the major holdings, and instead of being given greater social and political power, the workers merely received a larger fraction of the fruits of their own labors.

Only with respect to the third point did Otto Strasser's Black Front live up to its ideological claims. Here the spiritual awakening of the nation required that it be purged of all alien cultural and ideological manifestations. A reversion to the classical, the traditional German values meant a rejection of all that had caused Germany to get involved with foreign developments on the international scene. Culture, defined in its narrow Germanic application, was contrasted with civilization, the mechanistic development of the Romance countries. Correspondingly, all beliefs that had a greater than solely German relevance, such as Roman Catholicism and Freemasonry, were considered anti-Germanic and divisive. At the head of these alien influences were the Jews and Judaism. The Jews, as a people whose history and cultural development could be traced to other than German sources, were singled out as the hostile agents in all of Germany's problems.[23] Yet it is undoubtedly true that the Strassers despised the vulgar anti-Semitism of a man like Streicher, and Gregor Strasser stated categorically that Nazis did not desire persecution of the Jews, but only a "clean division" between them and the Germans.[24] Nevertheless, even Gregor Strasser called the Jews a "people composed of cheats" and said that they had practiced usury in the time of Moses.[25] On the whole, however, it can be concluded that their more specific social program lessened the preoccupation with the Jewish menace. With the Strassers in control the German revolution might perhaps have been kept from turning into an "anti-Jewish revolution." The brothers differed from Hitler in degree, though they also accepted ideas of racial purity.

Perhaps because the Volkish ideas were so important to their program, it ended up by stressing a spiritual transformation, a recapturing of the German soul. The attempts at social reform, important though they were, succumbed to the onslaught of the Volkish ideology. Metaphysics triumphed, for all these men were revolutionaries whose weapons lacked a concrete and practicable social and economic sharpness. They turned inward instead.

The Strassers, however, were not alone in their aspirations; others, with some of whom we have already become familiar, also shared similar goals. The idea of regenerating the corporatist structure of society, of conducting a purely spiritual and internal revolution, had adherents among those involved with the workers as well as among the higher echelons of state and society. For instance, Alfred Krebs of the DHV was joined by a fellow union leader sympathetic to the Volkish viewpoint. Max Habermann believed that Germany could attain her most "natural" form of political and economic organization only if she reverted to a corporatist state. He attempted to put his ideas into practice by entering into discussion with the Catholic trade-union movement, for he knew that many of its members were sympathetic.[26] More immediately influential, von Papen and members of his staff at a critical moment looked favorably on corporatism. In 1933, at the very moment when the Nazi-DNVP coalition government was formed, von Papen announced his sympathy with the corporatist position.[27] Of course, this did not carry with it a concomitant endorsement of social change or "third way" revolutions; rather, it was an attempt to stay the power of the fanatical nationalists, to preserve the *status quo*, and possibly to bring about a return to a non-industrial past. Edgar Jung, von Papen's chief theoretician, provided the most succinct analysis of the step, when he declared that the "new" Reich must be like that of the Middle Ages, that medieval society should serve as the model for constructing the organic Volk of the future.[28] Of course, von Papen's and Jung's beliefs did not include the Volkish desire for the union of the individual soul with the community of the Volk, the fusion which the DHV and other Volkish thinkers hoped would be effected by such a social order. They hoped instead for the re-establishment of the powers of the aristocracy based on heredity, tradition, and culture.

In the 1920's the advocates of the spiritualist and corporatist revolution were joined by segments of the Deutschnationale Volkspartei, which, through its economic specialist, Paul Bang, advocated the implementation of principles of corporatism in the economic field. Such a course, Bang asserted, would destroy the power of the labor unions and, in the interest of the nation, bring together the employer and the worker in industrial *Bünde*. In these, the employers, as the natural leaders, would assume the role of *Führers*, from among whom would be chosen, again by a natural process of selection, the most competent national leader.[29]

These advocates of a revived corporatism as well as the German revolutionaries sincerely wished for a change in German society. That they failed indicates that they made a serious tactical mistake. They underestimated the resourcefulness of Hitler and the temper of the times, which demanded a more concrete, even though fanatical, program and a simpler objectification of the ideology.

But we must not succumb to the temptation of judging these men retrospectively, in the light of Hitler's later triumph. Moreover, Hitler and his immediate adherents were not without sympathy for parts of the Strasser program or even the scheme advocated by Paul Bang of the DNVP. But in all instances Hitler accepted them only on condition that they reflected his leadership-oriented ideology. Correspondingly, Hitler did not permit the development of a hierarchical *Ständestaat* (a state structured according to estates) as an alternative national system. A chamber organized according to professions or occupations, if it should exist at all, would have economic functions only. The hierarchy he devised was to be based on party membership and spiritual contributions to the betterment of the Volk. Men must be placed in the Volk structure according to their grasp of its nature and destiny, not because of their professions.[30] Moreover, economic ability was not to be equated with an equal ability in the field of national leadership; that was to be reserved for the charismatic, spiritual leader alone. This was the reason why Hitler abandoned the original *bündisch* course of the party and transformed it into a mass movement with a freewheeling leadership ideal. This change also facilitated his alliance with the bourgeoisie and the circles of high finance. In 1929, while Strasser was challenging Hitler's authority, the Nazi leader was wooing the steel barons of the Ruhr and impressing them with a very "sensible" speech.

The German revolutionaries lost out to Hitler not only because of their failure of nerve, but also because Hitler no longer needed to rely on a narrow base for the "third way" alternative. By the late 1920's he could count for support from the masses on up to the financiers and the haute bourgeoisie. Yet Hitler also embraced the idea of a German revolution and used the "third way" as well. But now what had been implicit among all the "German socialists" became explicit. Here one could have one's cake and eat it too: the revolution so many Germans desired, but one which would not disturb social or economic relationships. A spiritual revolution could be supported by all classes without fear and trembling. Indeed, by stressing the spiritual over the economic and social realities, this was the ideal revolution for those who might have suffered under a traditional revolutionary upsurge.

Hitler took this opportunity, toward which all of Volkish history had led, and exploited it. Indeed, he drove it to its logical conclusion, for he gave it a concrete direction. Whereas the Strassers and Krebs only confused people with their halfway economic programs, and van den Bruck was vague about the "idea" Germany must attain, Hitler changed all this. The German revolution became the anti-Jewish revolution. The mass enthusiasm which over half a century of Volkish agitation had made explosive, and which, if not resolved, could become dangerous to its own creators, was shifted away from the real social and economic grievances and channeled into anti-Semitism. The Jew was made to bear the brunt and, although this too had been standard in the Volkish movement, Hitler made it stick.

Here then was the source of Hitler's success: his ability to transform the revolutionary longings and grievances of a large sector of the populace into an anti-Jewish revolution. Not the big capitalist or the economic middleman, but the Jew, was made the incarnation of the enemy. In his deft and ingenious distinction between Jewish and German capitalism, Hitler saved the capitalist structure of Germany from sure ruin and, in effect, preserved it. Meanwhile, the Jews were eliminated as an economic force, leaving behind their investments, inventories, and wealth. In the process they also shifted the guilt from the true source of Germany's crisis: the malfunctioning of the German capitalist structure, the lost war, and the frustrations of the past century. This is not to assert that Hitler's anti-Semitism was simply an opportunist device for attaining and retaining power. On the contrary, it was precisely because it was a sincerely held belief whose dynamism succeeded in holding the nation spellbound that Hitler could steer his party to victory.

The German revolution was that "idealism of deeds" which Volkish thought had always advocated. To be sure, there were similar ideas in other nations. In Belgium, for example, the fascist Rexists maintained that "every revolution has a mystical character." [31] But only in Germany had Volkish thought prepared a specific content for this mysticism which enabled Hitler to dramatize and personalize his revolution. The slogan "The Jews are our misfortune" conjured up the whole ideology which has been our concern, and the centrality of the Jew to this ideology prepared the way for Hitler's rise to power.

CHAPTER 17

The Anti-Jewish Revolution

IN THE HANDS of Adolf Hitler the German revolution was transformed into an anti-Jewish revolution. A basic ingredient of the Volkish ideology had ripened to a point where it could be plucked by the Nazis to be successfully assimilated into their own political maneuverings and used to increase their popular appeal.

With the appearance of Hitler on the political scene, followed as it was by a successful dissemination of a whole political program, the theme of anti-Semitism acquired a new dimension. Although anti-Semitism had flourished for more than fifty years, Hitler transformed it into a political vehicle, and the soundness of his move was attested by its favorable reception by the public. Now not only were Volkish leaders lecturing on the incompatible spiritual qualities of the two peoples, and theologians of race stressing the anthropological differences, but a political leader possessing a charismatic appeal was demanding that something be done about it, that, indeed, only if the Jews were eradicated could Germany regain her lost glory and achieve greatness in the future. What was the ideological store Hitler drew upon? Who were his immediate teachers and whom did he inspire to follow in his footsteps in a society which was already thoroughly drenched with the anti-Semitic stereotype? It is to these questions we must now turn by directing ourselves to the mind of Hitler, his immediate antecedents, and his disciples.

Many historians, seeking the source of Hitler's anti-Jewish obsession, have turned to the writings of the "classical" anti-Semites or to the ideologies of such people as Guido von List and Lanz von Liebenfels, both from Vienna. But to little avail. First of all, there is no evidence that Hitler read all the literature on the subject of the Volk and the Jews. It is more likely that he would listen to and be influenced by people who carried the message directly across the land and preached it at assemblies in Vienna, Linz, and other centers. And secondly, even if he did read books and journals on the subject, we do not know which ones. Thus, while he might have read Lanz von Liebenfels' *Ostara, Zeitschrift für Blonde (Journal for Blond People)*, a notoriously racist journal, we really have no proof.[1] Therefore it seems best to give full weight to Hitler's own testimony as to the development of his fanatical hatred of the Jews. For from whatever particular sources Hitler may have imbibed his ideas in his youth, much more important is the fact that he could have gotten them from the whole range of the Volkish movement. The interesting point is how he himself considered a system of thought which was already widespread and what he eventually made of it.

Hitler traced his anti-Semitism to an encounter with East European Jewry. Early in his life, as he traveled from the sheltered town of Linz to the metropolis of Vienna, he experienced, he claims, a horrible fright induced by the strange, forbidding dress and appearance of such Jews. He reacted with a feeling of horror to these strange beings who were crisscrossing the land to settle down, to multiply, and to dominate, displacing the genuine Germans.[2] Consciously or unconsciously, the pages of *Mein Kampf* summarize the stereotype of the ghetto Jew as this had grown up in Volkish thought. Here was the "strangeness" which proved the existence of a Jewish world conspiracy, the lack of morality which was translated into an absence of "idealistic feeling." The Jews were not a people of culture, the soil was for them a mere object of exploitation, and lustfulness took the part of true and rooted beliefs.[3]

This view of the Jews became bound up with Hitler's hatred of Vienna itself. He loathed the city, and precisely that part of it which was most civilized excited his greatest loathing. No doubt it is at this point that his anti-urbanism became basic to his attitude toward life.[4] This took the usual Volkish forms, including the glorification of the peasant, but it focused on the Jewish stereotype.

These facets of his thought existed before the war, but it was the war experience and what followed in Munich which gave them their particular dynamic. The Jews who dominated the Räterepublik, Communists as he thought them to be, reinforced the image of the Jew as he recalled it in *Mein Kampf* from his Viennese days. Hitler became the Volkish orator only after the war, but even before the war he had contacts with Volkish groups. His life in Vienna, lived in bitter poverty, brought him these contacts. Through them he could feel himself a member of an elite, in tune with what he called the "aristocratic precepts of nature," even while sleeping in his flophouse bunk.[5]

But Hitler's political astuteness also played an important role. He recognized the tactical value of anti-Semitic agitation. Later, when he himself was on the way to fulfilling his ambitions, he remembered the part that anti-Semitism had played in the successful career of the Viennese Lord Mayor Karl Lueger, and wrote of him, in *Mein Kampf,* as the "most powerful mayor of all time." But among all these factors none would seem to be a strong enough stimulus to have driven him to use anti-Semitism as *the* vehicle to political power. We may instead say that his hatred of the Jews was a deep emotional commitment and that its moral ingredient gave the political program just the right amount of respectability. It was not a mere tactic.

When Hitler transferred his interest to Munich and there became engaged in the intellectual life of the down-and-outers, his anti-Semitism also took an upward turn. In his early days of dabbling in politics, he came under the influence of Dietrich Eckart and remained close to him until Eckart's death in 1923. This important figure in the Volkish movement played the key role in crystallizing Hitler's political attitudes. At the time Hitler met him, Eckart was the publisher of *Auf Gut Deutsch,* a magazine which attracted the leading writers of the Volkish movement. Among the contributors whom Hitler is certain to have read were such men as Theodor Fritsch, Alfred Rosenberg, Ellegard Ellerbeck, the poet of the Germanic sun religion, and Ernst Wachler, who had revived the Germanic open-air theater. On the whole the journal was marked by the overbearing presence of anti-Semitic articles, many of them composed by Eckart himself, while others were reprinted from Lehmann's newspaper *Deutschlands Erneuerung.*

Eckart was very influential in the development of the anti-Semitic dynamic within the ranks of the young Workers' party. He reinforced Hitler's abhorrence of Jews as a mysterious, strange, and conspiring people, supplementing Hitler's ideas in some areas, while creating a more fanatical foundation for their development in others. While Hitler had already shared some of Eckart's beliefs, most of them were as yet only vague, unformulated convictions. Eckart plumbed deeper and connected the removal of the Jewish menace with the resuscitation of the Volk. He was to make Hitler view the problem as he himself viewed it: it transcended all others in importance, and its solution would bring to an end the Volk's period of trial. Or, as he stated it: "The Jewish question is the chief problem of humanity, in which, indeed, every one of its other problems is contained. Nothing on earth could remain darkened if one could throw light on the secret of [the Jews]." [6] And in what way did the Jews achieve their domination of mankind? Eckart repeated all the Volkish ideas on this question: by depriving mankind of its sentient soul, by injecting the cold, materialistic serum of Judaism into the institutions of man, and by conspiring to assume power over the Gentile world.[7]

Eckart took himself seriously, fanatically so. Lacking any other steady source of income (except for his adaptation of *Peer Gynt* to a Volkish message in which the peasant hero portrayed a Faustian figure), Eckart devoted himself fully to distributing and collecting money for *Auf Gut Deutsch*. The publication had not been popular with the masses, and Eckart resorted to distributing it personally to commuters on crowded trains in Munich. It was especially here that he tended to push, and perhaps with reason, the anti-Semitic special issues.[8]

Such then was the man and party member who befriended Hitler when he joined the small body of men who then constituted the National Socialist party. The two formed a team in which Hitler was the avid and quickly learning disciple. Eckart's tutelage proved to be indispensable in devising the tactics which the Führer later employed to gain control over the embryonic party. Thus it is indeed surprising that historians have failed to give Eckart due credit for his contribution to the viability of National Socialism. There is, of course, an explanation: historians have regarded him as too marginal, too much of a crank. But, and again we must reiterate this, in the Volkish movement he was no more marginal than Lagarde, Langbehn, or Ludwig Schemann, all of whom were equally frustrated and obsessed, and lived solely for the dissemination of what they believed to be the truth. Eckart was even more successful in that he found a disciple capable and ruthless enough to implement the faith of his master. Then, too, he introduced Hitler to Alfred Rosenberg, who in his limited and pedantic way continued the party's anti-Semitic momentum as an indispensable part of the ideology.

That Hitler had learned well from Eckart was shown during the party's first great internal crisis. In 1921, the six-thousand-member party was confronted with a division of emphasis: the issue was nationalism versus Gottfried Feder's socialism, which consisted in putting an end to all charging of interest. Where was the stress to be placed? Hitler adroitly avoided coming to grips with the problem, a clever tactic that he followed until, having silenced the Strasser group, he could declare for a German nationalism that did not destroy the bourgeoisie or capitalist institutions. Instead, he brought up the issue of the Jews and launched into a diatribe against their religion, race, and culture that was climaxed by the demand that force be used to counter the Jewish threat. There was no disagreement within the party: rather, the members united behind him and the separatist tendencies were buried for the time being in the enthusiasm for the anti-Jewish revolution. With this issue, Hitler had found the basis for uniting, emotionally and ideologically, the small and fanatical party, an issue which transcended the insoluble problem of nationalism versus socialism. With this issue, Hitler emerged victorious as party leader on July 29, 1921.[9]

The anti-Semitism embraced by Hitler was not just an opportunistic device, however, but a deeply felt conviction strengthened by a personal commitment to the whole Volkish outlook. And even though it was part of a spiritual disposition, an attitude toward life that was founded on belief in an irrational cosmology, life forces, and nature mysticism (and consequently could have been derided as the outlook of a mentally deranged person), it was real nonetheless. That these notions were real enough to have an impact on the public only indicates that the populace was relatively familiar with them, that they had existed prior to the advent of Hitler. Indeed, Hitler did not invent them; he was the direct heir of the Volkish movement. It was his strength to have grasped that the mass of Germans was highly receptive to the peculiarly Volkish anti-Semitic rationalizations of the nation's problems. Moreover, it is in Hitler's ability to rise above the sectarianism that had weakened the Volkish appeal that we must search for the uniqueness of the Nazi continuation of the traditional Volkish ideology. Hitler was able to translate the Volkish beliefs into a mass movement because he combined them with a pragmatic approach to politics. As he wrote in *Mein Kampf:* "A world view can be right a thousand times, but it will be without significance for the life of the Volk if it does not combine with the goals of a fighting movement, a political party." [10] For Hitler all belief became political belief, but this did not abolish the ideology itself. His criticisms of the Volkish movement do not touch the basic presuppositions, but instead concentrate upon their ineffectiveness: he condemns the earlier ideologues because they were "mere wandering scholars" [11] or because they escaped into the metaphysical world of pure feeling.

The last accusation relates, once more, to Hitler's desire to make the ideology into a living reality. This meant, for him, being as clear as possible: "To be German means to have clarity." [12] How proud he is in *Mein Kampf* for boiling the ideology down to twenty-five points! He understood that one needed a clear objectification of ideas in order to activate a mass movement. In addition, one needed discipline and organization. That Hitler was vitally interested in problems of organization is no argument that he was a mere power-seeking pragmatist. For organization, as well as propaganda, was a means to the end of translating into reality that Volkish thought which he believed to be an "inner necessity" of life. It was the combination of Volkish attitudes and a preoccupation with means in the person of a consummate politician that gave the National Socialists a dynamism and a relevance which none of the rival Volkish groups could equal. The focus upon the Jew. besides being politically useful, gave clarity to the ideology. This was precisely the combination which carried Hitler's mass movement forward to victory. Anti-Semitism had always been part of the Volkish attitude, and one of the most conspicuous parts. It was the combination of organization and the anti-Jewish revolution which proved so effective in Hitler's rise to power.

What had served to unite the party did similar service on the national level. The spiritual activism and fanatical dedication which the Nazi leadership brought to the theme of anti-Semitism appealed to the mass of German voters, from the unemployed to the industrialists and bankers. From the time Hitler made anti-Semitism the focal point of the party right up to his assumption of power, the German revolution was transformed into the anti-Jewish revolution. It served as a rallying point which, in its national application, provided the all too negative-sounding Volkish anti-capitalism and anti-Marxism with a positive framework. Grounded in the mysteries of race, nature, and cultural identity, the anti-Jewish revolutionaries claimed to be the defenders of Germanic creativity and not just mere preservers of the *status quo ante*. With the slogan "What is required is instinct and a will!" [13] Hitler increasingly achieved greater popularity as he directed the revolution.

Although we have stressed the overtly anti-Semitic aspects of the Nazi appeal as dating from the inter-party dispute of 1921, it was not until later that the theme emerged shorn of all socialist pretensions. For some time before the final victory of 1933, the program of the National Socialists still dressed up its anti-Semitism in national *socialist* goals. In an attempt to direct his appeal to the working masses, as Mussolini had done, Hitler supported a platform that included the "anti-capitalist longings" of Gottfried Feder's "socialism." And there is no doubt that he endorsed the "leftist" belief among the party members that the "bourgeoisie were finished" and that he raged at the betrayal of the nation by the middle class, indicting its money hunger and materialism for destroying the heroic will of the Volk.[14] However, this attitude became increasingly troublesome. The leadership of the party was not at all united on the appropriateness of the anti-capitalist image the party had created for itself. Hitler gradually realized that he, like the other Volkish leaders, could expect only scant support from the industrial and class-conscious workers, for their long-time socialist tradition directed them elsewhere. There was nothing left but to ameliorate the anti-capitalist direction and retrench along the line of anti-Semitism. Without funds, which had to come from industrial, financial, and individual bourgeois concerns, there would be no movement, there would be no favorable election returns, there would be no German transformation, socialist or otherwise. In the end, Hitler opted for legitimacy, for the bourgeoisie and against the pernicious forces of the Jewish hydra. With this shift, the overtly anti-bourgeois emphasis slowly subsided and at best remained ambivalent.

Whereas some Jewish observers during this period attributed the rise of the National Socialist party to despair over the economic situation, to bitterness, pessimism, and inherent longings of a growing section of the population,[15] one paper, representing the views of the Jewish university fraternities, disagreed. In its analysis it astutely recognized the essence of the anti-Marxist and anti-capitalist front. It is true, the paper acknowledged, that the Nazis were sincerely fighting Marxism and attacking profit-hungry capitalism, but they also identified both evils with the Jews. Reducing the Nazi program to its bare essentials, the paper asserted: "We, the Jews, are the enemies!" [16] The student paper was in a good position to know. Exposed as they were to constant harassment by their Gentile, German, self-styled Aryan classmates, the Jewish students were quicker than their elders to perceive the basis of Hitler's appeal among German youth. And they were correct. Youth viewed his call for the purification of all alien ingredients as its own idealistic task and readily made all necessary sacrifices in the name of it.[17]

The fears of the fraternity paper were borne out. Hitler was true to his promise not to relent on the anti-Semitic diatribes. They grew more extreme and became central to his program. This has been regarded as proving the psychopathic nature of the Nazi movement—not only for Hitler himself but for his followers as well. Thus a man like Julius Streicher was given free reign to express his sexual neuroses and frustrations through his obsession with the Jews. And we see still others who, acting out their primitive feelings of hate, gave in to the social urge and directed them at the Jews.[18] Of course, deep psychological disorders did underlie much of the manifestation of loyalty to the party. These disorders were real and pernicious enough but by themselves they do not explain the excesses of the party and the implementation of the anti-Jewish programs. Though the appeal of Nazism may well have been due to its release of primitive drives by providing them satisfaction in institutionalized hatred of the Jews,[19] this is by no means the primary reason for the party's success. The psychological view of the party's dynamic anti-Semitism can provide clues in individual cases—or in all cases from the point of view that all of men's actions are open to psychological explanation—but we are misled if we regard it as the sole or even the primary answer, for it tends to view National Socialism as a mere aberration that resolved a specific, temporary crisis. And what is more, it would maintain that anti-Semitism could have been eliminated by redirecting the psychic drives of Germany's maladjusted people. But there is a greater failing inherent in the psychological interpretation: it denies the endemic nature of anti-Semitism and regards it as a transitory phenomenon fulfilling certain psychological needs which could have been gratified by any other minority had the Jews not existed.

It should be apparent by now that we contest the validity of this approach to the recent history of Germany. It ignores the historical, social, and ideological character of anti-Semitism, which, as part of the Volkish movement, had been institutionalized and provided many of the German people with a particular framework for viewing the world and man's place in it. The immense and continuing popularity of the literary works we have analyzed, the trends of thought exhibited by the painters and youth, all attest to the fact that the existence of anti-Semitism was not dependent upon any single crisis; rather, it permeated all national questions. Consequently, the Volkish ideology cannot be viewed as a transient phenomenon; it was a new religion whose roots, like those of all religions and faiths, not only entered man's subconscious but penetrated deeper and became a whole new way of life. In the end, these feelings became tradition itself, readily acceptable and constituting weighty evidence for the sanctity of the Volkish purpose. Hitler only promised to fulfill a concept of life which had permeated much of the nation before he ever entered the scene.

That the appeal of anti-Semitism was more widespread and did not depend on psychopathy for its acceptance can be seen in the way that the Jew was pictured. Whereas the image of the particular, individual Jew might be sufficient to satisfy the frustrations of a mentally disturbed person, this "individualization" would fail to achieve the desired end in a political ideology. For the image of the Jew to arouse any feelings, pro or con, he had to be generalized, abstracted, depersonalized. It is always possible for the personal, individual case to contradict a general assertion by providing living, concrete proof to the contrary. For the Jews to become the foils of a mass movement, they had to be converted into objectified symbols so as to become other than human beings. Moreover, mass agitation demanded simplicity and consistency and consequently did not readily countenance subtle distinctions which might have excluded some Jews from condemnation. Hitler followed the path of his Volkish predecessors when he presented the Jewish evil not in its flesh-and-blood aspects but as an abstracted stereotype.

The growing abstraction of the Jew reflected the growing process of his depersonalization. Once the Jew had been denied a soul and genuine emotions, once his religion had been categorized as a fossil without ethical content, he was well on the way to being dehumanized. And who could feel any sorrow for or commiserate with an entity that had lost all human dimensions? Once a population had accepted this depiction of the Jew, it was possible to regard him as a cipher, as a figure that aroused no human compassion—only the large numbers of the martyred dead would stagger the imagination.

Hitler was greatly assisted in perpetuating this view of the Jews by the reapplication of the racial theories. Hitler himself used such theories to further the abstraction of the "Jew" and to serve as a basis for denying him his individuality. As early as 1919 he denied that anti-Semitism could be based upon one's feelings toward the individual Jew, unfavorable though this was bound to be. Instead, the evils for which the Jew stood were a "fact" of his race.[20] Hermann Rauschning has recalled that for Hitler "the Jew was a principle." [21] We have seen how at the turn of the century Theodor Fritsch made the identical distinction between the individual Jew and "the Jew" as an abstraction.[22] Here, once more, the Volkish tradition had prepared the way for a stereotype which transcended any concrete contact Jew and Gentile might have between them.

Purporting to be scientifically sound, racial theories built on the Volkish heritage. In this manner they had two ostensible virtues: they were "scientific" (and therefore respectable) as well as traditional. Through these ideas of race, the ideology of anti-Semitism was brought closer to earth, made more concrete, while the Jewish stereotype was given a more explicit objectification. We must again note here that though they pretended to be scientific, in the end these theories embraced all those features which had emerged from the romantic preoccupation with the German soul.

During the rise of Hitler, Hans F. K. Günther[23] became the leading proponent of the doctrine of race (though after the Second

World War he was "de-Nazified"). His books were greatly successful and before Hitler's assumption of power he was given a chair at
the University of Jena, where the students gave him a tumultuous
welcome. Concerned with the future well-being of the Volk, Günther made his literary debut with the publication of *Ritter, Tod und
Teufel* (*The Knight, Death, and the Devil*) (1921), in which he proclaimed the advent of the heroic saviour of the German nation.
This book was followed by the famous *Rassenkunde des deutschen
Volkes* (*Racial Science of the German People*) (1922), which was
reprinted fifteen times prior to 1933, and by *Rassenkunde des jüdischen Volkes* (*Racial Science of the Jewish People*) (1930). Both
works showed pretensions to erudition, in the copious footnotes, the
marshaling of evidence, and the careful phrasing of the text. But
in spite of these trappings of objectivity, the racial images portrayed
in both works made generalizations along the lines set by the prevailing Germanic ideology.

Like the Volkish racial theorists preceding him, Günther contended that the racial type objectifies the physical representation of
man's inner drives and nature.[24] Thus he moved from anthropological
considerations to metaphysical categories of racial beauty and soul.
The racial scheme demanded a hierarchy of perfect types. Günther
wisely recognized that no pure types existed: there were only less
imperfect, less impure types. He placed the Aryans at the pinnacle of
racial development. They were the most pure, the most beautiful, and the most creative. The lowest echelons, characteristically
enough, were occupied by the Jews, who differed sharply from the
Nordics. Their outward appearance, represented by slouched bodies,
bent shoulders, a tendency to obesity, and thick, lustfully sensual
lips, was the very opposite of the slender and statuesque German.
The physical stereotype was supplemented by a catalogue of what
purported to be typical Jewish gestures and traits for the purpose of
documenting the Jewish preoccupation with materialism, power,
and economic gain.[25]

The applicability and popularity of these racial theories was further enhanced by the controversy that developed between three
rival racial theorists. In the early thirties, Günther, already well established and recognized, entered into an argument as to what constituted valid racial criteria with L. F. Clauss, whose book *Die
nordische Seele* (*The Nordic Soul*) (1930) held that outward appearance was not essential, though desirable, in the typing of the Aryan
personality, and with Siegfried Passarge, whose *Das Judentum als
landschaftskundliches und ethnologisches Problem* (*The Jew as a
Landscape and Ethnological Problem*) (1929)[26] placed special empha-

sis on the environmental determinants of racial typology, repeating, typically enough, that soul-less Judaism was an urban religion. Though no single interpretation emerged victorious, the interchange, exposing the weaknesses in racial anthropology, produced a more pernicious result: from now on the Nazi ideologists could determine who was and who was not a Jew simply on the basis of their own subjective judgment. And since only a few Jews existed who could objectify in their persons the racial descriptions attributed to them, the subjective criteria could be applied to all Jews regardless of appearance or cultural identity, as well as to half Jews, without the fear of popular disapproval.

This "breakdown" of the supposedly "objective" criteria of racial typology was in full agreement with the needs of the Nazis' mass movement ideology. The leadership had to retain the prerogative of deciding how and when the criteria would be applied. For there were times when it had to make exceptions to the rule in order to gain a momentary advantage, or when it had to plead an ambiguity so as not to alienate powerful sections of support. Through this development, natural to a politically centered mass movement, a pragmatic note was injected into racial criteria, though they were no less sincerely held. As the particularized stereotype of the Jew was contested in theory and reality, the advocates of a racist anthropology gravitated toward more pragmatic criteria of racial character. Now, though individuals in a race might differ, or, as Clauss would have it, "black hair and small stature could contain thin and blond souls," [27] a more profound component set them apart from other peoples. This component could be defined in mystical terms as racial spirit, racial soul, or racial disposition, all categories that could be interpreted according to the personal or ideological inclinations of the leadership. Thus, Göring, much more cynical than Hitler, could repeat Lueger's remark: "I determine who is a Jew!" As a matter of fact, this supposed right was little used. Hitler felt differently where the Jews were concerned. When, in March 1933, the Italian ambassador, on behalf of Mussolini, urged Hitler to abandon the persecution of the Jews, the result was a "complete failure." Hitler expressed great admiration for the Duce, but in the same breath accused the Italian leader of knowing nothing about the Jewish question. Among the reasons for persevering against the Jews, such as their leadership in the Bolshevist cause, Hitler emphasized their cowardice and falsehood—components of the international Jewish psychology. Thus a threat of force against them obtained immediate results.[28]

While the scientific criteria of Jewishness became more spiritual, the spiritual anti-Semitism of the Nazi party and its adherents grew increasingly corporeal. Violence and cruelty against the Jews became distinct and important parts of the mass ideology, geared as it was to the emotional expression of its revolutionary urge. Hitler advocated the application of force against the Jewish menace as early as 1921.[29] The cry *"Juda, Verrecke"* ("Jews, drop dead") became commonplace. More bloody and correspondingly popular were the phrases of a verse sung by the smartly stepping SA troops as they marched through the streets: "When Jewish blood drips from the knife." In these crude slogans we can see the climax of that dehumanization of the Jews, associated with ideas of force, which we have discussed in previous chapters. The Nuremberg Laws of Jewish exclusion (1934), in their legalistic terms, also threatened violence, or punishment, against Jews for being Jews. As the Nazi government solidified its position of control, for a brief period it did attempt to settle the Jewish problem by means of legislation and encouraging Jews to emigrate. Hitler knew how to bide his time, how to exploit his captives in a multitude of ways, and how to build his program so that it could be effected with the greatest facility and with the cooperation of the population and the executioners.

Publications continued to arouse popular sentiment against the Jews throughout the land during the Third Reich. They kept alive the fire of anti-Semitism exactly to the degree necessary to implement measures for national ends. Pictures, films, lectures, and novels encouraged cruelty against Jews on all levels. For instance, Eher, the party's official publishing house, issued several novels in which anti-Jewish cruelty was the central theme. One of them, for example, published in 1936, glorified the murder of Walther Rathenau, while another idealized the deeds of Germanic Aryans against alien Jews.[30] *Der Stürmer*, Streicher's anti-Semitic sheet, published the most vitriolic attacks. It is little wonder then that when Hitler launched the campaign for the eradication of Jewry, he met with little opposition, little disillusionment in those he used for the purpose.

While it is true that the anti-Semitism of the Nazis had a practical intent—the elimination of the Jew as an economic and political force —it also rested its case on purely spiritual, ideological, and cultural grounds. The anti-Jewish dynamic that made itself felt in the streets, in political meetings, and in legal decrees, also made great headway through various spiritualist beliefs, theosophical religions which had a Volkish tradition, and within the body of a Germanic Christianity, as we saw in an earlier chapter. The party itself sheltered a notorious believer in spiritualistic forces. Heinrich Himmler believed in *karma* and was convinced that he was the reincarnation of Henry the Fowler. Indeed his whole thought was saturated with the nature mysticism which has been so often discussed in these pages.[31] Nor was Hitler himself free from it. Rauschning tells how Hitler occupied himself passionately with works such as those of the nature mystic Edgar Dacque.[32] Dacque wrote of a nature somnambulism. He believed that the magical forces of nature break through in man's dreams though his culture has wrongly sublimated them. This contact with the life force, springing from nature, is the only valid introduction to the cosmos.[33] Obviously there is a connection between Hitler's reading and the New Romantic ideology. No wonder that he told Rauschning that knowledge must once again take on the characteristics of a "secret science." [34] What a contrast the supposed Jewish materialism formed with such a world view!

The theosophical impetus also grew in popularity—in the form of a positive renunciation of a Judaicized Christianity and the adoption of a purely Germanic faith. Many Nazis embraced these variations of earlier Volkish precepts and turned toward sun worship. In its most palpable form, however, this trend attempted to link itself to Germanic Christianity and even presumed, as in Artur Dinter's attempt in 1927, to effect the "completion of the Protestant Reformation." [35] Dinter, the Nazi leader of Thuringia until he left the party in 1929,[36] was prominent in defining the spiritualistic basis of the new Germanic faith. His *Die Sünde wieder den Geist* (*Sin Against the Spirit*) (1921) postulated the theory that humans were only reifications of a "world of spirits" and only by striving to regain contact with the cosmic forces could they fully appreciate their racial uniqueness. In his *Die Sünde wieder die Liebe* (*Sin Against Love*) (1922), the world was described as peopled by spirits and among these the Jews were the "fallen spirits" led downward by Lucifer.[37] Thus the spiritualistic trend of the Volkish movement climaxed once more in this Nazi leader, as it had before him in such men as Langbehn and Fidus.

Even as early as *Mein Kampf* Hitler severely criticized such Volkish "religious reformers." Considering Hitler's own view of nature mysticism and the "secret science," this might seem contradictory. However, his reasons for such criticism are illuminating. The Volkish leaders in general were in his eyes "sectarians" who must be crushed by the true "movement," but specifically these reformers weakened the fight against the common enemy: Jewry. They scattered the forces that were needed to wage this battle.[38] Basically, Hitler's criticism of such men as Dinter was that they failed to focus their ideology on the Jews. This leads once more to our thesis that Hitler transformed the German revolution, of which many Volkish adherents dreamt, into an anti-Jewish revolution, and thereby concretized and objectified an ideology that had been too vague for the purposes of a mass movement.

The spiritualist and theosophical ideas were thus relegated to the background and their adherents silenced or ignored. Despite the fact that prominent members—such as Himmler, Rosenberg, Darré, and even Hitler himself—held private versions of the same beliefs, the party, in general, accepted officially only the anti-Jewish emphasis of the spiritualistic cults and Germanic Christianity.

For a time, during their rise to power and immediately afterward, the Nazi party encouraged dissident church groups which had broken with the established churches because of racial and ideological differences. The Judaic aspects of the Christian Church came under special attack and the church dogma was indicted for its lack of a Germanic context. The Old Testament had to be discarded, while the New Testament had to be salvaged by extracting all the "foreign" elements, leaving the basic "Germanic" figures intact. Christ had to be redefined as an Aryan and the dogma had to be read with a Germanic application. Moreover, the nationalism of some of the early church reformers had to be stressed, and Luther, consequently, was regarded more as a Germanic prophet of a Nordic religion than merely the purifier of a decadent church. Among the Aryan groups which advocated such a revision of Christianity, the Bund für Deutsche Kirche (Bund for a German Church) gained early prominence and received support from the Nazi party during its struggle with the established churches. However, the party soon found itself saddled with a possible liability, and when it started to patch up the rift with the Catholics and Protestants, it withdrew its support from the Bund.

The anti-Semitic impetus of the early party and the official anti-Semitism of the Third Reich was more pernicious when it entered into the dogma of the established churches. Many ecclesiastics, both Protestant and Catholic, felt a personal allegiance to the party, the state, and the Germanic ideology and openly voiced their convictions from the pulpit. Others believed that the German task, like that of the Holy Crusade, could be accommodated within the Christian dogma. Still others saw in the Nazi victory a revitalization of the German spirit and were grateful to the party, its ideology, and its leaders. Wilhelm Niemöller, a man of high intelligence, soon to become a leader in the Protestant resistance, has recalled with considerable frankness what May Day 1933 meant to him: then, with the Nazis in office and Germany sure of becoming a true *Volks-gemeinschaft* (community of the Volk), that day became "a day of joy, a day which aroused new hopes." [39] Throughout the country many congregations, devout Catholics and Protestants, joined the festivities, marched alongside the proudly victorious Nazi troops, and saw no conflict between their faiths and the Nazi ideology. With a few exceptions, among which the Dahlemer Pfarrernotbund (Dahlem Emergency Association of Ministers), organized by Martin Niemöller in 1934, was the most prominent, the congregations accepted the state directive that a Jew, regardless of his conversion or baptism into another faith, remained a Jew. That this effectively denied the validity of the sacrament of baptism did not prevent its acceptance by many a diocese.

Personally and as the leader of the state, Hitler attempted to extricate himself from direct conflict with the churches—especially the Catholic Church, whose Concordat had done so much for his prestige—and believed that, in the last resort, the religion of the Volk would triumph over Christianity. Thus Hitler's own declarations, made after his seizure of power, that he would not interfere with the Protestant and Catholic churches, but wished them well, must be taken as a tactical maneuver. For he proceeded to seek control over the Protestant Church and the attacks upon the Catholic Church, which increased as time went on, were not stopped. However, neither of the churches opposed him during his first year in power, for they still believed in his promises.[40] Not until 1934 did some resistance start, but never did the vast majority of the clergy join in. It is important to note the lack of resistance to Hitler during the first year: opposition to the ideology and what it stood for was apparently not strong enough by itself to produce protests against a regime committed to anti-Semitic and Volkish action. For some churchmen Hitler meant the end of chaos and the avoidance of a possible civil war, to others a bulwark against leftism, and to still others the mystical nature of the Volkish ideology would make believing respectable again and fill the churches.

But where Hitler abstained from direct interference except when it was necessary in the interests of the state, men such as Himmler, Rosenberg, and Darré kept alive the fires of a Nordic race-conscious Christianity. And the established churches, whether taken in by Hitler's seeming unconcern or whether they succumbed to the ideology, kept themselves alive by preaching on the civic duties of their flocks, endorsing peace and order and the observance of the nation's "laws," and by marching side by side with the men of the various

Nazi party organizations, absolving their transgressions, and appeasing their consciences.

To whom, then, did this anti-Jewish revolution, the de-Semitized Christianity, and the active anti-Jewish programs appeal? On one level, it appealed to a large percentage of the German population; on another level, it appealed to a bourgeois sentiment which was shared by most people regardless of class: obedience to the state. Many people overlooked Nazi and Volkish excesses because they regarded the rest of the ideology as pragmatic and respectable. And so it was, or at least purported to be. Bourgeois respectability and traditionalism were successfully woven into the ideological fabric of the Nazis, who, upon assuming power, took to championing the Volkish concepts of rootedness, puritan morality, and bourgeois tastes, ethics, and values. Professor Hans Neumann stated the case well when he spoke at the ceremony, in May 1933, of the burning of "degenerate literature": "We want a literature which treats as holy the pious bonds of family, *Heimat*, Volk, and blood, indeed, all the revered bonds [which bind men together]." [41] Hitler's revolution did not envisage the destruction of traditional personal bonds, just as he did not contemplate revolutionizing the capitalist economic structure.

By 1934 the Nazis had eliminated the extremists within the Volkish movement and within their own ranks. All things offensive to bourgeois ethics were rooted out of the party. The sexual license of some of the Volkish groups and the early National Socialists was abolished. Nude bathing, introduced by the Youth Movement, which had become somewhat popular as a reaffirmation of naturalness and genuineness, offended bourgeois sensibilities, and Göring had it outlawed in Prussia soon after the Nazis came to power. [42] Similarly, the *Bünde*, whose principles of Eros and male companionship Hitler had fought against early in his party career, were dissolved. Thus we might say that, from both a Volkish and a radically National Socialist point of view, the Nazi party had tailored the Germanic ideology to bourgeois standards.

From the moment when the Jew was designated as the enemy of the party and the Volk, the bourgeoisie were saved from a social and economic revolution, and in fact were actively brought into the transformation of the nation. They could proudly share in what Hitler, in 1933, proclaimed the "greatest Germanic racial revolution in world history." [43] Indeed, it was the bourgeoisie whom Hitler exhorted to become more courageous, to transcend their bourgeois limitations, and to fight against Jewish capital and Jewish communism. The revolution was anti-bourgeois insofar as it was directed against the Jew; while it was anti-Communist when it attacked both the Jews and the German Marxists, linking them in the Marxist-Jewish conspiracy. In its attack on the Communists, it was supported by middle-class hates and fears, while its "anti-bourgeois" drive set up a double standard, distinguishing between native and Jewish bourgeoisie.

This double standard, by which the middle class became the executor of the revolution, is made clear by a single example. Rudolf Höss, the commandant of the Auschwitz concentration camp, was undoubtedly the greatest mass murderer known to history. Yet his autobiography reveals a rather normal, pedestrian bourgeois existence. In the same breath in which he acknowledges himself a professional killer, he also describes a normal family life, tells of his kindness to children and his fondness of animals. In one passage his Jewish prisoners march to their death surrounded by flowering apple trees and the beauties of springtime. In the same passage he also gives vent to emotions, not of pity for the condemned Jews, but of concern for his own family.[44] That is just the point: the revolution was "displaced" toward the Jews and could thus protect and further bourgeois values.

The same double standard that worked in Höss was also present, if much less spectacularly, in the bourgeoisie as a whole. Adhering to their principle of the inviolability of private property when it affected their own interests, they religiously ignored this principle when Jewish property was involved. Arson was punishable by law, but when a synagogue was burned down the culprits were immune —if not commended. Thus the Nazis succeeded in fulfilling their promise to end the bourgeois reign—but only as it applied to Jews!

In the end Hitler had his German revolution. Long before, in 1920, he had outlined what sort of a revolution this was to be. Not a political revolution (for 1918 had shown what this could do in Germany), not an economic revolution (for the terrible example of Russia was before his eyes), but a "revolution of attitudes and feeling" (*Revolution der Gesinnung*).[45] Thus the Jew became the focus of the ideology, just as he had been for most of the earlier Volkish thinkers. Although some of the Nazi goals may have differed from those advocated by individuals and groups in the Volkish movement, most elements of Volkish anti-Semitism were a vital part of the Nazi program. In fact, many who had advocated a purely Volkish goal saw that National Socialism represented the most practical vehicle for achieving it. Many from the Youth Movement and the *Bünde* abandoned their earlier resistance and hostility and marched side by side with the brown-shirted Nazis. For these people, with their Volkish precepts, Hitler was not a stranger, not an innovator, but an adapter, a molder, who gave the prevailing Volkish theories a new edge, a more dynamic emphasis. But that edge was also dynamic enough to sweep the whole Volkish movement into the shadow of the Nazi party. Hitler's revolution, then, found large segments of the population ready for his message; and though that message may seem to us outlandish, best studied by psychologists, this was not how the admiring crowds regarded their leader, nor how historians must deal with National Socialism in retrospect.

CHAPTER 18

Conclusion

In our time two major revolutionary movements have made their mark upon Europe: the Marxist and the fascist. Like Marxism, fascism spread throughout Europe, and the various fascisms shared common elements, deriving from a commonly felt need to transcend a banal bourgeois world. All fascisms attempted to capture and direct bourgeois dissatisfaction with existing industrial and political reality, a dissatisfaction which began to take a concrete revolutionary form late in the nineteenth century. At that time, youth in particular attempted to escape from the "materialist" society in which they had been reared, and tried to find a new meaning in life, a new dynamic which would enable them to recapture their own individuality. On one level this revolt led to a battle against conventions, but on another it attempted to find a new sense of "belonging" that might be combined with the revolt to which they were committed. Fascism was far from being purely nihilistic; indeed, the discovery of a positive ideology was what enabled some fascists to succeed while their more "negative" ideological *confrères* failed.

In this book we have tried to analyze the kind of identity which this revolt achieved in Germany. The flight from reality which was the final result of the crisis of German ideology took a specific form in that nation, although the same urge can also be found in all the fascisms of western Europe. By realizing the extent to which German fascism differed from the rest, even on this level, we can understand the uniqueness of the movement of thought which led toward National Socialism. This is not to deny that all fascisms had certain features in common. Fascists everywhere spurned existing social and economic systems in favor of an irrational world view which sought both individuality and belonging at a new level. This irrational world view was itself objectified in the form of a new religion with its own mysticism and its own liturgical rites. José Primo de Rivera, the founder of the Spanish *Falange,* believed that "peoples have never been moved by anyone save poets," and it is small wonder that he castigated those, like the Bolsheviks, who were preoccupied with the viability of economic systems.[1] For Rivera, revolutions must have a mystical meaning. Likewise, in northern Europe, Léon Degrelle, the Belgian fascist leader, called every revolution "mystical in character" and asserted that events are dominated more by ideas and sentiments than by economic laws.[2] In France, the publicist Marcel Déat denied that the French Revolution had been in any way materialist, and contended that its philosophy was as idealistic as that of Germany.[3] All these western fascisms exhibited a flight from reality into the realm of an emotional and mystical ideology. They were all a part of the "displaced revolution" which moved from a rejection of reality to a glorification of ideology.

Moreover, in this manner these fascisms were able to retain the existing social structure, including property rights, and at the same time preach revolution. Existing society was supposedly rejected *in toto* and fascist thought centered instead upon the "new fascist man." Robert Brasillach, the French fascist, described this new hero: he wants a pure nation and a pure race; he loves to be a part of huge gatherings of men where the rhythm of the army or of the crowd beats as one pulsating heart. He does not believe in justice which exhausts itself in words, but rather appeals to that justice which rules by force. From that force springs joy. For Brasillach, fascism is not a political or economic doctrine, but an *esprit* and, above all, the spirit of joy.[4] There is little here with which the men we have discussed could have disagreed. Little wonder that Brasillach, after witnessing the Nuremberg *Reichsparteitag* (the celebration of the Nazi party at Nuremberg), asked himself: Can we Frenchmen share in this someday?[5] Similarly, Marcel Déat saw in National Socialism "a young, ardent and irresistible collective belief, against a civilization of fragmented and contradictory ideas."[6]

Nonetheless, we must not allow these similarities to disguise the profound difference between German fascism and the others of western Europe. For in the end, both Brasillach and Déat were disappointed, as were others who had earlier been enthusiastic about the true Nazi revolution. Marc Augier, who had founded the French youth movement of the 1930's, Les Auberges de la Jeunesse, and had become a most enthusiastic collaborator with Nazism, concluded that Hitler's ideology was too Germanic, and not universal enough in its fascist appeal.[7] The reasons for such disillusionment are clear, and they hold true for the other fascisms outside Germany as well.

The German revolution was too deeply anchored in its own restricted mystical ideology. The "anti-Jewish revolution" had displaced too many considerations which other fascists prized. These others attempted to put a greater emphasis upon the "anti-capitalist longings," especially in France (though always in a vague way), but above all, they exalted a Nietzschean love for action. This activism served at times to detach the "idealism" from the "deeds" which the Germans believed must go together. Thus, Drieu La Rochelle, the only French fascist writer of true distinction, could write that the Nietzschean, the model for his fascist man, believes in a provisional world which can be transformed and can explode at any moment.[8] The contrast between this view and the passionate German belief in eternal verities must be clear.

Such joyous activism made it impossible to channel the dynamic into merely anti-Jewish directions. Anti-Semitism was "instinctive" for the French, as Brasillach said, but it was never dominant.[9] The contrast between the issue devoted to the Jews by the French fascist newspaper *Je Suis Partout* and *Der Stürmer*'s approach to the problem is significant. Both agreed that the Jews were not a religious community but a separate people; however, the French newspaper added that one can have good relations with a foreign people and disclaimed any intention of being "xenophobic." While here the usual connection was made between Jews and Soviets, and even the pictures showed a common stereotype, there was no reference to brutality, certainly not to ritual murder, and indeed the Germans were criticized for dwelling too much on the "metaphysics of race."[10] Even this most radical of French anti-Semitic newspapers balked at accepting ideas that had become "official" in Germany.

Neither the manifesto of Degrelle's Belgian Rexists nor that of the Dutch National Socialists mentioned "the Jewish question," and Italian fascism followed the same course. The deputy leader of the Dutch Nazi party told a German National Socialist that his organization had no Aryan clause, although no friends of the Jews were to be found among its members.[11] This accurately describes the attitudes of these fascisms. While they tended (with the notable exception of the Italian movement before 1937) to be anti-Semitic, this was never a primary consideration.

Drieu La Rochelle sums up the attitude of the fascists of his generation toward ideology. In *Gilles* (1939), the only fascist novel ever to achieve popularity on the other side of the Rhine, he declares fascism to be not a program for action, not a doctrine, but a method. As he put it on another occasion, a program is something for tomorrow, while the struggle itself is what counts today.[12] Drieu La

Rochelle exemplifies a spirit of revolt, an urge for action which was common among youth at the turn of the century, but which in France, in contrast to the situation in Germany, was never controlled by a coherent ideology. Little wonder that French fascism remained restricted to an isolated group of intellectuals. The urge for joyous action was also primary in Belgian Rexism, the fascist movement founded by Degrelle, though here it was combined with an emphasis upon the family and the soil, an element which was notably absent from the movement in France.

These comparisons between German fascism and its counterparts in other western European nations are highly instructive, for they demonstrate that though fascism had spread throughout Europe, the German variety came to be unique. It was unique not only in the way it managed to displace the revolutionary impetus, but also in the primacy of the ideology of the Volk, nature, and race. The revolutionary impetus produced an ideological reaction throughout the continent, but the German crisis was *sui generis*, besides being more deeply rooted in the national fabric. Nowhere else was the ideology planted so deep or for such a long time. Nowhere else was the fascist dynamic embedded in such an effective ideology. How typical that when other fascisms, such as that of France, looked to Nazi Germany to bring about a real revolution, they always acted on a profound misunderstanding of the German phenomenon. National Socialism had tamed the activism which the other fascists prized and absorbed it into its Volkish and New Romantic ideology. Deeply rooted, as it was, in a specific German heritage, it could hardly serve as an aid to the fascist movements in other countries. It is typical in this regard that Hitler condemned the futurism which the Duce supported in Italy. With its emphasis upon action, futurism was at loggerheads with the "simple and plain enjoyment" advocated by the Nazis. As late as 1937, the fascist Marinetti, the founder of futurism, publicly accused Hitler of believing in a photographic stasis.[13] But that static ideal was, after all, nothing more than an expression of the eternal German verities which were "given" for all time. Thus Volkish writers had condemned the poet Heinrich Heine for not knowing the "good and the beautiful" but always reaching out for "the better, the more beautiful." In Nazi eyes such an attitude would lead to the wrong sort of revolution.

The divergence of German fascism from the other fascisms reflects the difference between German thought and that of the other western European nations. It was precisely through the ideology which we have discussed that this unfortunate nation came to repudiate a European heritage which was still alive elsewhere: that of the rationalism of the Enlightenment and the social radicalism of the French Revolution. Moreover, this repudiation was intimately connected with a general opposition to modernity which withdrew into itself, for what Eugen Diederichs and others had called the awakening of German individuality was both a flight from present reality and a flight from a European tradition. Other western fascisms tried to reach out to each other, but if National Socialism did this it was to further subversion on foreign soil for its own ends, not out of a deeply felt longing for a larger unity. Even today, when the still-existing Volkish movement clothes itself in the mantle of a "new Europe," the ideology is still that of the Volk tied to a mystical concept of nature on the one hand and to the cosmos on the other. Nothing has changed save for a rhetorical reference to European unity.

In 1936, Carl Gustav Jung said that for the first time it had dawned upon humanity that something not external to man can, nevertheless, be the truth.[14] It had dawned upon mankind long before this, however, and indeed had formed the foundation for European fascism. Looking at Germany, Jung saw the autonomous factors of the human soul embodied in collective phenomena. He believed that where the masses are in motion, men cease to be in control, and Jung saw the free play of the archetypes of the "collective unconscious" at work in Nazism. On the basis of these observations, Jung predicted that National Socialism was only the initial step in a development whose extent and result we could not begin to imagine.[15] From the point of view of the autonomy of the unconscious, the future was indeed awesome and frightening, especially at that time, when National Socialism had triumphed and was enjoying success after success.

But was Jung's view tenable? To be sure, throughout the Germanic ideology one finds a preoccupation with the *Ur* forces, the primeval instincts, combined with a mystically oriented dynamic. But this is only one side of the picture. National Socialism, the whole Volkish movement, was analogous to a religion, and the movement acted as if belief in the faith would grant the disillusioned a comfort and a sense of belonging which society could never provide. Yet the movement was not wholly centered upon the outpouring of the longings of the soul, as Jung would have us believe. The ideology was formalized. The archetypes were not allowed free play. And as the ideology was tamed, it came to express itself through an internal logic of its own which took on concrete, outward forms.

Georges Sorel had said disparagingly that intellectuals never know what to do with the phenomenon of religion in history. They could not deny its historical importance, nor could they explain it.[16] He held that men are motivated by irrational myths whose truth or falsehood is irrelevant to their appeal. It is hardly surprising to find that Sorel was a great source of inspiration for the fascists. But even the most irrational religion, to become effective, must express itself through outward forms. To move masses of men it must objectify itself. In the end the outward forms may become so important that they determine the content of the faith. This is what happened in Germany, both through the way in which the ideology was objectified and through the dominant role that the leader came to occupy. Moreover, the ideas of discipline and organization which Hitler stressed in place of "fanaticism" not only led to a more effective objectification of the ideology but also provided the basis for an awesome political effectiveness. The so-called eternal verities of nature, Volk, and race were channeled toward definite objects, consciously directed by the leadership.

The irrational is made concrete through rational acts within the terms of its own ideological framework. These rational acts are implemented by a political pragmatism as well as by the use of modern technology. But always the ideology provides the basic presuppositions and the eventual goal. For the enemy is powerful and will not shirk from the fight.

That the Volkish ideology, wedded as it was to anti-modernity, could be absorbed by the modern mass movement techniques of National Socialism led to its final realization. To be sure, if it had not been for very real grievances and frustrations, both on a personal level and on the national level, Germany's development in modern times might have taken a different turn. But the most important question is: Why did millions of people respond to the Volkish call? To this we have tried to give an answer.

NOTES

Notes

INTRODUCTION
(Pages 1–10)

1. Martin Broszat, "Die völkische Ideologie und der Nationalsocialismus," *Deutsche Rundschau*, 84 Jahrg., Heft 1 (January 1958), p. 67.
2. *Ibid.*, p. 58.
3. Oswald Spengler, *The Decline of the West* (New York, 1926), Vol. I, pp. 356 ff.
4. Gerhard Ritter, "Historical Foundations of the Rise of National Socialism," in *The Third Reich* (London, 1955), p. 386.
5. *Ibid.*, p. 384.
6. This is the view of the former National Socialist cultural expert Herbert Böhme. See his *Bekenntnis eines freien Mannes* (Munich, 1950), p. 67. Here it serves as an excuse for a present-day Volkish leader.
7. For example, the *Thunderbolt*, the newspaper of the National States' Rights party, sometimes reprints Volkish sources which are, today, difficult to obtain in Germany itself. Recently it offered to its readers the famous 1934 number of *Der Stürmer*, which accused Jews of ritual murder—in German!

CHAPTER 1
(Pages 13–20)

1. Otto Gmelin, "Landschaft und Seele," *Die Tat*, 17 Jahrg., Heft 1 (April 1925), p. 32.
2. Elizabeth Kriegelstein, "Vom landschaftlichen Erlebnis," *Preussische Jahrbücher*, Band 157 (July–September 1914), p. 6.

3. Friedrich Ratzel, "Die Deutsche Landschaft," *Deutsche Rundschau*, LXXXVIII (July–September 1896), p. 347.

4. Adolf Rapp, *Der Deutsche Gedanke* (Bonn, 1920), p. 235.

5. W. H. Riehl, *Land und Leute*, 6th edition (Stuttgart, 1867), p. 88.

6. *Ibid.*, p. 71.

7. For example, Hannah Gädecke, in *Wilhelm Heinrich Riehls Gedanken über Volk und Staat* (Dissertation, Heidelberg, 1934), p. 4, points out that for Riehl the medieval privileges of the nobility were the roots of a truly legal state (*Rechtsstaat*).

8. Gerhard Loose, "The Peasant in Wilhelm Heinrich Riehl's Sociological and Novelistic Writings," *The Germanic Review*, Vol. XV (1940), p. 265.

9. Riehl, *Land und Leute*, p. 99.

10. Riehl, *Die bürgerliche Gesellschaft*, 5th edition (Stuttgart, 1858), p. 349.

11. *Ibid.*, pp. 272 ff.

12. Riehl, *Land und Leute*, p. 96.

13. *Ibid.*, pp. 97-98.

14. Tüdel Weller, *Rabauken! Peter Mönkemann hat sich durch* (Munich, 1938), p. 114; Nathaniel Jünger, *Volk in Gefahr* (Wismar I, Mecklenburg, 1921), pp. 352-53.

15. Quoted in Victor Klemperer, *LTI* (Berlin, 1947), p. 240.

16. W. Harless, in *Marquartsteiner Blätter*, 2 Sondernummer (October 1933), n. p.

17. Riehl, *Die bürgerliche Gesellschaft*, p. 58.

18. Berthold Auerbach, *Sämtliche Schwarzwälder Dorfgeschichten* (Stuttgart, 1884), VII, p. 114.

19. This is best typified by the story "Joseph im Schnee," *ibid.*, pp. 3-110.

20. Graf Harry von Kessler, *Tagebücher 1918-1936* (Frankfurt, 1961), p. 525.

21. Hermann Löns, *Der Wehrwolf* (Jena, 1917), p. 239.

22. *Ibid.*, p. 14.

23. *Ibid.*

24. Wilhelm von Polenz, *Der Büttnerbauer* (Berlin, n.d.), p. 352. The most detailed discussion of such literature about peasant and Jew is in Wilhelm Stoffers, *Juden und Ghetto in der Deutschen Literatur zum Ausgang des Weltkrieges* (Nijmegen, 1939), esp. pp. 356 ff.

25. Heinrich von Treitschke, *Deutsche Geschichte im Neunzehnten Jahrhundert* (Leipzig, 1895), Band IV, p. 434.

26. Karl Beyer, *Jüdischer Intellect und Deutscher Glaube* (Leipzig, 1933), pp. 12, 17.

27. Wolfgang Menzel, *Deutsche Dichtung* (Stuttgart, 1859), Vol. III, pp. 465-66.

CHAPTER 2
(Pages 31–51)

1. Fritz Stern's *The Politics of Cultural Despair* (Berkeley and Los Angeles, 1961) is the best treatment of Langbehn and Lagarde.
2. The most thorough biography of Lagarde is Ludwig Schemann, *Paul de Lagarde* (Leipzig, 1919). Robert W. Lougee's *Paul de Lagarde* (Cambridge, Mass., 1962) also provides a good biographical treatment.
3. Paul de Lagarde, *Deutsche Schriften*, 4th edition (Göttingen, n. d.), p. 14.
4. *Ibid.*, p. 20.
5. *Ibid.*, p. 24.
6. Lougee, *op. cit.*, p. 129.
7. Lagarde, "Religion der Zunkunft," *Deutsche Schriften*, pp. 217 ff.
8. *Ibid.*, pp. 75, 76.
9. *Ibid.*, pp. 243, 247.
10. Klara Boesch, *Paul de Lagarde* (Augsburg, 1924), p. 52.
11. Lougee, *op. cit.*, pp. 171, 175, 183.
12. Lagarde, *Deutsche Schriften*, p. 11.
13. *Ibid.*, p. 13.
14. Boesch, *op. cit.*, p. 96.
15. Lagarde, *Deutsche Schriften*, p. 36.
16. *Ibid.*, pp. 245-46, 247.
17. Stern, *op. cit.*, p. 28.
18. Lagarde, *Deutsche Schriften*, pp. 22 ff.
19. Lougee, *op. cit.*, pp. 213-14.
20. Stern, *op. cit.*, p. 63.
21. See, for example, Lougee, *op. cit.*, Ch. 6.
22. Eugen Diederichs, *Aus meinem Leben* (Leipzig, 1927), p. 50.
23. Benedikt Momme Nissen, *Der Rembrandtdeutsche* (Freiburg, 1926), p. 73.
24. *Ibid.*, p. 43.
25. Julius Langbehn, *Rembrandt als Erzieher* (Leipzig, 1900), p. 203.
26. Cf. George L. Mosse, "The Mystical Origins of National Socialism," *Journal of the History of Ideas*, Vol. XXII, No. 1 (January-March 1961), pp. 81-96.
27. G. Trobridge, *Swedenborg Life and Teaching* (New York, 1938), pp. 176, 68.
28. *Ibid.*, p. 141.
29. Langbehn, *op. cit.* (1890), p. 88.
30. *Ibid.*, p. 98.

31. *Ibid.*, pp. 88 ff.
32. Langbehn, *op. cit.* (1900), p. 353.
33. *Ibid.*, p. 131.
34. Nissen, *op. cit.*, p. 109.
35. Langbehn, *op. cit.* (1900), pp. 130-31.
36. Nissen, *op. cit.*, pp. 114-15.
37. Langbehn, *op. cit.* (1900), p. 315.
38. Stern, *op. cit.*, p. 142; Nissen, *op. cit.*, p. 110.
39. Stern, *op. cit.* p. 141.
40. Nissen, *op. cit.*, p. 35.
41. *Ibid.*, p. 37.
42. *Ibid.*, p. 213.
43. Langbehn, *op. cit.* (1890), p. 303.
44. Nissen, *op. cit.*, p. 241.
45. *M. von Egidy sein Leben und Werk,* ed. by Heinrich Driesmans (Dresden, 1900), Vol. II, p. 99.
46. *Ibid.*, pp. 87 ff.
47. *Ibid.*, p. 101.
48. *Ibid.*, p. 100.
49. *Ibid.*, p. 87.
50. *Ibid.*, pp. 93, 97.
51. *Ibid.*, pp. 107, 110.
52. *Ibid.*, pp. 110, 112.
53. See above, page 160-168.
54. Paul Geheeb, the founder of the Odenwaldschule, was a true disciple of Egidy, but of his humanitarianism not his Volkish thought. See Walter Schäfer, *Paul Geheeb* (Stuttgart, n.d.), pp. 18 ff.
55. See above, page 111-112.
56. Quoted in *Mitteilungen des Vereins zur Abwehr des Antisemitismus* (hereafter cited as *Mitteilungen*), 22 Jahrg., No. 21 (October 1912), p. 159.
57. Driesmans, *op. cit.*, p. 104.
58. *Ibid.*, p. 103.
59. Moritz von Egidy to Theodor Fritsch (November 6, 1895), in *Hammer Festschrift* (Leipzig, 1926), p. 81.
60. "Anklageschrift des königlichen Konsistoriums von Westphalen, 10. Oktober, 1911," Traub Nachlass 35 (Bundesarchiv, Koblenz), p. 57.
61. Traub Nachlass 64a (Bundesarchiv, Koblenz). For a good reflection of Jatho's ideas, see Gottfried Traub, *Staatschristentum oder Volkskirche* (Jena, 1911).

CHAPTER 3
(Pages 52–66)

1. Conversation with Wolfgang Kroug, September 28, 1961.
2. Conversation with Gustav Wyneken, September 30, 1961.
3. *Ibid.*
4. Eugen Diederichs, *Selbstdarstellung,* "Der Deutsche Buchhandel der Gegenwart in Selbstdarstellungen" (Leipzig, 1927), p. 38.
5. Eugen Diederichs, *Politik des Geistes* (Jena, 1920), p. 28.
6. For the gift of Diederichs' publisher's catalogues, which are programmatical in nature, I want to thank the University Library of Jena.
7. *Eugen Diederichs, Leben und Werke,* ed. by Lulu von Strauss und Torney (Jena, 1936), p. 84.
8. Diederichs, *Selbstdarstellung,* p. 21.
9. *Ibid.,* 52.
10. *Eugen Diederichs, Leben und Werke,* p. 332.
11. Diederichs, *Selbstdarstellung,* p. 69.
12. Diederichs, "Die geistigen Aufgaben von heute morgen und über-Morgen," *Die Tat,* 19 Jahrg., Heft 9 (December 1927), p. 650.
13. Diederichs, *Selbstdarstellung,* p. 86.
14. *Eugen Diederichs, Leben und Werke,* p. 104.
15. Eugen Diederichs, "Besitzen wir eine Deutsche Stammeskunde?" *Die Tat,* 18 Jahrg., Heft 7 (October 1926), p. 548.
16. *Eugen Diederichs, Leben und Werke,* p. 196.
17. Eugen Diederichs, *Politik des Geistes,* p. 60.
18. Eugen Diederichs, "Nationalismus und Weltbürgertum," *Die Tat,* 13 Jahrg., Heft 9 (December 1921), p. 42.
19. *Ibid.,* p. 50.
20. Eugen Diederichs, "Antisemitismus," *Die Tat,* 14 Jahrg., Heft 8 (November 1922), pp. 607, 609.
21. *Eugen Diederichs, Leben und Werke,* p. 72.
22. *Ibid.,* p. 452.
23. *Erste Gesamtaustellung der Werke von Fidus zu seinem 60. Geburtstage* (Woltersdorf bei Erkner, 1928), pp. 9, 11.
24. *Eugen Diederichs, Leben und Werke,* p. 267.
25. Among others there is a reprint of Theodor Däubler's hymn to the sun (1910), *Klüter Blätter,* 10 Jahrg., Mappe 5/6 (1956), p. 17; and Johann von Leers, "Reich und Sonnenordnung," *Der Weg,* No. 9 (1955), pp. 555 ff.
26. Diederichs, *Selbstdarstellung,* p. 68.
27. *Eugen Diederichs, Leben und Werke,* p. 84.
28. *Ibid.,* p. 73.

29. See *Sera in Memoriam* (Jena, 1919).
30. The phrase is from Lagarde. Diederichs, *Selbstdarstellung*, p. 52.
31. Eugen Diederichs, "Die fehlende Instanz," *Die Tat,* 18 Jahrg., Heft 10 (January 1927), p. 790.
32. Diederichs, *Politik des Geistes*, p. 38.
33. *Ibid.*, pp. 39, 30.
34. See *Die Tat,* 13 Jahrg., Heft 12 (1921), p. 930; Diederichs in turn castigated the Pan-Germans for stressing race instead of metaphysics. *Politik des Geistes*, p. 59.
35. Diederichs, *Politik des Geistes*, p. 30.
36. *Ibid.*, p. 39.
37. Diederichs, *Selbstdarstellung*, pp. 19, 21.
38. *Ibid.*, p. 68.
39. *Gewissen*, 10 Jahrg., Heft 30 (July 22, 1928).
40. See Richard Benz, "Sechzig Jahre Eugen Diederichs Verlag," *Welt und Wort*, 2 Jahrg. (1956), p. 335.
41. Martin Buber, *Reden über das Judentum* (Berlin, 1932), p. 139.
42. *Ibid.*, pp. 133, 136.
43. Arthur Bonus, *Vom neuen Mythos* (Jena, 1911), p. 51.
44. *Ibid.*, p. 49.
45. *Ibid.*, p. 41.
46. *Ibid.*, pp. 58-59.
47. *Ibid.*, p. 9.
48. Arthur Bonus, *Religiöse Spannungen* (Jena, 1912), p. 52.
49. Bonus, *Vom neuen Mythos*, p. 58.
50. Hans Kohn, *Martin Buber* (Köln, 1961), p. 96.

CHAPTER 4
(Pages 67–87)

1. Adolf Rapp, *Der Deutsche Gedanke* (Bonn, 1920), pp. 217, 234.
2. Houston Stewart Chamberlain, *Die Grundlagen des 19. Jahrhunderts* (Munich, 1932), Vol. I, p. 509.
3. *Ibid.*, pp. 507-08.
4. *Ibid.*, pp. 342 ff.
5. Rapp, *op. cit.*, pp. 212 ff.
6. Felix Dahn, *Erinnerungen* (Leipzig, 1892), Vol. III, p. 425.
7. *Ibid.*, Vol. IV, pp. 1, 43.
8. See George L. Mosse, "The Image of the Jew in German Popular Culture: Felix Dahn and Gustav Freytag," *Year Book II of the Leo Baeck Institute* (London, 1957), pp. 218-27.

9. Eugen Diederichs, "Antisemitismus," *Die Tat*, 14 Jahrg., Heft 8 (November 1922), p. 607.

10. Dahn, *op. cit.*, Vol. IV, pp. 1, 590; Vol. II, p. 185.

11. Werner Lenz, "Unsere Ahnen: Nomaden oder Dauersiedler?" *Westdeutsche Bauernzeitung* (Köln, October 21, 1934), n. p.

12. Eugen Dühring, *Die Judenfrage* (Nowawes-Neuendorf, 1901), p. 32.

13. C. H. Carus, *Über die Ungleichheit verschiedener Menschenstämme für höhere geistige Entwicklung* (n. p., 1849).

14. Johann von Leers, "Reich und Sonnenordnung," *Der Weg*, No. 9 (1955), pp. 555 ff. For racial rhythm and rhythm of the sun, see also *Judenkenner*, Folge 32 (September 25, 1935), n. p.

15. Emil Hulbricht, *Christentum oder Heimatreligion?* (Freiberg i. Sa, 1931), p. 9.

16. For example, Fritz Bley, in *Deutsche Tageszeitung*, No. 9. Quoted in *Mitteilungen*, 18 Jahrg., No. 2 (March 11, 1908), p. 88; Hans Hauptmann, *Jesus der Arier* (Munich, 1931).

17. Leers, *op. cit.*, p. 558.

18. For a discussion of List, Schuler, and Tarnhari, see George L. Mosse, "The Mystical Origins of National Socialism," *Journal of the History of Ideas*, Vol. XXII, No. 1 (January–March 1961), pp. 81-96.

19. Johannes Baltzli, *Guido von List* (Vienna, 1917), pp. 26, 27.

20. *Ibid.*, pp. 79, 185.

21. E. Pichel, *Georg Schönerer* (Vienna, 1923), Vol. IV, pp. 550, 552-53, 573.

22. Baltzli, *op. cit.*, pp. 132, 138.

23. *Jahrbuch des Deutschnationalen Handelsgehilfen Verband* (1917), pp. 203-06. Some leaders were members of the List Society; see Baltzli, *op. cit.*, p. 84.

24. Franziska zu Reventlow, *Herrn Dames Aufzeichnungen* (Munich, 1958), p. 138.

25. See Alfred Schuler, *Fragmente und Vorträge aus den Nachlass*, with an introduction by Ludwig Klages (Leipzig, 1940), p. 92.

26. Claude David, *Stefan George* (Paris, 1952), p. 200.

27. Schuler, *op. cit.*, pp. 33 ff.

28. Baltzli, *op. cit.*, pp. 47, 155.

29. Documents about Tarnhari can be found in ZSGI-45/I (Bundesarchiv, Koblenz).

30. Reventlow, *op. cit.*, p. 186.

31. Hermann Burte, *Samson* (Leipzig, 1920).

32. *Sieben Reden von Burte* (Strassburg, 1943), pp. 30-31.

33. Hans Friedrich Blunck, *Licht auf den Zügeln* (Mannheim, 1953), Vol. I, p. 437.

34. *Ibid.*, pp. 100, 120.

35. See, for example, his rejection of "dilettante racial science." Blunck, "Zur Rassenbildungsfrage," *Die Tat*, 19 Jahrg., Heft 1 (April 1927), pp. 47-50.

36. For his theories, see Ernst Wachler, *Die Heimat als Quelle der Bildung* (Leipzig, n.d.). He was also close to the List Society; Baltzli, *op. cit.*, p. 46 n.

37. Karl-August Götz, "Der Grundsatz des Thingdienstes," *Der Deutsche Student* (December 1935), p. 693.

38. *Ibid.*, p. 690.

39. Wachler, *op. cit.*, p. 47.

40. *Mitteilungen*, 37 Jahrg. (March 1927), p. 34.

41. *Mitteilungen*, 29 Jahrg. (April 30, 1919), p. 71; *Mitteilungen* (September 18, 1919), p. 144.

42. *Auf Gut Deutsch*, 1 Jahrg. (September 5, 1919), p. 443.

43. *Mitteilungen*, 29 Jahrg. (April 30, 1919), p. 71.

44. Alfred Rosenberg, *Letzte Aufzeichnungen* (Göttingen: 1954), p. 95.

45. *Mitteilungen*, 29 Jahrg. (April 30, 1919), p. 71.

46. Alfred Köppen, "Hermann Hendrichs und seine Tempelkunst," *Westermanns Monatschefte*, Vol. 103, II, Heft 617 (February 1908), pp. 659, 660, 662.

47. Fidus, "Völkische Kunst und Tempelkunst," *Der Junge Deutsche*, 1 Jahrg., Heft 2 (May 1919), pp. 20-21.

48. *Erste Gesammtaustellung der Werke von Fidus zu seinem 60. Geburtstage* (Woltersdorf bei Erkner, 1928), p. 9.

49. Fidus, "Völkische Kunst und Tempelkunst," p. 20.

50. *Erste Gesammtdarstellung*, p. 11.

51. *Jahrbuch des Deutschnationalen Handelsgehilfen Verband* (1917), pp. 181-92, together with an article on Fidus and theosophy.

52. Fidus to Adolf Damaschke (February 18, 1943), Damaschke Nachlass, Bestand 21 (Bundesarchiv, Koblenz).

53. Wolfgang Willrich, *Säuberung des Kunsttempels* (Munich, 1937), p. 133.

54. *The Memoirs of Doctor Felix Kersten* (New York, 1946), p. 151.

55. This is the point of the attack on theosophy by Hans Sturm, *Entlarvte Dunkelmänner* (Berlin, 1935); and of Hans Schröder in *Jukenkenner*, Folge 17 (June 12, 1935), p. 3.

CHAPTER 5
(Pages 88–107)

1. These general ideas of a developing racism have been analyzed by George L. Mosse, *The Culture of Western Europe* (Chicago, 1961), pp. 73-93.

2. *Ibid.*, pp. 73 ff.
3. Ludwig Schemann, *Fünfundzwanzig Jahre Gobineau-Vereinigung* (Strassburg and Berlin, 1919), p. 3.
4. *Ibid.*, pp. 31-32.
5. *Ibid.*, p. vi.
6. *Ibid.*, pp. 7, 21.
7. Alfred Kruck, *Geschichte des Alldeutschen Verbandes* (Wiesbaden, 1954), p. 18.
8. Ludwig Schemann, *Lebensfahrten eines Deutschen* (Leipzig, 1925), p. 62.
9. *Ibid.*, p. 397.
10. Ludwig Schemann, *Wolfgang Kapp und das Märzunternehmen vom Jahre 1920: ein Wort der Sühne* (Munich, 1937).
11. See *Westdeutscher Beobachter* (February 18, 1938), n.p.
12. H. S. Chamberlain, *Die Grundlagen des XIX. Jahrhunderts* (Munich, 1932); see esp. Vol. I, pp. 25 ff.; Vol. II, p. 967; Vol. I, p. 558.
13. *Ibid.*, Vol. II, p. 1056.
14. *Ibid.*, Vol. I, p. 75.
15. *Ibid.*, Vol. I, pp. 229 ff.
16. *Ibid.*, Vol. I, p. 236.
17. R. Burger-Villingen, *Geheimnis der Menschenform* (Leipzig, 1912), p. 17; four editions of this work appeared by 1935.
18. *Ibid.*, p. 19.
19. This and the following paragraph present summaries from the two volumes of Chamberlain's *Grundlagen des XIX. Jahrhunderts.*
20. *Ibid.*, Vol. I, pp. 581-83.
21. *Ibid.*, Vol. II, pp. 918 ff.
22. *Ibid.*, Vol. II, p. 863.
23. Karl Pearson, "Charles Darwin, 1809-1882," in *The Making of Modern Europe*, ed. by Herman Ausuble (New York, 1951), p. 764.
24. Gisela Meyer-Heydenhagen, "Zum 80. Geburtstage des Grafen Georges Vacher de Lapouge," *Rasse*, 2 Jahrg. (1935), p. 41.
25. On this, see the fundamental article by Fritz Bolle: "Darwinismus und Zeitgeist," *Zeitschrift für Religions- und Geistesgeschichte*, Heft 2, Band 14 (1962), esp. pp. 163-76.
26. *Ibid.*, p. 167.
27. *Ibid.*, 166-67; Hedwig Conrad-Martinus, *Utopien der Menschenzüchtung* (Munich, 1955), pp. 74 ff.
28. Georg Lukacs, *La Déstruction de la Raison* (Paris, 1959), p. 256.
29. Ludwig Woltmann, *Politische Anthropologie*, ed. by Otto Reche (Leipzig, 1936), pp. 16-17, 267.
30. *Ibid.*, pp. 86-87.
31. *Ibid.*, pp. 132-33.

32. *Ibid.*, p. 289.
33. *Ibid.*, p. 355.
34. *Ibid.*, p. 384.
35. *Ibid.*, p. 322.
36. *Ibid.*, p. 134.
37. *Ibid.*, p. 392.
38. *Ibid.*, p. 388.
39. *Ibid.*, p. 380.
40. *Ibid.*, p. 251.
41. *Ibid.*, p. 181.
42. *Ibid.*, p. 350.
43. Ludwig Woltmann, *Die Germanen und die Renaissance von Italien* (Leipzig, 1905), p. 4.
44. Woltmann, *Politische Anthropologie*, p. 47, n. 26.
45. See the same remark, *ibid.*, p. 175, n. 107.
46. Ludwig Wilser, *Rassentheorien* (Stuttgart, 1908), pp. 17, 21.
47. *Ibid.*, p. 5; Woltmann, *Politische Anthropologie*, pp. 293-94.
48. Hermann Popert, *Helmut Harringa* (Dresden, 1923), p. 8. This is the 47th edition. The novel sold 320,000 copies up to then.
49. *Ibid.*, p. 172.
50. A. Lürssen, "Rassenhygene," *Vortrupp*, 2 Jahrg., No. 9 (May 1, 1913), p. 280.
51. I.e., his speech at the preparatory meeting on the Hanstein, *Vortrupp*, 2 Jahrg., No. 22 (November 16, 1913), pp. 686 ff.
52. Hermann Popert in *Vortrupp*, 7 Jahrg., No. 24 (December 24, 1918), p. 495.
53. *Die Sonne*, 10 Jahrg., Heft 10 (Gilbhart, October 1933), p. 517.

CHAPTER 6
(*Pages 108–125*)

1. Adolf Damaschke, *Die Bodenreform* (Jena, 1912). The book first appeared in 1902. Chapter 1: "Weder Mammonismus noch Kommunismus."
2. *Ibid.*, p. 63.
3. H. S. Chamberlain to Damaschke (February 9, 1916). Adolf Damaschke, Nachlass, Bestand 21 (Bundesarchiv, Koblenz).
4. Franz Oppenheimer, *Erlebtes, Erstrebtes, Erreichtes* (Berlin, 1931), p. 153.
5. *Flugschrift der Freiland-Freigeld Bewegung* (1919). This carries a swastika at its head.

6. Adolf Damaschke, *Aus meinem Leben* (Leipzig, 1924), pp. 288-96.

7. See "Eden, 40 Jahre, 1893-1933," *Eden*, 28 Jahrg., Festnummer 5-6 (May-June 1933). At that date the settlement included some 950 people; p. 99.

8. Oppenheimer, *op. cit.*, p. 161.

9. *Landesgemeinde*, Heft 3 (October 1917), p. 105, reprints the program of the "Edener Gilde."

10. See Carl Russwurm, *Das Germanische Grundgesetz von der Freiheit des Menschen und der Welt* (Leipzig, 1916).

11. "Eden 40 Jahre," pp. 102-103.

12. Herman Rosemann, "Erster Siegfried Ruf," *Der Zwiespruch*, 3 Jahrg., No. 7 (February 11, 1921), p. 3.

13. *Mitteilungen*, 18 Jahrg., No. 32 (August 5, 1908), p. 241.

14. Rudolf Linke, "Freie Liebe oder Zucht? Von Muck zu Mittgart," *Der Junge Deutsche*, 3 Jahrg., Heft 8-9 (July 1921), p. 125.

15. "Dr. Willibald Hentschel zu seinem 75. Geburtstage," *Die Sonne*, 10 Jahrg., Heft 2 (Nebelungen, November 1933), p. 575.

16. Willibald Hentschel, *Varuna* (Leipzig, 1907), pp. 602, 604.

17. *Ibid.*, pp. 607 ff., sketches the proposed settlement. For Hentschel as pupil of Haeckel, see Theodor Fritsch in *Die Sonne*, 10 Jahrg. Heft 2 (Nebelungen, November 1933), p. 574. Hentschel had also belonged to Stöcker's Deutschsoziale party and knew Stöcker personally.

18. Willibald Hentschel, *Vom aufsteigenden Leben* (Leipzig, 1913), p. 24.

19. *Mitteilungen*, 22 Jahrg., No. 21 (October 9, 1912), p. 165.

20. *Mitteilungen*, 22 Jahrg., No. 19 (September 11, 1912), pp. 146-47.

21. *Ibid.*

22. The novel was: Margaret Hunkel, *Freia und Frauwa, eine Sage der Zunkunft* (Leipzig, 1918).

23. Hentschel, *Vom aufsteigenden Leben*, pp. 91, 93.

24. Manfred Fuchs, *Probleme des Wirtschaftsstils von Lebensgemeinschaften* (Göttingen, 1957), p. 66.

25. Quoted in Achim Saemer, *Die Wurzeln der Artamanenbewegung* (Staatsarbeit, Münster, 1959), p. 3. (Typescript at Archiv der Jugendbewegung, Burg Ludwigstein.)

26. *Ibid.*, pp. 6, 50.

27. Ludwig Woltmann, *Politische Anthropologie* (Leipzig, 1936), p. 322.

28. Rudolf Proksch, "Artamanen," *Wille und Macht*, 7 Jahrg., Heft 5 (March 1, 1939), p. 22.

29. For example, in *Der Weltkampf*, 4 Jahrg. (1927), p. 432.

30. Saemer, *op. cit.*, pp. 42-48; Schmidt-Wodder, "Bauernhochschule aus Deutsch-Germanischem Geist," *Deutschvölkisches Jahrbuch 1922* (Weimar, 1922), pp. 67-70; Bruno Tanzmann in *Auf Gut Deutsch*, 7 Jahrg. (July 31, 1919), p. 375.

31. Heinrich Himmler, "Völkische Bauerpolitik," Himmler 186, Reel 98, in Special Collection, Selected Materials, Hoover Institution.

32. Fuchs, *op. cit.*, p. 78.

33. Elizabeth Fleiner, *Siedlungsversuche der Nachkriegszeit* (Heidelberg, 1931), p. 137.

34. Proksch, *op. cit.*, p. 21; Saemer, *op. cit.*, p. 43.

35. *Ibid.*, pp. 22, 23.

36. Saemer, *op. cit.*, p. 71.

37. Walther Darré, *Neuadel aus Blut und Boden* (Munich, 1936), p. 141.

38. Proksch, *op. cit.*, p. 22. The correspondence has been seen by Walter Lacqueur in the U. S. Document Center in Berlin. See also Lacqueur's *Young Germany* (London, 1962), p. 192.

39. Fuchs, *op. cit.*, p. 79.

40. The membership figures can be worked out from Fuchs, *op. cit.*, who gives the most complete account of the settlements, though he omits some with which we are concerned. Fuchs lists twenty-one settlements.

41. Carl Reinhold Petter, *Die siegende Sonne* (Danzig, 1924), pp. 7, 44.

42. Fuchs, *op. cit.*, p. 43; prospectus of *Frei-Deutschland* ed. by Ernst Hunkel (n. d.); Fleiner, *op. cit.*, p. 121.

43. Georg Becker, *Die Siedlung der Deutschen Jugendbewegung* (Dissertation, Köln, 1929), p. 62.

44. Fuchs, *op. cit.*, p. 44.

45. *Ibid.*, p. 38.

46. *Ibid.*, p. 40.

47. *Ibid.*, p. 98.

48. Friedrich Schöll, *Landerziehungsheim und Schulsiedlung im Dritten Reich* (Eisenach, 1936), p. 152. (First published in 1933.)

49. "Die Siedlung," supplement to *Zwiespruch*, 4 Jahrg., No. 3 (August 16, 1922), p. 1.

50. Schöll, *op. cit.*, p. 10.

51. Hermann Harless, "Ein Rückblick," *Marquartsteiner Blätter* (October 1937), p. 6; Fuchs, *op. cit.*, p. 55.

52. Fleiner, *op. cit.*, p. 144.

53. Bernhard Funk, "Zionismus oder Jude als Staatenbilder," *Deutschlands Erneuerung*, 6 Jahrg., Heft 6 (June 1922), p. 360.

54. *Deutsches Tageblatt*, June 21, 1928, p. 162.

55. Jaakov Simon, "Umrisse unseres Menschenbildes," *Binjam* (Sammelschrift des Habonim) (Berlin, March, 1935), pp. 36, 42.

56. Franz Oppenheimer, who was important in Eden, was also, for a time, important in establishing *Kibbutzim* in Israel. He was directly influenced by Hertzka and Henry George, a fanatic for free land and not markedly touched by other ideological considerations. He was in

Palestine in 1911 at Herzl's suggestion. *Erlebtes, Erstrebtes, Erreichtes,* pp. 165 ff.

CHAPTER 7
(Pages 126–145)

1. Christian Wilhelm Dohm, *Über die bürgerliche Verbesserung der Juden* (Berlin and Stettin, 1783), Part II, pp. 152, 174.

2. Wilhelm Stoffers, *Juden und Ghetto in der Deutschen Literatur bis zum Ausgang des Weltkrieges* (Nijmegen, 1939), pp. 413, 478.

3. George L. Mosse, "The Image of the Jew in German Popular Culture: Felix Dahn and Gustav Freytag," *Year Book II of the Leo Baeck Institute* (London, 1957), pp. 218 ff.

4. George L. Mosse, "Culture, Civilization and German Anti-Semitism," *Judaism,* Vol. VII, No. 3 (Summer 1958), pp. 257-58.

5. *Die Judenfrage vor dem Preussischen Landtag* (Berlin, 1880), p. 72.

6. Stoffers, *op. cit.,* p. 390.

7. Dohm, *op. cit.,* p. 172.

8. Paul de Lagarde, *Deutsche Schriften* (Göttingen, n.d.), pp. 23, 24.

9. August Rohling, *Talmud Jude,* retranslated by Karl Paasch from the French edition, foreword by Eduard Drumont (Leipzig, 1890). The publisher was Theodor Fritsch.

10. W. ten Boon, *Die Enstehung des modernen Rasse-Antisemitismus* (Leipzig, 1928), p. 11.

11. Eugen Dühring, *Die Judenfrage* (Nowawes-Neuendorf, 1901), pp. 37 ff.

12. *Ibid.,* pp. 32, 33.

13. P. G. J. Pulzer, *Anti-Semitism in Germany and Austria, 1867-1918* (Dissertation, Cambridge University, 1960), pp. 68-69. Now published as *The Rise of Political Anti-Semitism in Germany and Austria* (New York, 1964).

14. Walter Frank, *Hofprediger Stöcker und die christlichsoziale Bewegung* (Hamburg, 1935), p. 80.

15. Otto Böckel, *Die Juden-die Könige unserer Zeit!* (Berlin, 1901), *passim.*

16. Frank, *op. cit.,* p. 237.

17. *Neue Preussische Kreuzzeitung,* No. 279 (June 19, 1889), n. p.

18. Walter Frank calls it "ländliche Sozialdemokratie unter nationaler Maske," *op. cit.,* p. 238.

19. Theodor Fritsch, "Antisemit oder Judenschimpfer?" *Hammer* (1904), p. 2.

20. *Korrespondenz—Blatt des Verbandes der Deutschen Juden,* No. 6 (January 1910), p. 9.
21. W. Giese, *Die Judenfrage am Ende des XIX. Jahrhunderts* (Berlin, 1899), p. 15. This was a report to the Soziale Reformpartei in Hamburg.
22. Pulzer, *op. cit.,* pp. 285 ff.
23. Theodor Heuss, *Friedrich Naumann* (Berlin, 1937), p. 41.
24. *Die Weissen Blätter,* 2 Jahrg., Heft 2 (November 1915), pp. 1408-10.
25. Heinrich Pudor, *Was tun wir mit den Juden?* (Flugzettel, 1922); *Der Sinn des Hakenkreuzes* (Hellerau, n.d.) praises both Fidus and Tanzmann, p. 34.
26. Graf von Reventlow in *Der Jud ist schuld?* (Vienna, 1932), pp. 14, 38.
27. *Die Geheimnisse der Weisen von Zion,* ed. by Gottfried zu Beek (i.e., Müller von Hausen) (Charlottenburg, 1919), pp. 236 ff.
28. *Mitteilungen,* 30 Jahrg. (December 1928), p. 170; Daniel Fryman (Heinrich Class) *Wenn ich der Kaiser wär* (Leipzig, 1914), p. 76.
29. Karl Paasch, "Eine Jüdisch-Deutsche Gesandschaft und ihre Helfer," *Antisemiten Spiegel* (Danzig, 1892), p. 300. Similar ideas are expressed by the Austrian deputy Schneider in *Antisemiten Spiegel* (Danzig, 1900), p. 10.
30. Herman Ahlwardt, *Der Verzweiflungskampf der arischen Völker mit dem Judentum* (Berlin, 1890), p. 239.
31. *Ibid.,* pp. 35-36.
32. *Ibid.,* p. 241.
33. Stoffers, *op. cit.,* p. 664.
34. *Ibid.,* p. 33.
35. F. Roderich-Stoltheim (Theodor Fritsch), *Die Juden im Handel* (Steglitz, 1913), pp. 229 ff.
36. Cited in Wilhelm Michels, *Verrat an Deutschtum* (Hannover and Leipzig, 1932), p. 5.
37. Theodor Fritsch, *Handbuch der Judenfrage* (Leipzig, 1933), pp. 54, 72 ff., 290 ff.
38. Fritsch, *Die Juden im Handel,* pp. 3-5.
39. I.e., Adolf Wahrmund, *Das Gesetz des Nomadentums und die heutige Judenherrschaft* (Leipzig, 1887).
40. Letter of Dr. Engel, Hamburg (January 22, 1914), No. 223, Akte 1889 (Hamburg) (Jewish National Archives, Jerusalem); No. 310, Akte 1889 (Hamburg) (Jewish National Archives).
41. Reichsakte betreffend Antisemitismus, L 382073 (Bundesarchiv, Koblenz).
42. Cited in *Festschrift zum fünfundzwanzig jährigen Bestehen des Hammers* (Leipzig, 1926), p. 39 n.

43. Hermann Guach, *Neue Grundlagen der Rassenforschung* (Leipzig, 1933), n. p.
44. RK. NSDAP. Parteien 12, Band 5, L 530301, L 530299 (Bundesarchiv, Koblenz).
45. Lily Braun, *Memoiren einer Sozialistin* (Berlin, 1911), Vol. I, p. 459.
46. *Akten der Wiener Isr. Kultusgemeinde*, 50/3 (Jewish National Archives, Jerusalem).
47. Wilhelm Jacobson an den Deutsch-Israelitischen Gemeindebund, 14/4/1900, M.I/19 (Jewish National Archives, Jerusalem).
48. *Wiener Kultusgemeinde*, 50/3 (Jewish National Archives, Jerusalem).
49. *Bericht der Israelitischen Erziehungsanstalt zu Ahlem* (1904), pp. 4-5.
50. *Ibid.*, p. 8.
51. Isidor Wolff, *Die Verbreitung des Turnens unter den Juden* (Berlin, 1907), p. 5.
52. Max Warburg to Aby Warburg (February 28, 1913), Akte 1830 (Hamburg), 866b, fsc. 3 (Jewish National Archives, Jerusalem).

CHAPTER 8

(*Pages 149–170*)

1. See above, pp. 210-217.
2. Fritz Stern, *The Politics of Cultural Despair* (Berkeley and Los Angeles, 1961), p. 291.
3. Erich Weymar, *Das Selbstverständnis der Deutschen* (Stuttgart, 1961), *passim*.
4. See above, pp. 268-269.
5. See, for example, Weymar, *op. cit.*, p. 157.
6. *Ibid.*, p. 30.
7. Ernst Linde, "Über die Entfernung des Religionsunterrichts aus der Schule," *Neue Bahnen*, Heft 5 (February 1906), p. 212.
8. *Mitteilungen*, 22 Jahrg., No. 2 (March 27, 1912), p. 56.
9. *Neue Preussische Kreuzzeitung*, No. 270 (June 13, 1889), n. p.
10. *Antisemiten Spiegel* (Berlin, 1911), p. 101.
11. *C. V. Zeitung*, Vol. X (January 2, 1931), p. 3; *ibid.*, Vol. X (January 23, 1931), pp. 37-38.
12. Petition to Graf Taafe (March 1889), 50/3 (Jewish National Archives, Jerusalem).
13. Interview with former teacher, October 12, 1962.
14. Ernst Siecke, *Die Judenfrage und der Gymnasiallehrer* (Berlin, 1880), pp. 13, 19.

15. Karl Fischer, *Antisemiten und Gymnasiallehrer: ein Protest* (Berlin, 1881), p. 6.
16. Franz Oppenheimer, *Erlebtes, Erstrebtes, Erreichtes* (Berlin, 1931), p. 60. See also above, p. 196.
17. See Bernhard Förster, *Deutsche Colonien* (Leipzig, 1885).
18. Ludwig Gurlitt, *Der Deutsche und sein Vaterland* (Berlin, 1906), p. 98.
19. Ludwig Gurlitt, "Schüler-Schauspiele," *Bühne und Welt*, Vol. IX (1907), pp. 454, 411.
20. Ludwig Gurlitt, *Erziehungslehre* (Berlin, 1909), *passim*.
21. Gurlitt, *Der Deutsche und sein Vaterland*, pp. 15, 18.
22. Gurlitt, *Erziehungslehre*, p. 135.
23. *Ibid.*, p. 19; for the peasantry as the basis of national life, see *Der Deutsche und sein Vaterland*, p. 4.
24. Ludwig Gurlitt, "Geschichtsunterricht," *Junge Menschen*, 1 Jahrg., Heft 7 (April 7, 1920), p. 52.
25. Ludwig Gurlitt, "Friedrich Paulsen als mein Richter," *Neue Bahnen*, 18 Jahrg., Heft 10 (July 1907), p. 449.
26. Gurlitt, *Der Deutsche und sein Vaterland*, pp. 11, 12, 67.
27. Ludwig Gurlitt, *Die Schule* (Frankfurt, 1907), pp. 8, 42, 45, 46, 48.
28. Gurlitt, *Der Deutsche und sein Vaterland*, p. 92.
29. "Zum Andenken," by some graduates of the K.K.I. *Staatsgymnasium* in Graz (Siegfried Bernfeld Collection, Hoover Institution), p. 190.
30. E. Saupe, "Professor Gurlitt über die Reform des Erziehungswesens," *Zeitschrift für Experimentelle Pädagogik*, Vol. X (Leipzig, 1910), p. 275.
31. Gurlitt, *Der Deutsche und sein Vaterland*, p. viii.
32. Alfred Andreesen, *Hermann Lietz* (Munich, 1934), pp. 84-85. In 1901 Lietz denied that his schools had anything "specifically English" about them: "Fragebogen von Lietz ausgefüllt" (1901), Wyneken Archiv (Archiv der Jugendbewegung, Burg Ludwigstein).
33. *Ibid.*
34. Hermann Lietz, *Die Ersten drei Deutschen Land-Erziehungsheime* (Vecknested am Harz, 1920), p. 10; Otto von Greyerz, "Landerziehungsheime," *Kunstwart*, Vol. XXVI, Heft 15 (May, 1913), p. 180.
35. Interview with Mrs. Hermann Lietz, Gaienhofen, August 19, 1961. See also Lietz himself, "Fragebogen," where he stresses his birth as the son of a farmer and states that he fit his knowledge into this heritage.
36. See "Fragebogen," where he rejects the importance of football for the school; Hermann Lietz, "Ein Rückblick auf Entstehung, Eigenart und Entwicklung der Deutschen Landerziehungsheime nach 15 Jahren ihres bestehens," *Das Fünfzehnte Jahr in Deutschen Landerziehungs*

Heimen (Leipzig, 1913), p. 7. In 1898 he described the ideal plan for a school: 5 hours intellectual labor, 1 hour games, 2 hours practical work, 2 hours for singing and instruments and art, 4 hours recreation, "Die Erziehungsschule der Zunkunft," *Die Nation*, 15 Jahrg., No. 25 (March 19, 1898), p. 363.

37. Hermann Harless, "Ein Rückblick," *Marquartsteiner Blätter* (October 1937), p. 4; Gustav Wyneken, "Erinnerungen an Hermann Lietz" (hereafter cited as "Hermann Lietz"), typewritten ms., Wyneken Archiv (Archiv der Jugendbewegung, Burg Ludwigstein), p. 38.

38. Hermann Lietz, "Wie soll der Lehrplan für unsere Deutschen Mittelschulen gestaltet werden?" *D.L.E.H.* (Leipzig, 1910), p. 6.

39. Lietz, "Ein Rückblick . . . ," pp. 9-10.

40. Lietz, "Wie soll der Lehrplan . . . ," p. 11; "Ein Rückblick . . . ," p. 10.

41. Hermann Lietz, *Lebenserinnerungen* (Weimar, 1935), pp. 41, 47.

42. Hermann Lietz, "Aus dem Gebiete des Unterrichts in den D.L.E.H.," *D.L.E.H.* (Leipzig, 1909), p. 40; Hermann Lietz, *Des Vaterlandes Not und Hoffnung* (Haubinda, 1934), pp. 71, 80.

43. Lietz, "Aus dem Gebiet des Unterrichts . . . ," p. 39.

44. Lietz, *Des Vaterlandes Not und Hoffnung*, p. 80; *Lebenserinnerungen*, pp. 189 ff. (Feldansprache, 1915).

45. Wyneken, "Hermann Lietz," p. 19.

46. "Leben und Entwicklung in den D.L.E.H.," *D.L.E.H.* (Leipzig, 1912), p. 9; "Aus den Deutschen Landerziehungsheimen," *D.L.E.H.* (Leipzig, 1911), p. 14.

47. Hermann Lietz, "Wie soll der Lehrplan . . . ," p. 18; Alfred Andreesen, *Hermann Lietz*, p. 131. Wyneken wrote later that "everything was didactic moralism"—"Hermann Lietz," p. 55.

48. Lietz, *Lebenserinnerungen*, p. 133; "Wie soll der Lehrplan . . . ," p. 39.

49. Andreesen, *Hermann Lietz*, p. 111; Wyneken, "Hermann Lietz," p. 54; Lietz, *Lebenserinnerungen*, p. 94.

50. Lietz, *Lebenserinnerungen*, p. 194.

51. Hermann Lietz in *Leben und Arbeit*, Vol. I (1919), p. 67. This is a report of a discussion on education at Haubinda.

52. Hermann Lietz, "Das Landwaisenheim an der Ilse," *Das Fünfzehnte Jahr in Deutschen Landerziehungs Heimen* (Leipzig, 1913), pp. 26-27.

53. Lietz, *Lebenserinnerungen*, p. 115: Wyneken, "Hermann Lietz," p. 40.

54. Erich von Mendelssohn, *Nacht und Tag* (Leipzig, 1914), *passim*.

55. Lietz, *Lebenserinnerungen*, p. 115.

56. Interview with Gustav Wyneken, September 30, 1961.

57. Theodor Lessing, "Eine Deutsche Schulreform," *Beilage zur Allgemeinen Zeitung*, No. 288 (December 17, 1902), p. 519.

58. Lessing, *op. cit.* (December 16, 1902), p. 507.
59. Lietz, *Lebenserinnerungen,* p. 115.
60. "Beschlüsse der Allgemeinen Lehrerversammlung," *D.L.E.H.,* 14 Jahrg. (Leipzig, 1912), p. 34.
61. Hermann Lietz to Gustav Wyneken, December 8, 1901 (Wyneken Archiv); Lietz, *Lebenserinnerungen,* p. 162.
62. Interview with Mrs. Hermann Lietz, Gaienhofen, October 19, 1961.
63. Lietz, *Des Vaterlandes Not und Hoffnung,* pp. 25, 89-91, 196.
64. *Auf Gut Deutsch,* Vol. I (July 31, 1919), pp. 370-75.
65. Adam Kuckhoff, "Hermann Lietz und die Deutschen Landerziehungsheime," *Die Tat,* 17 Jahrg., Heft 4 (July 1925), p. 282.
66. Alfred Andreesen, "Innenpolitische Lage," *Leben und Arbeit,* Vol. XVIII, Heft 1 (1919), p. 31. Yet after Rathenau's murder he gave a favorable address about him in "Chapell," *Die Jahresarbeiten der Primaner am Deutschen Landerziehungsheim Bieberstein* (Vecknestedt am Harz, 1924), p. 71.
67. Interview with Mrs. Hermann Lietz, Gaienhofen, October 19, 1961.
68. In *Leben und Arbeit,* Vol. XXVIII (1935), p. 7; Alfred Andreesen, "Deutsche und Englische Gemeinschaftserziehung," *Internationale Zeitschrift für Erziehung,* Vol. VII (1938), p. 109.
69. Martin Luserke, "Landerziehungsheime," *Die Tat,* 17 Jahrg., Heft 11 (February 1926).
70. Martin Luserke, *Der Eiserne Morgen* (Potsdam, 1938), p. 497.
71. Kurt Hahn, *Erziehung zur Verantwortung* (Stuttgart, n.d.), *passim.*
72. For example, the school at Bad Berka, *Der Kronacher Bund,* Vol. XVIII, Heft 8-9 (May 1929), p. 179.
73. Hermann Lietz, "Erziehung zu Gesundheit, Kraft, Reinheit," *Der Junge Deutsche,* Vol. I, Heft 3 (June 1919), p. 25; Oberlehrer Streicher, "Die Deutschen Landerziehungsheime," *Wandervogel Führerzeitung,* Heft 13 (December 1913), pp. 256-60. This was the periodical of the racist minority of the Youth Movement. Mrs. Lietz believes that Hermann Lietz was much too busy to give any great thought to the Youth Movement. (Interview, Gaienhofen, October 19, 1961.) One youth leader held that Lietz went to Leipzig in protest against the Meissner meeting: *Karl Brügman in Memoriam* (Tübinger, 1954), n. p.

CHAPTER 9
(Pages 171-189)

1. On the movement as a whole see Walter Z. Laqueur, *Young Germany, A History of the German Youth Movement* (London, 1961).

Of special use for detail, despite its National Socialist slant, is Heinrich Ahrens, *Die Deutsche Wandervogelbewegung von den Anfängen bis zum Weltkrieg* (Hamburg, 1939).

2. Hans Blüher, *Wandervogel, Geschichte einer Jugendbewegung* (Berlin, 1916), Vol. I, p. 73. (First published in 1912.)

3. *Ibid.*, p. 124.

4. Frank Fischer, *Wandern und Schauen, Gesammelte Aufsätze* (Hartenstein i. S., 1921), p. 53; Ernst Michael Jovy, *Deutsche Jugendbewegung und Nationalsozialismus* (Inaugural Dissertation, Köln, 1952), pp. 100, 102, 37.

5. See *Wandervogel*, 6 Jahrg., Heft 7 (Heuet, July 1911), pp. 159 ff.

6. *Der Sämann*, Heft 12 (1914), pp. 431-32.

7. *Nachrichtenblatt des Wandervogels*, 1 Jahrg., No. 2 (November 1904), p. 14.

8. Blüher, *op. cit.*, p. 143.

9. *Ibid.*, p. 73.

10. Ahrens, *op. cit.*, p. 19.

11. Hans-Gerd Rabe, "Geschichte des Wandervogels Osnabrück" (typewritten ms., Archiv der Jugendbewegung, Burg Ludwigstein, 1960), p. 76. The date of this description is 1913.

12. Fritz Hellmuth, "Erinnerungen an Karl Fischer" (Archiv der Jugendbewegung, Burg Ludwigstein, 1957), n. p.

13. *Wandervogel*, No. 5-6 (1917).

14. Blüher, *op. cit.*, p. 144.

15. Georg Götsch, "Sibirischer Winter," *Westermanns Monatshefte*, 67 Jahrg. (September 1923), p. 372.

16. *Ibid.*, p. 369; Fischer, *op. cit.*, p. 36.

17. Gerhard Ziemer, "Die macht der Lieder," "Festschrift zur Übergabe des Hans Breuer Hauses," *Blätter von Greifenstein*, 5 Folge (April 1960), pp. 21-23.

18. Hans Blüher, *Die Deutsche Wandervogelbewegung als erotisches Phänomen* (Prien, 1918), pp. 25, 27, 70, 75. (First published in 1912.)

19. *Der Vortrupp*, 2 Jahrg., No. 1 (January 1, 1913), pp. 3, 4.

20. Blüher, *Wandervogel . . .* , Vol. II, p. 45.

21. *Deutsche Zeitung* (October 8, 1924), n. p.

22. Friedrich Bärwald, *Das Erlebnis des Staates in der Deutschen Jugendbewegung* (Berlin, 1921), pp. 16 ff.

23. Blüher, *Wandervogel . . .* , Vol. I, *passim*.

24. *Der Anfang*, 2 Jahrg., Heft 2-3 (June 1914), pp. 66, 67.

25. Georg Schmidt in a review of Blüher's *Wandervogel . . .* , *Wandervogel Führerzeitung*, Heft 3 (February 1913), pp. 45 ff.

26. H. E. Schomburg, *Der Wandervogel, seine Freunde und seine Gegner* (Wolfenbüttel, 1917), p. 44.

27. Semmelroth in *Wandervogel* (August 1906), pp. 1-3.
28. *Der Anfang*, 1 Jahrg., Heft 7 (November 1913), pp. 196, 197; *ibid.* (September 1913), pp. 129-30; *Freideutscher Jugendtag 1913* (Hamburg, 1919), pp. 25-27; Adolf Grabowski and Walther Koch, *Die Freideutsche Jugendbewegung* (Gotha, 1920), pp. 17-18.
29. Hans Breuer, "Herbstschau 1913," *Wandervogel*, 8 Jahrg., Heft 10 (October 1913), pp. 282, 284.
30. Walter Gron, in *Freideutsche Jugend*, 6 Jahrg., Heft 12 (1920), pp. 386, 388.
31. "Von Deutsch-Jüdischer Jugend," supplement to the *C. V. Zeitung*, 2 Jahrg., No. 8 (October 29, 1926).
32. *Wandervogel Führerzeitung*, 2 Jahrg., Heft 4-5 (April–May 1914), p. 83.
33. *Ibid.*, 2 Jahrg., Heft 6 (June 1914), p. 111.
34. Blüher, *Wandervogel* . . . , Vol. I, p. 98.
35. Karl Bückmann, *Jugendbewegung und Judenfrage* (Leipzig, 1918?), pp. 8, 22, 28.
36. *Freideutsche Jugend*, 2 Jahrg., Heft 10-11 (October–November 1916), pp. 300-01.
37. Moses Calvary, "Blau-Weiss" (1916), *Das Neue Judentum* (Berlin, 1936), pp. 79, 80.
38. Kurt Blumenfeld, *Erlebte Judenfrage* (Stuttgart, 1962), p. 43.
39. Fritz Kost at the meeting of former Blau Weiss, Naharia, Israel, May 18, 1962 (according to my notes of his speech).
40. *Freideutsche Jugend*, 2 Jahrg., Heft 10-11 (October–November 1916), p. 143.
41. Cited in Ahrens, *op. cit.*, p. 195, No. 43.
42. *Ibid.*, p. 196.
43. "Österreichische Nummer," *Wandervogel*, 13 Jahrg., Heft 5-6 (1918), p. 125.
44. For Wyneken's ideas, see Ulrich Panter, *Gustav Wyneken* (Weinheim/Bergstr., 1960).
45. Gustav Wyneken, "Der Kampf für die Jugend," *Gesammelte Aufsätze* (Jena, 1920), pp. 263 ff.
46. *Ibid.*, pp. 44, 45, 48.
47. *Der Anfang*, 1 Jahrg., Heft 3 (March 1911), p. 51.
48. *Ibid.*, No. 12 (May 1909), n. p. (The numeration of *Der Anfang* is highly erratic. I cite it as it occurs in the magazine.)
49. *Ibid.*, No. 15 (February 1910), p. 46.
50. Interview with Gustav Wyneken, Göttingen, September 7, 1961.
51. Willi Geisler in *Wandervogel*, 2 Jahrg., Heft 10 (Gibhart/Nebelungen, October–November 1916), p. 207.
52. Max Adler, *Neue Menschen* (Berlin, 1924), pp. 122-27.

53. *Die Geusen*, 1 Jahrg., Heft 3-4 (May 1920), pp. 69-70. See also Hans-Gerd Rabe, *op. cit.*, p. 94.
54. "Um Wyneken," *Freideutsche Jugend*, 7 Jahrg. (October 10, 1921), p. 62.
55. Interview with Gustav Wyneken, Göttingen, September 7, 1961.
56. *Ibid.*
57. Of a hundred leaders analyzed, the background was almost exclusively middle class. Walther Jantzen, "Die soziologische Herkunft der Führungsschicht der Deutschen Jugendbewegung," *Ranke Gesellschaft Jahrbuch* (n. d., but after 1946), Vol. III, pp. 127-35.
58. See Chapter 11.

CHAPTER 10
(*Pages 190–203*)

1. For the *Akademische Vereinigung*, see Wolfgang Kroug, *Sein zum Tode* (Godesberg, 1955).
2. See O. F. Scheurer, *Burschenschaft und Judenfrage* (Berlin, 1927).
3. Ludwig Quidde, *Die Antisemitenagitation und die Deutsche Studenschaft* (Göttingen, 1881), p. 12. Quidde was later the long-time (1914-29) president of the German League for Human Rights (Deutsche Liga für Menschenrechte).
4. *Akademische Blätter*, "Festnummer 1881-1931," 46 Jahrg., Heft 4 (July 1931), p. 110.
5. Theodor Heuss, *Friedrich Naumann* (Berlin, 1937), p. 41.
6. *Akademische Blätter*, *op. cit.*, p. 101.
7. *Neue Preussische Kreuzzeitung*, No. 32 (January 19, 1889), n. p.
8. *Akademische Blätter*, 44 Jahrg., Heft 1 (April 1933), p. 15. Except that the Kyffhäuser Bund apparently had some Jewish members (who had to leave in 1933)—but this only after 1918. See Sigfrid Rosenberger in *Schild*, 12 Jahrg., No. 19 (October 13, 1933), p. 168.
9. Scheuer, *op. cit.*, p. 40.
10. *Ibid.*, pp. 40, 49.
11. *Ibid.*, p. 49.
12. P. J. G. Pulzer, *Antisemitism in Germany and Austria, 1867-1918* (Dissertation, Cambridge University, 1960), p. 285.
13. Herwig (E. Pichel), *Georg Schönerer* (Vienna, 1923), Vol. IV, p. 434, No. 2.
14. Pulzer, *op. cit.*, p. 331.
15. Scheuer, *op. cit.*, pp. 42-43.
16. *Ibid.*, pp. 55, 58.
17. Quidde, *op. cit.*, p. 15.

18. *Ibid.*, p. 16.
19. *Ibid.*, pp. 16, 12, 17; Quidde, *op. cit.* (Göttingen, 1881), p. 7 (a different edition, published anonymously).
20. *Mitteilungen*, 17 Jahrg., No. 7 (February 13, 1907), pp. 53 ff.
21. Harry Graf Kessler, *Tagebücher*, 1919-1937 (Frankfurt, 1961), p. 328.
22. Reprinted in "Von Deutsch-Jüdischer Jugend," supplement to *C. V. Zeitung*, 2 Jahrg., No. 8 (October 1926), p. 32.
23. Ernst Fränkel, *Viadrina suspensa! Vivat Thuringia! 40 Jahre Kampf für Recht und Ehre* (Breslau, 1926), p. 33.
24. *Antisemiten Spiegel* (Frankfurt, 1911), p. 175.
25. Fränkel, *op. cit.*, pp. 43, 47.
26. *Jüdische Jugend*, Heft 1 (1919), pp. 7-8.
27. Reuwen Michael, "Grätz contra Treitschke," *Bulletin of the Leo Baeck Institute*, 4 Jahrg., No. 16 (December 1961), pp. 301-23. An excellent discussion of Treitschke on the Jewish question, which we have followed.
28. See below, page 55.
29. Heinrich von Treitschke, *Deutsche Geschichte im Neuzehnten Jahr-Hundert* (Leipzig, 1920), Vol. V, p. 387.
30. Michael, *op. cit.*, p. 306.
31. See Treitschke, *op. cit.*, p. 23.
32. *C. V. Zeitung*, 9 Jahrg. (June 27, 1930), p. 286; *ibid.* (August 15, 1930), p. 433.

CHAPTER 11
(*Pages 204-217*)

1. See Jost Hermand, "Gralsmotive um die Jahrhundertwende," *Deutsche Vierteljahrsschrift für Literaturwissenschaft und Geistesgeschichte,* 36 Jahrg., Heft 4 (1962), pp. 521-43.
2. Arthur Bonus, *Vom neuen Mythos* (Jena, 1911), pp. 6 ff., 40 ff.
3. Willibald Hentschel, *Varuna* (Leipzig, 1907), p. 520.
4. Bonus, *op. cit.*, pp. 72, 73, 83, 96.
5. Ernst Bertram, *Nietzsche* (Berlin, 1919), esp. pp. 1-16.
6. *Ibid.*, pp. 79, 347, 44.
7. *Ibid.*, p. 79.
8. *Ibid.*, p. 347.
9. Alfred Bäumler, *Nietzsche der Philosoph und Politiker* (Leipzig, 1931).
10. Bertram, *op. cit.*, p. 352.
11. Nietzsche letter cited in *Hammer Festschrift* (Leipzig, 1926), p. 77.
12. Karl Münster, "Ritter, Tod und Teufel," *Wille und Macht*, 4 Jahrg.,

Heft 8 (April 15, 1936), pp. 14-16. The portrait of Hitler is reproduced by Joseph Wulf, *Die Bildenden Künste im Dritten Reich* (Gütersloh, 1963), Plate 31. For another Nazi invocation of "the knight, death, and the devil," a print of which was given to Hitler as a "symbolic present" at the first Reichsparteitag, see Wulf, p. 176.

13. Wilhelm Schloz, *Landhunger* (Heidelberg, 1931), p. 99.
14. *Völkischer Beobachter* (Vienna), No. 261 (December 3, 1938), n.p.
15. Walther Darré, *Das Bauerntum als Lebensquelle der nordischen Rasse* (Munich, 1937), first published in 1929, makes much use of Günther's book; see especially p. 97.
16. Hans F. K. Günther, *Ritter, Tod und Teufel, Der heldische Gedanke* (Munich, 1924), *passim*.
17. "Junge Deutsche Dichtung," *Wille und Macht*, 3 Jahrg., Heft 20 (October 15, 1935), p. 14.
18. *Klüter Blätter*, Heft 11-12 (Mappe A), II (1954), I.
19. François-René de Chateaubriand, *The Beauties of Christianity* (London, 1813), Vol. II, pp. 267-68.
20. *Stefan George in Selbstzeugnissen und Bilddokumenten*, ed. by Franz Schonauer (Hamburg, 1960), p. 24.
21. For a description of the festivities, see Franziska zu Reventlow, *Herrn Dames Aufzeichnungen* (Munich, 1958).
22. *Stefan George in Selbstzeugnissen*, p. 123.
23. *Ibid.*, p. 139.
24. *Ibid.*, p. 113.
25. *Ibid.*, pp. 92 ff.
26. *Ibid.*, p. 128.
27. See Ludwig Klages, *Der Geist als Widersacher der Seele* (Munich and Bonn, 1960), first published in 1929. See also his *Die psychologischen Errungenschaften Nietzsches* (Leipzig, 1928). For Alfred Schuler, see below, pages 75-76.
28. Hans Blüher, *Die Rolle der Erotik in der männlichen Gesellschaft* (Jena, 1921), Vol. I, pp. 75-76.
29. *Ibid.*, pp. 29, 37, 143 ff.
30. *Ibid.*, pp. 29-31.
31. *Ibid.*, p. 25.
32. *Ibid.*, pp. 241 ff.
33. *Ibid.*, p. 4; Vol. II, p. 219.
34. *Ibid.*, Vol. I, p. 182.
35. Typically enough the Jews are said to suffer from weakness in forming *Bünde* ("Männerbundschwäche"), for they are not a Volk. *Ibid.*, Vol. II, p. 170 n. Blüher's book is now available in a modern edition (Stuttgart, 1962).
36. The best summary of Weininger is in Theodor Lessing, *Der Jüdische*

Selbsthass (Berlin, 1930), pp. 80-100. More favorable is Hans Kohn, *Karl Kraus–Arthur Schnitzler–Otto Weininger* (Tübingen, 1960).

37. Georg Lomer, *Wir und die Juden im Licht der Astrologie* (Hannover, 1928), p. 9.

38. Lothar Helbing, *Der dritte Humanismus* (Berlin, 1935), p. 89; first published in 1928. Blüher, *op. cit.*, Vol. II, p. 170 n.

39. Albert Krebs, "Partei und Gesellschaft," *Nationalsozialistische Briefe*, 4 Jahrg., Heft to (November 15, 1928), p. 150.

40. Quoted in Karl O. Paetel, *Das Bild vom Menschen in der Deutschen Jugendführung* (Bad Godesberg, 1954), p. 30.

41. Georg Franz-Willing, *Die Hitlerbewegung* (Hamburg, 1962), p. 82. Krebs, *op. cit.* Krebs was, at that time, a follower of the Strassers.

CHAPTER 12
(*Pages 218–233*)

1. Max Wundt, *Was heisst Völkisch?* (Langensalza, 1924), pp. 6, 8, 9.

2. Alfred Kruck, *Geschichte des Alldeutschen Verbandes* (Wiesbaden, 1954), p. ii.

3. See *ibid.*, p. 200.

4. For a general discussion of Pan-German aims, see *ibid.*, *passim.* Hugenberg is discussed in greater detail above, pages 248-252.

5. Wolfgang Mommsen, *Max Weber und die Deutsche Politik* (Tübingen, 1959), pp. 62-63.

6. *Mitteilungen*, 38 Jahrg. (December 1928), p. 170.

7. See Heinrich Class, *Wider den Strom* (Leipzig, 1932).

8. Kruck, *op. cit.*, p. 18.

9. Daniel Fryman (Heinrich Class), *Wenn ich der Kaiser wär* (Leipzig, 1914), pp. 263, 135, 49.

10. *Ibid.*, pp. 21, 59.

11. The review of Hentschel's *Varuna* praises the basic idea but criticizes the exaggerations and fantasies with which it is embellished. *Alldeutsche Blätter*, 17 Jahrg., No. 43 (October 26, 1907), pp. 371-72.

12. *Ibid.*, p. 372.

13. Class, *Wenn ich der Kaiser wär*, pp. 60-63.

14. See Kruck, *op. cit.*, p. 210.

15. Class, *Wenn ich der Kaiser wär*, p. 30.

16. *Ibid.*, p. 76.

17. *Mitteilungen*, 38 Jahrg. (December 1928), p. 170; *ibid.* (April 1928), p. 55.

18. Otto Bonhard, *Geschichte des Alldeutschen Verbandes* (Leipzig, 1920), p. 262.

19. Ludwig Kuhlenbeck, *Das Evangelium der Rasse* (Prenzlau, 1905), p. 55.

20. Ludwig Kuhlenbeck in *Zwanzig Jahre Alldeutscher Arbeit und Kämpfe* (Leipzig, 1910), p. 273.

21. *Eugen Diederichs Verlagskatalog* (Jena, n. d.), p. ii.

22. Kruck, *op. cit.*, pp. 168-69.

23. M. R. Gerstenhauer, *Der völkische Gedanke in Vergangenheit und Zunkunft* (Leipzig, 1933), p. 63; Kruck, *op. cit.*, p. 132. As a further cross connection, the secretary of the *Bund*, Alfred Roth, was also one of the founders of the white-collar union Deutschnationale Handlungsgehilfen Verband, for which see Chapter 14.

24. Class was one of three deputy editors, while Lehmann was a leading member of the Pan-Germans. Heinrich Class, "Julius Friedrich Lehmann und der Alldeutsche Verband," *Deutschlands Erneuerung*, Vol. V (1935), pp. 58-60.

25. *Deutsche Zeitung* (October 19, 1924), n. p.

26. Kruck, *op. cit.*, pp. 192, 203.

27. *Ibid.*, p. 216.

28. See Konrad Heiden, *Geschichte des Nationalsozialismus* (Berlin, 1932), p. 6.

29. Kruck, *op. cit.*, p. 211.

30. "Satzungen des Fichtebundes," ZSGI-153/1 (Bundesarchiv, Koblenz); Ottger Gräfe to Wilhelm Schwaner (8 Ernting, August 1916), in Alfred Ehrenstreich, "Zeugnisse der Freundschaft," Rathenau Nachlass No. 6 (Bundesarchiv, Koblenz).

31. Franz Schauwecker, "Begriff und Wesen des Völkischen," *Blätter für Deutsches Schrifttum*, Heft 3 (December 1928), p. 31.

32. Ernst von Salomon, *Der Fragebogen* (Hamburg, 1951), p. 154.

33. Ernst H. Posse, *Die politischen Kampfbünde Deutschlands* (Berlin, 1931), pp. 45 ff.

34. *Ibid.*, p. 13.

35. *Ibid.*, p. 50.

36. K. Hornung, *Der Jungdeutsche Orden* (Düsseldorf, 1958), p. 80.

37. *Ibid.*, p. 51, n. 2.

38. See Artur Mahraun, *Der Aufbruch* (Berlin, 1924), p. 23; where he rejects the unfruitful anti-Semitism of the DNVP, while, of course, retaining the Aryan clause for his own organization.

39. Rudolf von Sebottendorf, *Bevor Hitler kam* (Munich, 1933), pp. 33, 52.

40. Georg Franz-Willing, *Die Hitlerbewegung* (Hamburg, 1962), Vol. I, p. 82.

41. Reinhold Wulle, *Die Sendung des Nordens* (Leipzig, 1931), pp. 220, 176.

42. Wulle's own summary of *ibid.* as advertisement at end of his *Das Schuldbuch der Republik* (Rostock, 1932).

43. RK Grossdeutsche (Deutschvölkische) Freiheitspartei, Band 2, 9263; RKA Parteien 10, Band 2, RK 11332 (Bundesarchiv, Koblenz).

44. Reinhold Wulle, "Denkschrift" (für von Papen), RK 10896, Parteien 10, Band 2, p. 4 (Bundesarchiv, Koblenz).

45. Wulle, reprinted in *Der Ring*, Heft 27 (June 2, 1933), pp. 355-56.

46. Wulle, "Denkschrift," pp. 3, 4.

47. *Der Ring*, p. 355.

48. Rudolf Pechel, *Deutscher Widerstand* (Zurich, 1947), pp. 73-74.

49. *Deutsche Zeitung* (October 2, 1924), *passim*.

50. *Wahlblatt des Völkischen-Nationalen Blocks* (May 20, 1929). The party discussed themes such as: "Despite the opposition of Jewish democracy and Roman fascism we will work toward the true German state." *Deutsche Nachrichten*, 7 Jahrg. (September 25, 1932), n. p.

51. Albrecht von Gräfe-Goldebee to Herrn Kruse (February 15, 1932), Kl. Erw. No. 327 (Bundesarchiv, Koblenz).

52. As one example, in 1923 National Socialist membership cards were found among members of the Deutsch-Völkische Freiheitspartei: "Der Reichskommisar für Überwachung der öffentlichen Ordnung" (December 20, 1923), RK 14264/23 (Bundesarchiv, Koblenz), p. 5.

53. Wulle is one of these. See Pechel, *op. cit.* Walter Hammer claims that Wulle received preferred treatment in the concentration camp of Sachsenhausen, where he spent two years: "Jugendbewegung im Würgegriff der Gestapo," ms. (September 5, 1961) (Archiv Walter Hammer im Archiv der Jugendbewegung, Burg Ludwigstein).

CHAPTER 13
(*Pages 237–253*)

1. For the Bund der Landwirte see *Antisemiten Spiegel* (1900), pp. 63-67.

2. At the first party convention (1920) Kunze not only attacked the Jews but also the moderate party leadership under Oskar Hergt. His speech was well received among the rank and file. *Berliner Tageblatt* 50 Jahrg. (October 10, 1921), n. p.

3. Gottfried Traub, "Memoiren," 218, Traub Nachlass, 64 (Bundesarchiv, Koblenz).

4. Albert Reich, *Dietrich Eckart* (Munich, 1933), p. 92; Melanie Lehmann, *Verleger J. F Lehmann: ein Leben im Kampf für Deutsch-*

land (Munich, 1935), p. 43; *Mitteilungen*, 30 Jahrg., No. 6 (March 30, 1920), p. 46.

5. For an essentially correct, if biased, account, see Ludwig Schemann, *Wolfgang Kapp und das Märzunternehmen vom Jahre 1920* (Munich, 1937).
6. *Mitteilungen*, 18 Jahrg., No. 50 (December 9, 1908), p. 395.
7. *Ibid.*, 29 Jahrg., No. 25 (December 10, 1919), p. 189.
8. *Kreuz Zeitung*, No. 488 (October 31, 1922), n. p.
9. *Berliner Tageblatt*, 50 Jahrg. (November 28, 1921), n. p.
10. *Mitteilungen*, 33 Jahrg., No. 11-12 (June 5, 1923), p. 24. The local party groups were Hannover, Bavaria, Mecklenburg, Pomerania, Hamburg, and Potsdam II.
11. Werner Liebe, *Die Deutschnationale Volkspartei 1918-1924* (Düsseldorf, 1956), p. 95.
12. *Mitteilungen*, 38 Jahrg. (April 1928), p. 47.
13. *Der Nationale Wille*, ed. by Max Weiss (Essen, 1928), p. 42.
14. *Hier eure Führer* (1928); *Kohn Sorten* (1919). The stereotypes are identical with those used in the famous "Judennummer" of Dietrich Eckart's *Auf Gut Deutsch;* see Reich, *op. cit.*, p. 92.
15. *Männer und Frauen Gross-Berlins!* (1920); *Deutschen Männern und Frauen vor dem 7. Dezember sagen müssen* (1924).
16. *Räumt auf damit!* (c. 1932).
17. *Mitteilungen*, 29 Jahrg., No. 21 (October 16, 1919), p. 153.
18. *Ibid.*, 38 Jahrg. (June 1, 1928).
19. *Taschenbuch der Deutschnationalen Volkspartei* (Berlin, 1929), p. 9.
20. From material of the DNVP at the Potsdam Archives, kindly communicated to me by Philip M. Wiener.
21. Schemann, *op. cit.*, p. 199, n. 1; *70,000 Ostjuden füllen Berliner Wohnungen* (c. 1932).
22. Cited in Artur Mahraun, *Der Aufbruch* (Berlin, 1929), p. 22.
23. *Reichskanzelei Akten betreffend Antisemitismus*, L 382346 (Bundesarchiv, Koblenz).
24. This is one of the theses of the National Socialist Walter Frank, *Hofprediger Adolf Stöcker und die christlichsoziale Bewegung* (Hamburg, 1935).
25. Walter Gerhart, *Um des Reiches Zukunft. Nationale Wiedergeburt oder politische Reaktion?* (Freiburg, 1932), p. 153. RKA, Band 2, Parteien 10, RK 6406/24 (Bundesarchiv, Koblenz).
26. In a review of Frank, *op. cit.* in *Sammlung*, No. 128 (1928), n. p. (*Sammlung* is a supplement to the *Münchner-Augsburger Abendzeitung*).
27. "Memoiren," 278, Traub Nachlass 64 (Bundesarchiv, Koblenz).

28. "Auf der Pfingstwarte," *Vossische Zeitung*, No. 297 (June 11, 1916), *passim*.
29. See *Eiserne Blätter*, published by Traub, *passim*.
30. *Münchner-Augsburger Abendzeitung*, No. 33 (February 4, 1932), n. p.
31. "Tagebuch Notizen über die Hitlerzeit," p. 10, Traub Nachlass 63 (Bundesarchiv, Koblenz).
32. *Ibid.*, p. 7.
33. Anon., *Begriff und Wesen des Völkischen* (Leipzig, 1929), p. 28.
34. Paul Bang, "Sozialpolitik," *Unsere Partei*, 10 Jahrg., No. 13 (July 1, 1932), p. 171.
35. Paul Bang, *Deutsche Wirtschaftsziele* (Langensalza, 1926), pp. 140, 171, 157, 91.
36. *Ibid.*, p. 100.
37. *Der Nationale Wille*, pp. 71-72, 81.
38. A. Hugenberg, *Streiflichter aus Vergangenheit und Gegenwart* (Berlin, 1927), p. 5.
39. *Ibid.*, pp. 5, 6. *Unsere Partei*, 9 Jahrg., No. 18-19 (October 1931), p. 226.
40. *Deutsches Tageblatt*, 8 Jahrg., No. 165 (July 17, 1928), n. p. *Mitteilungen*, 42 Jahrg., No. 10 (December 1932), p. 225.
41. The book is Fritz Bley, *Am Grabe des Deutschen Volkes* (Berlin, 1919).
42. *Michel*, 15 Jahrg. (April 30, 1933), n. p.
43. *Unsere Partei*, No. 18-19 (October 1, 1931), p. 226.
44. Graf Westarp, *Konservative Politik* (Berlin, 1935), p. 338.
45. *Germania*, No. 669 (December 27, 1922), n. p.; Georg Franz-Willing, *Die Hitlerbewegung* (Hamburg, 1962), p. 228.
46. Otto Meesmann to Friedrich Middelhauve (May 20, 1953), Traub Nachlass 67 (Bundesarchiv, Koblenz).
47. *Deutsche Zeitung* (April 15, 1932), n. p.
48. *RKA* DNVP, Band 2, Parteien 2, L 529918 (Bundesarchiv, Koblenz).
49. Memorandum by Otto Meesmann, March 1953, pp. 5, 6, Traub Nachlass 67 (Bundesarchiv, Koblenz).
50. Hugenberg in 1926, quoted in his obituary, *Die Gegenwart* (April 1, 1950), p. 7.
51. "Schreiben Hugenbergs zweck Entlassung aus seinen Ämtern," p. 2, Traub Nachlass I (Bundesarchiv, Koblenz).
52. Hugenberg to Traub (December 11, 1941), Traub Nachlass I (Bundesarchiv, Koblenz).
53. *Mitteilungen*, 38 Jahrg. (April 1928), p. 47.

CHAPTER 14
(Pages 254-265)

1. Ernst H. Posse, *Die politischen Kampfbünde Deutschlands* (Berlin, 1931), p. 23.
2. *Ibid.*, pp. 32, 34.
3. *Braunschweiger Landeszeitung*, No. 184 (July 4, 1924), p. 7.
4. *Der Stahlhelm*, No. 8 (February 23, 1928), lead article. All references are to the Brunswick edition, to be found in the Niedersächsisches Landesarchiv, Wolffenbüttel.
5. *Ibid.*, No. 20 (July 17, 1924), n.p.
6. *Ibid.*, No. 23 (August 7, 1924), n.p.
7. *Ibid.*, No. 20 (July 17, 1924), n.p.
8. Letter to Julius Beutz (January 11, 1932) (Potsdam/DZA I/Stahlhelm/273/[Judenfrage] 34). I owe this reference to Philip M. Wiener.
9. *Der Stahlhelm*, No. 10 (May 8, 1924), n.p.
10. *Stahlhelm Zeitung*, No. 4-5 (February 2, 1928), n.p.
11. *Die Junge Nation*, No. 51-52 (December 22, 1932), n.p.
12. *Der Stahlhelm*, No. 8 (February 23, 1928), n.p.
13. *Die Junge Nation*, No. 20 (May 25, 1933), n.p.
14. Cited in Michael Jovy, *Deutsche Jugendbewegung und National Socialismus* (Inaugural Dissertation, Köln, 1952), p. 144.
15. *Stahlhelm Zeitung*, No. 2 (March 15, 1928), n.p.
16. See *C. V. Zeitung*, 5 Jahrg. (April 1, 1926), p. 193. Brunswick was certainly such a region. It was stated in a speech there before the women's auxiliary (Königin Luise Bund) that Jews are not human. *Mitteilungen*, 39 Jahrg. (November 1929), p. 176; see also adult education curriculum cited above, p. 256.
17. *Die Junge Nation*, No. 8 (February 25, 1932), n.p.
18. *Ibid.*, No. 29 (July 21, 1932), n.p.
19. Seldte in the early twenties had held that on the field of battle every soul goes to heaven, whether it be Protestant, Catholic, or Jewish; quoted in *Ludendorfs Volkswarte* (February 22, 1931), n.p.
20. *Deutsche Handelswacht*, 36 Jahrg., No. 3 (February 10, 1929), p. 43.
21. Membership figures given in *ibid.*, 39 Jahrg., No. 4 (March 25, 1932).
22. *C. V. Zeitung*, 5 Jahrg. (January 8, 1926), p. 16.
23. *Deutsche Handelswacht*, 14 Jahrg., No. 14 (July 15, 1907), p. 271; Richard Döring and Bruno Plintz, *Der Deutschnationale Handelsgehilfen Verband in der Reichshauptstadt* (Hamburg, n.d.), p. 109.
24. Advertising in *Deutsche Handelswacht*, 14 Jahrg., No. 13 (July 2, 1907), p. 263; Döring and Plintz, *op. cit.*, p. 55.

25. See A. Zimmermann, "Die Juden und die Deutsche Handlungs-gehilfen Bewegung," *Die Handelswacht*, 38 Jahrg. (all numbers of 1931).

26. Rudolf Brochardt, *Deutsche Literatur im Kampfe um ihr Recht* (Munich, 1931), pp. 12-13.

27. For these activities, see *ibid.*, p. 32.

28. See *Jahrbuch* (1931), p. 44.

29. Max Habermann in *Deutsche Handelswacht*, 37 Jahrg., No. 21 (November 10, 1930), p. 415.

30. *Ibid.*

31. *Der Jud ist schuld?* (Vienna, 1932), p. 269.

32. *Jahrbuch* (1912), p. 129.

33. Georg Franz-Willing, *Die Hitlerbewegung* (Hamburg, 1962), p. 29.

34. Lambach attacked DNVP monarchism, which led to his resignation. With Blechly he seemed to have hoped to unite the Christian trade unions into an effective political group. Otto Schmidt/Hannover, *Umdenken oder Anarchie* (Göttingen, 1959), pp. 230-31.

35. Albert Krebs to Adolf Hitler (February 6, 1930), p. 3. Krebs Nach-lass, "Partei, Privat" (Bundesarchiv, Koblenz).

36. "Leitung des DHV und der Ring National Sozialistischer DHV'er" (December 18, 1929), Krebs Nachlass, "Partei, Privat" (Bundes-archiv, Koblenz).

37. Albert Krebs, "Tagebuch," p. 12 (Bundesarchiv, Koblenz).

38. *Ibid.*, p. 22.

39. Unlike many other Volkish groups, the DHV could not accept von Papen as a chancellor and strong man; together with Hugenberg and Bang he was characterized as "reactionary." *Deutsche Handelswacht*, 40 Jahrg., No. 1 (January 14, 1933), p. 1; *ibid.*, 40 Jahrg., No. 2 (February 13, 1933).

40. A. Ciller, *Vorläufer des Nationalsozialismus* (Vienna, 1932), pp. 23-26, 48.

41. *Ibid.*, p. 109.

42. Cited in Friedrich Hielscher, *Fünfzig Jahre unter Deutschen* (Ham-burg, 1954), p. 52.

43. August Winnig, *Der weite Weg* (Hamburg, 1932), p. 392.

44. *Ibid.*, p. 228; Ciller, *op. cit.*, p. 129.

45. Cited in Ciller, *op. cit.*, p. 129.

46. At least Winnig was close to the *Bünde*. Otto-Ernst Schüddekopf, *Linke Leute von Rechts* (Stuttgart, 1960), p. 211.

47. August Winnig, *Aus zwanzig Jahren* (Hamburg, 1951), p. 124; Her-bert Böhme, *Bekenntnis eines freien Mannes* (Munich, 1960), pp. 81, 183.

48. August Winnig, *Das Reich als Republik* (Stuttgart, 1929), p. 286.

49. *Deutsche Handelswacht*, 38 Jahrg., No. 2 (January 25, 1931), p. 31.
50. For his career, see Winnig, *Aus zwanzig Jahren*.

CHAPTER 15
(*Pages 266–279*)

1. Friedrich Glum, *Der Nationalsozialismus* (Munich, 1962), p. 157.
2. Order of November 8, 1920.
3. *Mitteilungen*, 29 Jahrg., No. 5 (March 3, 1919), p. 39; Adam Röder in the *C. V. Zeitung*, 5 Jahrg. (March 5, 1926), p. 122. See also Siegfried Bernfeld's opinion that schoolteachers were totally committed to the right in a "crushing majority": *Das Tagebuch*, 8 Jahrg., Heft 4 (January 22, 1927), p. 144.
4. "Von Deutsch-Jüdischer Jugend," *C. V. Zeitung*, 2 Jahrg., No. 2 (February 19, 1926), p. 6.
5. Michael Muller-Claudius, *Rassenangst* (Berlin, 1920), *passim.*
6. See *C. V. Zeitung*, 11 Jahrg. (February 12, 1932), p. 57.
7. *K. C. Blätter*, 21 Jahrg. (December 1931).
8. "Von Deutsch-Jüdischer Jugend," *C. V. Zeitung*, 5 Jahrg. (February 19, 1926), p. 5; *ibid.* (January 15, 1926), p. 26.
9. Hermann Pinnow, *Geschichte des Deutschen Volkes von 1648 bis zur Gegenwart*, 10th edition (Leipzig, 1929), *passim.*
10. *Koch's Lehrbuch der Geschichte*, ed. by R. Volpers, 4th edition (Leipzig, 1927), Part IV, p. 129.
11. E. Wilmann, *Deutsche Geschichte*, 4th edition (Leipzig, 1930), p. 93.
12. Walther Gehl, *Geschichte für höhere Schulen*, 4th edition (Breslau, 1933), Heft 4, *passim.*
13. "Burschenschaftliche Blätter (1928)," quoted in *K.-C. Mitteilungen*, No. 8 (July 25, 1928), p. 68.
14. For this controversy see Hans Schlöner, "Studentenschaft und Weimarer Republik," *Unitas* (Köln), 94 Jahrg., Heft 12 (December 1954), pp. 14 ff.
15. See the cases of Cohn in Breslau and Gumbel in Heidelberg. Also the condemnation of professorial inactivity during the anti-Semitic riots against Naviasky in Munich, *K.-C. Blätter*, 20 Jahrg., Heft 2 (March 1930), p. 19.
16. *D. St. Pressedienst*, 8 Jahrg., No. 4 (March 14, 1934), p. 2. By 1929 we have one estimate that 40 per cent of the students were Nazi: "Vertrauliche Beilage," *K.-C. Blätter*, No. 4 (November 1, 1929), p. 107.
17. By early 1932, nine out of the ten "Kreisleiter" were members of the NSDAP, *D. St.* 71 (Bundesarchiv, Frankfurt).

18. RK Akten NSDAP, Parteien 12, Band 3, 213 (Bundesarchiv, Koblenz).

19. Ernst Buske, quoted in Ernst Michael Jovy, *Deutsche Jugendbewegung und Nationalsozialismus* (Inaugural Dissertation, Köln, 1952), p. 197.

20. See Hermann Siefert, "Politische Vorstellungen und Versuche der Deutschen Freischaar," *Lebendiger Geist*, ed. by Helmut Diwald (Leiden, 1959), p. 180.

21. Jovy, *op. cit.*, p. 142.

22. Walter Z. Laqueur, *Young Germany* (London, 1962), p. 134; Martin Voelkel in "Der Naumburger Bund," Special Issue of *Weissen Ritters*, Band 5 (Pfingsten, 1925), pp. 33 ff.

23. See Adam Ritzhaupt, *Die "Neue Schaar" in Thüringen* (Jena, 1921).

24. Jovy, *op. cit.*, p. 225; conversation with F. L. Habel, October 1961.

25. Jovy, *op. cit.*, p. 214; *Älterenrundbrief des Bundes Wandervögel und Kronacher*, 11 Jahrg., Heft 3-4 (April 1, 1932), p. 7, is typical of such criticism. See also *Freischaar*, Heft 1, Band 5 (1932), p. 22.

26. Winfrid-Kiel in *Nationalsozialistische Monatshefte*, 1 Jahrg., Heft 2 (May 1930), p. 62.

27. On the *Bund* and leadership, see Felix Raabe, *Die bündische Jugend*, (Stuttgart, 1961), p. 101.

28. Seifert, *op. cit.*, p. 188.

29. Otto Michel in *Freideutsche Jugend*, 7 Jahrg., Heft 2 (February 1921), p. 56.

30. *Der Wanderer*, 28 Jahrg., Heft 1-2 (1933), p. 29.

31. Günther Ipsen in *Deutsche Freischaar*, Heft 5 (1929), p. 5.

32. For the ideology, see Edwin Fritz in *Der Falke*, Heft 2 (Hornung, 1931), p. 26; *Die Geusen*, 1 Jahrg., Heft 3-4 (March 1920), pp. 46 ff.

33. *Die Geusen*, 1 Jahrg., Heft 3-4 (May 1920), p. 51.

34. Karl Bösch in *Der Falke*, Heft 1 (1931), p. 1.

35. *Die Geusen*, 2 Jahrg., Heft 3-4 (Oster, 1921), p. 46.

36. Conversation with a former *Bündesführer* of the Adler und Falken in the Sudetenland, October 10, 1961.

37. Richard Bülk to Alfred Krebs (June 2, 1930), Krebs Nachlass, "Partei, privat" (Bundesarchiv, Koblenz).

CHAPTER 16
(Pages 280–293)

1. Quoted in Fritz Stern, *The Politics of Cultural Despair* (Berkeley and Los Angeles, 1961), p. 258.

2. Möller van den Bruck, *Das Dritte Reich*, ed. by Hans Schwarz (Hamburg, 1931), p. 67.

3. Stern, *op. cit.*, p. 254.

4. Quoted in Hans-Joachim Schwierskott, *Arthur Möller van den Bruck und der revolutionäre Nationalismus in der Weimarer Republik* (Göttingen, 1962), p. 103.

5. See Stern, *op. cit.*, p. 258.

6. For these ideas, see Möller van den Bruck, *Das Dritte Reich*, first published in 1923 by the Hanseatische Verlagsanstalt, Hamburg, which was financially controlled by the DHV.

7. Edmond Vermeille, *Doctrinaires de la Révolution Allemande* (Paris, 1948), pp. 157-60.

8. Walter Gerhart (Waldemar Gurian) *Um des Reiches Zukunft* (Freiburg, 1932), p. 152.

9. Kurt Sontheimer, *Antidemokratisches Denken in der Weimarer Republik* (Munich, 1962), pp. 94 ff.

10. Möller van den Bruck, *Das Dritte Reich*, p. 5.

11. George L. Mosse, "The Corporate State and the Conservative Revolution in Weimar Germany," *Recueille Société Jean Bodin* (Brussels), to be published.

12. See Martin Voelkel in "Der Naumburger Bund," Special Issue of *Weissen Ritters*, 5 Jahrg. (Pfingsten, 1925), p. 38.

13. See Paul Krannhals, *Organisches Weltbild* (Munich, 1936), Vol. I, p. 31 (first published in 1928).

14. Neue Pfadfinder quoted in Hermann Seifert, "Politische Vorstellung und Versuche der Deutschen Freischaar," *Lebendiger Geist*, ed. by Helmut Diwald (Leiden, 1959), p. 197.

15. Carl Schmitt, *Staat, Bewegung, Volk* (Hamburg, 1934), *passim*.

16. Krannhals, *op. cit.*, p. 250.

17. Alfred Krebs, "Offener Brief an Ernst Niekisch," Krebs Nachlass, "Partei, privat" (Bundesarchiv, Koblenz); Alfred Krebs, "Tagebuch," March 30, 1932, p. 60, Krebs Nachlass (Bundesarchiv, Koblenz).

18. "Vierzehn Thesem der Deutschen Revolution," in Wilhelm Mommsen and Günther Franz, *Die Deutschen Partei-Programme* (Leipzig and Berlin, 1931), p. 118.

19. *Ibid.*, p. 117.

20. As to the dual allegiance, there is some evidence in Alfred Krebs, "Tagebuch" (October 17, 1930), p. 7, Krebs Nachlass (Bundesarchiv, Koblenz).

21. Otto-Ernst Schüddekopf, *Linke Leute von Rechts* (Stuttgart, 1960), pp. 196 ff.

22. *Ibid.*, pp. 319-20. See also Karl O. Paetel, "Otto Strasser und die 'Schwarze Front' des wahren Nationalsozialismus," *Politische Studien*, Heft 92, 8 Jahrg. (December 1957), pp. 269-82.

23. Mommsen and Franz, *op. cit.*, p. 118; Otto Strasser, *Aufbau der Deutschen Sozialismus* (Prague, 1936), pp. 77-78.

24. Otto Strasser, *Exil* (Munich, 1958), p. 37; Gregor Strasser, "Wesen und Ziel der Nationalsozialistischen Idee" (October 17, 1930), in Mommsen and Franz, *op. cit.*, p. 130.

25. Gregor Strasser in *Völkische Beobachter*, No. 283 (December 5, 1928), n. p. See also C. V. *Zeitung*, 10 Jahrg. (October 24, 1930), p. 560.

26. *Deutsche Handelswacht*, 37 Jahrg., No. 21 (November 10, 1930), p. 415; Otto Schmidt-Hannover, *Umdenken oder Anarchie* (Göttingen, 1959), pp. 230-31.

27. In *Der Ring*, Heft 9 (March 3, 1933), p. 149.

28. Edgar Jung, *Gegen die Herrschaft der Minderwertigen* (Leipzig, 1934), *passim*.

29. Paul Bang, *Deutsche Wirtschaftsziele* (Langensalza, 1926), pp. 171 ff.

30. Max Frauendorfer, *Der ständische Gedanke im Nationalsozialismus* (Munich, 1932), pp. 19-24.

31. Jean Denis, *Principes Rexistes* (Brussels, 1936), p. 17.

CHAPTER 17
(Pages 294–311)

1. Wilfried Daim, *Der Mann der Hitler die Ideen gab* (Munich, 1930), differs but, to me, not convincingly.

2. Adolf Hitler, *Mein Kampf* (Munich, 1933), Vol. I, p. 61.

3. *Ibid.*, pp. 330, 339.

4. Typically enough, when, in 1937, the representative exhibition of German art was held, 40 per cent of the paintings were landscapes and there were only two pictures with a factory motif. Hildegard Brenner, *Die Kunstpolitik des Nationalsozialismus* (Hamburg, 1963), pp. 112-113.

5. Hitler, *Mein Kampf*, Vol. I, p. 69.

6. Dietrich Eckart in *Auf Gut Deutsch*, 1 Jahrg. (1919), p. 18.

7. For example, "Das ist der Jude!" *Auf Gut Deutsch* (Summer, 1919?). This was said to have had a circulation of 100,000. Albert Reich, *Dietrich Eckart* (Munich, 1933), pp. 92-93.

8. See Reich, *op. cit.*, *passim*.

9. Georg Franz-Willing, *Die Hitlerbewegung* (Hamburg, 1962), p. 116.

10. Hitler, *Mein Kampf*, Vol. II, p. 418.

11. *Ibid.*, p. 395.

12. Speech at the opening of the House of German Art (1937), *The*

Speeches of Adolf Hitler, trans. by Norman Baynes (London, 1942), Vol. I, p. 587.

13. Walter Gerhart, *Um des Reiches Zukunft* (Freiburg, 1932), p. 99.

14. Hitler, *op. cit.*, Vol. II, p. 774.

15. *Mitteilungen*, 40 Jahrg. (October 1, 1930), p. 3.

16. *K.-C. Blätter*, 20 Jahrg., Heft 7 (August 1930), p. 104. Hans-Joachim Schöps believes that a large part of the Nazi vote in 1930 came from youth who earlier had been too young to vote. It follows that the real strength of the NSDAP cannot be exclusively measured by the votes it received in the 1920's. *Rückblicke* (Berlin, 1963), p. 204.

17. See Erich Wolff's analysis from a Republican point of view in *Älterenrundbrief des Bundes Wandervögel und Kronacher*, 10 Jahrg., Heft 1-2 (November 1930), pp. 17-19.

18. Winifred Martini and Hans Lamm (March 5, 1950), in Hans Lamm, *Über die innere und äussere Entwicklung des Deutschen Judentums im Dritten Reich* (Inaugural Dissertation, Erlangen, 1951), p. 97. Even so Martini puts first the Volkish direction which this dissimulation of drives took.

19. This is the thesis of Eva G. Reichmann, *Hostages of Civilization* (London, 1950).

20. Ernst Deuerlein, "Hitler's Eintritt in die Politik und die Reichswehr," *Vierteljahrschrift für Zeitgeschichte*, 7 Jahrg., Heft 2 (April 1959), p. 203.

21. Hermann Rauschning, *Gespräche mit Hitler* (New York, 1940), p. 220.

22. See below, p. 134. In Italy, Mussolini also found that to be successful racism has to treat the Jews as an abstraction. Renzo de Felice, *Storia degli ebrei italiani sotto il fascismo* (Turin, 1961), p. 257.

23. As reported in *Nation Europa*, 11 Jahrg., Heft 6 (June 1961), p. 67.

24. Hans F. K. Günther, *Rassenkunde des Deutschen Volkes* (Munich, 1923), p. 19.

25. Hans F. K. Günther, *Rassenkunde des Jüdischen Volkes* (Munich, 1930), pp. 163, 212 ff.

26. Siegfried Passarge, *Das Judentum als landschaftskundliches und ethnologisches Problem* (Munich, 1929), *passim*.

27. L. F. Clauss, *Die nordische Seele* (Munich, 1933), p. 9.

28. Renzo de Felice, *op. cit.*, pp. 148-49.

29. Franz-Willing, *op. cit.*, p. 87.

30. See Tüdel Weller, *Rabauken! Peter Mönkemann hat sich durch* (Munich, 1938); Hans Zöberlein, *Der Befehl des gewissens* (Munich, 1937), both published by the party publishing house. For other references, see George L. Mosse, "Culture, Civilization and Anti-Semi-

tism," *Judaism*, Vol. VII, No. 3 (Summer 1958), esp. p. 6, for Nazi detective stories.

31. Felix Kersten, *The Kersten Memoirs* (London, n.d.), pp. 296, 65.

32. Rauschning, *op. cit.*, p. 230. Rauschning does not mention that Dacque is the Munich scholar to whom Hitler refers, but from the description given, there can be no doubt that *Urwelt, Sage und Menschheit* is the book in question.

33. See Otto Gmelin, "Edgar Dacque," *Die Tat*, 20 Jahrg., Heft 8 (November 1928), pp. 589-92. Diederichs was Dacque's publisher.

34. Rauschning, *op. cit.*, p. 40.

35. Rosenberg's *Weltkampf* criticized Dinter's "197 Thesen zur Vollendung der Revolution," but wished it, nevertheless, a wide circulation. *Weltkampf*, 4 Jahrg. (1927), p. 285.

36. Not only for his beliefs. Dinter was editor of the *National-Socialist* in Weimar, which was a Strasser paper.

37. Artur Dinter, *Die Sünde wieder die Liebe* (Leipzig, 1922), p. 79.

38. Hitler, *op. cit.*, Vol. I, p. 397.

39. Wilhelm Niemöller, *Aus dem Leben eines Bekenntnis-Pfarrers* (Bielefeld, 1961), p. 2.

40. Guenter Lewy believes that, in part, the clergy, in cooperating, were responding to the enthusiasm of their parishioners. *The Catholic Church and Nazi Germany* (New York, 1964), p. 43.

41. Brenner, *op. cit.*, p. 188. A semi-official publication justifies monogamy on the basis that without it there can be no research into racial genealogy and that it gets rid of animalistic sexual drives. Moreover, whoever marries into money marries into a high level of biological inheritance, for money is obtained through personal ability. Hermann Pauli, *Deutsche Rassenhygene* (Görlitz, 1934), pp. 17, 19, 20.

42. *Der Deutsche Freikörperkultur*, No. 2 (February 1934), p. 20, fought back in the name of "pure Germanic nudism."

43. For example, on January 30, 1933; cited in *Frankfurter Neue Presse*, January 28, 1958.

44. Rudolf Höss, *Kommandant in Auschwitz* (Stuttgart, 1958), pp. 125, 129.

45. Deuerlein, *op. cit.*, p. 219.

CONCLUSION
(Pages 312-317)

1. Stanley G. Payne, *Falange* (Stanford, 1961), pp. 40, 90.

2. Jean Denis, *Principes Rexistes* (Brussels, 1936), pp. 17, 23.

3. Marcel Déat, "Révolution Française et Révolution Allemand," *Deutschland-Frankreich*, 2 Jahrg., No. 7 (1944), p. 10.

4. Robert Brasillach, *Notre Avant Guerre* (Paris, 1941), pp. 282, 283.

5. *Ibid.*, p. 276.

6. Quoted in Claude Varennes, *Le Destin de Marcel Déat* (Paris, 1948), p. 27.

7. Marc Augier, *Götter Dämmerung, Wende und Ende einer Zeit* (Buenos Aires, 1950), p. 116.

8. Drieu La Rochelle, *Socialisme Fasciste* (Paris, 1934), p. 72.

9. Brasillach, *op. cit.*, p. 189.

10. *Je Suis Partout*, 9 Jahrg., No. 381 (April 18, 1938), pp. 1, 2.

11. Helmut Otto, *Die Flämischen und Holländischen Nationalbewegungen* (Borna, Bez. Leipzig, 1936), p. 79.

12. Drieu La Rochelle, *Avec Droit* (Paris, 1937), p. 11.

13. *L'Oeuvre* (August 24, 1937) gave much prominence to this dispute in connection with the formation of the Berlin-Rome axis.

14. C. G. Jung, "Wotan" (1936), *Aufsätze zur Zeitgeschichte* (Zurich, 1946), p. 12.

15. *Ibid.*, pp. 19, 23.

16. Georges Sorel, *Reflections on Violence* (New York, 1961), p. 44.

Index